THEY CAST NO SHADOWS

THEY CAST NO SHADOWS

A collection of essays on the Illuminati, revisionist history, and suppressed technologies.

Brian Desborough

Writers Club Press

San Jose   New York   Lincoln   Shanghai

They Cast No Shadows
A collection of essays on the Illuminati, revisionist history,
and suppressed technologies.

Writers Club Press
an imprint of iUniverse, Inc.

For information address:
iUniverse, Inc.
5220 S. 16th St., Suite 200
Lincoln, NE 68512
www.iuniverse.com

ISBN: 0-595-21957-8

Printed in the United States of America

For Arizona Wilder, Mae Brussel, Credo Mutwa, April Oliver, Nikola Tesla, Wilhelm Reich, Victor Schauberger, Prof. Eric Laithwaite, Pope John-Paul 1st, Jack Smith, Yitzhak Rabin, Danny Cassalaro and the countless other free thinkers, investigative journalists and inventors, who suffered persecution in their attempt to make this a better world.

EPIGRAPH

What is ours we take tonight
As ring of fire burning bright
We stand behind the burning light
And cast no shadows in the night.
Words recited at Illuminati human sacrificial rituals.

CONTENTS

ACKNOWLEDGEMENTS

My heart-felt thanks are extended toward the numerous former Illuminati sex slaves and military assassins, all of them survivors of inhuman mind control projects, who have provided me with invaluable information regarding the covert criminal activities perpetrated by prominent members of the political, military and judicial establishments. Also to Zia Trin for proof reading the manuscript, and to Nicole Shoong for courageously publishing my politically sensitive articles in the *California Sun* newspaper. A big thank you to author David Icke for graciously allowing various articles of mine to appear on the website *davidicke.com.* I am indebted to Yoichi Omoto for providing me with information appertaining to esoteric aspects of Japanese history, and to Uri Dowbenko for journalistic insights. A very special thanks is due to the former Illuminati Mother Goddess Arizona Wilder, and also to the high-level Illuminati mind controlled survivor Cisco Wheeler, for their in-depth information regarding the present location of the Ark of the Covenant and their personal experiences at the hands of Josef Mengele. To that minor segment of humanity which treasonously elects to serve the Dragon, you will receive your just rewards in due course.

INTRODUCTION

"BE CAREFUL! Don't fry her brains—we need her!" exclaimed the United States Air Force officer, with an edge of anxious desperation in his voice, as he cast a concerned glance toward the civilian he knew as "Dr. Barrington".

"She's ours! She has always been ours, our uses are more important—you get what's left!" retorted the civilian angrily, in a voice as cold as his ice blue eyes. Subdued, the officer returned his gaze toward the blond haired woman of forty two years, writhing on a table as thousands of volts of electricity from electro-shock equipment surged through her brain.

The Air Force officer felt frustrated and humiliated; on several occasions, he and his psychiatric associates had unsuccessfully attempted to prevent the woman's mind control programming from unravelling. Now, the man posing as "Dr. Barrington" had insisted on directing the procedure himself. The officer was unaware of the civilian's true identity. All he knew was that here was a man possessing tremendous political clout, and when it came to advanced mind control programming techniques, "Barrington" was very, very good.

"Barrington" increased the voltage even higher, the rage in him bubbling to the surface. Not only was the woman on the table recovering memories of her years spent since infancy as a mind controlled occult slave, in an act of defiance, she had cut short her formerly knee length hair. How dare she! She was the only female member of the organization who was permitted to grow her hair to such a length, as a symbol of her elevated status. He and his associates had devoted many years, first selectively breeding her, then grooming her for her important role. Now she was attempting to extricate herself from their clutches.

Despite being lightly drugged, in order to minimize the muscular contractions induced by the electroshock trauma, the victim, in a gesture of spirited defiance, stared at the civilian, who exuded an aura of understated elegance. His suit would have done credit to a Savile Row tailor. She recognized his tanned, hawkish face, with its long, curved nose and topped with thinning silver hair brushed straight back from his high forehead.

To the general public, he was a member of a famous European family of international bankers, a cultured person of considerable charm. To the pain wracked victim however, he was the personification of evil—a creature she had observed participating in satanic rituals attended by members of the European oligarchy and various heads of state.

Little did the hapless victim know that she had been abducted and taken to a house of horrors located at Tyrone Avenue, in the California town of Van Nuys. To the casual passer-by, the white stuccoed house in a middle class urban area presented a picture of normalcy, except that its venetian blinds always remained tightly closed, even on the darkest of winter days.

Could such a nightmarish scenario really occur? Was it merely a product of a very disturbed mind? Sadly, the event did, in fact, occur. Even more sad is the fact that a national support group known as *Mothers Against Ritual Abuse* has received complaints made by other victims of mind control, who allegedly had been taken to the same house for reprogramming. This particular covert mind control facility is only one of many distributed throughout the world. Welcome to the real world, dear reader.

CHAPTER I

▼

OF WHAT USE IS KNOWLEDGE?

"The man with a new idea is a crank, until the new idea succeeds."

Mark Twain

The pursuit and expression of knowledge is, perhaps, the only form of labor which is not only endless, but pleasurable. In the ideal society there would be limitless potential for the aquisition of knowledge by all, in which the educational system would utilize both hemispheres of the brain in a balanced manner, in order to develop true renaissance thinkers. Perhaps the Roman philosopher Plotinus had such an educational system in mind when he suggested in the 3rd century A.D., that a person's education should include the following three aspects:

1. An education which addressed the social and civil needs of a just society.
2. An introspective study of one's inner self.
3. A study of human existence in the overall scheme of things.

Sadly, we have in our so called Global Village at the present time, not only appalling physical poverty, deliberately perpetrated by our genocidal oligarchic overlords, but also a poverty of knowledge which is free from false dogma.

There was a time in ancient Greece when the populace practiced what they termed *akreibic thinking,* each member of the adult populace thinking for themselves and rejecting unverifiable dogma. This was as it should be; unfortunately, things changed for the worse in the 5th century B.C. when Heraclitus, a proponent of totalitarianism, claimed that humankind was comprised of two groups—an intellectual and moral elite whom he termed the *aristoi,* and the *hoi-polloi,* the mindless, malleable masses.

Since the time of Heraclitus, the ruling oligarchical families have falsely considered themselves to be the *aristoi,* despite an abundance of evidence to the contrary, and have, therefore, established an educational system for the masses which is designed to fulfill two objectives: to generate wealth for the oligarchy, and the suppression of individual thought, for free thinking is necessary for the mental development of the well rounded renaissance person.

Through the centuries, education has become ever increasingly specialized, with the result that it is political suicide for a college professor to venture into a field of research beyond his or her narrowly defined field of expertise. In consequence, educators generally have become so compartmentalized within their own elected areas of expertise, that they lack the broad knowledge base which is necessary for the education of students.

We have to look no further than the fact that Egyptologists realize that the ancient Egyptian civilization lacked the customary developmental period, yet have failed to name the race of beings who provided Egypt with its ready-made culture. This academic short coming is attributable to two things: firstly, it is anathema for a member of academia to suggest that Planet Earth has been subjected to repeated cataclysmic upheavals, and secondly, Egyptologists are not permitted to research the culture of other races, e.g.the Phoenicians, if they wish to remain employed.

If we wish to discover the unknown, we must first know the known. By observing the world around us with unprejudiced eyes, it is readily apparent that both Earth and the planet Mars have been subjected to a cataclysmic event in geologically recent times, which is why recorded history only extends over the past six thousand years. As the research conducted by the author of this book reveals, it was the Phoenicians who undoubtedly re-established civilization in Egypt, and in some other geographic regions, after the last global catastrophe. Sadly, geologists, archaeologists and historians have ignored the abundance of evidence that this is so, because the facts do not fit the accepted chronological table of historical events, as dogmatically espoused by the academic establishment.

Historians go to great lengths to conceal from the populace the fact that the oligarchical families, together with well-known members of the establishment, comprise thirteen bloodlines whose roots are traceable to the Babylonian era. These bloodline familes comprise the hierarchy of a secret society known as the Illuminati (the Illuminated Ones). Contrary to the disinformation promulgated by academia, the Illuminati is not a short lived Bavarian secret society founded by Adam Weishaupt in 1776, but is, in actuality, the secret society which has ruled the world for millenniums, through its ability to control the historical, political and scientific flow of information to the masses.

Similarly, we find through observation, a mathematical unity and order which is common to all life forms, suggestive that a Supreme Intelligence influences an evolving universe, in order to prevent total chaos, yet permitting sufficient hazards to stimulate a purpose for existing in all creatures.

Throughout history, the Illuminati has attempted to inhibit humankind from understanding the actions of this Supreme Intelligence, by creating the major religions, a particularly insidious form of mind control. Thus, the Babylonian priesthood claimed that only the High Priest possessed the keys to the Kingdom of Heaven, and therefore was the only mortal empowered to communicate directly with God. Not surprisingly perhaps, the Babylonian High Priest was known as a *Ptr* (Peter)!

In this book, the author presents some of his thirty years of intensive biblical research,which has revealed, among other things, that the Israelites were not given dominion over Canaan by divine right, the mighty United Monarchy of David and Solomon appears to have been a myth, and new light is shed upon Qumran and the Dead Sea Scrolls.

Even though the Illuminati hierarchy has obfuscated the true history of the world, it maintains extremely accurate historical records for its own purposes. It exerts dominion over humanity through the use of millions of hapless individuals, who have been subjected to intensive mind control treatment, prior to being used either as programmed assassins, for use as sex slaves, for astral travel experiments, or to serve as highly trained psychics who perform at high level Illuminati satanic rituals.

Programmed to display intense loyalty toward their programmers, a few mind controlled individuals experience a disintegration of the programming upon the death of the programmer. In such cases, the programmed victim begins to recover true memories of prior experiences. By having a knowledge of Iluminati programming techniques, it is possible to access sensitive information deeply encoded in the mind files of highly placed Illuminati mind control survivors.

In addition to conducting research appertaining to the development of over unity (free energy) devices, the author has been involved in the research of geopolitics and also in the support of mind control survivors.

The multi-disciplinary background of the author of this book has enabled him to penetrate the innermost secrets of the Illuminati. In

consequence, you, dear reader, are afforded an unprecedented opportunity to learn the truth about such subjects as:

the present location of the Ark of the Covenant (not in Ethiopia) and
the Holy Grail (a pre-Christian cauldron, not a cup)
extraterrestrial species,
the covert on-going reception of interstellar intelligent communication.

On the political front, the reader will discover that President
Kennedy did not die at Dallas (a fact corroborated for the author by a
crew member of Kennedy's Air Force One aircraft). American readers
will be shocked to discover that the Constitution of the United States
was superceded in 1971 by a Title of Conveyance that transferred ownership of the united Sovereign States of America and her peoples to a
Water Resource Commission (only one congressional member objected
to the passage of this extremely covert and treasonous bill).

The author presents an in-depth analysis of the insidious on-going
social engineering (mind manipulation) projects perpetrated on behalf
of the Illuminati by the Tavistock Institute and its satellite organizations. These projects are intended to effect the political emasculation of
the public, in order to avert public resistance to the establishment of a
totalitarian global government.

While the author does not wish to foment anarchy or revolution, it is
self-evident from the above that as we enter a new century, we desper-
ately need to seek an enlightened conciousness with which to sever the
bonds which have tied us to our Illuminati overlords for so long.
Hopefully, this book will assist the readers in this task. Several of the
chapters in this book are essays which previously were published in the
California Sun newspaper and on the website *www.davidicke.com*.

▼

CHAPTER 2

HOW DID LIFE ON EARTH BEGIN?

"Don't try to improve on nature. Try, instead, to understand and protect it."

Wilhem Reich, M.D.

History, as we know it, is the interpretation of events recorded by scholars who reflect the bias of the dominant hierarchy; no historian is going to place his or her financial livelihood in jeopardy by biting the institutional hand that feeds them.

Thus, for instance, in recording the history of the Korean War, military historians have conveniently neglected to inform us that the real reason for President Truman's firing of General MacArthur was that the latter finally decided to disobey the edict ordering him to reveal his battle plans to the United Nations prior to each intended attack (Russians on the United Nations staff had been passing MacArthur's battle plans to the North Koreans). Historians also have failed to inform us that MacArthur accepted a multi-million dollar bribe in return for not prosecuting Japan's Emperor Hirohito as a war criminal.

Until a few decades ago, historians inevitably were males who either ignored, or deliberately obfuscated the role of women in history. To worsen matters, the insistence of academia toward a sharp demarcation between scholastic disciplines, has tended to foster an attitude of bigoted overspecialization in graduate students. Such myopic members of academia, finding only that which they seek, frequently overlook major discoveries accomplished beyond the ivory towers of academia.

In unravelling the origins of our planet's biogenesis, we will find our existing belief structures, built as they are on a foundation of incorrect dogma, which was forced upon us in our youth by our "educators", repeatedly challenged.

This essay accordingly is written in the hope that it will stimulate further investigation into history, religion and science by the lay person. Lest the reader be deterred from conducting such research due to a lack of "specialized" knowledge, it is well to note that no one has brought forth more creature comforts through their inventions than that great scientist Nikola Tesla. This self motivated original thinker worked entirely outside the realm of academia, and put to practical use theories regarded by academia as preposterous, e.g. the existence of ætheric energy (now reluctantly referred to by quantum physicists as the neutrino sea). In a similar vein, archaeologists maintained that the fabled city of Troy never existed, yet out of the mists of time, the ruins of Troy emerged, thanks to the unflinching efforts of amateur archaeologist Heinrich Schliemann.

Nobel physicist Erwin Schroedinger once stated: "Our present way of thinking does need to be amended perhaps by a bit of blood-transfusion from eastern thought." Eastern intellectual disciplines place heavy reliance upon the application of wisdom, a word which is derived from the Indo Aryan verb *"wied"* (to see). Conversely, our technology oriented western civilization of the present era has all but abandoned wisdom in its headlong rush to aquire knowledge, a word which stems from the root *"gno"* (to know) which, incidentally, also gave rise to the word "cunning".

In its haste to embrace eastern mysticism, a great deal of which is obtuse and mediocre, the New Age movement virtually has ignored western esoteric science, instead of integrating it with the better aspects of eastern studies.

In our investigation of the origins of life on Planet Earth, it is necessary to at least possess an overview of the different ways in which diverse life forms may have evolved. Unfortunately, this subject has been clouded by the battle raging between the Creationists and the Evolutionists, both factions permitting their ingrained biases to distort aquired knowledge. It is therefore imperative that we view this emotion evoking subject with knowledge tempered by at least a modicum of wisdom.

Evolutionists postulate that biological organisms originally evolved from a "primordial soup" consisting of organic molecules, created by geochemical means when the earth was very young. In the 1950's, Stanley Miller and Harold Urey at the University of Chicago, passed electrical sparks through a simulated primordial atmosphere. Sure enough, four amino acids were formed and the jubilant evolutionists believed that a continuation of the experiment would lead to the formation of RNA molecules. However, despite much additional experimentation since that time by other microbiologists, no nucleotides (the sub-units of RNA) have been synthesized, only simpler molecules which are generally discovered in tars.

It is a far cry, however, from the amino acids synthesized by Miller and Urey to functional proteins, even in the case of a simple protein like an insulin molecule, which contains twenty different amino acids configured in a specific order fifty amino acids in length. The probability of twenty different types of naturally occuring amino acids linking up in the correct sequence to form an insulin molecule, would be one chance in 20 to the 50th power, which is a virtual impossibility.

Such an improbability does not preclude the fact, however, that simple proteins can form naturally by means of random aggregations of amino acids. Sidney Fox demonstrated at the University of Miami that an aqueous solution of amino acids poured over hot lava rock will aggregate into the form of hollow proteinaceous spheres.

Amino acids possess the ability to rotate polarized light either to the right or to the left; moreover, a left-handed amino acid molecule, such as alanine, will convert to a right handed molecule if exposed to sufficient solar radiation. Given the considerable age of the earth, one would expect an approximately equal number of right and left handed amino acids to be found if life evolved as chance occurences of nature, yet almost all amino acids found in living things as protein constituents, are of the left handed form.

One type of molecular structure found in almost all terrestrial life forms are the porphyrins. Mammals are able to accept oxygen into the bloodstream because porphyrins possessing iron ions function as electron transfer catalysts. Plantlife on the other hand, require porphyrins which incorporate magnesium ions in order to accomplish photosynthesis. Since porphyrins are essential to life, it is interesting to note that porphyrins were discovered in the Orgueil meteorite in 1964 by two Canadian biochemists (Baker and Hodgson).

As ice comets traverse our solar system, they accumulate interstellar dust. Solar radiation melts some of the ice, thereby creating an organic soup from the various chemicals contained in the interstellar dust. In this manner, comets may function as chemical factories for the polymerization of chemicals into more complex precursors of life, such as porphyrins.

University of Hawaii scientists Claire Fulsome and Andrew Brittain have created protocellular molecules by means of electrical discharges. When the protocells were subjected to a primordial atmosphere of water, hydrogen and nitrogen, the cells were able to synthesize amino acids and various organic compounds, when irradiated with long wave

ultra violet light. The experiment demonstrated that such cells possessed metabolic capabilities even though they did not exhibit life as we
understand the meaning of the word.

Such protocells are a far cry from the incredible complexity of living
cells. Cyanobacteria, for example, have been found in rocks radiometri-
cally dated as being 3.8 million years old. Although single celled creatures, each cell contains billions of pieces of data—hardly an example of
a lifeform in its early evolutionary stage. Even such a primitive cell contains many complex mechanisms which are designed to prevent accidental evolutionary changes. DNA molecules are proof read by such
mechanisms in order to insure that RNA strand data is correct; incorrect DNA code sequences known as introns are removed by specific
enzymes. This is why evolutionary "missing links" never have been discovered, despite claims to the contrary by certain paleontologists, who
should know better. The British Museum of Natural History has seven
million fossils in its collection, yet has no transitional fossil types
among them.

Some anthropologists and paleontologists would have us believe
that they are descended from apes; be that as it may, no transitional fossil forms linking the remainder of humankind to ancestral apes have
been discovered. Paleontologists have presented an unsuspecting
public with a sorry litany of false claims that transitional forms between
apes and homosapiens have, indeed, been discovered. These include
Ramapithecus, later determined to be an early form of Orangutan. Eugene
Dubois'*Java Man* 's skull fragment was from a Gibbon. Dubois later
admitted finding two human skulls in the same location and of the
same age period.

Much media hype was given in 1974 to the discovery by Professor
Johanson of *"Lucy".* It was claimed that the skeletal remains included a
kneecap and pelvis which enabled the creature to walk upright. It was
later proven that the kneecap had been found a mile away from the
remainder of the bones, at a depth of two hundred feet. Moreover, the

ability to walk erect does not necessarily suggest a human trait, for the pigmy chimpanzee also possesses the same capability. Then came *Nebraska Man*. This spurious claim for the discovery of the missing link solely was made on the discovery of a single tooth! It was later determined that the tooth in question was from an extinct species of pig.

Many evolutionists claim that the fossil known as *Archaeopterix* is a transitional form between reptile and bird, the reptilian scales having been transformed into feathers. To claim that this was a transitional form stretches one's credulity to the limit, for scales are simply discrete folds in the skin of a reptile, whereas the feathers of *Archaeopterix* were as highly evolved as those of today's birds.

Admittedly, nature overcomes adversity by creating new taxa in a generation or two, but where are the transitional species in the paleontological shambles known as the fossil record? In the total absence of transitional life forms, we are forced to the inescapable conclusion that individual species did not evolve, but rather suddenly appeared, fully developed.

After having conducted extensive research into the development of so-called over-unity (free energy) devices, which function by harnessing the ætheric energy which pervades the cosmos, the author has arrived at the following postulate: an interrelationship exists between everything in the universe. Harmony within the universe is maintained by what we perceive as a cosmic canon of mathematical correspondences, originated by a concious creative agency which transcends the universe and is complete within itself.

It is quite probable that this creative intelligence, variously referred to as God, Al-lah, or Hillary Clinton, according to one's belief structure, administrates by means of a hierarchy of creative agencies immanent within nature, which assists at various transcendental levels in maintaining harmony throughout the cosmos.

If this postulate is correct, it is reasonable to expect that each heirarchical level is permitted a degree of freedom of expression unless, as in the present case of humanity, we cease to be in attunement with the cosmos and unwisely sow the seeds of our own destruction.

All too often, major scientific discoveries are rigidly suppressed by the academic establishment. A typical example of scientific suppression involved the biogenesis experiments of Andrew Crosse. A man of modest yet independent means, Crosse was an amateur scientist who owned a small estate in southwest England, at a time when the electrical discoveries of Michael Faraday were making headline news in the London newspapers.

In the autumn of 1837, Crosse attempted to grow crystals by passing an electric current over the surface of volcanic ironstone, which was kept wet with a solution of potassium silicate and hydrochloric acid. After fourteen days, minute white specks appeared on the stone, and over a period of several more days, adopted the form of insects—some with six and some with eight legs. On the twenty-eighth day, the insects were able to move their legs, and subsequently freed themselves from the stone the very next day.

Crosse repeated this remarkable experiment without the ironstone and obtained similar results, but could not reproduce the effect in his control experiment which omitted the electric current. Unfortunately for the pious and deeply religious Crosse, his experiments engendered a great deal of wrath among the clergy and members of academia, resulting in a suppression of Crosse's work, which has remained to the present time.

Undaunted by the furor, another amateur scientist, Donald Weeks, repeated the experiments, taking great pains to maintain a sterile and hermetically sealed environment for the experiment. Sure enough, living insects appeared in the highly acidic solution, but the controversy sparked by the Crosse experiments of the previous year, prevented Weeks from having his work published. To his credit, Michael Faraday announced to the Royal Society, an oligarchic institution established for the purpose of suppressing scientific discovery, that he had personally observed the creation of similar insects, termed *Acari,* in the course of conducting experiments of his own.

The significance of the Crosse experiments is that highly evolved insects were created in a very acidic environment that should have been too hostile to suppoert life. Moreover, an electrical current was essential for the creation of the creatures.

No rational explanation for the phenomena described has ever been proposed, which suggests that the creation of the insects possibly involves a principle of a very esoteric nature hitherto unknown.

The electromagnetic field generated by the electric current which flowed through the experimental solution, would have applied a weak stress upon the surrounding environment. It is known that the human brain is a transmitter and receiver of longitudinal scalar waves, which can travel vast distances through the universe. Could it be that scalar waves, generated by Crosse and Weeks, interacted with the electromagnetic field generated by the current flowing through the solution, thereby creating a pathway to a parallel realm of existence in which was stored the genetic data necessary for the materialization of such insects, in our realm of reality? That these were no ordinary insects was evident from the fact that they were not hatched from eggs, nor did they undergo a larval stage.

Some readers will be aquainted with psychotronic equipment, such as the unit developed by the late Thomas Hieronymous. Such devices form a mental link between the mind of the operator and another object; they have been proven to be remarkably effective for the erradication of agricultural pests. When a powerful orgone accumulator is connected to a psychotronic circuit, the mental powers of the operator are so greatly amplified that replicas of physical objects, which have been placed on the psychotronic unit, can be materialized (something that the Illuminati doesn't want you to know, dear reader). This suggests that the mind of Crosse may have been a crucial link in the biogenesis of the insects.

It has been experimentally demonstrated that when a very weak electrical current is passed through an aqueous solution, the water molecules will become charged with orgone energy (the term that the late Dr. Wilhem Reich applied to ætheric energy). The fact that Crosse, Weeks and Faraday all allegedly observed similar acari insects is puzzling, considering that no other species were created during the course of their respective experiments. Could it be that all three experimenters were in telepathic communication at a subconcious level, or mentally attuning to the same transcendental genetic data source? This is somewhat analogous to the fact that several inventors geographically remote from one another, frequently conceive of the same invention simultaneously, as if they all were tapping into an universal intelligence continuum.

Given the appropriate environment, it would appear possible that certain clays could promote the creation of chemical compounds which are precursors of primitive life forms. The discovery that clays and organic molecules have been found to coexist in some meteorites, has stimulated NASA to conduct research into the interface between organic molecules and clay at its Ames Research Center.

Clays are usually composed of layers of microscopic crystals that are linked by hydrogen bonds. Quartz and some other crystals emit a pulsed radiation in the ultraviolet region of the spectrum, which could be a synthesizing agent in the production of organic molecules, e.g. amino acids.

In order for clay to transform organic molecules into genetic material, the clay crystals would have to possess the capability of storing and regulating information. Curiously enough, this unique property came to light with the introduction of the nickel-cadmium battery. Such batteries will only recharge up to the level of the previous charge; in other words, if the battery initially was only charged to fifty percent of its capacity, successive charges will never exceed that level. This memory phenomenon occurs in the microscopic crystals that form between the battery plates.

Research conducted by Noam Lahav at Hebrew University, showed that clays possess the ability to link together molecules of the amino acid glycine, if the clays are subjected to repeated wetting and drying cycles. Clays are continuously being formed throughout the world by the weathering action on hard rocks. Moreover, we have noted that clays should provide a suitable environment for the creation of genetic material, especially since clays contain metallic ions which could stimulate the synthesized genetic material to mutate. Something is still missing from the equation, however.

That "something" was discovered in the 1930's by the previously mentioned Dr. Wilhem Reich. Like that prodigious inventor Nikola Tesla, Reich was a free-thinker of towering intellect; in keeping with most free thinkers throughout history, who possess the courage to challenge the false academic dogma of their day, he was considered a threat to the status quo of the oligarchic establishment. He was harrassed accordingly.

A former associate of Sigmund Freud, Reich's scientific research ran the gamut from psychotherapy to astrophysics, and he was a Nobel Prize nominee. His discovery that orgone energy was the animating principle in all life forms, prompted Reich to launch an in-depth study of its characteristics. This research led not only to new psychotherapeutic techniques, such as polarity therapy, but also to weather engineering and a novel method for removing atmospheric pollutants.

Applying his new-found understanding of orgone energy in yet another direction, Reich discovered a painless and very low-cost method for the treatment of cancer, which would have rendered the multi-billion dollar chemotherapy industry redundant. Not surprisingly, Reich was incarcerated in a federal prison and conveniently died under mysterious circumstances, only a few days prior to his parole hearing. The judge who sentenced him, presumably a political hack in collusion with the private corporation known as the American Medical Association (the latter hypocritically known to have received substantial financial donations from the tobacco industry) ordered Dr. Reich's published works to be publicly burned. And we thought that the Inquisition was a thing of the past.

Our immediate interest in Dr. Reich is his research appertaining to protozoal neo-biogenesis. Reich subjected earth and oceanic sand to intense heat; instead of becoming totally sterile, a filtrate obtained from this mixture contained microscopic organisms called vesicles, which emitted a bluish glow. Amazingly, these vesicles tended to merge together to form pulsating protozoa, which Reich suggested were the smallest units of living matter.

Dr. Reich's research into the origins of life has profound significance, for it suggests that, paradoxically, searing heat that destroys all life is also able to initiate the biogenesis of protozoal organisms, in the presence of microcrystalline materials. The ancient Vedic literature claims that fire swept the earth in antediluvian times, destroying most life. Such a cataclysm well could have occured if a giant solar flare swept the earth (some of the ancient mounds known as barrows, which are located in the vicinity of Stonehenge, in southern England, possess a vitrified surface, as if subjected to intense heat.). Such a fiery cataclysm well could have stimulated the creation of protozoa in clay deposits.

This brief overview of biogenesis should instill in readers possessing a creationist bias that humanity possesses the ability to generate life forms from seemingly inanimate substances, under certain conditions. On the other hand however, evolutionists should note that the failure to detect transitional life forms suggests that a higher agency apparently is involved in the process.

Is it even remotely possible that a Supreme Intelligence is disseminating information to all terrestrial physical matter from some remote region of the cosmos? According to the late Dr. Carl Sagan, a spokesperson for the organization calling itself the Search for

Extrater-restrial Intelligence (SETI) no evidence of intelligent inter-stellar communication has been observed.

Sagan's comments were blatant misinformation.[1] The first attempt to detect evidence of extraterrestrial life was *Project Ozma*, which was conducted at the National Radio Obsevatory located at Green Bank, West Virginia, in 1960. The targets were Tau Ceti and Epsilon Eridani. The project was abandoned after four weeks of negative results. The SETI program has used a sixty-four meter radio telescope in conjunction with electronic equipment capable of simultaneously scanning twenty-eight million channels.

In actuality, the SETI project primarily has served as a vehicle to covertly divert funds into "Black Budget" programs such as the Strategic Defense Initiative (SDI). A major function of the SDI is not the interception and destruction of nuclear missiles, as is popularly claimed, but rather the development of weaponry capable of destroying extraterrestrial craft deemed hostile by the United States National Reconaisssance Office. A typical SDI program was "Project Sealight"; scalar beam weaponry developed under this program for the primary purpose of destroying extraterrestrial craft was successfully tested at the Naval Weapons facility at Port Hueneme, California, during the past decade.

The notion that extraterrestrial intelligences, technologically more advanced than the human race, would waste their time communicating across vast expanses of the universe by means of radio signals is ludicrous. Conventional Marconi transverse radio waves travel at a velocity less than that of light. Hence, inordinately long time periods would be required to communicate between worlds many light years apart.

There is a simple means to resolve such a communication problem. In the late 19th. century, Nikola Tesla discovered methods for the transmission and reception of longitudinally-pulsed scalar waves of ætheric energy. It was found that such waves lack a time component; therefore, by employing such a waveform, it would be possible to communicate over vast intersellar distances instantaneously.

In 1962, a Los Angeles electronics engineer by the name of George Lawrence, was assigned the task of developing a transducer for missile applications. Among other requirements, the transducer would have to be resistant to electronic counter-measure jamming, while simultaneously sensing fluctuations in gravity, temperature and electromagnetic fields—capacities beyond the scope of electro-mechanical sensing systems.

Lawrence suspected that cellular material from living plants might offer such sensing capability. During his research Lawrence became aquainted with the experiments which had been conducted during the 1920's by the Russian histologist Alexander Gurwitsch, who had aimed the tip of an onion root at a similar onion root specimen. After several hours of exposure, the target onion root was found to have increased its cell division by twenty-five percent. Gurwitsch realized that the phenomenon had to be due to some type of radiation emanating from the other onion root. Only glass or gelatin blocked transmission of the rays, which Gurwitsch termed "mitogenetic radiation, since the rays caused mitosis (cell division).

Not surprisingly, the United States Academy of Sciences claimed that Gurwitsch's discovery was not reproducible, hinting that his results were due to an over-fertile imagination. This monstrous deception on the part of the academy was perpetrated despite the fact that researchers in Moscow, Berlin and Frankfurt had corroborated Gurwitsch's results.

Building on the success of the Gurwitsch experiments, George Lawrence developed a series of psycho-galvanic analyzers, which incorporated biologically-active transducers fabricated from thin wafers of quartz, which he had coated with plant proteins doped with organomethylglyoxol compounds. This enabled signals received by the transducer to be converted into quantitative electrical signals. Instead of feeding the electrical signals into a conventional pen recorder, Lawrence's prototype unit incorporated an audio oscillator, which emitted a steady tone; the tone changed to audible pulsations whenever the biological sensor detected signals from an external source.

Lawrence tested his device in the high desert of southern California in order to minimize electromagnetic interference from power lines or radio transmitters. Lawrence began his experiments in the desert by administering an electric shock to a tree located some distance from his instrument. This caused his device to respond noisily, thus verifying that his biosensing equipment was receiving information which was being transmitted by the distressed tree.

One day in 1971, Lawrence and his assistants took an afternoon break, leaving the biosensing equipment turned on, but left randomly pointing toward the sky. Suddenly, the steady audio tone changed to a series of pulsations. This could only mean that *the equipment was receiving signals from the cosmos!* Further refining his equipment, Dr. Lawrence was able to convert the received biodynamic signals into video images.

For the first time in recorded history, the scientist was able to observe interstellar information in a graphic format. Moreover, the perceived data was intelligent information, not just random noise. The only problem (which still remains) is that because the information received is not time dependent, each video frame contains the entire informational package, instead of the sequential information we perceive when we view a movie frame by frame. The information which plantlife is perceiving from the cosmos is of an *eidetic* nature, i.e. it is being received as complete packages.

At the present time, we lack the ability to interpret this intelligent communication. What is a certainty, is the fact that our global plantlife is constantly receiving intelligent communication from elsewhere in the cosmos. Whether the perceived information emanates from an advanced extraterrestrial race or from a central supreme intelligence has not been determined. Since plantlife has the ability to perceive such data, could it be that at a sub-concious level, humankind is also being instructed from a realm far, far away? [2]

CHAPTER 3

▼

WHERE WAS ATLANTIS?

There is no bar to knowledge greater
than contempt prior to examination.

—Herbert Spencer

The year 1584 was not particularly good for one Turkish pirate. It was the year that he was beheaded. Among the possessions which he left after his unfortunate demise was a strange portolan map, which had been made in 1513. Remarkably, the map, known as the *Piri Re'is*, depicted South America and a portion of Africa. Most remarkable of all was an outline of Antarctica devoid of ice; the map even indicated the location of bays in the portion of Antarctica known as Queen Maude Land. Amazingly, these individual bays, which currently are concealed by a thick layer of ice, were undetected until revealed by sonar soundings in 1949.

Medieval maps were notoriously inaccurate, yet a collection of such portolans compiled by E.E.Nordenskiold in 1889, were of such high accuracy that he became convinced that the maps in question had been redrawn from originals of very great antiquity.[1] One such portolan, known as the Haji Ahmed portolan, depicts an ice-free Antarctica and an accurate outline of America replete with the Baja Peninsula. Its ancient origins are attested to by the outline of a wide land bridge connecting Alaska and Siberia.

The accuracy of the portolan maps implies that they were redrawn from originals which had existed prior to the last ice age, their accuracy suggests that the cartographers who drew the original maps clearly were part of an advanced culture, not hunter-gatherers. That advanced civilizations existed prior to the last ice age is also attested to by the discovery of ancient manufactured artifacts, such as the nickel-alloy spheres that were discovered in pyrophilic rock in the Wonderstone silver mine, near Ottosdal, South Africa.[2] In addition, let us not ignore the Vedic literature of India, which describes ancient aerial craft known as Vimanas. These were claimed to have been developed by a black race known as the Dravidians. The maps and artifacts demonstrate that, contrary to what academia would have us believe, history is not linear, but in reality appears to be a series of advanced civilizations, each of which have devolved in the aftermath of a cataclysmic event.

Before investigating whether or not Atlantis ever existed, it is necessary to reconstruct known patterns of the very ancient past. Unfortunately, the earliest written texts only date from circa 3500 B.C.. Since it is apparent that the original maps upon which the portolans were based had to have been drawn prior to the last ice age, it behooves us to determine the approximate period in which the last ice age began.

Fortunately for our narrative, Admiral Byrd led a United States expedition to Antarctica in 1949. Core samples of ice obtained during the expedition, revealed that the last time that Antarctica was free from ice was more than six thousand years ago.

It is customary to find the maximum precipitation, in the form of rain or snow, in coastal regions, not near the center of a landmass, unless a major rainforest is present. This is not the case with either of the polar icecaps, where the ice is thickest near the center of both landmasses.

Another anomaly requiring explanation is that the Northern Yukon region remained free from ice during the last so-called ice age.

Professor Charles Hapgood postulates that the current polar land massess formerly were in warmer regions, and consequently ice-free. An excessive build-up of ice in the polar regions caused the earth's crust to slip, according to Hapgood, causing the landmasses to slide into their present polar locations. This theory recently has been adopted by author Randy Flemming.[3]

When lava flows begin to cool, the geomagnetic field strength becomes permanently locked into the lava's magnetite crystals. Core samples taken from ancient lava beds by members of the United States Geologic Service, have revealed that the earth's magnetic field drops to a zero value approximately every five hundred thousand years, then slowly rebuilds. The core samples also indicate that when the earth's magnetic field drops to zero, cataclysmic earth changes occur. These could be caused by a temporary cessation of the earth's rotation. Such an awesome event would, indeed, cause the earth's crust to slip, resulting in horrendous earthquakes, gigantic tidal waves and mountain building.

The writer feels that Hapgood's theory of earth crustal displacement caused by polar ice accumulation is flawed. In order to create such a massive accumulation of ice from regular snowfalls, incredible amounts of thermal energy would have to be generated in equatorial regions, in order to evaporate sufficient water to provide such prodigious snowfalls in the polar regions. Such a high magnitude of thermal energy probably would destroy all life forms in the equatorial zone.

We also must account for the fact that most of the Northern Yukon territory remained free from ice during the last ice age, and that mammoth elephants have been discovered in Siberia with undigested foliage in their mouths, inplying that they were flash-frozen during a very abnormal cataclysm—not necessarily of terrestrial origin. Arctic temperatures are not sufficiently low to accomplish the flash-freezing of large mammals; perhaps this is why the *Book of Job* pondered: "*Whence cometh the ice?"* This particular Old Testament book is believed to be an Arab work much older than the rest of the Bible.

A major anomaly of the past ignored by academia, is that botanist Nikolai Ivanovitch Vavilov studied more than fifty thousand wild plants collected from various global regions, and determined that they all originated in only eight different areas, all in mountainous terrain. This suggests that a major cataclysm obliterated life in lowland regions of the planet, sometime in the distant past.

Such an horrendous cataclysm would have changed the face of the earth, possibly destroying any advanced civilization in the process. A useful starting point for our quest is to ask ourselves why our planet not only occupies its present orbit, but why it occupies its specific location on its orbit; why isn't the earth fifty thousand miles further ahead or behind, at any given time period? The answer is to be found in the recently-developed theory of planetary orbital resonance.

A practical example of orbital resonance is to be found in the production of Chladni figures; these occur when lycopodium powder is sprinkled onto a vibrating disk. Wherever vibratory waves radiating outwards from the center of the disk encounter waves travelling toward the disk's center, a standing wave is generated. This wave interaction causes the powder to mound up into concentric circles on the surface of the disk. If the vibratory waves are of a single frequency, the powder circles will be equally spaced, one wavelength apart. If, however, the vibrations encompass a very broad spectrum of frequencies, the concentric circles will be spaced at octave intervals, thus forming an analog to the planetary orbital intervals of the solar system.[4]

If an object is placed on one of the concentric circles of powder, it will commence to orbit around the central axis of the disk, carried along by an energy flow created by radially-opposed vibrations. Each concentric circle of powder behaves as a vibrating circular string, producing a primary node point together with secondary nodes—the latter being formed by harmonic overtones. An object placed anywhere on the vibrating surface of the disk will be transported to a primary node, where it will commence to orbit, while lighter objects will migrate to one of the lesser nodes.

The solar system appears to be, in actuality, a gigantic Chladni structure, formed by standing waves created in the solar gravitational field through the interaction of a broad spectrum of ætheric waves. Each standing wave node will possess its own gravitational field, with planets being held at the primary nodes and objects of lesser mass, e.g. asteroids, being captured by secondary and tertiary nodes, which possess a lesser gravitational field. This suggests that a gravitational field is to be found at the nodal points of a galactic standing wave structure, regardless of whether or not a celestial object is occupying that location.

Astronomers claim that the solar system was created through the condensation of a spinning cloud of stellar dust. If this were the case, then the axes of all the planets which comprise our solar system should lie on the same plane of rotation, if the solar system has remained in a steady state since its formation. This is clearly not the case, however, for the polar axes of Earth and Mars are tilted almost thirty degrees from their orbital planes. Moreover, the polar axis of Uranus is more than ninety degrees out of alignment.

We must question why, if our solar system began as a rotating spiral nebula, is a very low-density planet, such as Saturn, orbiting at a much greater distance from the sun than the massive Jupiter, which possesses far greater angular momentum?

The above-cited solar anomalies lend credence to Dr. Immanuel Velikovsky's hypothesis that a gigantic comet entered our solar system, perturbing the polar axis of Uranus. The near-collision caused the comet to lose its tail, which coalesced into the ball of ice and gas we know as Saturn. This hypothesis accounts for its abnormally-low specific gravity. Careening at high speed towards the sun, the massive comet collided with a small planet, which disintegrated, thereby forming the asteroid belt.

Losing momentum as a result of the collision, the comet slowed sufficiently for capture by a vacant primary node of the solar system's
standing wave structure, adopting a Keplarian orbit as the new planet
Jupiter. It was the tremendous velocity of the comet immediately prior
to its transformation into the new planet Jupiter, that enabled the latter
to attain its present angular momentum. Jupiter's momentum is far
greater than that of the sun, even though the sun's diameter is ten times
larger than that of Jupiter—a feat unattainable if Jupiter were an original member of a steady-state solar system.

According to Velikovsky, the collision between the comet and the
small planet caused a large mass to be ejected from the comet, thus
forming a second comet, which finally went into orbit as Venus. This
would explain why ancient cultures held Venus in such awe. Native
American tribes sometimes performed human sacrifices whenever
Venus was particularly bright, and Greek mythology claimed that Venus
was born from the forehead of Zeus, who was associated with Jupiter.[5]

Some astrophysicists have speculated that Venus, while still an ice-
coated comet, temporarily was captured by the earth's gravitational
field for several orbits, but still possessed too much angular momentum, and consequently adopted its present orbit.

By combining this hypothesis with that of Velikovsky's, a rationale
for the previously-mentioned terrestrial anomalies is presented: if
Venus initially was formed as a comet arising from a collision that
spawned Jupiter, it is possible that Venus entrained large amounts of
water, which formed a thick coating of ice over its surface.

When two celestial bodies are on a collision course, the one with the
least mass begins to disintegrate when it reaches a distance between the
two bodies known as Roche's Limit. In this instance, the Venusian ice
coating would have disintegrated as the Venusian comet approached
Planet Earth; at a height of three hundred miles above the earth's
surface, the ice would have melted due to the comet's high velocity as it
encountered the friction of the earth's atmosphrere, only to freeze once

more as the moisture descended to a lower altitude. As the ice crystals passed through the Van Allen belt, the ice crystals would have become ionized, and therefore attracted to the earth's magnetic poles, which explains why the polar ice caps are closer to the geomagnetic poles than to the geographic axis.

Such a massive volume of ice crystals, raining down upon the polar regions from space, probably would have prevented the ice from elevating its temperature much above the black body radiation temperature of the upper atmosphere, which is approximately minus fifty degrees Fahrenheit. This in turn quite possibly could have lowered the jet stream to near ground level, which would account for ancient tales of phenomenal winds removing mountain tops. It would also provide a rational explanation for the fact that the arctic tundra contains billions of mammoth elephant bone fragments. One can visualize herds of hapless elephants being flash frozen, then torn to shreds by winds attaining velocities of many hundreds of miles per hour.

Chinese folklore claims that at the time of the global deluge, a terrible groaning noise was heard in the sky, which sounded like the word "Yahoo". So profound was the experience that one of the first historically-recorded Chinese emperors was named Yahou, in commemoration of the horrific event. Very significantly, the proto-Isreaelite Kenite tribe, domiciled in the Negev region, named their principal deit Yehu, which at a later date, etymologically gave rise to the fearsome and vengeance-wreaking deity "Yahwey".The awsome groaning noise well could have been the result of very powerful electrical capacitance discharges between Planet Earth and the temporarily orbiting comet Venus.

The writer accordingly suggests that a previously advanced civilization was destroyed in a cataclysmic celestial event, which involved the temporary orbital capture of Venus, still a comet, by Planet Earth; this catastrophe resulted in a simultaneous global flood and a reshaping of the earth's topography. Still possessing too much angular momentum to remain in a stable orbit around Earth, Venus eventually adopted its present orbit and became a planet. Recorded history can only be traced back little more than five thousand years, which suggests that the cataclysm occurred shortly prior to that period.

Significantly, Sumerian clay texts state that King Ziusudra was advised to construct a *Tibatu*—a ship designed to survive a capsize, in order to survive a predicted massive flood. The Babylonian chronicler and priest Berossus, also described a flood epic in his *Babylonian Antiquities,* in which he mentioned the construction of an ark possessing the capability of withstanding a capsizing. Sumerian textual data implies that King Ziusudra lived approximately 6800 years ago. This date fits favorably with the data obtained during Admiral Byrd's Antarctic expedition, which suggests that Antarctica was still ice-free 9000 years ago.

During the past century, several sightings of an ark have been made in the Ararat region formerly known as the Kingdom of Uratu. The remains of an ancient ship supposedly were observed there in 1917 by a Russian expedition, while another sighting was claimed by Ed Davis in 1943.

Claims have been made that the remains of what appears to have been an ark have been sighted embedded in a glacier on the slopes of Mount Ararat. In actuality, wood samples taken from the site carbon date to the mediæval era. This suggests that the remains are from the site of a mediæval monastery known to to have been constructed on the mountain by edict of St. Jacob. The wily monks sculpted a rock outcropping into the form of an ark, then sold what they claimed were timbers salvaged from the ark to gullible pilgrims. Naturally, the corrupt monks prevented visitors from approaching too close to the vicinity of the "ark". What is notable, however, is that salt crystals have been found on the mountain at the 6000 foot level, indicative that oceanic floodwaters once inundated the Ararat region at one time.

Even though St. Jacob's ark clearly is a grand deception, the same cannot be said for a curious structure that was the subject of an aerial photograph taken in the 1950's, by U2 pilot Gary Powers. The photograph showed that approximately fourteen miles south of Mount Ararat, an earthquake had resulted in soil slippage which revealed the outline of a large ship. An archaeological team explored the anomaly, never bothered to conduct a materials analysis, and promptly concluded that the site was of natural origins.

During the 1980's, American amateur archaeologist Ron Wyatt visited the site and collected samples of what he suspected were iron oxide and petrified wood. A laboratory analysis of the samples verified his suspicions; returning to the site, Wyatt and his team of assistants conducted a site exploration involving the use of metal detectors and interface radar instrumentation. Amazingly, the investigation revealed the outline of a ship which corresponded to the dimensions of the biblical ark!

A wooden ship of such great antiquity normally would be undetectable at the present time, if left exposed to the elements. In this case however, a lava eruption, followed by subsequent mudflows, had encapsulated the vessel, thereby facilitating the petrification of the wood and preserving the rusted remains of iron rivets.. Fortunately, the Turkish government has preserved the location as an historical site, for thanks to the superlative efforts of Mr. Wyatt, what could have been dismissed as yet another appocryphal tale, serves instead to corroborate the flood accounts depicted by Berossus and the authors of Genesis.

Mr. Wyatt claims to hace discovered fossilized animal dung at the sight. This should not necessarily be construed as corroboration of the accommodation of two of every species of creatures, as the Bible states—surely a logistical improbability. It is more likely that the ark occupants had a relatively small number of animals on board as a food supply for themselves. Let us not ignore the fact that some pre-flood civilizations appear to have possessed a very high degree of scientific knowledge. Is it not possible therefore, that the ark occupants took with them cell cultures from many different species of creatures, then cloned these particular species after the floodwaters had subsided? In addition, let us not discount the fact that possibly many similar vessels were constructed, which could account for ark sightings in disparate regions surrounding Mount Ararat.

Shortly after this chapter was commenced, the news media announced the discovery of a submerged house in the Black Sea; the discoverer was Commander Robert Ballard (USN Rtd.) noted for finding the wreck of the ill-fated Titanic. Ballard believes that the daub and wattle house was submerged during the global flood. Of great significance to our narrative is the fact that carbon dating suggests that the house is 7000 years old—further evidence that the global flood occurred less than 7000 years ago.

Imagine what would happen today if the global land masses were to be devastated by a series of cataclysmic earthquakes, and a deadly plague broke out worldwide, as the result of geophysical and biological warfare. Destruction of highways and airports, in addition to lack of manpower, would force the relatively few survivors to become hunter-gatherers of food, a task which would occupy most of their waking hours, thus preventing the education of children. Within a few generations, most surviving communities probably would have devolved to a primitive and superstitious level of existence. Even if some survivors remained literate, modern books, printed on acid paper, would have become brittle and useless after several decades, thereby expunging records of past history.

Even though the close passage of a celestial body, such as Venus, could account for our polar icecaps and the biblical global flood, as described above, the temperature of the snow and ice cascading down from space would not be sufficiently low as to cause the flash-freezing of mammoth elephants. If we are to comprehend the patterns of the past, we simply cannot ignore the problem of the flash-freezing of mammoth elephants, as academia has elected to do. Clearly some catastrophic event almost instantaneously lowered the ambient temperature to less than minus one hundred and fifty degrees Fahrenheit! This is the temperature at which flesh can be flash-frozen.

A possible mechanism for the rapid temperature drop may be deduced from the inventions of that great researcher Nikola Tesla. During the 1930's, Tesla invented a beam weapon which generated longitudinally-pulsed scalar waves. At a target distance equal to one quarter wavelength of of the weapon's resonant frequency emissions, the air in the target area would expand very rapidly, followed by a massive implosion, which possessed the capability of lowering the air temperature to absolute zero. As Venus temporarily orbited the earth, massive electrical discharges between the celestial body and the magnetic poles of Planet Earth well could have created an effect similar to that of Tesla's beam weapon. It should also be noted that developments of Tesla's Magnifying Transmitter currently are being employed by several major powers as geophysical warfare devices. In one particular mode, such weapons are capable of flash-freezing the inhabitants of cities located thousands of miles from the weapon in question.

Fossilized plants indicate that at one time, the earth experienced an uniform tropical climate. This would have been the case if a canopy of water vapor had enveloped the earth's atmosphere, as is suggested in the Book of Genesis. Such a water canopy immediately would have been condensed by the falling snow and ice from the temporarily-orbiting comet, which eventually became the planet we know as Venus.

Satellite images have revealed that every minute of the day and night, approximately twenty ice comets weighing approximately one hundred tons apiece, enter our atmosphere, thereby continually adding to the volume of water in our oceans. According to astrophysicist Dr. Louis Frank, the gentleman who first discovered the ice comets, our solar system is believed to be surrounded by a vast belt of ice comets.[6] According to Dr. Frank, some of these ice comets are perturbed by the passage of a tenth planet, whose orbit passess through the cometary belt (this is not the planet Marduk envisaged by author Zechariah Sitchen). Dr. Frank hypothesizes that every few million years, this tenth planet perturbs a gigantic ice comet so large that it crashes to earch, causing a major cataclysmic event. As Venus, in its cometary form, temporarily orbited our planet, there is a possibility that its mass as it traversed the comet belt, was sufficiently great as to knock one of these giant ice comets out of its orbit. If such a catastrophe did, in fact occur, the disintegrating ice coating of Venus, plummeting toward the earth's atmosphere, would accordingly be accompanied by the remains of such an ice comet. Such an event would explain why the earth's polar icecaps are so large.

If such a massive amount of snow and ice was suddenly deposited in the polar regions in this manner, it would flow radially outwards, travelling along valleys and avoiding mountains, which may be the reason why areas of the Northern Yukon region were not impacted by the last ice age. If the comet Venus lost its ice coating as it neared Earth, we would expect that the present-day Planet Venus would possess very little atmospheric water vapor. This was indeed verified in 1881 by the Pioneer space probe, as it entered the lower levels of the Venusian atmosphere.

It is also quite possible that the mass of Venus, possessing too much angular momentum to permanently remain in orbit around Planet Earth, perturbed the sun as the wayward comet streaked toward its final orbital location. If this occurred, the sun's perturbation well may have created very large solar flares, causing Earth's oceans to boil as the flares seared various regions of the earth. Much of the resultant steam well may have condensed and fallen as snow in the polar regions, thus adding to the mass of the polar ice caps.

If Venus did indeed orbit Planet Earth temporarily, its mass would have induced a major tidal wave in the earth's crust, creating new mountain ranges and causing the oceans to surge over continents, expunging most life forms.

During its temporary orbits around our planet, the close approach of the luminous comet Venus with its writhing tail, undoubtedly struck such terror among the global populace, that archetypal images of Venus in its role of Lucifer the light bringer, remain until the present era. Thus Illuminist Albert Pike, in his tutorial for 33rd Degree freemasons, known as *Morals and Dogma,* states that Christianity should only be applied in the masonic instruction given to masons of the lower degrees, but that the masonic hierarchy worships Lucifer. Similarly, the esoteric works of Alice Bailey, possibly written for the purpose of indoctrinating New Agers into the acceptance of eugenics and the New World Order, are published by the Lucis Trust, formerly the Lucifer Publishing Company (Bailey's husband was a 33rd degree mason).

Mexican myths suggest that the comet possessed a serpent-like tail and was adorned with appendages similar in appearance to feathers. Such appendages are referred to by astronomers as a comets "beard"; this cataclysmic event probably gave rise to the legend of the plumed serpent Quetzalcoatl. On its approach to earth, the comet's luminous coma apparently created the illusion of possessing two appendages like the horns of a bull, to the terrified viewers on Earth. Sanchuniathon, a contemporary of the Assyrian Queen Semiramis, wrote that Astarte (another appellation of Venus) had the head of a bull, while the oral tradition of the Samoans held that: "The planet Venus became wild and horns grew out of her head."

In describing the resultant cataclysm, the Mayans claimed that oceans inundated continents, volcanoes erupted, mountains rose and fell and a ferocious wind roared accross the face of the earth, sweeping away all forests and towns. The Mayans named this terrible wind Hurrakan, from which the word "hurricane" is derived.

It is a consensus of academia that the earth's topography has evolved in a uniformitarian manner, i.e. no global cataclysms have occurred in recent millenia. This belief structure obviously is incorrect, as is evidenced by the data presented in this chapter. Having suggested that such a global disaster did, in fact, occur only approximately six thousand, eight hundred years ago, which destroyed existing civilizations, including possibly the Atlantean one, it now behooves us to determine the location of Atlantis, if it ever existed.

Writers have provided us with a plethora of possible Atlantean locations, including Tantalus in Turkey, the Bosphorus, Cuba and the Amazonian floodplains of Bolivia. Another proposed location, which has received considerable attention in recent years, after first being suggested by Greek archaeologist Professor Galanopoulos, is the Mediterranean island of Crete. Admittedly its Minoan civilization virtually ended when much of the island was destroyed by a catastrophic eruption of its volcano, known as Thera, which occurred circa 1500 B.C.. The Minoan civilization was not an advanced original culture as described by Plato, however, since the island's wealth was simply derived by virtue of its geographical location as a strategic intermediary stage in the trade route between the Ottomani culture of the Carpathian Basin to the north, and its terminus in Egypt. A major problem is that the above cited possible locations for Atlantis are too small to correlate with the vast geographical continent described by Plato.

The most popular site claimed for the location of the fabled Atlantis is in the Atlantic Ocean, either off Bimini, as claimed by Edgar Cayce, or along the Mid Atlantic Ridge. Unfortunately, Cayce was not the infallible psychic, as claimed by some Cayce biographers; in fact, many of his predictions were extremely vague, while others were totally incorrect, such as his predictions that San Francisco, Los Angeles and New York would be destroyed and submerged before the end of the twentieth century. The author suggests that many of Cayce's predictions were influenced by the beliefs of his financial mentor, Arthur Lammers. Lammers was a Theosophist who, in turn, probably was influenced by the writings concerning Atlantis made by Theosophists Helena Blavatsky and W. Scott-Elliot.

The 19th century congressperson Ignatius Donnelly wrote an erudite book entitled *Atlantis: The Antediluvian World,* which became a best seller. He was prompted to write the book after learning of the discovery of the Mid Atlantic Ridge—a subterranean mountain range up to six hundred miles in width, which extends from Iceland to near the coast of Antarctica. Unfortunately for Donnelly, extensive underwater explorations of the Atlantic Ocean (which included numerous core drillings) have failed to locate the remains of any large cities.

It is not unreasonable to imagine that if the continent of Atlantis was as militarily powerful as claimed, it would possess either an empire, or a commonwealth. If this were indeed the case, a landmass as large as an ice-free Antarctica could suffice as either Atlantis itself, or as an Atlantean satrapy. Since it presently is covered with an ice coating up to a mile thick in places, it is unlikely that core drillings will yield any ancient artifacts in the forseeable future. Be that as it may, we have only two meaningful accounts of Atlantis and its purported location, which have survived from antiquitity.

The first of these accounts is to be found in the writings of Plato (427-347 B.C.). In his dialogue *Timaeus,* Plato reports on the visit to Egypt undertaken by the Greek legislator Solon circa 600 B.C.. Psonchis, an Egyptian high priest, revealed to Solon that at one time, an advanced civilization existed on a vast continent called Atlantis; the continent rapidly sank beneath the waves, together with most of its inhabitants, about 9000 years prior to the time of Solon. The cataclysm was preceded by "a deviation in their course of the bodies moving around the Earth and the Heavens....", a possible reference to the celestial catastrophe that spawned Venus as a comet. Plato's *Critias,* which was never completed, states that Psonchis, the high priest, relates to Solon that the Atlanteans were accomplished architects; their capital city was eleven miles in diameter and contained a series of wide canals in the form of concentric rings.

Was the story of Atlantis, as reported by Plato, fact or fiction? Many present-day scholars dismiss Plato's Atlantean account as a fable, but Solon, Timaeus and Critias all were real historical figures. Timaeus hailed from southern Italy and was an explorer and astronomer, while Critias, a cousin of Plato's mother, was a poet and astronomer, who was killed in a battle in 403 B.C.. Krantor, a disciple of Plato, purportedly travelled to Egypt in order to verify for himself Plato's Atlantean account. Visiting the Temple of Neith at the former Egyptian capital city of Sais, Krantor, who was a scholar at the Great Library of Alexandria, claimed to have seen tablets which confirmed Plato's account of Atlantis.

Some aspects of Plato's narrative are troubling to the author. Plato claimed that the Atlanteans were defeated in a battle by the Athenian troops. This would imply that the city of Athens existed more than nine thousand years prior to Plato's era—a date far older than the founding of the Greek city. Psonchis, the name of the Egyptian high priest visited by Solon, is a Greek derivation of "Sebek," an Egyptian water deity and the son of the Goddess Neith. One of the pre-dynastic deities, Neith was associated with the Waters of Chaos, possibly an allusion to the demise of Atlantis (the Greek Goddess Athena was a later personification). There is a possibility that the high priest had a different birth name, "Psonchis" being selected by Plato in order to present factual information in the form of an allegorical story.

According to Plato, the continent of Atlantis was located in the Atlantic Ocean beyond the Pillars of Heracles, and was larger than North Africa and Asia Minor combined. As was stated previously, extensive undersea exploration of the Atlantic seabed conducted by several individual nations, has failed to indicate the remains of possible major artifacts, other than a possible subterranean causeway and a purported pyramid observed in separate areas of the Carribean. Does this imply that Plato's claim that Atlantis was in the Atlantic Ocean was a fallacious statement? Not at all—it simply means that the typical writer on Atlantean matters has failed to conduct sufficient research, and consequently seeks the fabled continent in the wrong geographical region of the planet!

Exactly which region of the world was Plato referring to when he claimed that Atlantis had been situated in the Atlantic Ocean? A perusal of classical authors demonstrates that Aristotle (384-322B.C.) in his *De Coelo* states that the term "Atlantic Ocean" encompassed all the world's oceans, while Herodotus, who predated Plato by a century, claimed that the Atlantic Ocean was the ocean we now refer to as the Indian Ocean.

It therefore behooves us to refer to the only known extremely ancient historical body of knowledge which makes reference to the continent of Atlantis. This is the official history of the world, as meticulously kept for millenia by the historians of the Illuminati. Certain mind controlled Illuminati slaves who attain the exalted rank known as Mother of Darkness, are programmed to possess photographic memories, in order to perpetuate an oral tradition of maintaining an accurate history of the world. Such slaves are provided access to the world's most closely guarded repositories of ancient historical works, such as the Vatican Library and the works of antiquity found in certain Asian monasteries.

Occasionally, the mind control programming of a few high-level Illuminati slaves begins to unravel upon the death of their programmers. Through working in a support capacity in order to assist such hapless victims to escape the clutches of the Illuminati, the author has learned how to access much historical data believed by the arrogant Illuminati hierarchy to be irretrievable by members of humanity.

According to the official Illuminati history, Atlantis was a vast continent which divided the Indian and Pacific oceans. According to contemporary geologists, continents can be subjected to uplifting forces, but cannot sink. As previously stated in this essay, evidence of fossilized tropical plants has been found in all areas of this planet, suggestive that prior to the Noahic global flood, the atmospheric water canopy referred to in the Book of Genesis was an actuality.

Since the water vapor is a far more efficient greenhouse gas than carbon dioxide, the resultant greenhouse effect enveloping the planet at that time period would have created far more vegetation globally, than is existing at the present time.

The oxygen transpired by plantlife is derived from dissociation (splitting) of the water molecules in the vegetation, not from dissociation of carbon dioxide molecules during photosynthesis. In practical terms, this means that water taken in by plantlife is not recoverable as part of the normal hydrological cycle, since the hydrogen atoms contained in the dissociated water molecules are used in the formation of plant carbohydrates. At the present time, some six hundred billion tons of water are dissociated by land and marine plantlife annually.

This figure would have been far greater in Atlantean times, due to the luxuriant plantlife pervading all regions of Earth, which in turn would suggest that the oceans were much more shallow in those days. According to Illuminati global history, the vast Atlantean continent encompassed Japan to the north and Indonesia in the south. The continent would have included the land now covered by the South China Sea. Significantly, the depth of the South China Sea seldom exceeds three hundred feet.

In summation, evidence has been presented in this essay which suggests that Atlantis did, in fact, exist. It was a continent approximately three times the size of present-day India; moreover, it did not sink—most of its landmass simply was submerged when an enormous volume of ice of extraterrestrial origin was deposited in the polar regions. Japan, Indonesia, Malaysia and the Phillipines are the remnants of Atlantis which were not submerged, but had their topography modified by tidal waves and volcanic activity arising from the cataclysm.

The causal factor of this catastrophic event, according to the author's hypothesis, was an ice-coated comet, which orbited earth temporarily, creating geophysical havoc in the form of mountain building and volcanic activity. This horrendous event annihilated most terrestrial life-forms which existed at lower elevations of the planet. Agglomerations of Venusian rock may have been sufficiently insulated by a thick enough ice coating, as to withstand excessive frictional heating as it encountered Earth's atmosphere. If this were the case—the ice coating functioning as a sacrificial ablative insulator, then the rock may have contained deadly pathogens which caused certain terrestrial species of megafauna, such as the mastodon and diprotodon to become extinct. Even though paleontological evidence has revealed that mass extinctions of very large mammals occurred after the appearance on earth of humankind, it may mean that deadly pathogens released during the above-described catalysmic event were the causal factor in the hapless creatures demise, not that they were hunted to extinction by homosapiens. The author hopes that modern dating methods, e.g. the optical dating technique, which records tha last time that grains of quarz were exposed to sunlight, be used in order to determine such extinction periods.

The wayward comet eventually orbited the sun as the planet Venus, apparently perturbing Earth and Mars in the process. This explains why the Mars Pathfinder survey revealed that rocks on the Martian surface exhibited very little erosion, despite the occurrence of sandstorms, suggestive that the present Martian landscape is only a few thousand years old. The Krakatoa volcano, which erupted so explosively in the 19th. century, well may have been an extremely tall mountain during the Atlantean era—possibly the fabled Mount Atlas; the resultant cauldera would therefore have created the present-day Sunda Straights, which are located between Sumatra and Java.

The author's contention that Atlantis spanned both the Indian Ocean and the Pacific Ocean would appear to be in conflict with the claims of writers who believed that this was the site of other submerged continents.Thus the previously-mentioned Theosophist W. Scott-Elliot, after writing his book concerning Atlantis, wrote another book in which he claimed that he psychically perceived that there was a lost continent in the Pacific Ocean. Zoologist L.P. Sclater called this purported continent Lemuria, after the animal known as the lemur.

In 1926, a young Englishman by the name of James Churchward, had a book published called *The Lost Continent of Mu.* Churchward claimed that while in India, a Brahmin priest permitted him to copy ancient tablets which purported to describe a lost continent in the Pacific Ocean called Mu. According to Churchward, he later encountered a mining engineer named William Niven, who hailed from Scotland. Niven showed Churchward some engraved stone tablets which he had discovered in a Mexican village located near Acapulco. According to Churchward, the tablets were written in the same language as that on the tablets previously shown him by the Brahmin priest in India. Churchward claimed that the Mexican tablets had been written by Naacal priests, who had been sent to Central America from Mu.

Churchward wrote five books about the mysterious submerged continent of Mu, which have been regarded as fraudulent by some scholars, due to Churchward's failure to provide a meaningful location for the Indian temple that held the supposed tablets. There is a possibility that Churchward, lacking the ability to decipher the Mexican tablets which had been discovered by Niven, concocted the fictitious account of the Mu civilization after making the acquaintance of an elderly adventurer named Augustus Le Plongeon, who died in Algiers, in 1915.

A former lawyer, Le Plongeon and his English wife settled in Yucatan in 1873. After learning the Mayan language, Le Plongeon translated the Mayan text known as the *Troano Codex,* which significantly, according to Le Plongeon, described the cataclysmic submergence beneath the waves of an ancient continent that the Mayans called Mu.

What we appear to have then, are not two ancient continents—Atlantis in the present-day Atlantic Ocean and Mu in the Pacific, as is currently claimed by writers of the New Age genre, but in reality only one partially submerged continent situated in both the Indian and North Pacific Oceans!

If the global flood destroyed most life existing on the surface of Planet Earth, it presumably would have destroyed civilization as it existed in the pre-flood era. Surprisingly, a trace of a previous advanced culture is to be found in the remarkably advanced catamarans still sailed in the Pacific Ocean by the inhabitants of the Marianas Islands. These catamarans, locally known as proas, date back at least five thousand years; they not only possess an asymmetric hull, thus eliminating the necessity for a centerboard, a feature only reintroduced in the 20th century by catamaran designer Hobie Alter, but also incorporate a mast inclined at an acute angle, in order to provide a vertical lifting component to the hull.

The science of ethnomusicography also provides us with clues to incredibly complex music of great antiquity, such as very ancient clay flutes discovered in Central America capable of accommodating a musical scale consisting of eighty microtones. One would hope that traces of a very ancient culture would be found in the vicinity of the approriately-named Atlas Mountains of Morocco. This is indeed the case, for local woodwind musicians perform very complex music characterized by holding notes for incredibly long periods of time—a feat far beyond the capabilities of western trained musicians. The holding of such long notes is accomplished by boring a hole extending from behind the ear to the windpipe of the musician. The origins of this unique surgical procedure are lost in the mists of time, and could be a legacy from Atlantis, retained by migrating flood survivors.

According to the official Illuminati history of the world, which has been shielded from the general public for millenia, the Atlanteans were a race of reptilians and the overlords of humanity. Curiously, a very politically-oriented and powerful international cult exists at the present time. Known as the Mahikari, the cult was founded by Lt. Colonel Yoshikazu Okada, who was a member of the former Japanese Emperor's bodyguard. Lower cult members are given to believe that the cult is a New Age organization dedicated to spiritual matters. In reality, the Mahikari cult's heirarchy is composed of the financial power group that determines the political policies of the Japanese Government.

This power group believes that the world was ruled from Japan during the pre-flood era and that it is the destiny of the present Japanese Emperor to be the new global ruler. Japan has entered into a covert treaty with Russia, in which Russia has provided Japan with Tesla geophysical warfare technology, receiving advanced computer chips for Russian missiles in exchange. Since the author's hypothesis suggests that Japan once formed a part of the Atlantean continent, perhaps a new Atlantean global dictatorship will become a grim reality in the very near future, if the Mahikari cult succeeds in its endeavors.

CHAPTER 4

▼

THE GREAT PYRAMID MYSTERY: TOMB, OCCULT INITIATION CENTER— OR WHAT?

"Someday what we thought was myth will be found to contain the true history of the past, while what we always regarded as history will be relegated to a myth of our own making"
Gerald Massey, Egyptologist.

According to the aristocratic scholar Bertrand Russell, in his book *"Wisdom of the West"*, "Both Egypt and Babylon furnished some knowledge which the Greeks later took over. But neither developed Science of Philosophy. Whether this was due to a lack of native genius or to social conditions is not a fundamental question here." [1] This ill-informed comment is a graphic example of why we should refrain from implicitly trusting the information provided by academic "experts".

Most Egyptologists would have us believe that Egyptian civilization commenced circa 2995 B.C., was dominated by a necrophilic priesthood resistant to change and that construction of the the Great

Pyramid commenced about 2500 B.C., during the reign of the Pharoah Khufu (Cheops). They also claim that the Sphinx was created by Cheop's son Chefren.

A new perspective on early Egyptian culture was provided by the 1957 publication of the book *"Le Temple de l'Homme"*, written by R.A. Schwaller de Lubicz (1891-1961). Well versed in the esoteric arts (he taught Flamel a thing or two about transmutation) and influenced by the philosopher and mystic Henri Bergson, he spent several years in Egypt, devoting much of his time to a study of the Temple of Luxor, where he came to the realization that the civilization of ancient Egypt embraced an integrated corpus of sacred geometry, art, religion, science and philosophy, which enabled people to live in attunement with the cosmos. Moreover, his study of the Great Pyramid and the Sphinx revealed evidence of erosion by water, suggesting that the two huge edifices were of greater antiquity than was generally believed. An important point missed by earlier Egyptologists, but recognized by Schwaller, was that Egyptian hieroglyphs were not merely a phonetic script for the purpose of conveying information to a lay public, but possessed the dual function of also providing hermetic symbolism for the esoteric initiate.

His massive three-volume work was largely ignored until Egyptologist John Anthony West presented a lucid study of Schwaller de Lubicz's research in his 1987 book *"Serpent in the Sky"*.[2] Almost three decades ago, astronomer Virginia Trimble claimed that if the constellation of Orion (considered in ancient Egypt to be the celestial counterpart of their deity Osiris) is superimposed over the Giza Plateau, the three stars forming Orion's belt (Alnitak, Alnilam and Mintaka) are in alignment with the three pyramids (Khufu, Khafre and Menkaure). In 1994, a book by Egyptian-born amateur astronomer Robert Bauval was published, which also made the same claim. Furthermore, claimed Bauval, two other stars in the same constellation,

Saiph and Bellatrix, were in alignment with the remains of pyramids at Abu Ruwash and Zawyat al Aryan.[3]

Bauval later co-authored a book with journalist Graham Hancock, which concluded that since the Sphinx's erosion by water could not have occurred during historical times due to known lack of precipitation, it must have been built circa 10,500 B.C., in order to herald the dawning of the age of Leo.[4]

Through the use of the Global Positioning Satellite System, American astroarchaeologist Larry Hunter discovered that Bauval had incorrectly superimposed the Orion constellation over the Giza Plateau; he found, however, that when the star Rigel (Orion's left knee) was located over Abu Ruwash, and the star Betalgeuse (Orion's right shoulder) over Zawyat al Aryan, the constellation alignment became precise. Hunter subsequently determined that the stars erroneously sited by Bauval (Saiph and Bellatrix) plus two other stars in the same constellation, were in alignment with locations where Hunter discovered evidence of subterranean cyclopean stone structures.

Schwaller de Lubicz, West, Hunter, Bauval and Hancock all postulate that the Great Pyramid and the Sphinx were constructed by a technologically advanced race of beings who were not Egyptians, and may be Atlantean descendants. The above-cited authors consider the Great Pyramid's principal function to be that of an initiatory center involving necrophilic rites, in which a deceased Osiris is given immortality and, postulates Hunter, the shaft connecting the King's Chamber with the south face of the pyramid, was intended to serve as a portal for the ascent of Osiris' soul.

These authors were undoubtedly influenced by the Pyramid Texts inscribed on the tomb walls of 5th and 6th Dynasty pyramids, which are located at Saqqara, some ten miles to the south of Giza. The texts state that the ressurected Osiris became lord of a celestial realm adjacent to the Milky Way and known to the ancient Egyptians as the Duat. This region includes the Orion constellation.

The same authors also assume that the Great Pyramid was constructed in 2500 B.C. (The same date claimed by orthodox Egyptologists) because the north and south shafts emanating from the King's Chamber aligned at the meridian transit with the stars Alpha Draconis and Zeta Orionis respectively, during 2500 B.C.. This star alignment only lasted for approximately a century before and after this period.

The 2500 B.C. date for this star alignment presents a major problem in the above authors hypotheses, for in 1983, the Edgar Cayce Foundation, in an attempt to validate Cayce's claim that the Great Pyramid was built in 10,500 B.C. by Atlantean survivors of a cataclysm, commissioned the Radio Carbon Laboratory at Southern Methodist University to determine the age of seventy-two mortar samples taken from the great Pyramid.

Unlike earlier carbon dating methods, which often gave inaccurate results, the mortar samples in question contained charcoal believed to have been residue from the stonemason's campfires; for accuracy, the samples were calibrated by the tree-ring procedure. The results indicated a date for the mortar of 3000 B.C., thus putting the construction of the Great Pyramid at the dawn of the dynastic period, some 374 years earlier than the previously accepted date. This revised date invalidates the prediction of Edgar Cayce that the Great Pyramid was constructed circa 10,500 B.C. It also suggests that since the shafts emanating from the King's Chamber would fail to align with the previously-mentioned stars in 3000 B.C., the basic premise of Bauval, Hancock and Hunter regarding the purpose of the shafts, appears to be badly flawed. [5]

In contrast to the ornately-decorated temples and tombs known to have been constructed during the era of the pharoahs, the architecture of the Great Pyramid, with its stark, undecorated interior and use of massive stone blocks, is characteristic of an earlier time period. In fact, the Egyptian civilization, like that of the Indus Valley culture, lacks a period of development, suddenly mysteriously appearing, then gradually *devolving,* as a necrophilic priesthood aquired political control in Egypt. [6]

Commenting upon this mystery, John Anthony West stated: "A realistic approach to the mystery suggests alternatives that are unacceptable to the orthodox mind. The first is that Egyptian civilization did not develop insitu but was brought to Egypt by hypothetical conquerors. This alternative simply translates the mystery of a period of development to the as-yet-undiscovered homeland of these conquerors. The second alternative is that Egypt did not develop her civilization, but inherited it." [7]

That an advanced civilization once existed in prehistoric times is beyond doubt, as is evidenced not only by the incorporation of sacred geometry in the design of the Great Pyramid, but also by the Haji Ahmed portolan map. The map depicts the North American continent, replete with a wide natural landbridge connecting Alaska and Siberia, and an accurate outline of an ice-free Antarctica, suggesting that an ancient race possessed superb surveying and mapmaking skills.

A major anomaly of the past that has been ignored by academia, is the work of botanist Nikolai Ivanovitch Vavilov, described in the previous chapter, which suggests that a global cataclysm destroyed all vegetation in lowland regions of the planet.

In order to identify the mysterious and technologically advanced race who gave Egypt its civilization and bestowed a legacy in the form of the Great Pyramid, we must reconstruct the patterns of the past which currently are obscured by the mists of time. Previously we saw that a global flood and ice age apparently occurred simultaneously only 6,800 years ago; this catastrophic event literally changed the face of the earth, possibly destroying an advanced civilization in the process. After accomplishing this task, we must then establish a meaningful rationale for building the Great Pyramid.

The recent Mars Pathfinder mission has revealed that the rocks on the Martian landscape lack sufficient erosion to have been on the

Martian surface for more than 10,000 years, according to geologists. Martian anomalies are of particular importance; the Martian terrain is scarred with very deep canyons, which academia claims were gouged out by massive torrents of water, flowing thousands of miles accross the Martian surface and emanating from subterranean geothermal sources. Such reasoning is patently absurd, since the Martian surface is so incredibly cold that water would only flow for a very short distance from its source before freezing. Moreover, the near vacuum of the Martian atmosphere would cause water to instantly vaporize.

If the canyons of Mars were, indeed, created by large volumes of water, Mars at one time must have enjoyed a much warmer climate, implying that Mars previously orbited much closer to the sun. At the present time, Caucasians are able to exist quite comfortably in equatorial regions, rendering the necessity for dark pigmentation redundant. This implies that at one time, there was an era when the climate of Planet Earth was so hot that only dark-skinned races could survive on its surface, as would be the case if Earth once orbited closer to the sun. Not surprisingly perhaps, ancient skeletons discovered in the vicinity of Stonehenge and along the western coast of France, display the nasal fossae and steatopygic spinal deformation characteristic of many female Africans.

The author hypothesises that Planet Earth orbited closer to the sun at one time and that Mars originally occupied our present orbit. Possessing too much residual angular momentum to become a permanent satellite of our planet, Venus—originally a wayward comet, finally entered into its present orbit, displacing our planet in the process. The Earth in turn displaced Mars—the latter's present orbit being too far from the sun to sustain life on its surface. If the pyramidal structures in the Cydonia region of Mars prove to be artificial constructs, we are left to ponder whether the pyramid builders of Mars were sufficiently technologically advanced to abandon their planet and relocate on Earth, spawning the various Indo-Aryan cultures.

If this notion appears too preposterous, perhaps someone will explain why the Giza Plateau, upon which resides the Great Pyramid, was formerly named El-Kahira, a name etymologically derived from the Arabic noun El-Kahir, meaning Mars!

A great deal of recorded history has been deliberately distorted by Illuminati-controlled historians. Conversely, the Illuminati hierarchy maintains closely-guarded and accurate historical records for its own purposes. According to the Illuminati, the Aryan race originated in the Lyrian constellation prior to colonizing Mars and establishing high-technology outposts on Planet Earth.

The author accordingly suggests that a previously advanced civilization was destroyed in a cataclysmic celestial event involving Venus, which resulted in a simultaneous global flood and ice age, that re-shaped the topography of Earth. As stated in the previous chapter, the Sumerian monarch King Ziusudra, who purportedly lived 6,800 years ago, was advised to construct a ship capable of withstanding a capsize. We also noted in the previous chapter the metallic spheres that were discovered embedded in very ancient pyrophilic rock in the Wonderstone Silver Mine in South Africa.[8] It is evident that history is not linear, as academia would has us believe, but rather a series of cyclical series of advanced civilizations interspersed with periods of devolution.

In all probability, most of humanity did not survive the global flood and its accompanying ice age. In a short period of time, most of the survivors would have been reduced to hunter-gatherers, forced to live in mountainous regions at high elevations, until the floodwaters receded.

Procuring food would occupy most of the survivors time; within a few generations, most of the survivor's offspring would have forgotten how to read and write, as literacy devolved to an aboriginal level. Imagine the consequences if a self-contained cooperative, with the technology to produce its own food and water, survived the cataclysm, and after several decades ventured out among the illiterate hunter-gatherers and taught them the rudiments of agriculture and education. Such a group would be hailed as wizards; with the passage of time they would be elevated to the level of deities. This is what apparently happened to one group of technologically advanced flood survivors in the Middle East.

It is difficult to establish an accurate historical record of events preceding, and those occurring shortly after the global deluge, primarily due to the ambiguity of early textual material. The early post-flood Sumerian language *(emi-ku)* consisted of very specific pictographs, thus enabling us to identify a literal meaning for each pictograph. With the passage of time, and especially after the Babylonians adopted the Sumerian language, many meanings were assigned to the same pictograph. This is why it is imperative to refer back to the original pictograph, not to a highly stylized version of several centuries later.

Unfortunately, this later textual ambiguity has permitted mediocre scholars and Illuminati disinformers to present a very inaccurate picture of early post-flood history. Although pre-flood history is not really germane to this article, the Gilgamish texts (consisting of nine clay cylinders) are illustrative of this problem. The texts state that some two hundred persons assembled in a high valley on Mount Hermon, which is situated at the common border between Israel, Lebanon and Syria, and constructed a cedarwood dwelling.

They were under the leadership of Dinger en Lil Li (Enlil). *"Dinger"* implies that he was an heirarchical figure; the word *"Li"* was derived from a pictograph of a potted plant. The word *Lil"* originally was *"ge"*, meaning "of", but later was adopted by the Babylonians as meaning "air" or "wind". Hence the original translation, which suggested "Lord of agriculture", frequently is interpreted at the present time as "God of the air", which is incorrect.

To make matters worse, the pictograph *"Li"*, which originally depicted a potted plant, was turned on its side at a later date and embellished into a stylized ideogram, which bore no resemblance to a potted plant. Incredibly, author Zechariah Sitchen claims that this particular ideogram represents a two-stage rocketship and interprets the entire phrase as "The Righteous ones of the rocketship"!

The Gilgamesh Epic states that these beings established a farming community at a place they named *Edin,* the ideogram for which suggests a lofty plain with cascading water. They taught agriculture to the local natives, then later descended the mountain and migrated to Mesopotamia. With the passage of time, the group became deified. One group member, Ugmash, was involved with astronomy, later becoming deified as the sun-god Shamash by the Babylonians, and as Ogma by the Irish.

The writer hypothesizes that this group survived the flood by seeking refuge near the summit of Mount Hermon. As the floodwaters receded, the survivors, originally technologically advanced Aryan colonizers from Mars, descended to lower terrain and established the Edin community. These flood survivors, originally referred to in the Sumerian texts as *a-nan-na,* later became known as the *Anannage* or *Annunaki.*

We must not jump to the conclusion that these flood survivors were extraterrestrial humanoids, just because the Hebrew word *"nephilim"* means "those who descended", for the group had to descend the mountain at the commencement of their trek to Mesopotamia. Similarly, New Age authors have claimed that Ninkharsag—a female member of the group, was an extraterrestrial simply because clay figurines of her portray a being with very large eyes. This well may be artistic license, for the Pitt-Rivers collection of male fertility gods in England depict men with incredibly large genitalia, yet it never has been claimed that these represent space aliens. The same may be said for the very ancient female figurines from the Cyclades Islands, in which the breasts have been modified to represent a vagina—not a very biologically practical arrangement, even for an extraterrestrial being.

In order to avoid being considered part of the New Age lunatic fringe, the best we can deduce from the Gilgamesh Epic is that if they ever existed at all, we lack sufficient data to determine whether they were of human or extraterrestrial origin. This does not preclude the possibility, however, that the human race originally was created by an alien race, as some texts imply. Of course, that compels us to question who created the extraterrestrials.

For some strange reason, most historians assume that Mesopotamia was the cradle of post-flood civilization, but this is not necessarily the case. Consider the discovery of coppersmelting. Students are usually taught that copper first was discovered when a campfire was built over a deposit of copper ore, but such a feat is impossible, since a campfire does not attain the 1200 degrees Centigrade temperature that is necessary for the smelting process. In addition, most copper ore does not contain metallic copper; the ore has to be roasted and a suitable reducing agent added to the molten copper in order to convert the oxide present to metallic copper. Copper smelting clearly is too sophisticated a technology to have been developed by a primitive tribe. Presumably, the technology is a legacy from the pre-flood era, passed on by survivors of the cataclysm.

Until the present century, archaeologists believed that the European bronze industry was developed by Mycenean prospectors searching for new ore bodies, but this belief was dashed in 1907, when four laborers began digging a drainage ditch in the Carpathian Basin, a region where the countries of Czechoslovakia, Hungary and Romania meet at the headwaters of the Tisza River.

Approximately two feet beneath the surface of the sandy soil, the laborers discovered a cache of bronze weaponry, consisting of a sword and twelve battle axes. The sword was ornately decorated with the curvilinear scrollwork that is normally associated with Celtic and Mycenean jewellery. Bronze artifacts and the molds in which they were cast were found in the same locale, demonstrative that these were the product of a local bronze industry, not merely Mycenean imports. These items were the work of a culture known as the Otomani, and were manufactured more than a millenium prior to the dawning of the Celtic period.

The Otomani, who also were manufacturing iron objects during the early copper age, appear to be the first people after the flood to have used chariots with spoked wheels, and were probably the precursors of the Celts. The presence of iron artifacts implies that the Otomani knew how to slag off and refine iron as a by-product of copper smelting. The discovery of the early establishment of the Otomani culture means that the early historical record of Europe and the Middle East will have to be revised accordingly.[9]

The name Babylon conjures up images of hanging gardens, the Tower of Babel and the oligarchical couple Queen Semiramis and her husband Nimrod; they were the first recorded rulers of Babylonia, which was situated in the southern half of Mesopotamia (the northern half being Assyria).

Establishing the time period in which they reigned remains speculative; we are informed by the historians of antiquity that the father of Nimrod was the biblical Cush, also known as Bel or Belus. Since Cush was the grandson of Noah and the son of Ham, Babylon quite possibly was one of the first cities to have been built after the global deluge, a time when the last of the floodwaters were draining off the land. According to Josephus, Nimrod built the Tower of Babel as a place of refuge in the event of another calamitous flood: "….He would build it so high that the waters of another flood which the world might be afflicted, would not be able to submerge it."

Additional evidence that not many generations had elapsed since the deluge before the foundations of Babylon were laid, is to be found in the works of Diodorus Siculus and Plutarch, who both wrote of an era when Egypt was an inland sea. According to the historian Herodotus, Egypt was a marshland during the reign of its first ruler.

The offspring of the biblical Ham traditionally have been associated with Egypt; in fact, the biblical name for Egypt was Mizraim, which also was the name of one of Ham's sons. The Hebrew name *"Mizraim"* means "encloser of the sea", derived from *Tzr* "to enclose" and *"Im"*, meaning "sea". It has been claimed that during the reign of the first Egyptian ruler, often referred to as Menes, the land was drained by diverting the River Nile and enclosing its former course with an embankment (Schwaller de Lubicz concluded that the Nile was an artificial construction). It is quite probable, then, that Mizraim, whose name suggests that he was a skilled hydrologist, reclaimed Egypt from the floodwaters and became its first ruler, under the name of Menes.

Since Mizraim was the brother of Cush and, according to the Book of Genesis, Ch. 10, "Cush begat Nimrod", who was the founder of Babylon, the city must be one of the most ancient of all cities constructed after the Noahic flood. It is well to remember that the events depicted in Genesis were written many centuries after the fact. Even though Noah's descendants are portrayed as mortals in the Bible, in an earlier post-deluvial period they were hailed as deities. Thus Cush became deified as Hermes a synonym meaning "Son of Ham"; similarly the name *"Ham"* or *"Khem"*, meaning "the burnt one", has connotations of solar worship.

A curious jubilee medal, struck in 1825 by the authority of Pope Leo XII, depicted on the reverse side a woman symbolizing the Catholic Church, holding in her left hand a crucifix; her right hand held a cup and upon her head was the seven-rayed crown of Mithra, the Sun God (similar to the Mithraic crown on the Statue of Liberty). Surrounding the figure was the latin inscription *"Sedet Super Universum"* (the whole world is her seat). The figure is clearly a blatant depiction of Queen Semiramis and her Mystery religion, as characterised in the Book of Revelation 17:1-6, and is indicative of the true roots of Catholicism.

Early historians, such as Herodotus, claimed that religion, idolatory and the Mysteries all originated in Babylon. In a similar vein, the noted 19th century Assyriologist Sir Henry Layard, wrote: "Of the great antiquity of this primitive worship there is abundant evidence, and that it originated among the inhabitants of the Assyrian plains, we have the united testimony of sacred and profane history." The Babylonians believed in a supreme being and also in a Holy Trinity, which they symbolized by means of an equilateral triangle, the latter being adopted by the Catholic Church.

As in Papal Rome, worship of the Mother and Child was a dominant aspect of the Babylonian religious system. Queen Semiramis was deified as the Queen of Heaven and also as Rhea, the virgin mother of the gods, sometimes referred to as the Great Earth Mother. In another aspect, she was worshipped as Astarte, meaning "the woman who made towers"— a name possibly commemorating her role in the construction of the Tower of Babel. Her husband, the mighty ruler Nimrod, represented the dualistic role of God the Father and also as Ninus, the son of Semiramis. In the Old Testament (Ezekial 8:14) Ninus is represented as Tammuz, who, according to the writer Lanctantius, was crucified with a lamb at his feet, placed in a cave and found to have disappeared when a rock was removed from the cave's entrance, three day's later.

Nimrod was accorded the title Baal (the Lord) and his wife Semiramis bore the corresponding accolade Baalti (My Lady) the latin term for which is "Mea Domina", which, in a corrupted Italian form, is the popular "Madonna".

As the centuries rolled by, the Mother and Child myth adopted an air of universality, becoming Isis and her husband/son Horus in Egypt, Isi and Iswara in India, and as Cybele and Deoius in Asia. The first Jesuit missionaries to visit China were astounded to discover paintings of Shing Moo, the Chinese Holy Mother, depicted with an aura radiating about her head, and bearing a child in her arms.

The plethora of names accorded to Semiramis creates a linguistic nightmare through which researchers must tread with extreme caution. The task is well worth the effort however, for it demonstrates that the mythologies of many nations have their roots in the Babylonian legend. Thus the Greeks claimed that Kronos, equated by classical scholars with Saturn, was the brother of Rhea, the Greek mother of the gods, yet

Theophilus of Antioch stated that in the east, Kronus was known as Bel; a claim reinforced by the early Christian historian Eusebius, who wrote that the Assyrians called their first ruler Kronos. Since Kronos was the king of the Cyclops, who were known as tower builders, there is little doubt that the deity worshipped by the Greeks as Kronos, was none other than the Nimrod / Baal / Ninus of the Babylonians.

The name Kronos, signifying "the Horned One", is an appropriate appellation for Nimrod, who was often represented on Babylonian bas-reliefs as a bull. Layard presented a Babylonian relief depicting Nimrod wearing upon his head the horns of a slain bull; the lower half of Nimrod's body possessed a tail and cloven hooves. This representation of the Babylonian monarch bears a remarkable similarity to Zernebogus, a malevolent Celtic black-skinned deity replete with horns and tail. Zernebogus, meaning *"Seed of Cush,"* clearly another name for Nimrod, for the latter was the son of Cush and grandson of the biblical Ham, who purportedly was dark-skinned.

According to that most ancient of historians, Sancuniathon, Astarte (Semiramis) "….put on her own head a bull's head as an ensign of royalty," the horns symbolizing monarchical authority. Eventually this royal head adornment in Babylonia and Assyria took the form of a metal headband surmounted by three metallic horns, signifying regal power of a celestial origin. Thus was born the concept of a crown, or coronet, as a symbol of royalty. As the custom spread to India, the symbolic horns were superceded by a trio of leaves, which with the passage of time adopted the form of the fleur-de-lis.

In addition to her ascribed deified roles as Queen of Heaven and Virgin Mother of the Gods, Semiramis also represented the Holy Spirit; in her latter role, she graphically was depicted as a dove bearing an olive branch—the branch symbolizing her immaculately conceived son Tammuz. That the dove is holding an olive branch is not surprising, for the name *"Semiramis"* means "the branch bearer," derived from *"Ze"* (the) *"emir"* (branch) and *"amit"* (bearer).

The Mystery religion developed by the corrupt Babylonian priesthood, was designed to be all things to all of the populace, and accordingly, its rites embraced everything from baptism and sexual excesses, to drunken revelry and human sacrifice. A major Babylonian rite held in early spring, in order to commemorate the death and resurrection three days later of Tammuz, included offerings of buns inscribed with the solar cross. Easter is a derivation of "Ishtar," another of the many faces of Queen Semiramis (a later form of Ishtar was the Anglo-Saxon goddess Eostre).

The awesome havoc wrought by the comet Venus, as it temporarily orbited Earth, so traumatized the flood survivors that Venus left an indelible impression in the memory of the flood survivors and their descendants. Thus Sancuniathon assures us that Semiramis also was deified as the goddess Venus, whose sacred day was Friday; since the Babylonians regarded fish to be an aphrodisiac, it is not surprising that the fish became a sacred symbol of the Goddess of Love.

The husband of Semiramis also was venerated as a god associated with fish. As the fish-god Dagon, he was depicted as half-human, half-fish; when the composite creature was portrayed in profile on Babylonian bas-reliefs, the head of the open-mouthed fish formed a mitre above the head of the man. H.A. Ironside states that the Pope is "….the direct successor of the Babylonian mysteries and the servant of the fish-god Dagon, for whom he wears, like his idolatrous predecessors, the fisherman's ring."[10]

Nimrod also was deified as Eannus, the god with two faces, later known to the Romans as Janus, who was empowered to open the doors of heaven. It is from the word *"cardo"* meaning "hinge," that the term "Cardinal" is derived. In order to attain political control of the populace, the Babylonian priesthood claimed that Nimrod, in his role as Eannus, was the sole possessor of the keys which unlocked the doors of heaven, and accordingly, was the Creator's sole intermediary with the human race; any dogma not approved by Nimrod was therefore false.

To consolidate their new-found power, the Babylonian priesthood established a governing body known as the Grand Council of Pontiffs.

Like some religions of the present era, the religion of Babylonia consisted of an exoteric shell for the promulgation of false dogma for the superstitious masses, and an inner core of Mystery teachings concerning the Sacred Canon of Numbers and other esoteric subjects, for a select group of initiates. The Babylonian High Priest who instructed the initiates was known as a Peter, meaning "the Great Interpreter." Athens later continued the tradition by establishing the Eleusinian Mysteries, where candidates for initiation received instruction from a book known as the *"Pet Roma."* In Egypt, the deified Kush was known as *"Ptr-Roma."*

Not surprisingly perhaps, St Peter's feast-day traditionally was celebrated on the day when the sun entered Aquarius—previously the day when Eannus and his later Roman counterpart were honored. The writer suggests that devout Christians who find the foregoing passages troublesome, should not forsake their church, but rather attempt to make it a better place, e.g. by opening its doors to the homeless.

As we have seen, with the passage of time, Semiramis and Nimrod became deified under a plethora of names, each name representing a different aspect of the increasingly perverted religion concocted by the despotic priests of Baal. In their quest for power during the embronic years of the Babylonian civilization, the priesthood adopted the philosophy discussed by Machiavelli milleniums later in the *Discourses:* that humanity is moved by two principal things—love and fear. Unfortunately, the one who arouses fear gains more of a following and is more readily obeyed than the one who wins their affection.

Through the establishment of a religion which promulgated the worship of deities whom the public feared, the priesthood was able to attain dominion over the masses, who mistakenly grew to equate deity worship with love, a trait still prevalent among religious practitioners today, who fail to realize that it is not really possible to love a vengeful god, who might bring retribution to those who have the temerity to question biblical passages.

Of all the deified aspects of Nimrod, none struck more terror into the hearts of the superstitious populace of Babylonia than that of Moloch (later known to the Israelites as Tammuz) in whose honor the sadistic priesthood demanded ritual sacrifice by fire, of children. The name *"Tammuz"* in fact, is derived from the verbs *"tam"* (to perfect) and *"muz"* (to burn). When the Babylonian religion spread to Britain, the degenerate druidic "priests of the grove," in conducting the Beltane ritual (Mayday) burned a huge wicker effigy of a man, in the belly of which were hapless sacrificial victims.

Not surprisingly, St John's Eve falls on June 23rd, which was the day that the Feast of Tammuz was celebrated to commemorate the deity's ascension from the underworld. After his resurrection, he was known as Oannes, a version of the name "John"!

Every summer in the present era, some 1600 of America's leading bankers, politicians and captains of industry, gather at a heavily-guarded 2,700 acre retreat in Northern California known as Bohemia Grove. The bizarre procedings commence with the burning of a Celtic wicker effigy of a person. Even though a ceremony, whose central figure is an idol possessing a gruesome and bloody history, fill a balanced individual with revulsion, it must be remembered that many of the patrician members of the Bohemian Club are initiates of such Illuminati secret societies as the Skull and Bones. They covertly conduct the martial and mysterious rites of the solar deity Mithra, both at Yale University and at their island retreat in the Hudson River.

Significantly, the Bohemian Grove wicker ritual takes place beneath a huge sculpture of an owl. The owl was a symbol of Moloch and death. It also appears as a concealed micro engraving on the U.S. Dollar bill. A "snuff" movie, filmed on behalf of the Illuminati, features a young women being ritually murdered at the Grove. In keeping with most secret societies, the Bohemian Club has an inner core of initiates who are cognizant of the darker aspects of the organization, and a peripheral membership who are unaware of such activities. These lesser members and their guests attend various social gatherings at the Grove throughout much of the year, in order to present an aura of innocuous respectability.

In keeping with the present day Illuminati, the Babylonian priests were required to partake in the eating of human sacrificial offerings. In consequence, the term *"Cahna-Bal."* meaning "the priest" gave rise to the word *"cannibal."*

The worship of fire, serpents, and the sun, formed an integral part of the early religions of Babylonia, Persia, Egypt and also of the Israelites. The serpent was described as being "fiery," possibly being an archetypal memory of Venus, when it was still a comet with a luminous tail. The Phoenician writer Sancuniathon stated that the serpent was esteemed by the Egyptian deity Thoth, who considered it "….to be the most spiritual of all the reptiles, and to be of a fiery nature….upon which account this animal is introduced in the sacred rites and Mysteries."

The creation of a postdeluvial civilization evidently was a vast social undertaking, incorporating land reclamation and irrigation schemes, yet the Babylonian priesthood in later times credited the accomplishment to their pantheon of deities, in conjunction with the use of agrarian fertility magic.

This act perpetrated by the priesthood was a tragedy for humanity, for it culminated in the creation of a societal system in which the farmers and artisans became isolated from the oligarchy, who jealously guarded the secrets of cosmology and mathematics, presumably bequeathed them by the survivors of the global flood. In consequence, the lives of the ever increasingly superstitious populace became subjected to the dominating influence of magic, ritual and false religious dogma, resulting in a situation which is perpetrated to the present day, whereby religion is a subliminal barrier to truth and knowledge.

The refusal of the Babylonian priesthood to publicly disseminate the arcane knowledge aquired from the Noahic flood survivors, created not only a technologically stagnant civilization, but also gave rise to the formation of the first Mystery schools as repositories of this esoteric knowledge.

To the profane eyes of the typical Christian churchgoer, the magnificent Gothic cathedrals of Europe are merely structures whose sole function is to provide a covered facility, where Christians may congregate for the purpose of prayer. Nothing could be further from the truth, for the architects of the Frater Solomonis Mystery School who designed these wondrous structures, encoded within their configuration alchemy, numerology, astrology and sacred geometry, so that the esoteric initiate might facilitate attunement with the cosmos. Employing design techniques which embraced a profound knowledge of universal harmonic laws, this school of architects mysteriously appeared on the 11th century churchbuilding scene, flourished for three centuries, then equally abruptly, faded from history, leaving in its wake a legacy of sacred architecture never equalled.

Another group of mysterious architects and civilizers equally well-versed in the art of sacred geometry, appeared in prehistoric Egypt with similar abruptness. As writer Peter Tompkins has pointed out, Egyptian civilization was not a "development," it was a legacy. This legacy was bequeathed by an older and possibly more advanced civilization, probably pre-dating the global flood.

Unlike their counterparts in early Babylonia, who allowed a degenerate and rapacious priesthood to assume political control and suppress esoteric knowledge, the Egyptian civilizers, known as the *Shemsu Hor* (Companions of Horus) while admittedly shielding dangerous esoteric knowledge from the eyes of the profane, implemented a complex culture in which the everyday life of the masses was permeated by hermetic symbolism, in order to assist in living in attunement with the cosmos.

Thus, each hieroglyph not only depicted a physical object such as a bird or animal, but also conveyed a metaphysical *essence*, the serpent for instance, with its forked tongue, symbolizing the dualism of truth versus lies.

Egyptian art and architecture incorporated a numerical canon of proportion and harmony, particularly involving the Golden Section (1.618) designed to instill a sense of the sacred in the populace. To the early Egyptians, numbers were not only mathematical units, but rather expressions of complex vibratory waveforms which influence our lives. Thus the proportions of the inner sanctum of the Temple of Luxor are based upon the square root of five, five being the union of the first female number, two, and the first male number, three. Hence five signifys love. Moreover, all harmonic proportions can be derived from the roots of two, three and five. It is the vibratory interaction of these proportions that determines the physical form of the material world.

A major innovation which appeared in Egyptian Mystery school regalia was the introduction of the ceremonial apron, a custom later aquired by the Canaanite initiates of the Melchizadek priesthood, who began making their aprons from white lambskin, a practice later adopted by freemasons.

A peculiar aspect associated with the Middle Eastern civilizers and lawgivers of antiquity was that they were supposedly saved from a watery grave. Thus, Osiris was rescued from the river by his wife Isis, who was conveyed in a boat fashioned from reeds. Similarly, Sargon (a.k.a. Shargani, Cain) the Semitic founder of the Akkadian Dynasty (2360 B.C.) claimed: "My mother conceived me and bore me in secret. She put me in a little box of reeds, sealing its lid with pitch. She put me in the river....The river carried me away and brought me to Akki. Akki the drawer of water adopted me and brought me up as his son...." The Syrian ruler Mises experienced a similar event. According to Philo, Moses was named after the Egyptian word for water *(mou)*.

In ancient times, the manner in which a civilization evolved was largely determined by the nature of the local terrain and environment. Accordingly, the great civilizations of antiquity, such as those of Egypt and Mesopotamia, all possessed navigable rivers, replete with very wide floodplains which provided the basis for extensive agriculture. In time, a network of canals and dikes was constructed in order to control the distribution of floodwaters; these in turn required the establishment of a centralized government, in order to provide effective water resource management.

Possession of a navigable river which facilitates easy transportation, also enabled such a nation to develop national tax collection and military intelligence systems. Conversely, countries lacking navigable rivers, such as Canaan, were dependent upon rainfall-based agricultural economies, which tended to foster the establishment of city-states, instead of nations. Perhaps it was this dependency upon major rivers that led to the creation of the "rescue-from-a-watery-grave myth."

Since the Egyptian civilization emerged from the mists of time lacking a period of development, a phenomenon also apparent in the early Indus Vally culture of Asia, we have to address the question of who were these advanced people and where did they come from?

The ancient literary epics of the Indian sub-continent describe an advanced Indian civilization known as the Rama Empire, which purportedly existed at least 15,000 years ago, and was populated with a black race known as the Dravidians. The Vedic poems, believed to be the oldest of this large literary corpus, describes aircraft known as Vimanas, while the Mahabarata Epic refers to spherical aircraft. An ancient scientific treatise known as the *Samara Sutradhara,* contains 230 stanzas relating to the construction and flight details of such aircraft. According to Dr. Ruth Reyna of the University of Chandrigarh, ancient documents recently discovered in Tibet and sent to her university, contained instructions for the fabrication of spaceships called *Astras.*

The Mahabarata describes how the Dravidians eventually were defeated in an horrendous aerial battle by an invading race who flew in cigar-shaped craft, and used what appears to have been nuclear weapons. Significantly, the remains of the Indus Valley city of Mohenjodaro contained clay pottery which had been vitrified by intense heat, and skeletons which littered the streets were found to be quite radioactive. The Ramayana Epic even describes a battle on the moon. Curiously, many of the moon's craters have a vitrified surface, as though subjected to intense heat, yet do not contain meteoritic residue; this anomaly suggests that at some period in the past, the moon could have been blasted with beam weaponry.

As stated previously, the writer postulates that Mars was once populated by the Aryan race, some of whom visited Planet Earth prior to the flood; these visitors or colonizers became stranded on Earth when Mars was forced out of its previous orbit during the cataclysmic celestial event involving Venus. The relatively few earthbound Martians who survived the flood (presumably losing their technologically advanced equipment in the process) was the race who re-created the civilizations of the world after the flood, and became known as the Phoenicians.

If Mars previously occupied our present orbit, as described earlier in our narrative, its human inhabitants would not have required dark skins in order to withstand solar radiation. Significantly, it has been claimed by some scientists that when Caucasians are immersed in sensory-deprivation tanks for a prolonged period of time, their circadian rhythm has a frequency which corresponds to the rotational period of Mars.

Lending credence to this postulate, tenuous though it appears, are the pyramids discovered in the Cydonia region of Mars. If it is eventually determined that these pyramids are, indeed, artificial constructs, it is unlikely that pyramids were constructed on both planets without communication between the architects of both planets. In addition, infrared scans of the Martian landscape have revealed subterranean cavities which possess rectangular configurations, suggestive that they are not of natural origin. The author also suggests that prior to the Earth's temporary encounter with Venus, the dark-skinned Dravidians were defeated in a series of aerial battles by the reptilian inhabitants of Atlantis, who were the Illuminati.

The close encounter with Venus, which resulted in a global flood and ice age, submerged much of the vast Atlantean continent, temporarily destablizing the Illuminati reptilian dominion over the affairs of humanity. For some strange reason, most historians have overlooked, or elected to ignore, the overwhelming evidence that the principal body of humankind who initiated new cultures after the global deluge, were the Phoenicians.

A great deal of research into this matter was conducted by the late British anthropologist and linguist Professor L. Waddell. During many years spent in India, Waddell came to the realization that the list of ancient Indo Aryan kings in the Mahabarata Epic corresponded with the names of early Phoenician rulers!

In the Pali language of ancient India, these Indo Aryans referred to themselves as *Kattiyo Arryio,* while in Asia Minor and Syria-Phoenicia, the same race called themselves *Khatti-Arri,* the word *"Arri,"* from which *"Aryan"* is derived, means *"the Noble Ones."* The term *"Khatti"* became corrupted in the Bible to *"Heth"* and *"Hitt,"* when referring to the ruling race in Phoenicia and Canaan; with the addition of the latin affix *"ite,"* we get the modern word *"Hittite"* (in several of the Canaan city-states, Aryans ruled over a Semitic populace; Abraham purchased a burial plot for his wife in Canaan from Hittites).

The Phoenicians were great road builders, many of the roads radiated from their capital city Boghaz Koi, the traditional home of Saint George; their architecture incorporated the massive cyclopean masonry typical of pre-dynastic Egypt and Central America. Of significance is the fact that the Gilgamesh Epic claims that the first rulers of

Mesopotamia came from the Mount Hermon region, which was Phoenician territory.

The ruling Phoenician clan was the Barat, who gave their name to their tutelary goddess of water Barati. The Egyptian goddess of water was Bairti. Phoenician coins depict Barati sitting on a chair adorned with the red cross of Saint George; in one hand she holds a cornucopia, while holding the tiller of a ship in the other. She is the prototype Britannia and in the later Roman era, their goddess Fortuna.

The word *"British"* undoubtedly was derived from *"Brt"* (the Phoenician language lacked vowels) for Phoenician place names and inscriptians on standing stones and stone circles attest to the fact that the Phoenicians began colonizing Britain as early as 2900 B.C.. A typical example is the Newton Stone in Aberdeenshire, Scotland. The monolith bears a Phoenician text which translated to: "This Sun-Cross was raised to Bel by the Phoenician Ikar the Barat of Cilicia." British coins of the pre-Roman era often bore such words as Barat, Khatti or Indara, the latter being the Phoenician father-god, whose name gave rise to the Saint Andrew legend.

Being superb sailors, it is no wonder that Phoenician inscriptians have been found on coins, rocks and figurines in the American continent. Typical is a stone discovered in Brazil by Brandes University scholar Cyrus Gordon. The stone, known as the *Parahyba Text,* bears a Phoenician inscriptian describing a voyage by Phoenician merchants who had departed from the Mediterranean port of Sidon, during the 6th. century B.C..

It is a common practice for some poorly-trained New Age channelers to claim that they are receiving communication from Archangel Michael. Typically, such people are delusional and ill read on matters related to religious origins. In order to comprehend the genesis of the winged deity Michael, the reader must be aware that the homeland of the Phoenicians originally extended from the Mediterranean to Mesopotamia.

The earliest Phoenicians distinguished themselves from their nomadic serpent-worshipping aboriginal neighbors by their development of agriculture, which allowed them to pursue a higher level of civilization. The second Phoenician leader was so revered by his subjects for his introduction of the plough, that he later was deified as the archangel of their monotheistic solar cult, and given the name *Tas-Me-ki-gal,* meaning " The Door of Heaven".[11]

He is represented on both Phoenician and pre-Roman British coins as a winged human with an ear of grain. His association with agriculture is celebrated by Christians in the form of harvest festivals, which occur on Michaelmas Sunday. The deity is sometimes represented on Phoenician and Sumerian coins and seals by means of five circular impressions.

Schwaller de Lubicz pointed out that folklore has it that pre-dynastic Egypt was ruled by "venerables of the North." He also commented that many Egyptian statues had blue eyes, which is not surprising considering that the Phoenicians were Aryans, unlike their swarthy Semitic neighbors (Strabo commented that the Phoenicians were white-skinned). Sir Flinders Petrie claimed that the Phoenicians (whom he called Syrians) "....had a civilization equal or superior to that of Egypt, in taste and skill....Luxury far beyond that of the Egyptians, and technical work which could teach them rather than be taught."[12]

In view of the Phoenicians advanced culture and their capability to construct buildings which incorporated gigantic blocks of stone, the author suggests that it was the Phoenicians, not the Egyptians, who built the Great Pyramid. The reader may wonder why, if the Great Pyramid was constructed by the Phoenicians, there are no pyramids in their Phoenician homeland. In order to solve that puzzle, we first must determine the purpose for constructing the Great Pyramid in the first place. Admittedly, most Egyptologists assume that the structure was built for necrophilic purposes, but where is the lid to the stone "sarcophagus" in the King's Chamber? If it ever existed, it would have been too heavy for it to have been removed by tomb robbers, even if they had wished to steal it.

Egyptian tombs are ornately decorated, yet the King's Chamber in the Great Pyramid has bare walls. In addition, it previously has been pointed out in this narrative that the shafts emanating from the King's Chamber were not in alignment with any particular star system at the time of its construction, according to the carbon dating. If it was intended to serve as an initiation center, as New Agers believe, why were not steps provided in the steeply sloping Grand Gallery, in order to facilitate access to the King's Chamber? Occult initiations usually took place in laberinthine caves, as in the Rites of Mithra, so why go to the enormous expense of constructing a pyramid for this purpose, when there were caves available? We also to have to account for the fact that when the Great Pyramid was first explored on 820 A.D. by Caliph Al Mamoun, he reported that the pyramid's interior was encrusted with a deposit of salt and mud from the Nile.

In order to accurately determine the function of an object, one has to know what one is looking at. If an intrepid explorer were to come across the wreckage of an aircraft in a remote jungle region of New Guinea, he or she immediately would recognize it for what it really was. To a member of a local superstitious and primitive tribe however, the wreckage probably would be regarded as an object with religious connotations. The same applies to the Great Pyramid, for Egyptologists clearly do not comprehend its primary function, yet to an engineer with a knowledge of hydraulics, this should not present a problem, for the Great Pyramid clearly was designed to operate as a hydraulic ram!

Hydraulic rams are devices which pump water to higher elevations without the requirement of an external power source, deriving energy solely from oscillating columns of water and air cushions. After visiting and studying the Great Pyramid, an American, E.J. Kunkel, and an Austrian, Hermann Waldhauser, independently of each other concluded that the pyramid had been built to function as a ram. Kunkel later fabricated a sheet metal scale model of the Great Pyramid, which pumped water so surprisingly well that he subsequently patented the device; Waldhauser commissioned a fellow Austrian (Franz Hauber) to construct a scale working model of the pyramid in 1977, which also demonstrated its capability to pump water very efficiently.

It is not surprising that the Great Pyramid should serve a utilitarian, instead of a necrophilic function, for beneath the drifting sands of the greater Giza area, are the remains of townships cconstructed with limestone megaliths similar to those that comprise the core of the Great Pyramid. The high degree of erosion prevalent on these cyclopean stone blocks is a clear indication that they were installed at a much earlier date than the mud-brick pyramids, such as the one at Abu Ruwash, which exhibit little evidence of erosion.

This suggests that the megalithic townships of Egypt were constructed during the pre-dynastic era of Egypt—a period when the early colonizers of Egypt still possessed the technology necessary for the lifting of stone blocks weighing one hundred tons or greater. If these early colonizers possessed such advanced technology, they presumably would also require a means of delivering Nile water to their townships and farms, particularly during periods of drought. Hence the necessity for the Great Pyramid waterworks.

The Greek historian Herodotus claims that the great pyramid was surrounded by water, and that a subterranean duct connected the River Nile with the pyramid's interior. Both Kunkel and Waldhauser claim to have seen the remains of stone checkvalves during their visits to the Great pyramid. Significantly, the eight inch diameter sockets that accommodated the checkvalve trunnions, had been filled in with cement early in the 20th. Century, presumably in an attempt to conceal the pyramid's original function. Creating an air of mystery concerning the purpose for constructing the Great Pyramid in the first place, is more lucrative for the Egyptian tourist industry than revealing the pyramid's true utilitarian function.

The Great Pyramid's pumping sequence is quite straightforward. Water from the Nile flowed under gravity past a checkvalve in the sub-terranean chamber and up the well shaft past a second checkvalve. Air entrapped in the subterranean chamber became compressed, as water flowed past a loosely-fitting stone piston located in the descending passage.

A rope running from the piston, up the descending passage to the exterior of the pyramid was pulled, creating a suction in the water column. This action caused water to rise up the well shaft, past the second checkvalve. When the rope attached to the stone piston was relaxed, the water column began to oscillate due to the air trapped in the subter-ranean chamber behaving in the manner of an elastic air spring. The oscillating motion caused water to be sucked into the upper portions of the pyramid (water compressed under its own weight stores large amounts of potential kinetic energy in the form of elastic deformation).

The ascending water created a water oscillation to commence in the upper region of the pyramid, causing water to fill the Grand Gallery and compress air against the roof of the King's Chamber. The large vol-ume of entrapped air in the King's Chamber would cause a copius flow of water to emerge from the shafts known as the Ascension of Souls (the rapid oscillations would release the stored elastic deformation energy at high velocity).

The air trapped under high pressure in the various chambers of the pyramid, served the same function as the air spring in Nikola Tesla's isochronous oscillator, resulting in a smooth, continuous automatic operation (the rope only would be used for initiating the flow). The so-called sarcophagus in the King's chamber is known to emit a loud ringing sound when struck. Water initially entering the King's Chamber would force the "sarcophagus" against the roof of the chamber very rap-idly, presumably making sufficient noise as to inform the operators to cease pulling on the ropes. On the down stroke of the stone piston, the weight of the "sarcophagus" would assist in forcing the torrent of water past the outlet shafts.

That the early colonizers of Egypt possessed the ability to design an hydraulic ram is not surprising considering that their antediluvian ancestors apparently travelled in interstellar spacecraft, according to the Indian epics, and the extremely ancient Japanese literary work known as the Takenouchi. The real genius behind the design of the Great Pyramid however, is only apparent to those cognizant with the design of anti-gravitic and free-energy devices; only then does the rationale for locating it to the west of the Nile, and aligning it with the Orion Constellation become self-evident.

The early settlers of Egypt had a great reverence for nature and agri-culture, as is evidenced by the hieroglyph *"mer,"* meaning both "hoe" and "love". Ancient Egyptian texts reveal that soil was transported from the fertile east bank of the Nile and depostied on the relatively infertile west bank.[13] To be fertile, a soil must possess paramagnetic energy, i.e. it must be attracted to a magnetic field. Oxygen-breathing creatures are paramagnetic because oxygen is strongly paramagnetic; after death, the corpse becomes diamagnetic (diamagnetic substances such as quartz are repelled by magnetic fields).

Etymologist Professor Phillip Callahan has discovered that energy transmitted by the sun in the form of dipoles, is torn assunder through the action of solar flares, and arrives on earth in the form of monopoles. North monopoles are directly absorbed by vegetation, while paramag-netic rocks, e.g. granite and limestone, absorb south monopoles.

The Great Pyramid is composed of weakly paramagnetic limestone, together with a strongly paramagnetic pink granite King's Chamber. Such a massive amount of rock would accumulate a large charge of south monopole energy, which would slowly disperse through the soil of the surrounding countryside, where it would combine with the north monopole energy stored in the roots of plants (plants are diamagnetic) and serve as a component of photosynthesis. Experiments conducted by Professor Callahan verified the postulate of the late Dr. Freeman Cope that solar-emitted dipoles are a form of tachyons that travel faster than the speed of light.

For more than fifty years, United States Office of Naval Research scientists have studied petrovoltaic phenomena in geologic structures. Much of this reasearch, a great deal of which is still classified, was conducted by the late Townsend Brown, PhD., the developer of anti-gravitic and time-warping systems. Brown discovered that certain sectors of the sky emit gravity waves which are detected and absorbed by certain types of rock. The rocks convert a portion of the gravity waves into electricity. Another researcher, Dr. Lloyd Zirbes, found that whenever these waves slow to subluminal velocities, they form sub-atomic particles.

Petrovoltaic electricity was harnessed by that virtually-unknown 19th century genius Nathan Stubblefield. Before Marconi was able to transmit feeble Morse Code signals through the air, Stubblefield was transmitting loud and clear *vocal* dialogue through the ground with his wireless telephony system. Moreover, his sole electrical power source was derived from petrovoltaic energy. In another invention, he was able to harness sufficient energy from rocks to power electric motors and arc lamps. His most remarkable development was the conversion of rock electricity into a form which rose from the ground like bright sunlight.

During the 8th century A.D., Irish monks constructed tall, round towers from paramagnetic stone. Amazingly, these towers were designed to perform as waveguide antennas, tuned to detect gravity waves, which were converted to petrovoltaic electricity within the masonry of the structures, then trickled into the surrounding fields, in order to provide additional crop fertility. The towers were aligned to particular stars, mainly in the Drace Constellation.

The orientation of the Irish round towers provides a clue as to why the Great Pyramid was aligned with the Orion Constellation. In order to attract and collect sufficient quanta of gravity waves emanating from the Orion Constellation, the paramagnetic stone blocks of the pyramid had to be assembled into what is known in radio parlance as an end-fire array antenna. Adopting the configuration of the Irish round towers would not be practical, since the structure had to function as an hydraulic ram; a pyramid shape incorporating sacred geometry would, however, serve the purpose. In addition, a pyramidal shape is very earthquake resistant.

A very unique characteristic of water is that it possesses a memory, which is why homeopathic remedies work, even though the curative has been so diluted that no molecules of the substance remains in the water. Water in which the molecules are arranged in an hexagonal pattern is known as structured water; it has a much lower surface tension than regular water. Living cells must contain structured water in order to function efficiently; post-partum depression occurrs when a fetus removes too much structured water from the brain of the mother.

Water pumped through the Great Pyramid accordingly would be restructured, through contact with the accumulated gravity waves, as the water traversed its sinuous path through the pyramid. This would enhance the water's bioenergy and reduce its surface tension, thereby enabling it to wet the soil of the surrounding countryside more efficiently, thus increasing the yield of crops grown on the Giza Plateau. In addition, the oscillations induced in the water as it passed through the pyramid would cause discrete molecular structures to form in the water. A similar effect occurs when homeopathic remedies are succussed (impacted) during their manufacture. It should be noted that human cells only operate at peak efficiency if the water within the cells is structured; this is a principal secret to longevity.

It probably is no accident that the key dimensions of the Great Pyramid are harmonics of the Sacred Cubit (20.60 inches) for objects whose dimensions incorporate the cubit are in resonance with the cosmos. This would result in the generation of a life-enhancing energy field, which would stream from the external corners and apex of the pyramid, thus improving the local environment.[14]

No written article concerning the Great Pyramid would be complete without a discussion of construction methods. Sir Laurence Gardner, Chancellor of the Royal Court of the Dragon, claims that the pyramid's stone blocks were raised into position simply by placing white powdered gold on them, which caused them to levitate. The writer is very conversant with the manufacture from plagioclastic ores of this very unique two-dimensionally-structured material. Admittedly it warps the spacetime continuum and degravitates anything it contacts, but only at very elevated temperatures. At room temperature the material degravitates nothing.

The north face of the Great Pyramid appears to have large areas filled with random blocks of stone. This could imply that lock gates temporarily were installed on the north face during the construction period, to facilitate raising and positioning the colossal stone blocks by means of water power. In this case, water would have flowed under gravity via a flume from Lake Moeris. According to Herodotus, the lake, which had a shoreline in excess of four hundred miles, was an artificial construction which had two pyramids located in it. By supporting each stone block on a pontoon, even the largest blocks could be pushed with ease into their final location by only a few workers.

There are reports that Tibetan monks levitated rocks by a combination of chanting and the sounding of trumpets. Such a technique would appear too crude to have been employed by the sophisticated architects of the Great Pyramid. If they levitated stone blocks by sonic means, they well may have employed a method similar to that developed in the 19th century by the American John Keely, who performed levitation feats in front of witnesses, including members of the United States military, who lacked the vision to avail themselves of Keely's superb levitation system.

Although shrouded in secrecy, Keely's device, when placed on top of heavy objects, caused the object in question to levitate. The small device consisted of three gyroscopes connected with coiled tubes fabricated from gold, silver and platinum and tuned to specific frequencies. Keely also developed another small device that pulverized rocks by sonic means. Such a device could have been employed to hollow out the "sarcophagus" in the King's Chamber. Ultrasonic means currently are used to drill square holes in glass.[15]

Some tourists who venture into the interior of the Great Pyramid experience an altered state of awareness; such psychic events would be generated by virtue of the fact that the sacred geometry incorporated in the pyramid's design includes Fibonacci spirals.

Whenever such male and female spirals interact within the pyramid, a concentration of ætheric energy is generated, which tends to modify the neurochemistry of the psychically-sensitive, resulting in temporal lobe lability. This ætheric energy concentration is very prevalent in the short horizontal tunnel adjacent to the so-called Lower Burial Chamber, sometimes resulting in the innermost fears of visitors literally being manifested as physical reality. This particular tunnel is now closed to visitors due to several injuries and deaths purportedly having occurred there. The tunnel predates the construction of the Great Pyramid.

Another curious object at Giza is the Sphinx; much discussion has arisen concerning its antiquity. It is unlikely to have survived the global flood, with its accompanying earth changes, but its deeply eroded surface suggests that it predates the Great Pyramid.

Some of its erosion would have been caused by the heat from the fire pits along its sides, the remains of which still exist; however the walls of the Sphinx enclosure are also too deeply eroded for the Sphinx to be only the same age as the Great Pyramid. Its use still remains a mystery. However, it should be noted that ancient civilizations used to covertly indicate the concealed entrances to subterranean realms by sculpting a sphinx-like creature from solid rock, an example of which occurrs in the Santa Monica mountains of Southern California (with nearby heiroglyphs).

Curiously, the stela erected by Thutmosis IV circa 1400 B.C., located between the paws of the Sphinx, depicts a profile view of a sphinx sitting atop a plinth in which there is a door. According to Arab tradition, Salhouk, an antediluvian ruler, purportedly dreamt of an impending great flood, and had a subterranean vault constructed in what is now the vicinity of the Great Pyramid, into which he placed works on mathematics, science and astronomy.

It is popularly claimed that the Sphinx was made in the form of a reclining lion, and that therefore it was sculpted in the Age of Leo, which commenced circa 10,500 B.C.. The Sphinx's face appears to have been remodelled at a later date however, so we cannot know for certain that the creature's body is that of a lion. The body also bears an uncanny resemblance to that of a reclining Weimaramer dog, and is oriented toward the helical rising of Sirius, the Dog Star, during the summer solstice. Moreover, in pre-dynastic Egypt, the most venerated deity was Seth, not Thoth; Seth was associated with the Dog Star.

Seth was not villified as an evil entity until after the establishment in Egypt of the Illuminati sub-cult known as the Royal Court of the Dragon, which in later eras included such personages as Vlad the Impaler (Dracula) author Bram Stoker and the Elizabethan, Edward de Vere—the most probable author-in-chief of the Shakespearian corpus.

In summation, what the foregoing narrative suggests is that an Atlantean reptilian race defeated a technologically-advanced terrestrial black race, together with refugees or colonizers from Mars, the latter race subsequently establishing colonies on Earth. These colonists, known today as Aryans, became stranded here after their home planet changed its orbit and lost its ability to sustain life on its surface.

A few of the stranded Martian aliens survived the global flood and re-created civilization on Planet Earth, becoming known as the

Phoenicians. A branch of them established the Babylonian culture, which subsequently degenerated under a corrupt priesthood, but other Phoenicians successfully initiated an advanced civilization in Egypt during the pre-dynastic era. This group of Phoenicians constructed the Great Pyramid, whose principal function was the pumping of a restructured and life-enhancing bio-energetic water to the neighboring fields and townships on the Giza Plateau.

The pre-dynastic advanced culture of Egypt that was developed by the Phoenicians, declined after they were ousted by the Illuminati, who created the Royal Court of the Dragon. This is evidenced by the inability to continue the art of handling cyclopean blocks of stone. Around 1450 B.C., Phoenicia itself was conquered by Egyptian forces; large numbers of Phoenician artisans were transferred to Egypt. This event coincided with the introduction of blue-glazed beads, for which Egypt became famous, and ceased when Phoenicia regained its independence from Egypt circa 1250 B.C.. Similar blue beads have been found in the vicinity of Stonehenge. It is worth noting that the maternal grandfather of Akhen-aten was the Phoenician high-priest Yusa.

Historians usually refer to the Giza pyramids as a necropolis, even though no mummies have been discovered within the Great Pyramid. In order to maintain its authority over its membership, the Illuminati elite have placed great emphasis on the importance of rank and sacrificial ritual, yet place little importance on the Great pyramid as a ceremonial site. Regarding the Giza Plateau as the root chakra of the world, the Illuminati, on rare occasions, hold sodomy rituals within the Great Pyramid, preferring instead to hold most of their Egyptian rituals at the Valley of the Kings (at which gold masks are worn).

This lack of interest possibly suggests that the present-day Illuminati heirarchy are cognizant of the fact that the principal function of the Great Pyramid was merely to serve as a mechanical water pump, for the utilitarian purpose of supplying the city which now lies buried beneath the sands of the Giza Plateau.

Sadly, Egyptologists have neglecteted to access Illuminati history. Were they to do so, they would discover that the Ark of the Covenant still exists, not in Ethiopia (one of several fakes) but at a very covert subterranean facility in Egypt, awaiting its installation in the new Jerusalem Temple. According to Illuminati historians, the Ark of the Covenant does not contain the Ten Commandments, but rather something not from this planet. But that is a story for another time.

CHAPTER 5

▼

WHO WERE THE ISRAELITES?

"Hear O Israel; thou art to pass over the Jordan this day, to go in to dispossess nations great and mightier than thyself, cities great and fortified up to heaven."

Moses

Biblical history in the form that it has been presented to us, is not an accurate depiction of Middle Eastern antiquity, but is largely a synthetic creation of biblical scholars, whose interpretations of ancient events are all too often influenced by their own ideologies, and those of their theological and oligarchic overlords.

What we perceive as biblical and more recent history, is largely propaganda disseminated in order to legitimize the actions of the victors of bloody conflicts or coups. The vilification of England's King Richard III stems primarily from the pen of Sir Thomas More, who conveys the impression that he was a contemporary of the monarch. In actuality, he was less than six years old at the time of Richard's death; his writings were an attempt to legitimize the usurpation of the throne by the Tudors. This villification was extended in the Shakespearian play, in which the hapless monarch was portrayed as a hunchback with a withered arm. This inaccurate portrayal was perpetrated because in the Elizabethan era, it was popularly believed that a deformed person was evil.

During the past century, archaeological excavations in the Holy Land have revealed a more realistic portrayal of life in ancient Israel than that presented by successive generations of theologians, who have elected to obfuscate the true patterns of the past, in order to elevate their own importance in the overall scheme of things.

A great deal of innocent blood has been spilled in recent years in defence of Israeli claims that the State of Israel belongs to the Jews by virtue of divine right, as depicted in the Old Testament. Does it not behoove us therefore, to ascertain whether or not the Old Testament is accurate in this matter?[1]

The theocratic institution of Judaism has exerted a major geopolitical, spiritual and occult influence upon humankind, in part because it modified and popularised the Cabala (created by the Khwajagan) and the infamous Babylonian Talmud.[2] It is important to remember, dear reader, that the Old Testament was not written until after the conclusion of the Babylonian captivity period, which means that many events were not committed to writing until several centuries had elapsed. This is why claims such as the Israelite occupation of Canaan by means of conquest, as described in the Book of Joshua, lack credibility; in fact, if we deeply delve into the patterns of the past, it would appear that the genocidal activities of the psychopathic Joshua and Moses, as depicted in the Bible, never occurred.

Although the Bible displays many inaccuracies, therefore invalidating any pretence to being a divinely-inspired work, we should not ignore the Bible as an historical source, for it contains many nuggets of historical truth; it therefore behooves us not to throw the baby out with the bathwater.

According to the Old Testament, the patriarch Abraham led his band of proto-Israelites from the Mesopotamian city of Harran, to the land of Canaan. Several generations later, starvation forced the tribe to migrate to the land of Goshen. Goshen was an exceedingly fertile region located in the Nile Delta, where the Israelites co-existed peaceably with the Egyptians for a period of 430 years, before being forced to flee, in order to escape enslavement ordered by a new Egyptian monarch.

In order to reconstruct the historical origins of the Israelites, together with their religion, it is well to note that Judaism as we know it today, only dates back to the second century of the present era. It is claimed to be a continuation of Pharisaic teachings which were formulated during the aftermath of the Maccabean revolt (168-164 B.C.).

Archaeological evidence is indicative that Judaism, during its formative period, assimilated cultic beliefs aquired from neighboring peoples, and is, therefore, not the uniquely original religion that theological purists would have us believe.

In ancient times, the manner in which a civilization evolved was largely determined by the nature of the local terrain and environment. Thus, the great civilizations of antiquity, such as those of Egypt and the Indus Valley, all possessed navigable rivers, replete with very wide flood plains that provided the basis for extensive agriculture. Egypt is typical of a nation which evolved as a hydraulic civilization; each year between August and November, the level of the mighty Nile used to rise some fifteen to twenty five feet above normal, resulting in a floodplain up to seven miles in width. When the floodwaters receded, rich, fertile silt was deposited, which was then planted with barley, flax and wheat (conditions have changed for the worse since the construction of the Aswan Dam, whose construction was an act of sheer lunacy).

The Tigris and the Euphrates rivers similarly enabled the inhabitants of Mesopotamia to develop an hydraulic civilization, particularly since the Mesoptamian Valley is even wider than the corresponding Nile Valley. With the passage of time, a complex network of canals and dikes were constructed, in order to control the distribution of floodwaters. These in turn required the establishment of a centralized government, in order to provide effective water managemnt.

Possession of a navigable river which provides easy transportation, also enabled such nations to develop national tax collection and military intelligence systems; these in turn facilitated the creation of powerful armies. Conversely, countries lacking in navigable rivers, were dependent upon rainfall-based agricultural economies. These tended to foster the establishment of city-states instead of nations.

In perusing the Bible, one is given the impression that the River Jordan is a geographical feature of major importance, particularly in view of the fact that it is mentioned no fewer than 196 times! In actuality, the Jordan is little more than a wide stream, and the appellation "river"(nhr) is never assigned to it in the scriptures.

Located in the Great Rift Valley—a massive rupture of the Earth's crust extending from Turkey to North Africa, the Jordan, fed by melting snows, rises in the foothills of lofty Mount Hermon, which is situated at the boundary between Israel and Syria.[3] It plunges through a narrow gorge before entering the Sea of Galilee, some twenty five miles to the south. Exiting Galilee, the Jordan placidly meanders a sinuous path before discharging into the Dead Sea, for an overall distance of ninety miles as the crow flies, which pales in comparison with the more than four thousand mile length of the Nile.

Unlike the Nile, the floor of the Jordan Valley is devoid of vegetation, except for an almost impenetrable thicket of poplars, tamarisks and thorn bushes which line the banks. To make matters worse, the Jordan floods in the Spring, which is harvest time in the arrid regions of the Middle East. In consequence, the Jordan was incapable of sustaining an agricultural economy during the biblical era; this is why the geopolitical structure of Canaan developed in the form of independent city-states, devoid of a unifying central government.

Being so dependent upon rainfall, water was a scarce and hence a very valuable commodity in Canaan. In consequence, the prohibition against the eating of pork, as stated in both Deuteronomy and Leviticus, probably had little to do with the possibility of contracting trichinosis, but a lot to do with the fact that pigs, in addition to being difficult to herd, also consume more water than goats or cattle.

Despite being independently ruled, the cities of Canaan during the Bronze Age (which was superceded by the Iron Age circa 1200 B.C.) developed an integrated trading system which dealt in spices, gold, bronze implements and agricultural produce. Even the farmers and nomadic pastoralists appear to have entered into a symbiotic relationship, wherein the sheep and goats of the nomadic tribes grazed and fertilized the farmland, following the harvest.

It was the development of copper smelting that provided the impetus for the growth of international trade between the hierarchical nations during the Bronze Age. Thus, Egypt, rich in gold, but lacking a domestic source for silver ore, established a maritime trade with the silver smelting cities of the Aegean region.

In the previous chapter, we saw how the Otomani people of the Carpathian Basin had established a trading route, the southern portion of which terminated at the Black Sea, where it intersected with an eastern Mycenean trading route that had been established for the purpose of conducting trade with Mesopotamia. This was during the era in which the patriarch Abraham resided at the city of Haran, in the kingdom of Mari.

Located between the Tigris and the Euphrates rivers, Haran in the era of Abraham (which is believed by most biblical scholars to be 1900—1800 B.C.) was the seat of the Mari government; it was also one of the great wonders of its day, due primarily to the gigantic dimensions and splendor of its palace. This was sufficiently large to accommodate the entire administrative staff of the monarch.

The almost 24,000 texts unearthed at Mari reveal that the nation worshipped twenty four deities, and possessed a superb administrative system. Of masonic interest is the textual distcovery that some 2,000 of the nation's craftspeople were members of guilds.

Some of the texts cautioned about the necessity of protecting their farmlands from incursions by Semitic nomadic pastoralists and their herds, who disturbed the peaceful lives of the Mari populace, whose principal interests appeared to be commerce and religion.

Thanks to the sterling efforts of archaeologists such as Professor Parrot of Paris, Mari has revealed itself to us as a kingdom of considerable sophistication. It is highly unlikely therefore, that Abraham was an itinerant pastoralist, as the Bible would have us believe, particularly since he employed servants; this implies that he was a person of means.[4]

A disturbing parallel exists between the events occurring in the lives of Abraham and his kinfolk and the laws of the kingdom of Mittani, a nation-state sharing the northern border of the kingdom of Mari. According to texts that were discovered at Nuzi, an Mittani city located near the present-day Kirkut oilfield in Iraq, a childless couple could legally arrange for a surrogate mother to provide an heir. The Bible claims that Abraham's wife Sarah, being barren, procured the services of Hagar to fulfill this role.[5] In a similar manner, Jacob's wife Rachel, arranged for her maid Bilhah to be a surrogate mother.[6] Mittanni law also awarded inheritance rights to a person who possessed statues (teraphim) of the deceased; we are told that Rachel stole the teraphim of her father Laban.[7]

The Nuzi texts were written circa 1500 B.C., in other words, some four centuries after the purported time of Abraham. This suggests that either the Mari were the precursors of the Mitanni people, or that the biblical chronology is incorrect, and that Abraham was born at a later period. Abraham allegedly left Haran 645 years before the purported exodus of Israelite slaves from Egypt.

Be that as it may, the Mitanni nobility—known as Marya, were an Indo-Aryan warrior caste, referred to in the Bible as Horites; the Horites worshipped the Indian deities Mithra, the god of light, who was claimed to be the intermediary between the Creator and humankind, and Varuna, the god of cosmological order.

In view of the preoccupation of the Marya with horses and chariots, they probably were descended from a migratory branch of the previously mentioned Otomani people of the Carpathian Basin, who not only possessed superior smelting technology, but appear to have used chariots at a much earlier period than their Middle Eastern neighbors.

In consideration of the fact that Abraham possessed servants, he obviously was a person of influence, and quite possibly a member of the nobility. This supposition is reinforced by the fact that textual evidence claims that the Mari populace were hostile toward Semitic pastoralists. Emerging from the past, the excavated ruins are indicative that Haran was a very substantial city, even by today's standards. The image of Abraham and his kindred pastoralists dwelling in tents amidst the palaces, temples and related splendors of this majestic city of antiquity stretches one's credulity to the limit. Either the Patriarch was a tent-dwelling nomad living in a sparsely-populated pastoral region, or an affluent city dweller, but not both, as the Bible suggests.

Nearing the end of his life, Abraham, reluctant to see his son Isaac take a Canaanite for a bride, instructed his eldest servant to "….go into *my* country, and to *my* kindred and take a wife unto my son Isaac….And he arose and went to Mesopotamia, *unto the city of Nahor.*" [8] [emphasis added]. From this statement, we can ascertain that Abraham's original home was not Haran, or even Ur, but Nahor; moreover, it was the domicile of his relatives. Nahor was a city located in the Balikh Valley of Northern Mesopotamia, in the region that later became the kingdom of Mitanni. This is of great historical importance, for it suggests that *Abraham was an Indo Aryan Horite, not a Semite,* as is claimed by Arab and Jew alike.

We are informed in the Bible that Abraham and some of his relatives relocated to Canaan.[9] That this was not merely a visit is emphasised by the fact that they took all of their possessions with them. The six hundred mile trek would have taken them down the fertile Balikh Valley to Palmyra, then via the famous caravan route that extended all the way from Mesopotamia to Egypt. Along the way, they would have passed the site where Damascus, renowned for its spring blossoms, would later develop, and past the towering snow-clad peak of Mount Hermon and the hills of Galilee, before traversing the arid countryside of Canaan.

Canaan, in the era of Abraham, extended from Mount Hermon in the north, to the arid wilderness of the Negev region in the south, an overall distance of 150 miles. At its narrowest point, the width of Canaan was only 25 miles. The Canaanite aristocracy lived in small towns of only twenty acres or less in area; archaeological digs have revealed that these townships were very primitive, lacking in meaningful drainage and consisting of a fortified dwelling for the local ruler. This structure was surrounded by a haphazard collection of residential buildings. These Canaanite townships afforded little protection against marauding Bedouin tribesmen.

The inevitable question arises as to why Abraham would elect to leave the sophisticated city of Haran, with all its creature comforts, and undertake a long and hazardous journey to a primitive country of petty city states and hostile nomads. Even if he were an aristocrat on a diplomatic mission, he would not have taken all his worldly possessions with him, as the Bible claims.

The author therefore suggests that Abraham lived at a later time period than the 18th century B.C., as is claimed by a concensus of biblical scholars. The most probable reasons for Abraham to undertake such an arduous journey, particularly since his wife was advanced in years, were either that he and his relatives were fugitives from justice, or that a major disaster had befallen the kingdom of Mari.

Such a cataclysmic event did, indeed, occur circa 1700 B.C., when the Babylonian monarch Hammurabi conquered the kingdom of Mari, and left the magnificent city of Haran in ruins. Throughout history, it has been the custom of invading despots to massacre the hierarchy and intelligentsia of conquered nations, in order to minimize the possibility of a rebellion. Accordingly, it would be perfectly natural for the Patriarch and his relatives to flee for their lives if they were members of the Haran aristocracy, living during this later time period.

Now that we have constructed a more realistic picture of Abraham, let us rationalize why he would choose to relocate in the arid and primitive country of Canaan, instead of a more fertile region of the Middle East. The answer to this problem may be found in Egyptian texts that were discovered at Tel el Armana, in 1887. This major archaeological find comprises 377 diplomatic letters dating from the 15th century B.C., written by the rulers of Canaanite city states. Canaan, during the second millenium B.C., was an Egyptian satrapy; amazingly, the Tel el Amarna letters bore such signatures as Prince Indaruta and Prince Suwarduta. In other words, some of the Canaanite townships were administrated by Indo Aryan Horites!

Interestingly, some of the correspondence dealt with attacks on Canaanite townships that were perpetrated by nomadic Semitic tribes. If Abraham were a nomadic Semite, clearly he would not be welcome in Canaan; if, however, Abraham was an aristocratic Indo Aryan refugee, his presence in Canaan would not present a problem to the Horite princes.

Our only problem with this scenario is that Abraham supposedly possessed camels, according to the Bible. Camels were not domesticated until several centuries later. It is well to bear in mind, however, that early biblical history did not appear in written form until the Solomonic era at the earliest. With the passage of time, incorrect chronologies and embellishments occurred in the oral narratives. The possession of camels is almost certainly a false interpolation added to the narrative centuries later.

When his wife Sarah died, Abraham purchased a buriel site in Hebron from the Hittites.[10] Again we are faced with a problem if the event occurred in the 19th century B.C., as claimed by many biblical scholars, for the Hittite kingdom had not been established at that time period. The Hittes were in existence, however, during the 16th century B.C., the period in which Abraham lived, according to the author's hypothesis. The term "Hittite" is a Hebrew derivation of "Khatti"—the Aryan race we know as the Phoenicians, some of whom colonized India, where they were known as *Khattiyo Arrio,* meaning "ruler".

Since the Hittite kingdom's immediate neighbors were Canaan and the kingdom of Mitanni, both of whom, as we have seen, were administrated by Indo Aryans, it explains why the Hittites were able to own land in Canaan.

The Bible does not make it clear whether or not Abraham journeyed to Egypt, but there is archaeological evidence supportive of such a contention; the Bible does categorically state however, that his trek took him to Gerar, which is located in south-western Canaan, in the arrid region known as the Negev.

Mention of the Negev has an immense bearing on our narrative, for it is in this region of Canaan that the genesis of the future Israelite nation occurred, according to the author's hypothesis. Not surprisingly perhaps, since the author tends to march to a different drummer, this hypothesis is at variance with those of many biblical scholars, who believe that the earliest Israelite domain was the hill country of upper Galilee. In order to provide the reader with a balanced perspective of suggested Israelite origins, it behooves us briefly to examine some of these alternative hypotheses.

It is the consensus of contemporary biblical scholars that the Exodus, if it ever occurred at all, and the subsequent bloody conquest of Canaanite cities, is an unacceptable historical construct for the dawning of the Israelite nation. This is because there are too many archaelogical and chronological discrepancies: the destruction of individual Canaanite townships spanned too great a time period to have been the result of Joshua's purported genocidal military campaign. An alternate model was proposed during the 1920's by the German scholars Alt and Noth, who deduced from the previously mentioned Tel el Armana texts that the proto-Israelites were the people known as the *Apiru,* whom they theorized were hostile nomadic pastoralists who eventually destroyed the Canaanite city states. They suggested that the appellation "Hebrew" was, in fact, derived from *"Apiru".*

The major problem with this theory is that the Apiru primarily were troublesome renegades from affluent Canaanite and Syrian families, who hired themselves out as mercenaries; they never were pastoralists. The term *"Apiru"* is not linguistically associated with the term *"Ibri"* (Hebrew).[11]

During the 1960's, University of Michigan scholar George Mendenhall hypothesized that Apiru mercenaries instigated a revolt by peasants, who had become unified by monotheism after fleeing from the plains to the hills. Unfortunately, there is no archaeological evidence to verify such a major demographic shift from the plains to the hills during that particular period.

The latest theory, advanced by Israel Finkelstein of Tel Aviv University, proposes that an international recession diminished the market for the sheep and goats raised by the pastoralists. The economic setback accordingly forced the pastoralists to modify their lifestyle and become farmers.[12]

To be succesful, a militant peasant revolt has to be well funded and professionally directed. This was the case in the French Revolution, for example, where trained foreign mercenaries bore the brunt of the fighting, under the direction of the Jesuit dominated British East India Company. Similarly, the Angolan revolution was funded by the petroleum cartel (using the CEO of a major airplane manufacturer as the bagman) in order to oust small independent oil companies from the Angolan oilfields. It is highly unlikely that the Cuban revolution would have succeeded, had not Fidel Castro received CIA and Jesuit aid. There is no historical evidence that a well funded and highly-trained peasant army ever attacked and conquered any of the Canaanite city-states.

For a fledgling civilization to successfully develop, it must possess a strong market economy, as was the case with the coastal cities of Canaan, where Egyptian gold and spices were traded for copper and the unique purple dye that the Canaanites obtained from the murex shell-fish. The Canaanite peasants, eking out a meager living on their arid hill-country farms, clearly lacked the requisite product diversification which is necessary in order to establish such a strong economy, and sustain an affluent temple oriented priesthood, as is claimed by Finkelstein.

In summation, the presently advanced theories regarding the genesis of the Israelites lack too many important facets to be tenable, which is why it is advisable to research important subjects ourselves, instead of accepting the all too incorrect dogma foisted upon us by the academic establishment.

In order to develop a realistic construct for the origin of the Israelites, we must search for a clan, or closely-related group of people, who possessed manufacturing as well as farming skills, and who also were adept at marketing their wares. They must have lived in the southern region of Canaan, in the Negev and the surrounding hill country. They also must be aquainted with a monarchical system of government. We must also search for archaeological evidence of early Judaic temple relics, such as a brazen serpent or the remains of a tabernacle. If we can find biblical and archaeological references to such a society, we can be reasonably certain that we have discovered who really were the proto-Israelites.

Such a clan did, in fact, exist during the time of Abraham. Known as the Kenites, they were a branch of the Midianites, a federation of semi-nomadic clans whose territory extended from the Arabian Desert to the Negev. Unlike other Palestinian tribes who were ruled by chieftans, the Midianites possessed a monarchy which is referred to in the Bible.[13] They were also called the Ishmailites.[14] The Bible informs us that they were both shepherds and traders.[15] In addition, they were known to perform as middlemen in the gold and frankinscence markets.

The Kenite branch of the Midianites primarily were metal workers, as is evidenced by their name, which is derived from the root *"qvn"*, meaning "metalsmith" in Aramaic *(qvny)*. The Kenites probably developed their metalworking industry after they, or the Egyptians, discovered large copper and iron deposits in the Wadi el Arabah, which is located in southern Canaan.

Being skilled in both metalworking and animal husbandry, the only missing element needed to enable the clan to become a formidable marketing entity, was a person with vision and strong leadership qualities, such as Abraham. The Patriarch had exhibited such skills in undertaking the arduous trek to Canaan; we therefore need to seek biblical verification that Abraham knew the Midianites.

Abraham not only knew the Midianites—he married one named Keturah![16] Kenites feature prominently in the Old Testament: the apocryphal Moses married the daughter of a Kenite priest, also Jethro, who purportedly aided Moses in the wilderness and introduced the cult of the brazen serpent. Enoch was also associated with the Midianites, and the House of Rechab were Kenite relatives, some of whom resided at the copper-mining center of Ge Harashim.[17]

Some scholars hold that the Israelite deity Yahwey originally was the Kenite god Yahu. This is a most important claim, for ancient Chinese folklore states that Emperor Yahu ruled shortly after the last global flood. Unfortunately, most ancient Chinese records and classical works were destroyed by order of Emperor Tsin-Khin-Hong (246-209 B.C.). From mythologies and history that was rewritten at a later date, we are given to understand that a Chinese scholar by the name of Fu-hsi survived the flood and re-introduced the Tao (the way of the universe and nature, which begets all phenomena and creation).

Chinese folklore claims that Emperor Yahu was named in memory of a terrible groaning noise which permeated the sky and sounded like the word "yahu," during the time of the global flood; the noise may well have been an electrical capacitative discharge between Planet Earth and the comet Venus, as the latter temporarily orbited Earth.

So far, we have determined that the Kenites possessed the means for establishing an international market economy strong enough for them to create a nation state. All we have to do now is to find archaeological evidence of early religious artifacts possessing Judaic characteristics, and discovered in known Kenite territory.

During the early 20th century, many biblical scholars expressed doubt as to whether the legendary Tabernacle of the Israelites ever existed. These doubts were refuted in 1959, when Professor Benno Rothenberg, an Israeli of German birth, discovered a Midianite shrine at a copper mine in the Wadi-el-Arabah, which forms part of the Great Rift Valley. At the shrine were the remains of a tabernacle, very similar to the one described in the Old Testament. Also found at the shrine was a gold decorated brass serpent, the symbol of the Mother Goddess Astarte, who was identified with Queen Semiramis of Babylon, according to Athenagoras.

A brazen serpent purportedly was installed in the pre Solomonic temple at Jerusalem; other brass serpents of later date were also discovered at various shrines near Jerusalem, suggestive of the serpent's importance in early Israelite worship. According to ancient African lore, the serpent did not symbolize the planetary telluric energy currents, but was used as a symbol to covertly represent the shape shifting dragons, who were known to Africans as the chitauri (the dragon overlords of the human race allegedly forbade images of themselves to be made, hence the adoption of the serpent as a symbol).

In the north eastern sector of the Negev, at an elevation of 610 meters and overlooking the Dead Sea, lies the modern city of Arad, which was constructed in 1961 for the production of petrochemicals and fertilizer. A few miles away in former Kenite territory, are the remains of a fortress known to have been constructed during the Hyksos period (1730-1580 B.C.). If the author's contention that Abraham vacated Haran in 1700 B.C. is correct, it is quite feasible that the fortress, known as Tel el Milh, was constructed after the Patriarch had made contact with the Kenites. The township appears to have been settled by the Jerameelite family.[18]

The Bible claims that the offspring of Moses settled in the vicinity of Arad, which was mentioned by Eusebius in the 4th century A.D., and is situated about thirty kilometers to the northeast of Beersheba. Tel Arad was a large Early Bronze Age city that was fortified by a massive wall replete with semi-circular towers. This ancient city was destroyed circa 2700 B.C., and remained abandoned until the 11th century B.C., when a new settlement arose on the site. A century later, a temple was added. This particular temple is of extreme importance to authenticate Judaic history, for it is the oldest Israelite temple yet discovered.

The general configuration of the temple closely resembled that of King Solomon's Temple. Flanking the main hall were two stone slabs, which presumably functioned as the bases for two columns, similar to the Jachin and Boaz columns of Judaic and Masonic lore, which formed an important symbolic element in Solomon's temple. The outer court-yard of the Tel Arad temple contained a sacrificial alter five cubits square, *corresponding exactly with the dimensions of the biblical taberna-cle.*[19] Ink inscribed pottery shards (ostraca) found at the site bear the names of two biblical priestly families: Meremoth and Pashur.

Like the gradual materialization of a photograph in a tank of devel-oper, our investigation has finally revealed a realistic portrayal of the dawning era of the Israelite nation. All the necessary elements are there: the heavy emphasis that the Bible imparts upon the relationship between Abraham and the Kenites, the oldest known Israelite temple was located in Kenite territory, and the Kenites were adept metal workers and middlemen.

Archaeological surveys indicate that numerous hamlets and towns sprang up in the previously sparsely populated hill country of Canaan, the development commencing around the time that the author believes Abraham settled in the Negev. The author surmises that the increasing affluence and political stability of the Negev region, under the possible leadership of Abraham, gradually attracted the attention of pastoralists known as the Shosu, who were comprised of many tribal affinities, and who eventually settled in the hill country of Canaan.

If Abraham was indeed an Indo Aryan Horite, his standing with the Indo-Aryan rulers of the Canaanite city-states presumably would have been quite high, particularly if he were an aristocratic figure, or a person of means. This would have provided him with both the political and marketing clout necessary to establish the Kenites as a formidable commercial entity.

When we evaluate what we have so far gleaned of the commercial potential of the Kenites, we find a group whose industrial and agribusiness capabilities were no better than those of the Canaanite city states. Clearly an extra element was necessary in order to transform the Kenites and assimilated pastoralists into a powerful and united nation. The author believes that missing element to have been the Kenite development of the largest copper and iron smelting industry in the entire Middle East.

Commencing with the extensive copper smelting industry in the previously mentioned Wadi el Arabah, which remained operational until 1200 B.C., an even larger metal smelting operation, also located in Kenite territory, was discovered in 1937 by the distinguished American archaeologist Nelson Glueck. Near the shores of the Gulf of Aqabah, Glueck unearthed the remains of the biblical city of Ezion Geber, famed during the Solomonic era for its shipbuilding industry. Among the ruins, Glueck discovered the remains of a surprisingly modern-looking blast furnace, designed to utilize a forced draft that was induced by the incessant strong winds that swept over the surrounding desert.

The extremely large smelting pots and numerous copper and iron mines that were discovered in the vicinity, attest to the fact that here, in Kenite territory, was the center of a very major metal smelting industry. The profits derived from such a vast undertaking undoubtedly would have made the Kenite clan far more affluent than any Canaanite city state. As the wealth of the Kenites accumulated, their purchasing power would have enabled them to structure a formidable defense force, which in turn would tend to foster political alliances with neighboring tribes who were seeking protection from marauding bands of militant nomads.

Wealth also tends to foster cultural advances, hence the Bible informs us that Moses purportedly met his Kenite father-in-law priest in the Sinai wilderness. It was the same locale that the eminent British archaeologist Sir Flinders Petrie discovered fragments of clay texts; these bore a previously unkown form of writing. It was not until thirty years later, in 1948, that scholars were able to decipher the unique writing dating from 1500 B.C., which was revealed to be a dedication to the Goddess Baalath, and was the forerunner of our present Western alphabet. Once again, we find a connection between the Kenites and the birth of the Israelite nation.

As more of the Northern tribes became affiliated with the Kenites, it would have become necessary to locate the administrative and religious capital of the new nation to a more northerly city, in order to establish a centralized bureaucracy for the collection of taxes and direction of religious rites. This would have been the logical rationale for the abandonment of the Arad Temple, and the construction of a new temple at Jerusalem, during the Solomonic era. It must be remembered that Judaism is not a unique religion, but rather one that has retained elements of earlier religions, such as the incorporation of the tree calendar, as evidenced in the use of pomegranite wood in the manufacture of sacrificial offering spits, and the association of the menorah with the almond tree. Moreover, the pomegranite was the only fruit permitted within the Holy of Holies of the Temple.

Shortly after Abraham arrived in Canaan, Egypt, for the first time in its long and glorious history, was conquered by foreigners. These were Syrian and Canaanite tribes who were collectively known as the Hyksos; the victorious Hyksos established an administrative center in the fertile Nile Delta region, known in the Bible as the Land of Goshen. It is a matter of record that the Hyksos permitted starving Canaanites to settle in the Nile Delta, whenever Canaan experienced a famine.

We can therefore surmise that proto Israelite pastoralists migrated with their flocks to Egypt in migratory waves, whenever a prolonged drought occurred in Canaan, and co-existed with the native populace of Egypt. It is therefore possible that the biblical Joseph did, in fact, become Viceroy of Egypt, as the Bible claims, during the Hyksos dynasty. The only problem is that supposedly he was the son-in-law of Potiphar, a high-ranking official. Unfortunately, the name "Potiphar" only came into use during the 10th century B.C.. In addition, Joseph's family allegedly rode camels, which were not domesticated at that early date.

On a positive note however, an ancient Egyptian canal some two hundred miles in length, still transports water from the Nile to the fertile Faiyum region, where orchards are cloaked with a profusion of orange and peach blossoms in the springtime. Even today, the canal is known as *"Bahr Yusef"* (Joseph's Canal). Since the original Pentateuch did not appear in written form until the 10th century B.C. at the earliest, the oral tradition of the Joseph story is, in all probability, a composite of several events which span several centuries.

Two seemingly unrelated events occurred during the 15th. Century B.C.: The Hyksos long reign over the Egyptians came to an end following a bloody revolt by the Egyptians, also the hill farmers of Canaan abandoned their land in droves. Biblical scholars have failed to provide a rationale for both events. The author believes that both events may have had a common causality: one thousand miles away in the Aegian Sea, the island of Santorini volcanically exploded with a force many times greater than those which accompanied the eruptions of Krakatoa or Mount St. Helens in recent times. The Santorini disaster was precipitated by the explosive eruption and subsequent collapse, of the island's volcano Thera, causing two thirds of Santorini to plunge into the gigantic caldera.

The initial blast, of unimaginable intensity, rocked the nearby island of Crete, followed shortly after by the issuance of a stupendous cloud of pyroclastic ash, which engulfed the island to a depth of one hundred feet in some places; the cataclysmic event destroyed the island's Minoan civilization. As the island of Santorini collapsed into the gaping cauldera, the resultant tidal wave, some one hundred feet in height, bore down on the coastal regions of Canaan and Egypt, inundating the Nile Delta and depositing water-borne volcanic ash on the foothills of Canaan. The prevailing winds would have carried the sulfurous ash cloud over Canaan, creating major weather changes for several years, and leaving a countryside beset with famine.[20]

The disaster undoubtedly would have prompted a mass migration of Canaanite hill farmers to the Land of Goshen, which would have been too far south to have been affected to any great extent by the volcanic ash cloud. No doubt the tidal wave and resultant flooding would have severely disrupted the administrative and military capabilities of the Hyksos, thereby providing an opportunity for the Egyptians to rebel and overthrow their Hyksos overlords.

It is understandable why the proto Israelites would wish to settle in the fertile Land of Goshen and co-exist with the Egyptians, rather than return to the arid hill country of their native land. The co-existence appears to have proceeded harmoniously until the reign of Ramesses II ((1301-1234 B.C.) whose penchant for grandiose construction projects prompted him to commit the unfortunate Israelites to forced labor.

This was facilitated by the fact that most of the building sites were located in the Land of Goshen, where the proto Israelites grazed their herds.

We can surmise that some of the proto Israelites escaped servitude by fleeing to Canaan at the onset of the construction period (1290-1270 B.C.). If some of Abraham's relatives had, indeed, continued on to Egypt, instead of terminating their long trek from Haran to the Negev with Abraham, then the total length of the Israelites sojourn in Egypt would closely correspond to the time span indicated in the Bible (430 years). This timeline would only hold true however, if Abraham's party began their journey at the time of the destruction of Haran (circa 1700 B.C.) not two centuries earlier, as is claimed by most biblical scholars.

Obviously a mass escape from bondage by 600,000 Israelite men, plus their dependents and large herds of cattle, as claimed in the Bible, would have been intercepted at the border by the Egyptians, who maintained an efficient network of border outposts. The notion that such a vast number of refugees could covertly assemble without detection, then escape the clutches of the Egyptians, is absurd, a fact now acknowledged by leading Judaic scholars.

Even if we ignore the logistical nightmare which would be generated in attempting to provide sustenance for such a large body of people, during their forty-year sojourn in the wilderness, we cannot overlook the fact that wherever large numbers of people congregate, garbage is deposited with the same degree of certitude as death and taxes. Despite extensive archaeological excavations in the wilderness regions of Israel, including major searches by Israeli archaeologists, no artifacts older than the 10th century B.C. have ever been discovered in the region. Of the broken utensils and pottery, or the graves of hapless Israelites who perished prior to reaching the promised land, not a trace has been found, leaving scholars to reluctantly conclude that *the much vaunted Exodus simply never occurred.* This is of paramount importance geopolitically, *for it negates the Jewish claim to Palestinian territory based solely upon divine right.*

In all probability, the Exodus, if it ever happened at all, consisted of very small individual groups of runaway slaves, who fled eastward into Kenite territory in order to avoid the vigilant Egyptian border patrols, instead of taking the more direct caravan route into the coastal region of Canaan, which was once more under Egyptian rule. Much has recently been made by Christian Fundamentalists of the discovery of a sunken causeway in the Red Sea replete with Egyptian chariot wheels, thus "proving" that the biblical Exodus really took place. Unfortunately, the causeway appears to have sunk during the eruption of Thera, at a much earlier date than the purported Exodus. Even the claim that Ramesses kept slaves is based solely upon the discovery of a stele which depicts a worker being whipped by an overseer.[21]

In summation, the author is proposing that Indo Aryan refugees, of high social status, whose original home was the city of Nahor, intermarried with Semitic Kenites and founded the Israelite nation. The copper smelting technology and marketing expertise of the Kenites, in conjunction with local ore deposits, enabled the proto Israelites to establish themselves as the dominant copper producers in the Middle-East.

The resultant economic stability of the fledgling Israelites promulgated the peaceful assimilation of various other tribes of hill farmers and Shosu pastoralists. While existing Canaanite city states feuded among themselves, and were periodically attacked by foreign invaders, the Israelites quietly developed their overseas markets. They probably exported a great deal of their iron and copper to Asia, via the port of Ezion Geber (the biblical Eloth) situated on the shores of the Gulf of Aqabah.

In short, the Israelites were not the abominable psychopathic racists who attained a position of dominance by virtue of bloody conquest, as the Old Testament would have us believe, but instead, *peaceably advanced toward nationhood by virtue of their superior manufacturing and marketing skills.*

Doubtless such an hypothesis will generate unbridled fury among Judaic and Christian Fundamentalists alike, who, through their ignorance, implicitly believe in biblical infallibility, and appear to glorify in the rape, pillage and genocide that allegedly was incited by the psychopathic Moses and Joshua. To such unevolved specimens of humanity, the author suggests that they attempt to expand their myopic vision, in addition to seeking psychiatric help.

The religion of the early Israelites does not appear to possess any unique characteristics; the Ten Commandments closely parallel the moral laws of ancient Egypt, where the *Book of the Dead* and the *Teachings of Amenope* counsel one not to covet the wife or property of a neighbor, not to commit murder or ridicule people of diminutive stature. In keeping with the Israelites, the Athenians and the Egyptians considered themselves the Creator's chosen race.

We know very little regarding Judaism during its formative centuries, except that the Israelites embraced goddess worship. We glean from *II Maccabees* that even as late as 162 B.C., Jewish soldiers wore magical amulets. The Bible also informs us that during the post Solomonic period, human sacrifices still occurred in Israel.

Mention of goddess worship brings us to Solomon, who, according to the Bible, erected shrines throughout the land dedicated to the Goddess Ashtoreth. We are also told that the architectural design and construction of the Temple was directed by Hiram, who was loaned for the task by the goddess worshipping King of Tyre.

According to occult lore, Hiram was a member of a Mystery School known as the Dionysian Artificers, who had established esoteric lodges throughout the Mediterranean countries. This Mystery School was destined to found similar lodges in Europe at a later date, such as the Comacine Masters, even influencing the great Roman architect Vitrivius in the process.[22] A splinter group of architects known as the

Cassidens were active among the desert communities (Essenes, Zxadokites, etc.) during the 1st century A.D.. It was such Mystery Schools, with their closely-held esoteric knowledge of sacred geometry, that eventually spawned the Frater Solomonis Mystery School, founded by St. Bernard of Clairvaux and responsible for the design of the magnificent Gothic cathedrals. The design of the Gothic cathedrals incorporated not only conventional sacred geometry, but also magic squares, in order to render the cathedral interiors function as tuned resonant cavities.[23]

Unlike contemporary western religions, which embody the use of prayer, and also posssess philosophical overtones, the religion of the Israelites essentially was a temple cult, oriented primarily toward the practice of the sacrificial rite, prayer being considered a superfluous element.

The plethora of goddess oriented artifacts discovered throughout Israel, suggests that a strong matriarchal influence was extant among the populace, as the Israelites evolved toward nationhood—a concept clearly at variance with the patriarchal emphasis implied in the Pentateuch. In analyzing this apparent contradiction, we must take into consideration that the first five books of the Bible were not written until at least seven centuries after Abraham had entered Canaan. This is ample time for the oral transmission of Israelite history to have become distorted or, more likely, deliberately revised in order to falsely justify the necessity for the line of succession of the Israelite priesthood to remain permanently within the Levite tribe.

After the floodwaters of the global deluge had subsided somewhat, Yahwey informed Noah, according to the Bible, that the rainbow represented a covenant between Yahwey and Planet Earth. Note that this covenant was not addressed to a specific ethnic group, but to "....every living creature of all flesh." Yahwey later replaces the covenant with a new one addressed solely to Abraham and his descendants, in which Abraham is promised the Land of Canaan forever (Genesis 17.8). At an even later date, Yahwey yet again revises the covenant, this time addressing it to Moses, who is instructed to lead the Israelites to the promised land.

Such a display of capriciousness forces one to conclude that in order to rigidly enforce their religious and administrative authority over the Jewish populace, the levitical priesthood had to conceive and implement a deceptive ploy, which would persuade the Jews, after their release from their Babylonian captivity, to abandon their worship of various deities and offer exclusive allegiance to Yahwey. Hence the covenant myth, which significantly is explained in expanded form in Leviticus 26:3-5: "....if ye walk in my statutes and keep my commandments, and do them; Then I will give you rain in due season, and the land will yield her increase....". Needless to say, this covenant, which binds the nation in perpetuity, was composed of hollow words, for despite attempted adherence to the Mosaic Law, the Israelites suffered crop failures and oppression from foreign powers.

In conceiving of a deceptive masterplan worthy of a Machievelli, the Levitical priesthood was able to maintain its rapacious and repressive dominion over the god fearing populace for many centuries. Like the contract between the Devil and Dr. Faustus, the Levitical covenant in its final form permanently bound the Israelites to a vengeful deity.

How strange it is that Jews and Christians alike, subscribe to the existence of a Supreme Being, yet also believe that the Creator entered into an exclusive covenant with the Israelites—a body of people who, according to the Bible, committed genocide on a massive scale, in addition to participating in the ritual sacrifice of juveniles.

Eventually, belief in the Mosaic covenant formed such a powerful mindset among the post exilic Jews, that the covenant myth became the cementitious constituent which, through the centuries, has prompted Jews from very diverse backgrounds to tenaciously adhere to their elected religion. It is a tragedy for humanity that belief in such a false theocratic dogma has generated what is, in all probability, the most enduring and important cultural construct in recorded history. It has resulted in a great deal of unnecessary bloodshed, particularly during the 20th century, and is inevitably destined to foment even greater mayhem in the near future, if the Illuminati accomplishes its objective of fomenting a nuclear holocaust in the Middle East.[24]

The Old Testament exhibits a gradual, yet subtle shift toward thinly-disguised Mithraism—the patriarchal solar cult of the Indo Aryans, becoming very blatant in the Books of the Prophets, such as Habakkuk 3:3-4, where "...his brightness was as the light." Originally androgynous when worshipped in India centuries prior to his adoption by the Persians, Mithra shed his feminine aspect and became the militaristic god of monarchs and warriors. This change occurred after Macedonia was conquered by Darius 1st, King of Persia (521—485 B.C.).

The Israelite functions of priests and temple attendants became the exclusive domain of the Levite clan, who were entrusted with these positions as a reward for their supposed dedication in following the laws of the mythical Moses, according to the Bible. Paradoxically, Levitical followers of an Israelite named Korah had rebelled against Moses! Something is clearly amiss with the biblical history of the Israelites, suggestive that it was tampered with, presumably in order to justify the Levites seizing control of the priesthood. Such a ploy also would enable them to manipulate the wealth of Israel, particularly since the Temple held the nation's treasury; it also was the national center of commerce, as well as its religious focal point.

In all probability, the Levites seized political as well as religious authority through aligning themselves with a foreign power, and subsequently revising Israelite history to favor their own self aggrandizement. We must therefore search for a period in Israelite history which not only provided for such an opportunity, but also was an era which saw radical modifications to both religious and secular codes.

Such an opportunity arose in 587 B.C., when King Nebuchadnezzer conquered the towns and cities of Judah, destroying the Temple and deporting much of the populace to Babylon, where they remained for seventy years. Archaeological and historical research has revealed that although the devastation of Judah was severe, some of the populace, including priests, remained; a Jew named Gedaliah was apponted Governor of Judah by the Babylonians. This historical fact is of importance to our search, since the prophet Jeremiah and the remnants of the ruling class joined Gedaliah in Mizpa, a city to the north of Jerusalem. The fact that Gedaliah subsequently was assassinated by a Jewish nationalist for his complicity with the Babylonians, suggests that Jeremiah and his priestly associates were quislings. Interestingly, Jeremiah 51 claims that Babylon "....*shall become* a *dwelling place for dragons.*"

Levites returning to Judah after their long exilic period in Babylon, were in an unique postion to establish a dictatorship. Gone forever was the monarchical era established earlier, and there was no centralized administration or written national history. The Persian monarch Cyrus, who had released them from their captivity, even ordered them to rebuild the Temple.

Seizing their opportunity, the Levites apparently established a theocracy, introducing laws which incorporated religious and secular codes which were based upon those of their Babylonian captors. Feast days corresponded: thus Tisri of the Babylonians became the Feast of the Tabernacles; Nisan equated with the Passover, and Adar was similar to the Purim. *Until the Babylonian captivity, angels formed no part of Israelite life;* the angel myth had been created by Sumerian peasants after a mortal named Tas Mi-ki-gal became honored as *dragon slayer and Lord of Agriculture.*

With the passage of time, he was deified as Lord of the Air. To the superstitious Sumerians, this meant that he must have had feathered wings, in order to fly. And so began the myth of the person we know as Archangel Michael, whose agricultural genesis is celebrated by Christians with the Harvest Festival, held on Michaelmas Sunday. To the Sumerians, the lofty aloofness of their sun-god Ia provided the priesthood with the opportunity to appoint his powers on earth to his son Tas Mi-ki-gal, who subsequently became the overlord to a host of angels. Phoenician coins depict the winged figure and the name "Mikalu", while a Hittite seal illustrates a man, under attack by a dragon, appealing to the archangel for help. In this manner, the angelology of the Babylonians was eventually incorporated into the Jewish religion in the post-exilic years; the Jews also inherited the insidious Babylonian practice of usuary.

Cuneiform texts discovered in Babylon have revealed that during the reign of the Babylonian monarch King Kandalanu (648-625 B.C.) a Babylonian banker named Jacob Egibi was charging an interest rate of twenty percent for bank loans. This was shortly prior to the arrival in Babylon of the exiled Judeans, which occurred in 587 B.C.. It was during their seventy years spent in Mesopotamia that the Jews became aquainted with usurious money-lending practices; clay textual documents found in the Mesopotamian city of Nippur reveal that an exiled Judean family named Murushu had also been engaged in usurious money-lending, commencing in 587 B.C..

The Jewish sabbath became as strict and repressive as that of Babylonia, and possessed similar prohibitions regarding cooking and the lighting of fires on the Sabbath. Another adoption was the establishment of places of worship that were subservient to a central Temple authority; the rapacious Levites even authorized themselves to mint the coin of the realm! With the approval of their Persian overlords, the Levitical priesthood (descendants of Aaron) established their own repressive version of the Israelite religion as the law of the land, and the High Priest of the Temple became ruler of all the nation.

Reconstruction of the Temple and establishment of the new theocracy occurred during the reign of King Darius 1st of Persia. The ruler apparently expunged all traces of the feminine aspects of the deity Mithra, who, the legend claims, was the intermediary between the

Creator and humankind. Mithra was purportedly discovered as a baby by herdsmen, who had been guided by a star. Egyptian and Judean texts demonstrate that the Persian monarch played an active role in overseeing the religious activities of his satrapies.

It was the custom of conquering monarchs to introduce the attributes of their deity Mithra to the defeated nation, by attaching them to a local god, in order to avoid incurring the wrath of the defeated populace. Another ploy sometimes adopted by an invading monarch was an earnest plea to the gods of a city under seiege, to transfer their allegiance to the side of the invaders. To prevent such a ploy being used against them, a defensive measure later utilized by the Romans was the assigning of the name Appollo to Mithra, the god of their military forces.

In view of the above, it is quite possible that an understanding was reached between the cunning Levite clan and King Darius 1st, whereby the unscrupulous Levites were installed as rulers of the nation in perpetuity, in return for assigning the attributes of Mithra to the Israelite deity Yahwey. In effect, Yahwey, the god of the Kenites, was covertly displaced by the militaristic deity Mithra, only the deity's name remaining unchanged.

It is quite remarkable how quickly that new generations of Chinese, growing up under the yoke of communist indoctrination, abandoned the religious beliefs and ancestor worship of their elders. Similarly, the new generation of Jews, who grew up so influenced by Babylonian culture that they even forgot their native Hebrew tongue, would have lacked the ability to discern that the religion and history of their people being promulgated by the Levites, radically differed from that taught previously by the pre exilic priesthood. The immediate post exilic period was accordingly very opportune for the rapacious Levites to introduce a new, self aggrandizing code of religious and secular laws, without arousing undue suspicion, particularly if the new religion bore the approval of King Darius.

The coastal peninsula, some twelve kilometers north of the city of Tunis, is a prestigious residential area. Even the official residence of the President of Tunisia is located there today. Unfortunately, the present growing urban expansion has posed a major threat to the archaeological remains of what was one of the great maritime trading centers of the ancient world—the city of Carthage.

Founded in the 8th century B.C., as a Phoenician outpost and colony of the city of Tyre, Carthage possessed two large artificial harbors, replete with covered berths for commercial and naval ships. From this city, the stately Phoenician triremes plied their trade over far greater oceanic distances than establishment archaeologists would have us believe. A hoard of Carthaginian coins was discovered by Portuguese sailors during the 18th century A.D. In the Azores, some 800 miles off the European coast.

Dr. Mark McMenamin, a professor of geology at Mount Holyoke College in Massachusetts, became interested in this event, which induced him to conduct a study of Carthaginian currency. He discovered that Phoenician gold coinage bore minute markings corresponding to the outlines of several geographic regions, including South America. The professor's findings are supportive of bronze figurines which were discovered in 1641 by Jesuit priests residing near Minas Gerais, in Brazil.

Inscriptions on the figurines have been identified by Vatican scholars as Phoenician; the coins and figurines strongly suggest that the seafaring Phoenicians had established widespread trading relationships during the biblical era. Additional evidence that the Phoenicians had visited South America as trans oceanic traders, not as shipwrecked mariners, is provided by a stone discovered in Brazil more than a century ago. The stone, known as the *Parahyba Text,* bears a Phoenician inscription describing a voyage by Phoenician merchants, who had departed from the Mediterranean port of Sidon, during the 6th century B.C..[25]

At the same time that the city of Carthage was being built during the 8th century B.C., the Spanish coastal city of Tarshish prospered, as metallic ore mined by the Basque natives was traded to Phoenicians who had settled in the region; the local language, known as Tartessian, was a dialectical variant of Phoenician.[26]

Unlike the flimsy coastal hugging craft that plied the Mediterranean during the biblical era, the Phoenician ships of Tarshish, with their graceful swanlike bows and leather sails, were large ocean going vessels. Moreover, the Basque seafarers of Tarshish possessed exceptional navigational skills, which had evolved from their employment of a base-seven mathematical system, similar to that of the Irish Celts. The Basques, noted for their octagonal fields and incredibly difficult language, never have been given due credit for their major contribution to navigation and cartography (Juan de la Cosa Vizcaino was the Basque owner/navigator of Christopher Columbus's flagship, the *Santa Maria*, and also served as pilot on the epic voyages of Amerigo Vespucci and Vasco de Balboa).

This digressian from our narrative was necessary because it is interesting to conjecture the economic fate of the Kenite metal workers, after their local supply of copper ore had become exhausted. Ezekial reported that the merchants of Tarshish brought silver, tin, iron and lead to the city of Tyre for trade. In all probability, much of the imported metal was aquired by the Kenite metalsmiths, in exchange for copper from the Kenite foundries. Is it possible that the Kenites found a new supply of copper ore after their own mines became depleted? Could it have been smelted into copper ingots in North America by Kenites, then exported to Israel by means of Phoenician ships?

Curiously, 5000 ancient copper mines have been discovered on Michigan's Isle Royale. In total, some 500,000 tons of copper were smelted from Michigan ore in ancient times, yet the relatively small number of copper artifacts recovered from Native American burial mounds does not account for the prodigious volume of ore that was extracted from the Michigan mines. Strangely, some Native American gravesites were found to contain copper sheets formed into the shape of animal hides.

It was a common practice among European and Mediterranean Bronze Age cultures to cast their copper ingots into a configuration similar to that of an animal hide, the four leg-like protusions serving as convenient handles for lifting purposes. It is possible that the artifacts found in the Indian graves were beaten from native copper (which does not require smelting) by Indians who were influenced by the shape of the smelted ingots, in the belief that the latter possessed magical properties. Since the amount of North American copper ore which was mined in biblical times does not tally with the quantity of copper artifacts unearthed in North America, one is compelled to wonder whether any imported ore or copper found its way into the hands of Kenite craftspeople.[27]

Ignoring the vast discrepancy between the total weight of copper ore mined in Michigan, and the small number of artifacts discovered on North American soil, the archaeological establishment claims that the gigantic American mining effort was solely the work of a North American copper culture, without explaining what happened to the missing copper! Sadly, mainstream archaeologists also have elected to dismiss the abundant epigraphic evidence which very strongly suggests that the Phoenician merchants of Tarshish had established trading stations in North America more than two milleniums ago. Abundant epigraphic evidence in the form of inscribed stones, and structures bearing inscriptions in Tartessian and Oggam, have been discovered at New England sites.

A credible find occurred in 1982, when Russell Burrows discovered an ancient funerary cave in Southern Illinois. In addition to jewels and gold medallions, the funerary artifacts also included several thousand stone tablets bearing inscriptions in Tifinag, Phoenician and Oggam, and symbols denoting Bel and Tanith. Of particular note were

engravings of men wearing Phoenician-style hats, an Egyptian car-
touche and a Jewish menorah. In view of the above, it is quite possible
that the Kenite metal workers used North American copper after their
own mines had become depleted.

In completing our quest for the true origins of the Israelite nation,
we cannot ignore one important facet of the puzzle, for it has a direct
bearing upon the belief structure of many Christian fundamentalists
and Mormans.

These fundamentalists have adopted the so-called British Israelite
hypothesis, which claims that the princess Tea Tephi, a daughter of the
King of Judah, together with her retinue, settled in Ireland circa 1250
B.C.(the Bible merely states that she was taken to Egypt, which
incurred Yahwey's wrath). Some Danites, in addition to the other tribes
who comprised the northern kingom of Israel, after the division of the
nation, were taken into captivity by the Assyrians circa 740-721 B.C.,
and were relocated in the Caucasus region, where they became known
thereafter as "Caucasians", according to the fundamentalists.

They claim that the tribe of Dan subsequently migrated to Western
Europe. Therefore, according to the convoluted reasoning of the fundamentalists, the Anglo Saxons and people of Germanic stock are God's
chosen race, a reward for disseminating Christianity throughout the
world.

In consequence of this poisonous and distorted belief structure, a
great deal of anti-Jewish hate literature has been published by various
Christian Funamentalist groups. Since it is hoped that this book will
contribute toward interracial understanding and harmony, such a
claim by the Christian Fundamentalists and Mormons cannot go
unchallenged.

Recent archaeological excavations among the former Canaanite
coastal cities, have revealed ceramic containers from the Philistine era
(12th century B.C.). These containers, which differ from earlier
Canaanite vessels, possessed very thick walls in order to withstand the

rigors of maritime travel. They were discovered in the Levantine area known to have been occupied by the Danites; similar vessels also were found in Cyprus and at Tel Dan, an inland Danite stronghold of the Galilee region, described in the Bible as Sidonian (Phoenician) territory.

According to Genesis 49:16-17, the Danites, *lacking a known genealogy, were not related to the early Israelites.* In other words, the Danites were presumably members of the Sea Peoples group, known as the Danuna or Denyen to the Egyptians, who initially settled in Canaan circa 1175 B.C., according to an Egyptian wall relief at Medinet Habu, and were, in all probability, related to the Greek Sikeloi. There is a strong possibility that the Danites were Greeks who had participated in the Trojan war, and served as role models for the epics Goliath and Samson. Regrettably, space does not permit development of this hypothesis, attractive though it is. Additionally, we must not overlook the biblical statement that the Danites "....*dwell on ships*" (Judges 5:17) whereas the Israelites were not a seafaring race.

The claim that the Jewish princess Tea Tephi arrived in Ireland circa 1250 B.C., accompanied by the Stone of Scone, is clearly apocryphal. The ancient history of Ireland, as portrayed in the Lebor Gabála (a medieval monastic work) and such works as the Book of Ballymote, also is largely apochryphal, something Wiccans will not like to hear. This is why it is imperative to return to first principals in order to determine the source of such stories as the origin of the Stone of Scone. We must also avoid linguistic pitfalls when determining what early historians meant when they mentioned Ivernia or Hibernia (Ireland). This is because the coastal region of southern England extending from the county of Dorset to the Solent used to be named Iwerne, which is cognate with "Ivernia"; its inhabitants were known as the Gwyddel, often translated as "Irish".

In the interests of good scholarship, we must search for any other historical reference to a matriarchal figure possessing a ceremonial stone (preferably descended from a Middle-Eastern tribe or clan) whose arrival in Ireland substantially predated the era of Tea Tephi.

Our search for such a person begins not in Ireland, but at an elevation of 5,200 feet up the western flank of Mount Ararat, at the town of Van. Believed to have been founded by Queen Semiramis, according to Armenian tradition, it is located near Lake Van. In prehistoric times, this lake supplied the headwaters of both the Tigris and the Euphrates rivers.

The tribal people of antiquity who originally inhabited this region were short statured and dark haired, similar to the Picts of the Scottish border country and known variously as the Vans, Bans, Wans, Fens, Feins, or Faens. A serpent worshipping race,the Vans have become confused with the solar worshipping, fair-haired, blue eyed Phoenicians in Wiccan and New Age literature. The Vans tribal name became appended to the names of countries and townships which sprang up as they migrated westward to Britain and Ireland. Thus the ancient name of Britain was Alban, later Albion, and Paisley was originally Vanduara. Van Lake, in Wales was traditionally sacred to the Lady of the Lake.

According to tradition, a matriarch and her serpent worshipping clan landed in South Western Ireland at Duna Mark, which is in Bantry Bay, not later than 1000 B.C.. This time period predates that of Tea Tephi and that of the first Jewish diaspora. The matriarch's name was Ceasair, which is cognate with *"Kvasir"* (wise person of the sacred cauldron) mentioned in the Gothic Eddas. According to the Eddas, the matriarch of the Vans had a consort/son named Baldr, cognate with the "Balor of the evil eye," who was the champion of the Irish Feins (also known as the Fae). A later Irish hero was Fal—Fal's Hill being at the ancient capital Tara. Very significantly, Baldr, Balor and Fal were tribal champions and all were possessors of a magic stone. In later Irish legends, Fal's Stone cried out during the coronation of monarchs who were true heirs. It is purportedly the Stone of Scone which is used at the coronation of British monarchs.

In similar fashion, the legend of Saint Bridget appears to have been derived from the tale of the matriarchal sorceress Frigg, the "Mother of the Wolf of Fen," "Fen" being cognate with "Van." Frigg allegedly was the leader of a group of serpent cult priestesses known as "the Nine Maidens." Maiden Stone monoliths bearing serpent emblems are found in various parts of Britain.

According to the author's esteemed friend Mr. Credo Mutwa, the Sanusi and Official Historian of the Zulu Nation, ancient races were forbidden by their overlords to depict dragons, hence the adoption of serpents in lieu.

The last known clans of the Vans in Ireland were known as the Fomorians, and in the Eddas as the *"Baombur;"* purportedly they were defended by dragons. The serpent worshipping Fomorians were vanquished by the solar-worshipping army of Part-olon, circa 400 B.C.. Part-olon was a Phoenician, who, according to ancient British chronicles, arrived in Ireland from the Mediterranean via Scotland (a Phoenician seal depicts their arch deity Mikal defeating a winged dragon). A solar oriented army defeating a serpent tribe is probably the origin of the fable in which Saint Patrick rids Ireland of serpents, particularly since Saint Patrick allegedly was in Ireland during the same century as Part-olon.

It should be self-evident from the above that the key elements of the Tea Tephi tale are to be found in the earlier occupation of Ireland by the Vans.

British Israelism was the brainchild of Elizabethan occultist and spymaster John Dee, who signed his coded messages 007! This false religious dogma was revived in the 19th century by the British Crown and members of its government, in order to falsely claim that the British are really God's chosen people. This ploy was initiated as a public relations measure in order to elevate public acclaim for Queen Victoria, who had become unpopular due to her protracted seclusion following the death of her husband Prince Albert.

Major impetus to British Israelism was given by Queen Victoria's daughter Princess Alice, who became a patroness of the movement. The insidious doctrine of British Israelism accordingly was established in order to suggest that the British Monarchy was descended from the biblical House of David. This false ideology was reinforced in 1901, when an American freemason and British Israelism afficionado, the Reverend Charles Parham, created the Pentecostal Movement. Parham later lost his ministry after being charged with pederasty and became a speaker for the Ku Klux Klan. The forty different British Israelism organizations merged in 1919 to form the British Israel World Federation.

Observing the successful spread of Pentecostalism among the American black population, the British introduced Pentecostalism to South Africa's militant Zulu nation, as a pacification measure, in 1908. Throughout recorded history, the oligarchy has employed state regulated religions as a ploy to maintain a form of mind-control over the populace, as evidenced by the Cult of Apollo in Greece, and King Henry VIII appointing himself Pontifex Maximus, in order to regulate the religious belief structure of the English.

At the present time, the City of London crowd and British Intelligence, are using Christian Fundamentalism and the charismatic cults as a means to exert control over both the United States military and the Patriot Movement. Several leading Pentecostalists are former high-level military officers, such as General Ralph E. Haines, the former architect of *"Operation Gardenplot,"* intended for the military take-over of every American city if a state of national emergency is declared, and General Benton Partin, a founder of the Front Line Fellowship. The latter is a charismatic organization which is active in South Africa; participants include former South African commandos. Partin allegedly has received intelligence reports from a British Israel geopolitician.[28]

Another fundamentalist organization under oligarchical control is the International Christian Leadership, created by Colonel Sir Vivian Gabriel, a former British Air Commission Attaché in Washington, D.C., in order to exert influence over key members of society. During the 1950's, the organization's major sponsor was former Nazi S.S. Officer Prince Bernhard, at the time he was founding the notorius Bilderberg Group. According to one American newspaper, televangelist and Christian Fundamentalist Pat Robertson visited Zaire at the request of then President George H. Bush, in order to persuade the Zaire Government to transfer that nation's mining interests to foreign ownership. British mining companies subsequently funded the bloody coup led by the despotic Lauren Kabila, which resulted in the deaths of hundreds of thousands of Africans. After the coup, Robertson invited the dictator to be his guest in America.[29]

The Christian Fundamentalist movement, with its emphasis on British Israelism, is particularly dangerous at the present time, since fundamentalist extremists are urging the destruction of the Al Aqsa mosque—the third holiest Islamic location, which is situated atop Jerusalem's Temple Mount, so that reconstruction of the Jewish Temple can commence. Britain's Quator Coronati Freemasonic Research Lodge purportedly is the command center for both Jewish and Christian fundamentalist fanatics who are urging mayhem on the Temple Mount, in order to initiate a nuclear war which, in their warped minds, will hasten Armageddon. As we will see in a later chapter of this book, the Temples of Solomon and Herod were located at the Gihon Spring, not at the erroneously named Temple Mount, which was merely a Roman fortress in the biblical era.

Another insidious British Israelite activity in recent years has been the publication of books which erroneously claim that Mary Magdalene and her purported sister Martha, were both brides of Christ. These books claim that Mary fled Jerusalem in A.D. 70, and settled in France, where Mary's offspring allegedly married into the Frankish royal family, which later spawned the Merovingian bloodline.

This nonsensical tale appears to be a ploy to convince the public that the principal European royal families are direct descendants of the biblical house of David, and appears to be an attempt to legitimize the European Oligarchy as overlords of the New World Order official religion (which is being developed at a private estate in Crestone County, Colorado).

This charade began in France with the publication of thirteen poems entitled *Le Serpent Rouge*, in which Mary Magdelene possessed *"a celebrated vase."* All we know of Mary Magdalene from the Bible is that Christ puportedly cast seven devils out of her (Magdala was an ancient occult center). We are not informed whether or not he married her, or whether Martha was her sister.

The myth is extremely flawed. The direct Merovingian bloodline began with Merovee, who died in 458 A.D. and was succeeded by his son Childeric, whose tomb contained 300 gold bees. *The Merovingians claimed descent from the Trojans of Greece, not from the Jewish Davidic bloodline.* This claim is almost certainly correct, for according to Homer's *Iliad*, the Greek city of Troy was named in honor of Tros, whose father Dardanus, founded the city. His name suggests that he could have been of Danite descent. The Greek deity Zeus was depicted both as an eagle and also as a serpent, to which offerings of honey were made, possibly a connection with the Merovingian gold bees. Zeus was claimed to have been born in Arcadia, a name of esoteric importance to the Priory of Sion.

Arcadia was in the region known as Sparta. It is known that some Spartans migrated initially to Troy, then later to Southern France, before settling in the French province of Lorraine (the domicile of the current head of the Illuminati). In the apochryphal book *1 Maccabees*, a letter from Areus, King of Sparta, to the Jewish High Priest, states that the Spartans are "….of the race of Abraham." As we have seen, Abraham was most certainly an Indo Aryan Horite, not a Semite.

The letter ended by stating that the King's symbol was an eagle holding a dragon in its claws. This is very interesting, because the Danites flew a red and white standard bearing an eagle, and like the Spartans, grew their hair long. As was stated previously, the Danites were not related to the ancient Israelites; they also, in keeping with the Greeks, made offerings of honey, possibly denoting a tradition later symbolized by the Merovingian gold bees.

According to "Josephus," the Danites migrated to Lebanon, where they remained for 600 years before disappearing from recorded history. *What the above investigation appears to reveal however, is that the oligarchical families of Europe are not descended from the House of David (even the biblical story of David appears to be apocryphal) but from the Indo Aryan Danites.*

This would account for the long hair of Merovee; it also provides an explanation for the Hapsburg adoption of the eagle symbol and the gold bees. One author promoting this fallacious attempt to link the European monarchical bloodline with the House of David also appears to be an apologist for the consumption of menstrual blood—a revolting custom still performed by members of the Illuminati heirarchy, according to more than one observer of this habit. This same author also displays a penchant for griping that the House of Windsor usurped the rightful claim to the British Crown, which thankfully suggests that there is disharmony within the Illuminati ranks.

Fortunately for humanity, even the Christian Fundamentalists have rejected the nonsensical claims of such books, which present an indigestible stew consisting of a few nuggets of truth, immersed in misinformation and pabulum. Only the more ill-informed and gullible members of the New Age community have swallowed this concoction.

Over the centuries, the wrath of Christians has been directed toward the Jews, not only for their refusal to accept Christ, but also for the Jewish bigotted claim that the Jews are God's chosen elite, a claim based upon it being a reward for the Israelite adherence to the Mosaic Law. Such a claim is, of course, utter nonsense, since, according to the Bible, the Israelites under Moses and Joshua broke most of the Ten Commandments, during their alleged destruction of the Canaanite cities, in the so-called conquest period.

Established beliefs die hard, but it is hoped that the next generation of Jews will avoid the intolerant and hateful attitude of the radical Gush Emunim Jewish Fundamentalists, and instead adopt an enlightened attitude and realize that Israel is not theirs by divine right, and learn to co-exist with their Arab neighbors. The Old Testament is both a very flawed religious and secular history of the Israelites; the author accordingly hopes that the factual data presented in this chapter will assist in generating a paradigm shift in the mind set of younger Jews, toward a more accurate understanding of Israelite history.

In these times of growing anti Semitism, it is well to remember that Judaism, despite its false dogma, has afforded a sterling service by providing a focus for Jews during times of persecution, thereby maintaining cohesion among individual Jewish family units.

In concluding this chapter on a positive note, it appears to be a fortuitous characteristic of human nature that most people strive to make spiritual growth during their lifetime. What finer role model could we find for this task than a person whose first name simply means "Judahite." He was the late Sir Yehudi Menuhin. This consumate European violinist and gentle human being, not only provided the world with decades of wonderful music, but had selflessly given countless hours of his spare time to perform at fundraising benefits for the preservation and restoration of those most audacious and wondrous of structures—the Gothic cathedrals. It is no exaggeration to state that without the selfless efforts of this fine humanitarian, many of our Gothic edifices would, in all probability, be in ruins today.

CHAPTER 6

▼

DID JOSHUA, DAVID AND SOLOMON EVER EXIST?

"So the elders of Israel came to the king to Hebron before the Lord, and they annointed David king over Israel...."

(2 Samuel 5:3)

As stated in the previous chapter, archaeological evidence reveals that the Old Testament appears primarily to be an historical fable concocted by the Levites, either during, or shortly after their Babylonian captivity, in order to justify their establishment of a Judean theocracy. Similarly, the biblical account of the lives of Joshua, David and Solomon also appears to be largely apocryphal.

Deuteronomy claims that God commanded the Israelites to cross over the Jordan and dispossess "....great cities forified unto heaven." What God is this? Is it the Yahu of the Kenite proto Israelites, YHWH, or one of the gods mentioned in textual inscriptions discovered in the Negev hill country and in Judean territory, such as Jehova Terman and Jehova Shomron? And what about Mrs. God? These inscriptions send blessings in the name of Jehova and his Ashera! The inscriptions were written during the 8th century B.C., which suggests that during the alleged reign of King David (10th century B.C.) the kingdoms of Israel and Judea were not monotheistic, which strongly contradicts the Bible.

According to the Bible, David was a shepherd who was annointed the second king of Israel in the city of Hebron, upon the death of King Saul. He later captured Jerusalem from the Jebusites, his total reign lasting a total of forty years. Upon his death, he was succeeded by his son Solomon, who also very conveniently ruled for forty years.

During the 19th century, German biblical scholars, led by Julian Wellhausen, challenged the infallibility of the Old Testament, claiming that its historicity largely was a fable concocted for theological reasons. Possessing an opposing belief structure, American archaeologist Willian Albright, set out to prove the historical veracity of the Bible by conducting major digs during the 1920's at such key biblical sites as Meggido and Jericho. In particular, Albright and his associates were determined to prove the veracity of Joshua's conquest of Canaanite cities, and also to seek evidence of the "united monarchy" of David, which the Bible describes as the pinnacle of Israel's military and ecconomic power.

Alas for the efforts of Albright and numerous subsequent archaeologists, the great fortified Canaanite cities that Joshua supposedly conquered revealed themselves to be very small and largely unfortified settlements, whose culture declined over a period extending for several centuries, demonstrative that Joshua's conquest of Canaan never occurred.

The major constructions supposedly established under Solomon's direction at Hazor and Meggido never became a reality. Only 7.5. acres was fortified at Hazor, while Meggido lacked a fortified wall. In actuality, these supposedly major cities merely were very minor settlements.

Hebron, a city which dates from the third millenium B.C., allegedly was King David's capital before his supposed capture of Jerusalem. Recent excavations at the site, located at Tel Runeida, led to the discovery of artifacts of the 8th century B.C., but evidence of David's capital city of the 10th century B.C. is absent. Moreover, the site occupies an area of less than eight acres. Even if 10th century B.C. evidence is found at another part of the Tel, its area will still represent a minor settlement, not a city of significance.

The same situation applies to Jerusalem, known as the City of David: despite numerous excavations which have been conducted in Jerusalem for a period spanning more than a century, no structures dating from the period of David's purported united monarchy have been discovered.[1] Joab, King David's general, supposedly gained entry to Jerusalem by climbing up a water shaft and surprising the city's Jebusite populace. Seeking verification of the tale, some biblical scholars claim that this particular water shaft was one discovered in 1867 by British explorer Charles Warren (who later founded the Quator Coronati freemasonic lodge and participated in the Jack the Ripper murders). The shaft in question is a very ancient and natural karstic formation. Archaeologists Eli Shukron and Ronny Reich have recently stated that the upper end of the shaft was man made *after* the time of David's reign; therefore it could not have been used by David's General Joab to access the city.

Jerusalem's rich culture did not occur until after its northern rival Samaria was conquered in 722 B.C.. Since no evidence of David's purported substantial cities, nor evidence of his "united monarchy" have been discovered despite extensive archaeological searches, it is apparent that if David ever existed at all, he was a very minor and insignificant chieftan, not a monarch of substance. Even the story of David slaying Goliath is questionable, for not to be upstaged by David, David's nephew also killed a giant at Gath, according to *2 Samuel. Samuel* also claims that a Bethlehamite by the name of Elhanan killed a giant named Goliath during a battle at Gath. *I Chronicles* would have us believe that Elhanan also killed yet another giant by the name of Lahmi, who was Goliath's brother. War broke out again, this time at Gezer, and Sippai, a descendant of giants, was slain by Sibbecai.

In claiming descent from the Davidic bloodline, the British Israelites and the European oligarchy have backed a loser, due to the abundance of archaeological evidence illustrating that the mighty regional "united monarchy" of David never existed. Far better to have claimed descent from the Phoenicians, whose colonization of Britain in pre-Roman times is a given. Such a concept would, however, be anathema to the Illuminati, who were ancient adversaries of the Phoenicians, which is why the legend of Saint George slaying the dragon stems from Cappadocia, the central province of the Hitto Phoenics.

That the European oligarchic families and the Royal Order of the Dragon should also promote British Israelism is not surprising, when one considers that British Israelism was created by Elizabethan astrologer, occultist and spymaster John Dee, the father of modern Freemasonry. Dee received esoteric tuition from Rabbi Loew, the alleged creator of a golem (a humanoid). Loew was noted for his bizarre occult rituals involving cadavers stolen from graves. Sadly, British Israelism has a widespread following, which is a tragedy, for its afficionados exhibit the same disgraceful "holier than thou" elitism that pervades a large segment of the New Age community. Such elitism is often a precursor to wars fought in the name of God.

The author strongly urges all readers to closely monitor current archaeological digs occurring in Israel, for Kabbalistic rabbis and certain prominent Christian Fundamentalists are instrumental in promoting an on going search for the *Kalal*, containing the ashes of the magical red heifer, which is referenced in the so-called copper scroll and also in the Book of Numbers (19: 1-19).

According to Judaic tradition, the Temple cannot be reconstructed at Jerusalem until the ashes of the legendary red heifer are found. A senior Illuminati historian has informed the author that as a back-up plan, a very pure blooded red heifer currently is being raised. Since a seismic faultline traverses the Mount of Olives, the Illuminati are also planning to create a geophysically generated earthquake sufficiently strong to destroy the Islamic Al Aqsa mosque and the Dome of the Rock. The red heifer's ashes will then be used to purify the Temple Mount, prior to consecration of the new Temple.

A closely guarded secret of the Illuminati heirarchy is the fact that construction of the new Jerusalem Temple was commenced more than two decades ago. Since it is self evident that any attempt to construct the Temple on the misnamed Temple Mount (which is sacred to Arab and Jew alike) would result in unceasing bloodshed, the new Temple is located very deep underground. After it has been consecrated, the Temple is to be used solely by the Illuminati heirarchy, not by the Israeli populace, most of whom will undoubtedly die if the planned Middle East nuclear holocaust becomes a reality. The new Temple's Holy of Holies will house the Ark of the Covenant, which currently is hidden in a subterranean vault at Karnak, in Egypt (the Ethiopian and Japanese Arks being merely fakes).

During the 19th century of the present era, correspondence between Illuminists Albert Pike and Guiseppi Mazzini discussed Illuminati plans for the implementation of three global wars, which were to be precursors to the establishment of a totalitarian global government.

World War I was to be initiated by creating political differences between Britain and Germany. Communism would be implemented in Russia and used for the purpose of conquering other nations.

World War II would destroy the German Empire and foster sympathy for oppressed Jews, in order to establish the State of Israel. Communism was to be expanded until it equalled the strength of the Western Powers, at which time its growth would be checked.

World War III would be initiated by fomenting ideological differences between Arab and Jew. The other global powers will choose sides and destroy each other. The survivors, disillusioned with existing religions, will embrace the Illuminati Luciferic religion. Out of the chaos of war, a New World Order will be created.

The on-going search for the ashes of the fabled red heifer, currently is focussed on the region immediately north of the Wadi Qumran. In all probability, when the Illuminati timetable calls for an Arab/Israeli nuclear conflict, in order to precipitate World War III, the red heifer's ashes conveniently will be "discovered". This will provide the rationale for the destruction of the Al Aqsa mosque and the Dome of the Rock—an act guaranteed to initiate a nuclear Holy War (selected Jewish boys currently are undergoing training as future Temple priests).

How sad that most Israelis—descendents of Khazars who lacked Israelite or Judaic ancestral roots, have developed such a myopic mind-set that they remain in ignorance of the fact that present day Israel was built upon a quagmire of biblical falsehoods; the Israeli nation accordingly lacks a stable foundation. This chapter accordingly is oriented toward the current generation of Israeli college students, in the hope that they will research Israelite history for themselves, instead of accepting the false religious dogma directed toward them by a bigotted priesthood. Only then will they come to the realization that the land of Israel is not theirs by divine right, and learn to co-exist peacefully with their Arab neighbors and avert the Armageddon scenario planned for them by the Illuminati and their maniacal fundamentalist lackeys.

After this chapter was written, an explosive article by Jewish scholar Ze'ev Herzog appeared in the Israeli publication *Ha'aretz*. Entitled *"Deconstructing the walls of Jericho,"* the article began: "Following 70 years of intensive excavations in the Land of Israel, archaeologists have found out: the Patriarchs' acts are legendary, the Israelites did not sojurn in Egypt or make an exodus, they did not conquer the land. Neither is there any mention of the empire of David and Solomon, nor the source of a belief in the God of Israel. These facts have been known for years, but Israel is a stubborn people and nobody wants to hear about it."

The lengthy article by this scholar, who should be honored for his courage in daring to speak the truth, cites supportive archaeological data and continues: "….the great united monarchy [of David and Solomon] is an imaginary historiosophic creation, which was composed during the period of the Kingdom of Judea at the earliest. Perhaps the most decisive proof of this is the fact that we do not know the name of this kingdom….. The potency of tradition has now led some researchers to "discover" Mount Sinai in the northern Hijaz or, as already mentioned, at Mount Karkoum in the Negev. These central events in the history of the Israelites are not corroborated in documents external to the Bible or in archaeological findings. Most historians today agree that at best, the stay in Egypt and the exodus occurred in a few families and that their private story was expanded and "nationalized" to fit the needs of theological ideology."

CHAPTER 7

▼

WHO IS MITHRA?

"I remember that the priests of the fellow in the cap used at one time to say, "Our Capped One himself is a Christian."

Saint Augustine

By the time of the patriarch Abraham, a great deal of the esoteric knowledge disseminated by the survivors of the Noahic flood had been forgotten or suppressed. The later re-emergence of such technology as evidenced by the Round Towers of Celtic Ireland, and the incorporation of cosmogony in the architecture of Europe's Gothic cathedrals, suggests that an underground esoteric network sustained a working knowledge of esoteric science into the mediæval era. The network, however, apparently refrained from divulging their secrets to their rapacious priestly overlords.

Thus we can perceive the origins of one form of secret society, or Mystery School. In fact, it appears that the more esoteric aspects of temple architecture, involving sacred geometry, were transmitted by successive generations of Mystery Schools, commencing in antiquity with the Dionysian Artificers of the Middle East, who passed their covert technology to the Cassidens. The Cassidens were a little-known secret society of temple architects who were active among such Jewish Covenant groups as the Essenes and the Zadokites.

The tradition was inherited by the Roman Institute of Architects, and used by its famous member Marcus Vitrivius Pollio, who related temple architecture to harmonious human proportions. He also established a sacred canon of proportions based upon the numbers 3, 4 and 5 and their correspondences with musical root harmonies. This esoteric temple tradition re-emerged during the 11th century of the present era, in a Mystery School known as the *Fraters Solomonis,* whose architects created the great Gothic cathedrals of Europe. This latter secret society was founded by Saint Bernard of Clairvaux, the hidden financial and political power behind the Knights Templar.

That the principal objective in writing the Old and New Testaments was not spiritual enlightenment, but political control of the masses, is evident in the savage punishment meted out by Levite priest and Catholic Inquisitor alike, for the slightest supposed transgression of biblical law.

Fearful of a coup launched by a populace skilled in the esoteric sciences, the biblical authors roundly condemn any form of divination as being the emanation of Satan, yet a blind eye is turned toward the divinitory practices of the Levite priests. Exodus 22:18 succinctly states: "Wizards thou shalt not suffer to live," yet Genesis hypocrytically points out without censure, that Joseph, the son of Jacob, practised a form of divination known as hydromantia (gazing into a cup of liquid). Similarly, the 13th chapter of Genesis provides an extremely detailed narrative in which Jacob performed sympathetic magic, in order to best a Syrian in a cattles deal. Manasses, the 13th King of Judah (692-638 B.C.) unabashedly indulged in the revolting divinatory practice of extispicium, whereby omens are interpreted from the enrails of newly murdered boys.

In subjecting the masses to religious mind-deadening tyranny during the biblical era, the priestly overlords were under the delusion that they themselves possessed freedom of will, when in actuality, they were enslaved not only by the constraining demands of maintaining a dominating regime, but through being initiates of the oldest and most mysterious of all religions known to humanity—Mithraism.

Never in the annals of theological literature has there been such an concerted effort to conceal the true nature and history of a religion from the general public, than is the case with Mithraism. So thoroughly did the priestly hierarchy of the early Christian Church distort the history of Mithraism, that present day texts on the subject invariably inform us that Mithraism was a sun worshipping cult that was spawned in Persia during the time of Zoroaster. It is erroneously claimed that Mithraism became embodied into the Sol Invictus cult of the Romans and died during the early Christian era.

Nothing could be further from the truth. Mithra the Sun God was enshrined in the oldest religious work known, the Rig Veda, created by the Aryan invaders of India, where he was described as the *"God of Daylight."* Clay tablets discovered in 1907 at Boghazkoi, reveal that Mithra was worshipped in Mesopotamia as early as 1400 B.C..

For much of his life, Abraham lived in the region located on the northern border of Mesopotamia known as Mitanni. In his book *The Greatness that was Babylon,* Professor Saggs comments: "....the kings of Mitanni bore not Hurrian (Horite) but Indo European names, whilst the old Indian gods Mitra, Varunna and Indra were worshipped....All this points to the presence of an Aryan warrior caste ruling over a largely non Aryan population." Concurring with the professor, archaeologist O.R. Gurney writes: "It is thus clear in Mitanni a population of Hurrians was dominated by a ruling caste of Indo Aryans."

Armed with the knowledge that Mithraism was practiced in the Mitanni region of the Middle East during the 2nd millenium B.C., we are able to obtain a deeper insight into the mysterious reign of the

Egyption pharoah Akhenaten. No rational explanation has been provided by Egyptologists for what prompted the young monarch to establish his new capital at El Armana, where he created a monotheistic solar cult by eliminating the worship of all deities except Ra, whom he renamed Aten.

A strong clue to this puzzle is to be found in archival correspondence discovered at El Armana between Akhenaten and various Canaanite nobles. In discussing these letters, Werner Keller writes: "Though it may seem extraordinary, a third of these princely correspondents from Canaan have Indo-Aryan ancestry." In all probability, Akhenaten was introduced to the religion of Mithraism through this princely correspondence. In addition, let us not forget that Akhenaten's maternal grandfather Yuaa, was a Phoenician, and therefore Aryan, High Priest. Yuaa's tomb contained an ornately decorated chair, which depicted a goat and a sun-cross. The goat represented a sacred solar symbol of the Phoenician deity Indara (later Christianized as Saint Andrew). The Vedic literature also equates the goat with the sun and is referred to as the vanquisher of the Serpent Dragon of the Deep.[1]

Of great significance is an ancient Hittite (Phoenician) rock sculpture which depicts a goat wearing the Phrygian cap, long associated with Mithra. As we shall see, Mithraism was, and still is, an Illuminati sun worshipping cult of the oligarchy, organized along the lines of a masonic society. According to some scholars, Akhenaten's mother Ty, and wife Nefertete, were of Horite descent. If this hypothesis is valid, the pharoah would have been raised under a strong Mithraic influence.

Whenever the Aryans conquered a new country, they frequently substituted the name of the principal indigenous god for Mithra; if the deity were a goddess, Mithra became her consort. By adopting this ploy, the conquering oligarchy were able to continue worshipping their solar deity without arousing the ire of the local populace.

At the time of Akhenaten's ascendancy to the throne of Egypt, the principal deity in the Egyptian pantheon of gods and goddesses was

Amon-Re, to whom the temple complex at Karnak was dedicated. In establishing a new capital at Al Armana, not only was the new pharoah able to surreptitiously introduce Mithra under the guise of the established deity Ra, he was able to geographically distance himself from the priesthood of Amon, thereby diminishing the political clout of the former religious center.

As we have observed, Mithraism was introduced into the Middle East by the Aryans,.There is insufficient historiographic data available to ascertain the precise origins of Mithraism; what we do know however, is that whenever a treaty between Middle Eastern nations was signed, it was customary for the clay tablets to bear not only the signatures of the contracting parties, but also the names of deities of each respective kingdom. Among the archival material discovered at the Phoenician capital Boghazkoi, was a treaty between the nations of Hatti and Mitanni; appended to the text was the name Mithra as a divine witness to the covenant. Amazingly, the text then listed the names of Mithra's ancestors: Anu, Enlil, Ninlil, etc., the Aryan hierarchy of the Noahic flood survivors, who, according to Sumerian texts, descended Mount Hermon, presumably as the floodwaters receded, and farmed a lofty plain they named Edin, prior to colonizing Mesopotamia!

If Abraham and his Levitical descendants were members of the ruling Aryan oligarchy, should we not find traces of Mithraism in both the Old and New Testaments of the Bible? Indeed we should, and we find much more than mere traces, for the very backbone of the Bible is pure Mithraism. Just as we can never attune to the very essence of a residence by merely looking at its exterior, so we will never achieve a true understanding of the Bible, unless we are conversant with the fundamental tenets of Mithraism. What are we to make of Revelation 2:18 for instance, in which a person is given manna and a white stone which bears a secret inscription, unless we are cognizant of the fact that these items form an integral part of the initiatory ritual into the Mithraic brotherhood?

The earliest Mithraic lore suggests that Mithra was the benevolent intermediary between the creator and humanity, and was referred to as the Redeemer (the Celtic deity Esus was cast in a similar role). Mithra was also one of the seven Amshaspands, the first of the creative emanations of the Almighty, which correspond to the Seven Rays of Theosophy. Born in a cave, baby Mithra clothed himself with figleaves; he was visited by herdsmen bearing gifts, who had been guided to him by following a star.

Mithra was depicted as wearing a Phrygian cap, wielding a knife in one hand and holding a flaming torch aloft with the other. The Illuminati frequently use the flaming torch of Mithra as a subliminal symbol of their dominance over humankind. This is self-evident in the misnamed Statue of Liberty, donated by French freemasonry. The statue is even replete with the seven-rayed crown of Mithra! After the tragic death of Princess Diana in the Pont d'Alma tunnel, which is an ancient Merovingian sacrificial site, a large effigy of the Mithraic torch was erected over the portal of the tunnel, in order to covertly signify to Illuminati members of lower rank that Diana's death was a planned ritual sacrifice. We are told that Mithra subdued the sun, thus becoming the Sun God; he killed the primeval Bull of Life by plunging a knife into its side (symbolized in the crucifixion of Christ). From the blood of the dying bull sprang the first animals and vegetation, thus symbolizing resurrection.

Mithra was the protector of the first human couple against the Prince of Darkness, who caused a drought, according to the legend. The thirst of the proto humans was slaked when Mithra struck a rock and water gushed forth. A flood was later sent to engulf humanity, but the solar god taught one man and his family how to construct an ark. Prior to ascending to heaven in a fiery chariot à la Elijah, Mithra was given a communal Last Supper. In heaven, the Sun God was to preside over a Last Judgement, after which his faithful followers were to become immortal.

Mithra's birthday was December 25th, and his ascension was celebrated at Easter. Until the advent of Zoroaster, Mithra was regarded as a beneficent androgynous deity; he frequently underwent a name change in order to accommodate differing political situations, becoming at various times Atys, Appollo and Helios-Dionysos.

The principal objective of any secret cult is to establish a côterie of dedicated followers, whose individuality and former behavioral patterns either have been modified or expunged by means of sophisticated brain-washing techniques, as exemplified by the Society of Jesus (the Jesuits). Mithraism was the progenitor of all major mystery cults which have been formed throughout recorded history, whether they be the Eleusinian cult of ancient Greece, or Freemasonry of the present era. The mind-altering techniques first developed by the Mithraic priesthood, consisted of subjecting the candidate for initiation to prolonged periods of fear, anxiety, conflict and deprivation, in order to render the mind of the aspirant pliant and susceptible to the implanting of a totally new belief structure.

In its early form, Mithraism was restricted solely to members of the establishment; during the Julian period of the Roman Empire however, servants were also accepted as Mithraic candidates, provided that they were considered worthy of the Sun God's blessings.

Throughout history, the initiatory rites of Mithra have been conducted in a cave, or a replica of one. The candidate for initiation was subjected to a series of physical and emotional trials, which were designed to induce terror and emotional fatigue in the aspirant. The aspirant underwent trials by scourging, prolonged fasting, cold and exposure to physical danger. If the trials were completed successfully, the by now, mentally debilitated candidate, received counselling by a Mithraic priest on the need to exhibit personal loyalty, courage, invincibility and endurance at all times.

With the arduous ordeal behind him, the neophyte underwent a baptismal rite, which included immersion in water and the making of the sign of the cross upon the initiate's forehead. The rite of the Taurobolium followed, in which a bull's blood was sprinkled over the fledgling initiate, symbolic of resurrection.

Now a full fledged initiate of the first of twelve degrees of Mithraism (the Crow) the new Soldier of Mithra was given a white stone which was inscribed with a secret name. He then partook of a symbolic meal consisting of bread and wine in the company of twelve elders of the cult. A crown was offered to the new initiate, which he had to refuse, stating that the crown belongs to Mithra.

Religions only withstand the test of time if they continue to fulfill the requirements of that sector of society toward which they are oriented. Even though it is the most ancient of all known religions, Mithraism has endured to the present era as the religion of empire builders, simply because it possesses sufficient flexibility to be accommodating of local indigenous variations of the Sun God myth.

Approximately three thousand years ago, the Persian prophet Zoroaster developed his own version of Mithraism; this was later documented in the sacred work known as the *Zend-Avesta*. According to Zoroaster, the Supreme Being created seven Amshaspands, the first being light; twenty-eight additional emanations were then created, known as the *Izeds,* of whom Mithra was the overlord. His task was to oversee the actions of humankind.

The second emanation of the Creator, who was given the name Ahriman, became overly ambitious, and was banished to the Kingdom of Darkness, where he became the tempter of humanity; henceforth, there has been a relentless struggle between the powers of Light and Darkness. Ahriman purportedly slew the Primordial Bull, from whose blood sprang the first human couple. The woman was then tempted by the Prince of Darkness with offerings of fruit and milk—a literary ploy perpetrated by the authors of the Zend-Avesta with the clear intent of relegating women to a secondary role in society.

The supposed life of Zoroaster is, perhaps not surprisingly, reflected in the purported life of Christ. We are informed that Zoroaster was immaculately conceived; while still a baby he survived an assassination attempt by a Herod-like Turanian prince. The Holy Spirit of the Creator descended upon him at the age of thirty, and he subsequently was subjected to temptation by the Lord of Evil.

The Aryan conquest of the Middle East occurred in the form of a succession of migratory waves. One of these migrations was led by an Aryan noble called Hakham-Anish (wise man). Whether or not he was a close relative of Abraham is not recorded, but we do know that his descendants were the monarchs Cyrus and Darius. By the time of Cyrus' death in 529 B.C., the Persian Empire enveloped most of the Middle East, and the entire region was bathed in the radiance of the Sun God.

The reign of Cyrus is pivotal to our narrative, for it was during this period that the Jews underwent their Babylonian captivity. It is the opinion of the author that the Babylonian captivity of the Jews is one of the most significant events in recorded history. Not since the global flood has any other event resulted in such earth-shaking consequences for the human race, for a direct result of the exile was:

a)   The adoption of usuary banking practices by the Jews.

b)   The foundations of Judaism and Christianity.

c)   The writing of the Babylonian Talmud.

d)   All the major wars of the past two centuries.

Such a sweeping statement appears ludicrous of course, unless the reader is cognizant of the tremendous religious and social impression that Babylonian society made upon the Jewish captives. The Jews commenced their period of exile without any semblance of a structured religious or civic code, yet underwent an extraordinary societal transformation during their approximately seventy year sojurn in Babylon.

The claim made by the authors of the Old Testament that the religious creed known as Judaism was an unique gift bequeathed solely to the Israelites by Yahwey, is patently false, as was explained by the 19th century scholar C.W.King. In noting that the Jews used Mithraism as the basis of Judaism, King wrote: "It was from this very creed [Mithraism] that the Jews, during their long captivity of the Persian Empire (of which when restored to Palestine, they formed but one province) derived all the angelology of their religion, even to its minutest details, such as we find it flourishing in the times of the Second Kingdom. Not until then are they discovered to possess the belief in a future state; of rewards and punishments, the latter carried on in a fiery lake; the existence of a complete hierarchy of good and evil angels, taken almost verbatim from the lists given by the Zend-Avesta; the soul's immortality, and the Last Judgement—all of them essential parts of the Zoroastrian scheme, and recognized by Josephus as the fundamental doctrines of the Judaism of his own times."

The strict laws governing the observance of the Jewish Sabbath were obviously adopted from the manner in which the Babylonian Sabbath was observed: no food was to be cooked, nor clothing changed; medication was not to be administered and bathing or washing prohibited. Even the major Babylonian festivals later were plagiarized by the Jews, with the Festival of Zagmick becoming Purim, Tisri being transformed into the Feast of the Tabernacles, and even the Nisan eventually was celebrated as the Passover.

In the Babylonian religious system, local places of worship formed a network that was subservient to a centralized temple. We also see a parallel format adopted by Judaism, whereby a network of synagogues interfaced with the Temple of solomon (a synagogue is not considered a temple in Judaism).

As we have observed, the Sun God Mithra was worshipped under a variety of different names: to the Babylonians he was known as Tammuz, the Son of Light, a name probably derived from the Sumerian monarch Damuzi, who reigned circa 2500 B.C.. According to Sir James Frazier, "In the religious literature of Babylonia, Tammuz appears as the youthful spouse or lover of Ishtar, the great Mother Goddess, the embodiment of the reproductive energies of nature....every year Tammuz was believed to die, passing away from the cheerful earth to the gloomy subterranean world, and that every year his divine mistress journeyed in quest of him "to the land from which there is no returning"....Under the names of Osiris, Tammuz, Adonis, Attis, the peoples of Egypt and Western Asia represented the yearly decay of life, especially of vegetable life....The supposed death and resurrection of this oriental deity, a god of many names but of essentially one nature...."

In this death and resurrection myth, we see not only the origins of the Judaic practice of lamentation, but also the death of Christ dogma, so central to Christianity, for according to the Babylonian myth, Tammuz received a fatal wound in the side and was buried in a cave. On the third day following the burial, the large rock concealing the cave's entrance mysteriously had been removed, and the body of Tammuz was missing.

Not only did the Jews adopt the Jewish calendar, but they made the Babylonian Feast of Tammuz one of the two most important fasts of the Jewish year, in recognition of Tammuz, who "....was held to descend to the netherworld every year, in the month of June or July and then, after lamentations and various offerings, to be restored to life through the intermediation of his wife or mother, Ishtar,....The fourth month of the Babylonian year (July-August) was named after Tammuz, and this has been taken into the Jewish calendar." The Fast of Tammuz is a period when Orthodox Jews are forbidden to wash more than one's fingers "as an evil spirit rests on the fingers....". It is also a time for the intoning of special lamentations, a carryover from the Babylonian custom of weeping for the return of Tammuz from the underworld.

As a ploy to obfuscate the Mithraic origins of the Fast of Tammuz, the present day Judaic hierarchy claim that the fast commemorates the loss of the Jerusalem Temple. That Judaism is simply a blatant form of Mithraism and not a divine covenant between Yahwey and those of the

Jewish faith, is evident from the fact that even today, Jews practice the ceremony known as the "Blessing of the Sun," which is held on the first Wednesday of Nisan, every twenty-eight years.

Immediately after the bloody conclusion of the second World War, there arose a great public feeling of empathy toward those Jews who had suffered so terribly at the hands of their Nazi oppressors. As time passed, public empathy slowly turned to dismay and disgust, as Palestinians were driven from their homes by Israelis whose only claim to their newly aquired territory was a fictional biblical covenant. How ironic that today, the once persecuted Jews exhibit the same brutality toward the Palestinians that the Nazis demonstrated in the Jewish ghettos of Europe.

We all tend to personally act with the best of intentions, even if the end results are considered evil by others. The bloodlust that is prevalent among many Israeli settlers, especially those hailing from America, obviously emanates from some sort of irrational mindset. The author believes that the *Book of Esther* is a major causal factor for the subtle, yet deadly, behavioral conditioning of Israeli society, for the *Book of Esther* spawned the major Judaic festival known as Purim. If the Israeli public would refrain from behaving like the proverbial flock of sheep, and instead conduct their own investigation into the origins of their religious history, they would soon discover that the *Book of Esther* is totally devoid of factual data

According to the Old Testament, King Ahasueras, who resided in Elam, married Esther, the adopted daughter of Mordechai the Jew, without bothering to ascertain her nationality or family background, which was highly irregular to say the least. Mordechai committed a minor infraction which prompted Haman, the king's aide, to call for the extermination of all Jews residing in Elam; the genocide was to occurr on a day to be determined by the casting of lots.

Through subterfuge, Queen Esther persuades the king to allow her to issue a proclamation permitting the Jews to slay all the Elamites considered to be their enemies; this is tantamount to the First Lady of the United States authorizing Asian immigrants to slay all Americans that they disapproved of! On the 13th day of Adar, the Jews purportedly slaughtered thousands of Elamites.

Not only is the story of Esther thoroughly implausible, but there is no historical evidence that King Ahasueras ever existed. The *Book of Esther* undoubtedly is based upon the Babylonian New Year festival known as Zagmuk, which involved the casting of lots and excessive consumption of wine. The festival symbolized the victory of the Babylonian deity Marduk over the Elamite deity Humman; in the Old Testament version, Marduk becomes Mordechai, and Humman asumes the name Haman.

The Festival of Purim celebrates the supposed slaughter of the Elamites by the Jews; the *Book of Esther* is recited and the Talmud encourages celebrants to drink to excess.[1] The wicked Haman is sometimes burned in effigy. Purim probably evolved from the celebration of the victory of Judah Maccabeus over the Syrians, which became known as Marchodias' Day (probably in honor of Marduk) and was held on the 13th day of Adar.

As nonsensical as the story of Esther may appear to the Gentile, the alleged slaughter of the Elamites by the bloodlusting Jews is so indelibly etched in the psyche of practising Jews that "The Rabbis teach that in the future, in the days of the Messiah, all scripture will be abolished except for the *Book of Esther,* also all festivals except for the Feast of Purim."

Spiritual truths are able to withstand any degree of scrutiny, which only serves to draw suspicion to these Rabbis who level claims of anti-Semitism against anyone who questions whether a covenant between Yahwey and the Israelites ever existed.

Typical of the compassionless mindset engendered by Purim conditioning is an article by Rabbi Leon Spitz, which appeared in the *American Hebrew.* [2] Citing the *Book of Esther* as an example of the need for Jewish solidarity, Spitz, in a bloodthirsty tirade worthy of Hitler, called for the Jews to: "Exterminate anti-Semitic termites as our ancestors did 2,500 years ago." If all the scriptures are to be abolished except for the *Book of Esther,* isn't it a tragedy for humanity that the only remaining scripture bears no mention of the Creator, love or compassion?

CHAPTER 8

▼

QUMRAN

"He will atone for all the children of his generation, and he will be sent to all the children of his people....They will speak many words against him."
"Let not the nail approach him."

Qumran text 4Q541, fragments 9 and 24.

As was stated in Chapter 5, note 24, the eventual impetus for the creation of a Jewish homeland in Palestine during World War I came not from orthodox Jews, who regarded Zionism as a heresy, but from two British groups: the Protestants, who believed that a Jewish colonization of Palestine would expedite the Battle of Armageddon, and hence hasten the return of Christ, and the Circle of Initiates.

According to the Circle of Initiate's historian Professor Carroll Quigley, who himself was the mentor of President Clinton, the Circle of Initiates was devoted to the extension of the British Empire. The Circle was an Illuminati sub group and functioned as an oligarchical geopolitical think-tank. The enormous wealth of its members had been derived through their control of the opium and slave trades. Membership included Lord Bulwer Lytton, head of British Intelligence and the principal architect of Nazism. He also was Grand Master of the Scottish Rites masonic order, and the author of the novel *Rienzi*, which was adapted by Wagner for his first opera.

Lytton also was the mentor of medievalist John Ruskin, Theosophist Helena Blavatsky and satanist Aleister Crowley. Other Circle of Initiates members included Lord Milner—the mentor and financial backer of Lenin; Arthur Balfour, the future British Prime Minister; Cecil Rhodes, controlling stockholder of Anglo American Gold and the De Beers Corporation, and Lord Rothschild.

According to his will, Rhodes left his immense fortune: "....to establish a trust, to and for the establishment and promotion and development of a secret society, the true aim and and object shall be the extension of British rule throughout the world, the perfecting of a system of emmigration..." The will also specified that colonization of the Holy Land should be accomplished. A further goal of Rhodes was the awarding of Rhodes Scholarships to foreign students, who, even today, are unwittingly subjected to a sophisticated and intensive behavioral modification program, by members of the Tavistock Institute (Britain's psychological warfare unit) for the purpose of creating a British controlled fifth column among foreign governments. In view of the above, it is beyond the author's comprehension why Americans foolishly elect former Rhodes Scholars to public office.

Significantly, Circle member Arthur Balfour was a member by marriage of the oligarchic Cecil family, covert overlords of the British Monarchy since the period when a Cecil ancestor became the private secretary and lover of Queen Elizabeth 1st. Of even greater significance, many members of the British aristocracy are Jewish. Being a member of an occult secret society which was strongly influenced by the Jewish Cabala, Balfour was favorably disposed toward the establishment of a Jewish homeland in Palestine, if it would advance British colonial interests in the Middle East. Hypocritically, Balfour also sponsored anti immigration laws, which later prevented many Jews fleeing from Nazi persecution from entering Britain. Anticipating that Britain could wrest control of the Middle East from the crumbling Ottoman Empire at the conclusion of World War I, Balfour, the British Foreign Secretary at the time, after conferring with the Zionists, drafted the nebulous Balfour Declaration, which authorized the establishment of a Palestinian homeland for the Jews, despite the fact that at that time period, native born Jews and recent Jewish immigrants only owned 2.5% of Palestinian land (less than 5% of the Palestinian populace were native born Jews).

In keeping with the Rothschilds and the Jesuit-influenced Cecils, another aristocratic family prominent in the political and business affairs of Cecil Rhodes was the Montefiores. It so happened that fifteen years before Hertzl founded the World Zionist Organization, Claude Montefiore, the Jewish heir to the family fortune, was in need of an Rabbinic tutor. The successful candidate for the position—the brilliant Russian-born Solomon Schecter, was educated at a number of rabbinical seminaries *(yeshivot)* prior to studying Jewish history in Vienna and Berlin. In contrast to Berlin, Schecter found that London extended tolerance towards Jews; in 1890, he accepted the post of Lecturer in Talmud at Cambridge University.

It was during his tenure at Cambridge that Schecter was visited by two very erudite and remarkable Scottish widows: Agness and Margaret Gibson. In an era when any thought of the emancipation of women was merely a distant dream, these two self-reliant and inseparable ladies had already undertaken three risky camel treks from Cairo to Mount Sinai, in order to study ancient manuscripts at the monastery of Saint Catherine.

The two adventurers asked Schecter to examine ancient Hebrew texts which they had purchased in Cairo. Amazingly, one of the manuscript leaves was a text written during the 2nd century B.C., by the Jewish writer Ben Sira (Ecclesiasticus) which is included in the Catholic Bible.

Excited by the discovery, and suspecting that the texts previously had been stored in the ancient Ben Ezra synagogue, in Old Cairo, Schecter embarked for Egypt in December, 1896, in an endeavor to retrieve any manuscripts of importance that the synagogue might possess. After spending more than a month in the dusty and spider-ridden attic of the synagogue, Schecter returned to Cambridge with approximately 140,000 textual fragments.

Schecter had struck literary gold! Although the distinguished scholar later emmigrated to America in 1902, to be come President of the Jewish Theological Seminary of New York, he continued to study two incomplete manuscripts that had been copied during the 10th and 12th centuries of the present era. The original text from which both had been copied, had originally been written prior to the destruction of the second Jerusalem Temple, in the year 70 A.D..

The two incomplete, but fortunately overlapping texts, were written in biblical Hebrew, and comprise an historical codex known as the *Damascus Document*. According to the document, a Jewish sect that regarded itself as the True Israel, was formed during an "Age of Wrath," which occurred in approximately 196 B.C.. The group of dissidents, which was led by a "Teacher of Righteousness", was forced to flee from their native Judea to "the land of Damascus."

Many Jewish biblical texts were written on two levels—one for the general reader and the other for the esoteric initiate of a specific sect. Place names were frequently disguised in order to shield a secret meaning from the eyes of the profane. In the present case, the text also quotes a passage from the *Book of Amos* (5:26-27) referring to "Damascus," an obvious reference to Babylon. The same passage also occurrs in Acts 7:43, where the city in question is actually called Babylon.

When the sect arrived in Babylon, "God established his covenant forever..." (C.D. 6:19). During their sojurn in Babylon, the Teacher of Righteousness was expected by his disciples to return shortly as the Messiah. The documents, which are believed by some scholars to have been written in Babylon, includes a strict code of conduct for a fundamentalist Jewish community that is living in a Gentile environment. It also states that not all of the exiles returned to Judea: some remained in Babylon, their descendants in all probability being the founders of the sect known as the Kairites. This sect still exists at the present time. Others presumably settled in Alexandria, where they were referred to by the writer Philo as the Therapeuts.

The laws of the sect, as presented in the Damascus Document, and the contents of some of the Dead Sea Scrolls, strongly suggests that the sect who fled to Babylon were the original Essenes. The Essenes' later writings were discovered in caves at Qumran. Even the appellation "Teacher of Righteousness" occurrs in the Dead Sea Scroll known as the *Habakkuk Commentary;* moreover, fragments of nine copies of the Damascus Document have been discovered in the caves at Qumran.

In order to comprehend the circumstances that caused the sect to flee to Babylon during the "Age of Wrath," we briefly must observe the change in the political environment under which the Jews had lived since the Persian monarch Cyrus had freed them from their original Babylonian captivity, and they had begun the long trek back to their Judean homeland, in the Spring of 537 B.C..

According to the Old Testament, King Nebuchadnezzar's Babylonian army laid seige to Jerusalem in late 587 B.C.. After some eighteen months, the Babylonian battering rams breached the city walls and put Jerusalem to the torch, destroying the Temple in the process. At the core of the original city, known today as the City of David, where today ancient ritual purity baths *(mikva'ot)* are sadly neglected and strewn with garbage, archaeologists have discovered a thick ash layer and piles of stones which had been dislodged from the city walls by the battering rams.

The Old Testament states that the Jews who survived the flames and the ensuing massacre, were taken to Babylon by Nebuzaradan, the Babylonian captain of the guard; only a few peasants were permitted to remain to tend the land, Judea remaining desolate for fifty years. This is a blatant falsehood, which serves to demonstrate that the Bible was not a divinely inspired work. Archaeological digs at other Judean cities have revealed very little evidence of destruction during the era of the Babylonian exile. In fact, relatively few of the Judean population were taken into captivity—some Judean cities even expanding under Babylonian rule, indicative of good economic times. This was especially true of the Judean city of Mizpah, which was used by the Babylonians as an administrative center. That King Nebuchadnezzar would permit a large segment of the Jewish populace to remain in Judea makes good strategic sense, for he would need large amounts of produce grown in Judea for feeding his army during his campaigns against Egypt. The close geographic proximity of Judea to Egypt would minimize the risk of food spoilage while in transit.

For the following two centuries after the return of the Jews from their Babylonian exile, the Persian overlords of Jerusalem permitted the High Priest of the rebuilt Temple to be appointed from the Levitical descendants of Zadok. The absence of cultural artifacts or large buildings dating from this period, suggests that the inhabitants of Judea underwent a prolonged period of economic hardship under the yoke of Persian rule.

Persian dominion over Judea came to an abrupt end when the Persian monarch Darius 3rd was defeated in 333 B.C. at Issus, by the Macedonian ruler and Mithra worshipper Alexander the Great. Alexander went on to establish a vast empire extending from Egypt to the Indus Valley.

Alexander adopted a laissez-faire policy toward the governing of his newly won satrapies. Hence, Jews residing in the new city of Alexandria were accorded equal status with the conquering Greeks, and even formed a national association (politeuma). The cosmopolitan environment stimulated a cross fertilization of ideas between Jew and Greek, resulting in Alexandria becoming one of the great cultural centers of antiquity. In contrast, the Judean populace were still being subjected to the stultifying theocratic administration of the Temple priesthood. As that most erudite of biblical scholars, the late Professor Elias J. Bickerman noted: "Alexander's arrival did not change anything in Jerusalem except the name of the pagan sovereign. The rulers of the people, the tribute, the status of the Temple, all remained as they had been under the Persian kings."[1]

And so the minuscule nation of Judea tenaciously adhered to its inflexible theocratic traditions and slumbered amidst an Hellenistic empire rampant with progressive ideas. Gone was the lucrative copper smelting industry of the Kenites, the decline of which appears to have followed the ascendancy of the Jerusalem priesthood. Now the economy of Judea revolved around the Temple, which became the nation's principal consumer of both farm and craft products. So great was the slaughter of sacrificial animals, that their hides made the Temple the focal point of the Judean leather trade.

After the death of Alexander at the early age of thirty three, his empire was divided into three separate kingdoms, which extended from Asia Minor to the Indian border, and to Judea and the Ptolemaic kingdom of Egypt.

One customarily expects bureaucratic red tape to exert a negative influence upon the upward mobility of a nation's citizenry; however, the Greek administrative system demanded that no Jewish goods were to enter the marketplace without the appropriate paperwork—even the lowliest peasant was unable to sell produce prior to presenting the ever present tax collector with a properly written petition *(enteuxis)*.

No longer were the Temple priests the sole arbiters of Jewish religious and secular law, for the Greek overlords were unwilling to permit the wily priesthood to rule on matters appertaining to the Temple treasury. Thus was created the necessity for a new class of Jews—the professional scribes *(sopherim)* who were required not only to be fluent in the Greek language, but also had to possess sufficient expertise to draft contracts and divorce papers. Lacking legal skills, the rank and file Jewish priests eventually were supplanted by the scribes as interpreters of the Mosaic Law, thereby enabling some of the more senior sopherim to aquire positions of privilege within the Temple hierarchy, by the year 200 B.C..

The author speculates that the "Age of Wrath" commenced when the Seleucid monarch Antiochus III vanquished Ptolemy V and conquered Judea in 195 B.C.. It was a crushing blow for the Levitical priesthood; already deprived of much of their political clout under the previous Ptolemaic regime, the Temple priests were powerless to prevent the rapid Hellenization of the Judaic populace, which was fostered by the new Seleucid rulers.

Not only were the Jews participating in athletic events dedicated to Zeus and Appollo, they had adopted the Greek style of competing completely naked! It is therefore understandable that the lesser members of the priesthood, together with the more pious of their followers, should undertake a self-imposed exhile in Babylon. In addition, this exodus was prompted also, in all probability, by the rapid increase in the number of Zadokite priests during the Hellenistic era. Since the Temple priesthood derived its income primarily from the tithes of worshippers and agricultural levies, the lower echelons of the burgeoning Temple staff undoubtedly saw their quality of life diminish, as increasing numbers of Jews forsook their traditional religion and embraced the gods of their foreign overlords.

Life was not particularly trouble-free for Antiochus IV, who ascended the throne of the Seleucid Empire in 175 B.C.. The Syrian monarch was gravely concerned over the threat posed to his kingdom by the spread of Judaism. Admittedly the tyrannical Levites governed Palestine, which had become an adjunct of the Seleucid Empire, on his behalf, but the only Israelites domiciled in Palestine were the tribes of Benjamin and Judah. The other former ten Israelite tribes had been dispersed throughout the Middle East and Europe, several centuries earlier, and were proliferating rapidly. Antiochus felt that the religion of Judaism was the unifying element in Jewish solidarity throughout the Seleucid Empire; if all the Jews could be persuaded to adopt the Greek lifestyle, the king reasoned, Judaism would dissipate, together with the threat posed by Jewish solidarity.

Not content with plundering the Temple treasury, Antiochus IV despatched an armed force under the command of his chief tax collector Appolonius, to sack Jerusalem in 168 B.C., "....when he had taken the spoils of the city....and pulled down the houses and walls thereof on every side." [2] Even worse, it was made a capital offense to engage in religious ceremonies, and the Temple was re-dedicated to Zeus. In addition, the Zadokite line of High Priests, unbroken since the Solomonic era, was terminated following the ousting of the High priest Onias 3rd, by his brother Jesus, who promptly adopted the Greek name Jason. Jason promoted the Hellenization of the Jews and later was deposed by Menelaus.

This was an extremely significant turn of events for Judaism, due to the fact that Menelaus was not a Levite, and therefore not of the lineage of the priestly caste. Menelaus became the first of a line of quisling collaborationist High Priests known as the Saducees. Concerned solely with their own wealth and privileges, this new priestly caste demonstrated extreme servility, initially to the Seleucids, then to the Roman Empire.

Subsequently, the position of High Priest went to the highest bidder, regardless of whether or not the successful candidate was of the Zadokite lineage. Angered by the Hellenization of Jewish society, the author of II Maccabees commented: "Harsh and utterly grievous was the onslaught of evil. For the Temple was filled with debauchery."

Refusing to worship foreign gods, Mattatias, a village priest living twenty miles from Jerusalem, together with his five sons, formed a guerrilla movement. It was under the military leadership of Mattatius' eldest son Judas Maccabeus. After many ferocious battles, the Jewish rebels

eventually drove the Seleucids from Judea—a victory which is still commemorated in the celebration of Hanukkah.

The war over, Judas Maccabeus appointed himself High Priest, even
though he was not of the Zadokite lineage, thereby initiating the
Hasmonean line of Jewish rulers, and entered into a diplomatic treaty
with Rome. He formed a theocratic opposition group initially known as
the Hassidim, and later as the Pharisees. Angered by the usurpation of
the high priesthood by one not of the Zadokite line of descent, and also
alarmed at the increasing Hellenization of the nation, many of the former priestly hierarchy "zealous for the Law", formed their own religious
sects, not only in Judean towns and villages, but also in desert regions of
Judea.

The Dead Sea Scrolls make mention of a "Wicked Priest". The true
identity of this particular person has never been determined by biblical
scholars. The author suspects that the High Priest who earned the
intense animosity of these various religious sects was Simon the
Hasmonean, who ruled Judea from 142 to 134 B.C.. Simon became
both ruler of Judea and its High Priest after defeating Antiochus
Epiphanes. Antiochus had housed his Syrian troops in a garrison adjacent to the Temple known as the *Akra*.

The *Akra* citadel was located adjacent to the Temple, according to I
Maccabees and "Josephus," on a crescent-shaped ridge known as Mount
Zion. The Temple had fallen into severe disrepair during the rule of
Antiochus; upon ascending to the throne of Judea, Simon the
Hasmonean decided to construct a new Temple on the same site,
because the existing Temple, in addition to having been desecrated by
the Syrian troops, was also impure, due to the sacrificing of pigs on its
alter during the reign of Antiochus. Since the *Akra* obscured and overlooked the Temple due to its height, Simon ordered its destruction.
Jewish workers purportedly toiled day and night for three years, not
only in demolishing the *Akra* citadel, but also in removing Mount Zion
down to bedrock. A new citadel was then constructed approximately

one third of a mile north of the Temple. Later, Herod the Great drastically enlarged the new citadel, naming it Fort Antonia. Today it is mistakenly known as the *Temple Mount* and also as the *Haram esh-Sharif.*

Simon appears to have been held in high esteem by the populace of Judea; to priests of Levitical descent however, Simon was hated, not only because he was not of the Zadokite lineage, but also because he had committed an unpardonable sin in removing Mount Zion and using the soil to provide fill dirt for the building of a new township known as Upper Jerusalem. Mount Zion, being taller than the other hills in the environs of Jerusalem, was a landmark and therefore had been regarded as a seat of Yahwey by the Levitical priesthood. It was the levelling of Mount Zion by Simon that irked a minority of the priesthood; in actuality, Mount Zion's elevation primarily was due to the fact that several townships of antiquity had been successively built on it, thus gradually increasing its height.

Caught in the middle between the greedy Saducees (founded by Sadoc, a student of Antigonus Schohaeus) and the religiously intransigent Pharisees (created by Pharez, a proponent of predestination) were the economically alienated Jewish masses, who had little hope of improving their wretched existence.

The subsequent Galilean uprising under the leadership of Judas of Galilee, a priestly Pharisee, was a particularly virulent one, due to the religious fanaticism of the militants, who were known as zealots. It was inevitable that such an affront to the presumed invincibility of Rome would provoke a violent response. Retribution was swift and bloody: a Roman army swept through Galilee putting the city of Sepphoris to the torch, and sending the entire populace into slavery. The vengeful Centurions then loosed their wrath upon Jerusalem; by the time that the revolt was quelled, some 2,000 hapless revolutionaries paid for their short-lived attempt at freedom by dying on the cross.

Even though the uprising had been ruthlessly crushed, the various covenant sects collectively known as the Zealots, continued to fan the flames of discontent, so much so that in A.D. 66, the entire nation of Judea erupted in revolt against Rome. Once again, the Roman army successfully negated the Jewish bid for freedom, destroying Jerusalem and sacking the Temple in the process. The destruction of Jerusalem was so complete that the Roman General Titus, who later became Emperor, marvelled that no one would believe that a city had ever existed there. Even the foundation stones of the Temple were removed, so that Roman soldiers could recover the Temple gold which had melted during the conflagration and had collected in rivulets between the stones. Thereafter, the Temple site became a garbage dump. The only structure left unscathed by the Romans was their immense garrison, called Fort Antonia, now renamed the Temple Mount because most Jews and Christians mistakenly believe that it was the site of the Temple. The revolt was finally suppressed in 73 A.D., when the Zealot heirarchy purportedly committed mass suicide in the desert fortress of Masada (a questionable event which may never have happened).

It was in this turbulent era that many of the Dead Sea Scrolls were apparently written by members of these various sects. The story of the chance discovery of more than eight hundred texts in the caves of the Wadi Qumran and at other Dead Sea locations, in 1947, by Bedouin herdsmen, is well known and need not be repeated here. Until their discovery, it was not possible to discern how Rabbinic Judaism and Christianity evolved from the numerous forms of Judaism, e.g. Phariseeism, Saduceeism, etc., which vied for religious supremacy in the three centuries prior to the destruction of the Temple in 70 A.D. Fortunately, about 75% of the recovered scrolls are of a non biblical nature, many reflecting the the ideologies of various religious sects. These provide us with an insight into the fact that in the pre-rabbinic era, the inhabitants of Judea embraced many forms of religion, some of them displaying pronounced overtones of occultism, solar worship and messianism.

The dry riverbed known by its Arabic name of Wadi Qumran, is situated on the desolate northwestern shore of the Dead Sea. The caves where many of the texts were discovered, are in cliffs which rise precipitously from the floor of the wadi to an arid, treeless plateau which overlooks the Dead Sea to the East, and beyond to the biblical land of Moab, now called Jordan. On the plateau are the remains of an ancient complex of buildings which date to the 8th century B.C.. These ruins were excavated between 1951 and 1956 by the late Dominican priest Father Roland Devaux, who was assigned the task of forming an international team of scholars for the purpose of deciphering the scrolls and scroll fragments.

The most important manuscript discovery of the 20th century, the Dead Sea scrolls have generated a veritable cottage industry for biblical scholars, who have written several thousand volumes and articles concerning scroll related matters. It is the consensus of opinion of these scholars that the Khirbet Qumran ruins are what is left of a monastery that was occupied in biblical times by the Jewish religious sect known as the Essenes. The Essenes, claim these scholars, diligently wrote the Dead Sea scrolls in a large room of the "monastery" referred to by Father Devaux as a scriptorium. Some scholars also suggest that the scrolls were hurriedly secreted in the nearby caves for safekeeping, during the Jewish rebellion against Rome in 70 A.D..

While such speculations initially appear attractive, there are too many pieces of the puzzle that do not fit the picture portayed by Father Devaux, of the monastic Essenes industriously writing their texts in the scriptorium overlooking the Dead Sea. In order to avoid the pitfall of assuming that just because the scrolls were discovered in close proximity to the ruined Qumran building complex, they must have been written there, it is incumbent upon us first to determine whether or not the complex was a suitable habitat for a Jewish religious sect that strictly adhered to the Holy Law, then study the physical and textual appearance of the scrolls.

Archaeological evidence is indicative that construction at Khirbet
Qumran commenced during the 8th century B.C.. The first construction phase consisted initially of cisterns for the storage of rainwater (the
only water source available at the site) a multistoried tower and surrounding rooms. The buildings possessed a roof structure of palm
trunks overlain with reeds, then plastered with marl, a roofing system
sometimes still employed in present-day Israel.

The charred remains of the roofs at Qumran attest to the fact that the
complex once was destroyed by fire shortly following commencement
of the reign of King Herod the Great, who ruled from 37 B.C. to 4 A.D..
Qumran thereafter remained unoccupied until the site was renovated
and subsequently enlarged during the administration of the ethnarc
Archelaus (4.B.C.- 6 A.D.).

The corpus of sectarian laws presented in the Dead Sea Scrolls,
makes it abundantly clear that the failure of the Hellenized Temple
priesthood to adhere strictly to the religious rituals, as specified under
the Torah, prompted the deposed priestly descendants of Aaron and
their pious followers to create the Essenic cult.

One would expect that a religiously oriented group of priests, who
forsook the creature comforts of Temple life for a spartan existence in a
commune, would display traits of good fellowship and compassion
toward those less fortunate, yet this was not the case. The scrolls
demonstrate that the Covenanters (a collective term for all the various
dissident priestly sects, e.g. the Essenes, Zadokites, Siccarii, etc.) were
not only religious fanatics, but also chauvinistic bigots.

Handicapped people were not permitted to join the sect; some scrolls
imply that members were permitted to marry, but other texts claim that
women are harbingers of evil and lower than animals, which only goes
to demonstrate what every woman since the time of Eve suspects: all
men are pigs! Purification rituals transformed personal hygiene into a
fetish, a ploy presumably conceived by the priestly hierarchy as a mode
of behavioral modification: ritual baths (mikveh) could only be taken in

flowing water. In arid surroundings, water from a flowing source had to be transported to an ancillary pool located adjacent to the ritual bathwater, in order to purify it.

The longest scroll discovered in the Qumran caves is twenty seven feet in length. Known as the *Temple Scroll,* it is quite possibly a missing sixth book of the Torah; it contains strict laws appertaining to ritual cleanliness, in addition to dimensional details of a new Temple, festivals and monarchical statutes. The dimensions and layout of a temple referred to in the scroll are at variance with details of the reconstructed Temple of Simon, which may also contribute to the hostility displayed toward Simon the Hasmonean by the Covenanters. According to the Temple Scroll, people suffering from a discharge, or leprosy, had to be confined to areas downwind of Jerusalem, for it was believed that leprosy was an airborne disease. The scroll also bans the construction of toilets near a dwelling.

Sectarians who violated such religious edicts faced dire consequences. We would surmise therefore, that Essene communities would be located near a spring, in order to obtain a ready source of flowing water for ritual bathing purposes. Additionally, we would not expect to discover latrines in the vicinity of their habitat. In order to remain in a state of ritual purity, a Covenanter was also obliged to distance himself from human corpses and cemetaries.

How amazing it is therefore, that communal dwellers "zealous for the Law" and obsessed with ritual purity, should elect to take up residence at Khirbet Qumran—an arid marl bluff devoid of vegetation and flowing water! The ruins do not even contain a reserve pool for the storage of previously-flowing water, so vital for their baptismal and ritual bathing rites. Equally fantastic is the fact that the Qumran building complex adjoin a cemetary containing more than one thousand graves.

It was the custom for Essenes to apply frankinscence to their linen garments, a practice which left a deposit of calcium carbonate in the vessel used for laundering the clothing, yet no such deposits have been found in the Qumran cisterns. One also has to wonder why many thousands of scroll fragments littered the floors of the Qumran caves, yet not a single fragment has been found among the ruins.

In the northwest sector of the ruins are the remains of a number of stalls; since they are too narrow to have housed beasts of burden, they were, in all probability, latrines. In commenting on the Essenes, Pliny the Elder (23-79 A.D.) stated: "On the west side of the Dead Sea, but out of range of the exhalations of the coast, is the solitary tribe of Essenes, which is remarkable beyond all other tribes in the whole world, as it has no women and has renounced all sexual desire, has no money, and has only palm trees for company....Lying below the Essenes was formerly the town of Engedi...."[3]

In view of the above, could it be that countless biblical scholars are incorrect in assuming that the sect lived at Khirbet Qumran? Common sense suggests that it would be extremely difficult, if not impossible, for the sect to live adjacent to a cemetary and latrines and without easy access to flowing water, yet remain in a state of ritual purity. For Essenes to reside at such a location, which would mean violating the Mosaic Law, makes no sense when an oasis replete with flowing spring water and vegetation, known as Ein Feshka, was only a little more than a mile further south of Khirbet Qumran.

Although some Covenanters formed sects in Judean towns and villages, where access to flowing water for ritual bathing purposes would readily be available, a most suitable site for a commune on the west bank of the Dead Sea would be at the Ein Feshka oasis. In addition to possessing spring water and vegetation (including palm trees) it also contains the ruins of a Graeco-Roman style villa which was constructed during the reign of King Herod the Great. Moreover, a calcium carbonate deposit was discovered in several shallow basins at the site, suggestive that a Covenant sect did indeed reside at Ein Feshka, and also laundered garments impregnated with frankinscence. This presumably was the site of the Essene commune referred to by Pliny the Elder.

Even though Khirbet Qumran was devoid of water except for stored rainwater, and therefore unsuitable for the growing of produce, the ample supply of springwater at Ein Feshka obviously would have facilitated the growing of produce and the grazing of sheep and goats, thus enabling a commune to be self-sufficient. Even today, Ein Feshka is used as a rest and recreation area by the Israeli Mossad intelligence organization.

Either the priestly sect displayed extraordinarily poor judgement in electing to establish their commune adjacent to latrines and a cemetary or, what is more credible, they possessed the good sense to reside at Ein Feshka or at some equally suitable locale, but not, under any circumstances, at Khirbet Qumran. The fact that so many Dead Sea scholars have concluded that a covenant sect should have elected to occupy the building complex at Khirbet Qumran is demonstrative of the myopic vision of many members of academia.

Unfortunately for society at large, most of whom believe the conclusions of "experts," the belief that Essenes wrote biblical scrolls in the "scriptorium" at Qumran is very widespread. Clearly Father Devaux and his archaeological team elected only to consider the Qumran archaeological evidence which possibly fitted Devaux's hypothesis that the Qumran facility had served as a monastery. In the process, the archaeological team ignored important artifacts which demonstrated that the complex had been used for non-theological purposes—something we will evaluate later in this chapter.

Turning now to the riddle of the Dead Sea Scrolls, it is the consensus of scholars that the scrolls that were discovered in the Qumran caves comprised the library of the alleged Qumran sectarians, even though some of the scrolls were written at other locations, such as the desert fortress at Masada. Even in the unlikely event that the sectarians resided at Qumran, we must ask ourselves why they used the nearby caves as a library, instead of the spacious rooms at the Khirbet Qumran building complex.

Some scholars have suggested that the scrolls were hastily hidden in the caves for protection when the Roman General Titus and his troops over-ran the area during the Zealot uprising in 67 A.D., yet this suggestion lacks credibility, since the caves entrances are readily visible to anyone travelling along the floor of the adjacent wadi. Moreover, Qumran cave number four has holes bored into its walls for shelf supports, scarcely the time consuming operation one undertakes when hurrying to escape detection by soldiers. It is also highly unlikely that all of the desert dwelling Covenanters were killed by the Romans, so why were the scrolls left to slowly decay in the caves after the uprising had subsided?

The author feels that a more secure hiding place for the scrolls would have been the caves which are situated in the complex of wadis that extend from Jericho to Jerusalem. These particular caves, which are not visible from the wadi floor, were modified by Zealots under the command of Simon bar Giora in 69 A.D., during the first Jewish revolt against Rome (66-70 A.D.). The original cave entrances were blocked by rocks, after which concealed entrances were added. These were accessible only by rappelling down the precipitous cliffs, in order to provide a safe refuge, not only for jews, but also for valuable documents.

Since these caves were modified as part of the Jewish regional defense plan, it follows that the Covenanters would have had ample time to deposit their precious scrolls there, where the chances of escaping detection by Roman military patrols were far greater than at Qumran.

Is it not possible therefore, to conjecture that the Qumran caves were selected solely because of their extremely low humidity? Significantly, some of the Dead Sea Scrolls have deteriorated badly since being transferred, following their discovery, to the more humid environment of Jerusalem.

In order to offer a rational explanation for depositing the scrolls in the Qumran caves, we must take into consideration the physical condition of the Qumran cave's contents when the Bedouin herdsmen made their initial momentous discovery. When originally deposited in the eleven Qumran caves, the scrolls had been placed in clay containers, most of which had broken prior to their discovery by the herdsmen. Strewn amidst the pottery sherds and scroll fragments were date pits.

One edge of some of the scrolls had the appearance of either having been slashed with a knife, while others bore a charred wavy edge, as though the end of the scroll had been passed through a flame. It is the prescence of date pits, and the mutilated condition of some of the scrolls, that provides us with the rationale for depositing the scrolls in the Qumran caves.

It was a requirement of the priesthood that sacred items declared redundant could not be destroyed, particularly in the case of texts which contained holy names *(shemot)* but were to be consigned to a suitable repository known as a *geniza*. Prior to discarding, it was customary to slash one end of a scroll with a knife, or pass one end through a flame in order to leave a charred edge. Peasants who were too poor to provide animals or doves as sacrificial offerings to the Temple, were permitted to offer dates instead. After the dates had been eaten by the Temple priests, the date pits were considered sacred items and accordingly deposited in a geniza. In all cases, the items intended for shipment to a geniza had to be placed in clay jars, which were then sealed.

Texts which had been written on parchment made from animal skins, were also deposited in genizas if the animals had not been ritually sacrificed, and therefore considered impure. This probably accounts for the large number of leather scroll bindings which were discovered in Qumran caves four and eight. In consideration of the fact that the Qumran caves contained scrolls which had been mutilated at one end, or possessed a charred wavy edge, together with date pits and pottery sherds, it is self-evident that the Qumran caves clearly were used by the Temple priesthood as a sacred garbage dump!

This is why some of the texts discovered at Qumran are inconsistent with the Essene doctrine of pacifism, such as the *War Scroll,* for example, which is filled with militant statements and curses. Scroll fragment 4Q448, which extolls the praises of Jonathan, the Maccabean monarch, also is contrary to the political ideology of the Covenanters, who considered the Maccabeans as priestly usurpers.

Just as the Vatican employs a very formidable intelligence organization, so did the Temple priesthood during the Hasmonean and Herodian eras, not merely to identify citizens who failed to pay Temple tithes, but also to ascertain the location and size of dissident sects. During their intelligence gathering duties, Temple operatives undoubtedly procured sectarian scrolls, particularly since the militant Covenanters regarded the Temple heirarchy as usurpers. We may draw a parallel here with the Vatican library, which houses the world's largest collection of pornographic literature among its proscribed books.

Father Devaux presented us with a picture of Essene "monks" happily writing texts in the Qumran "scriptorium," yet we do not conjure up the image of a lascivious College of Cardinals busily churning out pornographic literature in the Vatican, just because pornographic works are to be found there. During World War II, a portion of the Vatican library was transferred to Paris for safekeeping. This is demonstrative that sometimes a large corpus of religious texts is transported many miles from its original location, when deemed necessary, and may contain works not reflective of that particular religious order's doctrine.

The Saducees were the dominant Judaic religious faction during the Herodian period, but later were supplanted by the Pharisees. The Rabbinical Judaism of the present era is based upon Pharasaic doctrine, which reflects more flexibility in religious matters than that of the earlier Zadokite tradition of the conservative Covenanters. Since some of the Dead Sea Scrolls are polemics against the Pharisees, it is understandable why the latter would wish to suppress such subversive texts.

Early Christianity was faced with a similar problem, which they attempted to solve by assassinating the brilliant Gnostic teacher

Hypatia, and burning the renowned library at Alexandria, in order to suppress the spread of Gnosticism.

Prevented by the Holy Law from burning the subversive sectarian texts, the author speculates that the Pharisees did the next best thing by consigning such material to the Qumran caves sometime after the advent of the Rabbinical era (circa 200 A.D.) a period when the Pharisees were in full political power. The items destined for the Qumran geniza would have included not only subversive scrolls, but also date pits and texts copied from the Pentateuch which possibly were written on parchment of questionable purity; sacred texts containing errata also would be deemed geniza material.

Very significantly, the *Jewish Encyclopedia* states that a geniza was: "….a place for the putting away of all kinds of sacred articles, such as sacred books no longer usable, as well as the books of the Saducees and heretics, and other writings of which the sages disapproved…."

The scrolls discovered in the Qumran caves had carefully been placed in clay pots and sealed, a common geniza practice, which also mitigates against their having been hastily concealed as a temporary wartime measure. Clay pottery found in the caves is similar to the type discovered amidst the Khirbet Qumran ruins, suggestive of a link between the two locations—a mystery that will be addressed later in this chapter.

In order to solve the riddle of Qumran, we must develop an hypothesis which encompasses *all* of the available archaeological evidence, not merely select data which fits, while ignoring facts which are troublesome—a ploy which some of the scholars appear to have adopted in order to promote their pet theories.

Accordingly we must provide a rationale for the purpose for the ruined tower, and why a large number of dishes were discovered at Khirbet Qumran, suggestive that the facility housed a considerable number of occupants following the second phase of construction, yet only two inkwells were discovered at the site—an inadequate number if scribes worked there. It has been suggested by Belgian scholars Robert

Donceel-Voute and his wife Pauline, that the ruins are the remains of a luxurious villa. Their speculation primarily was based upon the discovery of delicate glass unguentaria, elegant urns and two flat circular stones, the latter quite possibly being bases for ornate columns. The circular stone bases present a particular problem which we must solve, for if indeed they were column bases, no columns or column capitals have been found during archaeological digs at the site.

Since these mysterious stones lack grooves, they are unlikely to have served as millstones, even though they each possess a hole through their axes, capable of accommodating a shaft. The author speculates that these stones were, indeed column bases, and were brought to the site in an effort to upgrade the architectural esthetics of the complex. The remodelling effort, according to the author's hypothesis, was curtailed prior to the arrival of the columns and capitals. Columns experience great difficulty in withstanding the high lateral loads imparted upon them during an earthquake. An earthquake that occurred shortly prior to the arrival of the columns may have prompted the architect to have abanoned that phase of the remodelling project.

According to the Old Testament, a major earthquake did in fact occurr in the vicinity during the 8th. Century B.C.. "Josephus" (believed to be the pseudonym of a member of Rome's powerful Piso family) claimed that one also occurred in Judea during the 1st century B.C.. We also must question why a private luxury residence would possess a tower and be constructed on such an inhospitable site, adjacent to a large cemetary.

The author suggests that the primary reason for selecting the inhospitable plateau at Khirbet Qumran as the site of the building complex was a geopolitical one. This was the fact that the high elevation of the site provided a sweeping view over the surrounding desert. From the complex's tower, not only the floor of the Wadi Qumran would be visible, but a panoramic view of the northern shore of the Dead Sea would also present itself. Therefore we must inquire why should a sweeping view be of paramount importance to the site owners, when construction commenced at Khirbet Qumran in the 8th century B.C., particularly since the necessary provision of storage cisterns for rainwater would add considerably to the construction costs.

We are able to shed light on the mystery of Khirbet Qumran when we become aware that Judea entered into an era of considerable prosperity and political stability during the reign of King Uzziah, during the 8th century B.C.. Uzziah successfully recaptured former Judean territory, including the city of Elath, which was located on the shore of the Red Sea. He also fortified Jerusalem and intensified the strength of the Judean army. Uzziah also undertook the economic development of the arid hill country and desert regions of Judea. Very significantly, we are informed in *2 Chronicles 26:10* that he "....built towers in the Steppe and digged many cisterns; for he had large herds...."

This biblical passage provides the rationale for the initial construction phase at Khirbet Qumran, which included cisterns, single-storied buildings and a tower. Of particular note is the fact that Qumran is situated in the Steppe country the arid Judean hill country which extends the full length of the western shore of the Dead Sea.

The design of the earliest buildings at Qumran is similar to that of others constructed throughout Judea during the 7th and 8th centuries B.C.. By constructing the building complex high atop the Qumran bluff, a commanding view, not only of herds grazing in the wadi below, but also of the northern shorline of the dead Sea, would be afforded. Such a commanding panoramic view would provide early warning of any impending attack by nomadic tribesmen, for this was a period when the River Jordan constituted the eastern border of Judea.

In all probability, the Khirbet Qumran complex originally served as an administrative center for King Uzziah's ranching operation in the Steppe country, the lesser herdsmen living in tents. Forked sticks were discovered in some of the nearby caves, and probably served as tent poles. If the author's speculation is correct, then because of its commanding panoramic view, the complex also served as the headquarters for a mounted border patrol. One noted scholar has suggested that Qumran was a fortress, a hypothesis that the author finds untenable, for a mounted border patrol is an interception force, not requiring a fortified headquarters.

Due to its elevated position in relation to the Dead Sea coastal region, which extends in a northerly direction toward Jericho, the Qumran tower need not have been more than two stories in height, in order to function as part of the national communication system noted in *Jeremiah 6:1* and also in the *Lachish Papers*. Constructed in the 7th And 8th centuries B.C., the communication system consisted of a network of beacons which were strategically located, so that fire beacons placed at the summit of each tower could be lit as a warning of impending danger. The remains of a typical tower of this type are to be found at French Hill, in northern Jerusalem.

The Qumran tower undoubtedly would have been used to communicate with the building at Vered Jericho, which consisted of several rooms and twin towers which flanked the entrance. This structure presumably served as a border outpost, in order to monitor travellers on the road from the Dead Sea area to Jericho. In keeping with the Qumran complex, this structure was built at an arid location that was devoid of water.

An unusual aspect of the cemetary at Qumran is that the majority of the bodies of men, women and children interred there, are oriented with their feet facing the north. This is in contrast with the traditional Jewish custom of burying corpses in an east-west direction. Scholars who postulate that Khirbet Qumran was a monastery, skirt the thorny question of why its ultra conservative residents elected to break with religious tradition and bury their dead in such an uncustomary orientation.

So far, our investigation suggests that the Khirbet Qumran complex never was used as a monastery. Could it possibly be that the orientation of the graves was intended to serve as a warning to Jewish travellers that Qumran was a ritually impure place?

A very strong clue that this well may have been the case is provided in *2 Chronicles,* which informs us that during his long reign (785-734 B.C.) King Uzziah was stricken with leprosy and banished from Jerusalem to: "….a house set apart." His son Jotham became regent and ruled in his place. In all probability, King Uzziah took up residence at a fortress built in the 8th century B.C., two miles south of Jerusalem. Discovered in 1959 by Professor Aharoni of Hebrew University, the ruins contained artifacts symbolizing the goddess Astarte, which demonstrates that even oligarchic Jews worshipped deities other than Yahwey.

The author theorizes that upon contracting leprosy, lepers were hired as members of the monarch's staff, since Jews had an abhorrence of leprosy and similar contagious diseases. Under normal circumstances, King Uzzia would have been buried in the cemetary of the House of David, in accordance with halakhic tradition, but due to his affliction, he was buried "….in the field of burial which belonged to the kings; for they said he was a leper."[4]

At a later date, his bones were transferred to the Mount of Olives, according to an Aramaic inscription of the Second Temple period. Since the monarch was a leper, it is conceivable that unafflicted Jews would refrain from becoming members of Uzziah's staff, in which case lepers would be hired to serve in administrative capacities at Khirbet Qumran. In other words, the facility became a leper colony!

As the Bible makes abundantly clear, the Jewish abhorrence of leprosy necessitated Uzziah's burial, not in the cemetary traditionally reserved for monarchs of the incorrectly termed Davidic lineage, but: "….in a field of burial," presumably a cemetary intended for the burial of people who had died from contagious diseases.

King Uzziah lived ten years after contracting leprosy; if, during the final decade of his life, the king's hired help consisted primarily of lepers, it is quite conceivable that Qumran, being downwind of Jerusalem, became a leper colony—its cemetary being the biblical "field of burial."

Presumably some of the lepers were from wealthy families, hence the presence at the Qumran complex of expensive urns and fine glass unguentaria for containing perfumes. Even though such artifacts admittedly could be found in a temple, it is highly unlikely that they would be found at Qumran, if the complex housed Covenanters, living the spartan lifestyle depicted in the Dead Sea Scrolls. The author therefore suggests that the north/south orientation of the graves at Qumran, served as a warning to Jewish travellers that the occupants had died from contagious diseases.

In summation, we have examined data in this chapter suggestive that the Qumran caves served as a geniza, commencing sometime after the Pharisees had become the dominant Jewish religious sect, and that the Qumran buildings had originally served as an administrative center and military border outpost, prior to becoming a leper colony. Although its role as a border outpost would have become redundant after the Judean border was relocated east of the Dead Sea, the Qumran tower probably was used as a communications beacon for several centuries.

If the desert sectarians did not reside at Khirbet Qumran, where did they live? The author postulates that a small desert community of Covenanters resided south of Qumran at the previously-mentioned oasis known as Ein Feshka, during the Herodian era. Everything fits— the availability of fresh flowing water for the ritual baths, the Essene location replete with palm trees depicted by Pliny the Elder, and the prescence of a calcium carbonate residue from the laundering of linen garments impregnated with frankincense, are consistent with the postulate.

The problem we must now address is why would religious sectarians allegedly obsessed with ritual purity, elect to reside at Ein Feshka, an oasis located little more than a mile south of the Qumran leper colony?

Fortunately for us, "Josephus" states that Herod the Great held the Essenes in high esteem; this is understandable since the religious beliefs of the conservative Essenes were reflective of those of Herod's ruling Saducees. In addition, one of Herod's aides was an Essene.

Given the favorable attitude displayed toward the Essenes by Herod the Great, and that the Ein Feshka ruins date from the Herodian era, the author suggests that Herod agreed to the ritual purification of the Qumran complex through incineration, prior to construction of a sectarian dwelling for the Essenes at Ein Feshka. As we have observed, archaeologists have estimated that the Qumran buildings were destroyed by fire during the early years of the reign of Herod the Great; reconstruction did not commence until after the monarch's death.

If the Qumran lepers were evicted from Qumran by Herod the Great, where did they go? Presumably they would have been restricted to a locale downwind of Jerusalem (the prevailing wind in Jerusalem blows from the northwest). A suitable location therefore would be near the western shore of the Dead Sea, and not too close to the newly-constructed Essene habitat at Ein Feshka.

Naturally the ruins of such a relocation site would possess a cemetary with graves oriented in a north/south direction, instead of the customary east / west orientation traditionally adopted by Jews in biblical times. Nine miles south of Qumran, at En el Ghuweir, is an ancient cemetary in which the graves are, indeed, oriented in a north/south direction. Adjacent to the cemetary are the ruins of a settlement, which very notably, date from the Herodian period.

An analysis of the coins discovered at Qumran suggests that the site was refurbished and reoccupied from aproximately 4 A.D. until it was destroyed again in 68 A.D., this time by Roman troops who were engaged in the suppression of the Zealot revolt. Exactly whom the occupants of Qumran were during these intervening years is difficult to ascertain, due to a lack of relevant data. The presence of arrowheads inside of the ruins suggests that they belonged to the residents, and were not fired by Roman archers during the quelling of a revolt. This premise is reinforced by the discovery of a forge and attendant water supply at the site; this implies that the arrowheads probably were manufactured there.

Such militaristic overtones suggest that Qumran was occupied during this turbulent period by personnel whose function it was to maintain surveillance over militant zealot factions, who were active in the area. Almost all of the coins discovered at the site dating through this period were Jewish, not Roman, implying that the complex possibly was occupied by a Jewish militia acting under the direction of the Procurator of Judea. A number of Jewish and Roman coins dating from 67 A.D. (The second year of the first Jewish revolt) discovered at the site, in addition to the presence of some Roman arrowheads, suggests that the complex was occupied during the hostilities by Zealots. The Zealots subsequently were defeated by troops under the command of the Roman general Titus. It is believed that two of Titus' legions were active in the region bounded by Jericho, Qumran and the Wadi Farah during this period; this is not surprising, since the area was a hotbed of Jewish militant activity, fomented by the rebel leader Simon bar Giora.

The author speculates that Khirbet Qumran, or what remained of the complex following the Roman assault, was occupied for the final time at the dawn of the Rabbinical era. This was the period following the adoption by the Judaic priesthood of the Pharisaic tradition, when it became politically-expedient to consign anti-Pharisaic texts to a geniza.

The Qumran occupants during this final phase presumably were potters, who made the uniquely-styled clay pots into which the scrolls were placed, prior to their internment in the Qumran caves. Manufacturing the clay pots at Qumran would have avoided the additional shipping weight and space in the wagons, which would have been incurred if the pots had been transported from Jerusalem, together with the scrolls and other material destined for the geniza, particularly since a pottery already existed at Qumran. Doubtless the clay pot filled with animal bones that was discovered in the Qumran ruins, comprised the remains of a priestly sacrificial meal, which somehow had been over-looked when the other geniza items had been deposited in the caves.

As to the Dead Sea Scrolls themselves, perhaps the *Copper Scroll* is the most enigmatic. The scroll describes sixty four places where more than one hundred tons of precious metal were purportedly hidden. It describes hiding places in the Jordan Valley near Jericho, e.g. in the cave next to the fountain belonging to the House of Hakkoz. The Hakkoz family did indeed own an estate in the Jordan Valley, and were a priestly family. Upon returning from the Babylonian exile, the family was unable to substantiate their genealogy, according to *Nehemiah 7: 61-65*, and accordingly were relieved of their priestly duties. *Ezra 8;33* claims that Meremoth was entrusted to be the Temple treasurer; he was a member of the Hakkoz family. The treasure referred to probably accrued from Temple tithes at the time of the Zealot uprising. The scroll itself dates from around 70 A.D..

The previously-mentioned scholar, the brilliant Solomon Schecter, was a close friend of Cyrus Adler, the founder of the American Jewish Commitee. Adler, whose research demonstrated that Jews, during the biblical era, were involved in Satanic practices and polytheism, hired archaeologist E.L. Sukenic, who later became head of the Hagganah intelligence agency—the forerunner of the Mossad. Sukenik's son was Yigal Yadin, who popularized the *Temple Scroll,* which called for reor-ganizing Israel around a newly constructed Temple. Through his popu-larizing of the Dead Sea Scrolls, which called for a war between the *Sons of Light* and the *Sons of Darkness,* during an apocalyptic period, to be followed by the return of both a princely and a priestly Messiah, Yadin conditioned the minds of Jews into dividing the Middle East into two armed camps.

In 1977, Yadin formed the Democratic Movement for Change with Ariel Sharon, out of which was spawned the Likkud Party, which ended the various Labor Party coalitions which had ruled Israel since 1948. This change ushered in the huge expansion of settlements in the Occupied Territories, as a precursor to destroying the Al Aqsa mosque situated on the Temple Mount. Shortly after the end of the Six Day War in 1967, Yadin allegedly discovered a scroll during excavations at the ruined fortress at Masada. The scroll purportedly was signed by one of the defenders named Jesus of Genessareth (Galilee). The scroll allegedly was stolen and made its way via Pakistan to Russia, where the Soviets purportedly used it to blackmail the Vatican. The Jesus mentioned on the scroll may well have been the son of the Zealot leader Judas of Gamalah, who lived east of Galilee.

Many authors, particularly those of the new Age genre, have portrayed the sectarian authors of the Dead Sea Scrolls as spiritually evolved pacifists; the texts themselves refute this characterization, portraying the initiates as militant fundamentalists and religious fanatics, with a marked disdain for women and the physically handicapped.

Possibly the most remarkable characteristic of the Dead sea scrolls is the striking similarity which certain scroll passages bear to doctrines espoused in the New Testament: sectarian views concerning divorce, and condemnation of marriages with a niece, correspond respectively with *Mark 10:6* and *6:17*. The New Testament and the sectarian texts both embrace the Zoroastrian dualistic principles of light and darkness, and allude to those treading the path of righteousness as "Sons of Light." [5] Both also subscribe to the immortality of the soul, [6] baptism and a final judgement *(mishpat)*. Whereas Christianity anticipates the eschatological return of a single princely Messiah, the scroll known as the *Manual of Discipline* refers to two Messiahs—a Messiah of the Aaronic lineage and a Messiah of Israel.[7] Curiously, another scroll fragment makes reference to only a single Messiah, signifying either an evolution of messianic doctrine, or that the text's author was an initiate of a different sectarian community. [8]

In view of the above similarities, we are compelled to arrive at the inescapable conclusion that key Christian doctrines were derived from the Dead Sea Scrolls. These in turn appear to have been the written works, not of a single sect, but of fissiparous Judaic sects differing in minor aspects of heteropraxis, yet unified through their militancy toward their successive Hellenistic and Roman overlords.

Too little factual information is available concerning Judaism during the 1st century A.D., for us to determine whether or not the early Christian Church was a continuation of the sectarian New Covenant, or the creation of a parallel sect which espoused similar doctrines. We have seen in an earlier chapter of this book that the Saint Peter story was a myth originated by the Babylonian priesthood, in order to put distance between a dictatorial priesthood and the masses. In light of such shameful dogma perpetrated by the Babylonian priesthood, is there any factual data which proves the historical existence of Jesus Christ, or was he yet another mythical figure who never lived, created for the sake of expediency? In the next chapter we will explore the esoteric aspects of the Covenant sects and the geopolitical reasons for the creation of Christianity.

CHAPTER 9

▼

WAS THE LIFE OF JESUS A FABLE?

"The hidden Sophia which we teach in our mysteries is the Sophia that God predestined to be for our glory before the ages began. She is the Sophia that none of the masters of this age have ever known."

Corinthians, 2: 8

To be successful, a religious sect must adopt the role of the proverbial "tar baby," to which those members of the public who are either unwilling or unable to think for themselves, adhere. The successful religious cult accordingly promotes an unethical escatological doctrine based upon fear and authoritarianism, which promises salvation for the faithful sectarians and eternal damnation for the remainder of humanity. In addition, religions tend to wither if they fail to incorporate an unverifiable mystery story, such as the imminent return of a divine Messiah.

Christianity and the Covenant sects all adopted such a doctrinal format; most significantly, at the very core of each format, carefully screened from profane eyes, lay occultic lore of the type that was revealed only to the higher echelons of Mystery School initiates. In other words, the hierarchy of both Christian and Covenant sects were Mystery School initiates. In keeping with the most powerful secret societies of today, the covert activities of the Mystery School hierarchies during the biblical era, were shielded from scrutiny by the public, whose attention was misdirected toward an outer circle consisting of lesser sectarians, from whom the true arcane knowledge and motives of the sect's hierarchy were with-held. By adopting this ploy, the sect presented the outward appearance of a spiritually-oriented group of pious believers, who were disinterested in the material affairs of the world.

Typical of the inner arcane core activities of the Judean Covenant sects was their use of a secret code, termed the *Atbash Cipher* by that erudite biblical scholar Dr. Hugh Schonfeld. He discovered that several of the Dead Sea Scrolls were encrypted with this particular cipher. By applying the cipher to the name "Baphomet," the scholar found that the name precisely decoded to "Sophia"—which is the Greek name for the black Mother Goddess of Wisdom who, like her doppleganger sisters Isis, and Mary, the mother of Jesus, was awarded the appelation "Queen of Heaven."

The Dead Sea Scrolls reveal that at least some of the Covenant sects functioned as Mystery Schools, or secret societies, as is evidenced by references to solar worship, and the practice of divination by means of facial features *(physiognomics)* [1] or by studying the paths of thunderstorms *(brontologia)*.[2] A pentagram and what appears to be an occult incantation inscribed in charcoal, were discovered on the walls of a cave in the complex of wadis which extend from Jerusalem to Jericho.[3] An additional inscription in Aramaic reveals that the writer occupied the cave towards the end of the second Temple period (70 A.D.). Of significance, a pentagram with additional pentagrams inscribed inside the body of the figure was a messianic symbol that was adopted by sectarians.

In all probability, many of the occult practices embraced by the leaders of the Covenant sects lacked meaningful substance, and were merely employed as a ruse to impress gullible novitiates. The same cannot be

said for members of a Mystery School who were active among some of
the Covenant sects. These were the Cassidens (also known as the
Kassidens). Some members of the secret society of architects known as
the Dionysian Articifers, who purportedly were loaned by the King of
Tyre for the purpose of designing and overseeing the construction of
the Temple, eventually settled in Judea and founded the Cassidens sect.
Unlike the ill informed masonic groups of the present era, the
Cassidens inherited the truly esoteric science of sacred geometry, and
have been claimed by some writers to have founded the Essenes.

Sacred geometry, which comprised the core teaching of any genuine
Mystery School of antiquity, was incorporated into the design of buildings that enabled them to function as resonant cavities, which were
attuned to the dynamic energies that pervade the cosmos. This is the
same energy continuum that was harnessed some two thousand years
later by Nikola Tesla and other scientific pioneers, who elected to conduct their research beyond the stultifying confines of academia.

The basic tenets of sacred geometry were taught in ancient Mystery
Schools in countries as geographically diverse as India, Britain and
Egypt. This strongly suggests that such institutions functioned not as
individual entities, but rather as a transnational network. Such a suggestion implies that the more esoterically-oriented of the Covenant
sects operated not as individual religious communities, but were in
communication with the Mystery Schools of other nations.

A prime example of such an esoteric relationship is to be found on
the island of Kyushu, in southern Japan. The ancient Heidate Jingu
shrine, which is located on the island, contains five masks, each one
painted a different color. Curiously, the colors are the same as the ones
on the logo representing the Olympic Games. Even more odd is a very
ancient artifact known in Japan as a "water crystal." This curious object
is in the form of a short stem, to which is attached two contiguous crystal spheres. Amazingly, this curio allegedly was presented to the
Japanese in antiquity by the Israelites! Since the proto Israelites known

as the Kenites were exporters of copper, it is possible that Phoenician ships carrying copper sailed from the Gulf of Aqaba to Japan, and brought the water crystal with them as a gift to the Japanese Emperor.

One fact that the Illuminati hierarchy has tried to conceal from the public is that on the Japanese island of Shikoku, which lies just north of Kyushu, is a mountain known as Tsurugi-San. This sacred mountain is the private domain of the Japanese Emperor, and is associated with the Atlantean overlords who ruled the world prior to the global flood. An Illuminati ritual periodically is held on this sacred mountain, which features a replica of the Ark of the Covenant, suspended by two poles and borne by men.

Further support for the hypothesis that an transnational interrelationship existed between ancient Mystery Schools, was the discovery of the Gunderstrup Cauldron—a superb example of the silversmith's art. This bowl, which was discovered in a Jutland peat bog, is decorated with pan-cultural deities. Attached to the exterior of the large cauldron, which was beaten from a single silver ingot, are a number of silver plates, which were fashioned by the repouseé technque. This suggests that the bowl was fabricated in the Thracian region of south western Europe—a region which specialized in repouseé work. Embossed on the plates are depictions of such Indian goddesses as Lakshmi and Hariti; also portrayed are elephants and the horned Celtic deity Cerununnos, the latter deity being depicted in the lotus pose.[4]

The transcultural nature of the Gunderstrup figures strongly suggests that the cauldron was fabricated by members of an itinerant guild of silversmiths who possessed transnational connections which extended from Europe to India. In addition, the yogic posture of the Celtic deity, which bears a remarkable resemblance to a figure depicted on an Indus Valley seal, implies that the silversmith's guild possessed arcane knowledge of a shamanic, or Mystery School nature.

The Gunderstrup cauldron was fabricated 150 B.C., a period when the Judean Covenant sects were active. Since the cauldron demonstrates the transnational character of the silversmith's guilds, is it not possible that communication occurred between Covenant Mystery Schools, such as the Cassidens, and their Celtic counterparts?

Unfortunately, the Mystery Schools of antiquity seldom committed key arcane knowledge to writing, so there does not appear to be any historical evidence of fraternization between esoterically oriented Celts and Jews, a situation rendered worse by the Old Testament emphasis on the exclusivity of the Jews as Yahwey's chosen elite, suggestive of racial insularity. Be that as it may, the Bible does make several veiled references to the black Mother Goddess Sophia. Sophia's Celtic counterparts were the black goddess known as the Cailleach, and Ceridwen, keeper of the Grail, which in pre Christian times took the symbolic form of a Cauldron of Knowledge. According to a high level Illuminati informant, this particular jewel encrusted cauldron is in the custody of the Hapsburg family. The lore of the Goddess of Wisdom is much in evidence in the *Book of Proverbs:* "Wisdom cries aloud in the street, in the markets she raises her voice….." [5] *Proverbs* also asserts that Sophia was the first manifestation and companion of Yahwey: "The Lord created me at the beginning of his work, the first of his acts of old…." [6]

The Jewish philosopher Aristabulus of Paneas assigned the numeral seven to Sophia "….representing the true Sabbath rest which may be enjoyed by the followers of Wisdom." [7] In a similar vein, *Proverbs* infers: "Wisdom has built her house, she has set up her seven pillars."[8]

The transnational character of esoteric beliefs is in evidence when we note that the Egyptian cult of Isis claims that the goddess manifested herself in the sun's rays. A similar notion appears in the pseudopigraphical work *"The Wisdom of Solomon,"* written by a Hellenized Jew who lived in Alexandria, and claimed that Sophia was a radiance of everlasting light.[9]

There has been a tendency throughout history for power brokers to be initiates of Mystery Schools or secret societies. Such was the case with the Celts, where the Druids not merely comprised the priesthood, where they directed the oral transmission of esoteric knowledge, but also were the administrative, economic and judicial overlords of the pan-tribal Celtic world. In other words, the druidic heirarchy were priestly statesmen who, by establishing an inter-tribal network of Mystery Colleges, were able to unify the diverse Celtic tribes into a theocratic hegemony.

Contact between Celt and Jew almost certainly occurred when Judea became part of the Hellenistic Empire, and educated Jews, particularly scribes who performed bureaucratic functions, undertook journeys to Asia Minor, where they would be likely to encounter some of the 20,000 Celts who had settled in Galatia circa 270 B.C.. [10]

An exchange of arcane knowledge during such encounters would have been facilitated through the use of an esperanto type of language, known as *koiné*, which enjoyed common usage throughout Asia Minor and the Levant during that period. Such esoterically inclined Jews also would have met members of the Mystery School known as the Ionians, whose initiates had settled in Asia Minor. Allegedly, they were responsible for the design of the temple dedicated to the goddess Diana at Ephesus; the Ionians were associated with the previously mentioned Dionysian Artificers, who had designed Solomon's Temple.

The content of the Dead Sea Scrolls makes it self-evident that at least some of the Covenanters possessed the type of arcane knowledge common to Mystery Schools. As was demonstrated earlier in this chapter, it is also abundantly clear that there is a great similarity between certain Dead Sea Scroll passages and New Testament verses: the *Sermon on the Mount* (Mathew 5:7) is another prime example, where such phrases as "turning the other cheek" and "poor in spirit" are also to be found in the *Manual of Discipline.* [11] and the scroll known as the *War of the Sons of Light Against the Sons of Darkness* [12] respectively, yet are not to be found in any other religious writings of that period. Many similarities also occur in their ritual and community practices, together with the pronounced emphasis on the imminent Messianic return.

It is a matter of historical record that the Palestine of the 1st century A.D. was a country awash with political upheaval and bloodshed. Such tumult obviously would leave an indelible impression in the minds of Jewish writers, yet the New Testament creates the distinct impression that all was peaceful in Judea—the Jews being quite contented with their wretched lifestyle; only Roman authors, or Roman sympathizers would convey such a distorted image, which brings us to the problem of the true authorship of the New Testament.

We cannot claim that the Dead Sea scrolls and the *New Testament* scriptures constitute parallel developments arising from an earlier form of Judaism, for it should be noted that there is a total lack of factual evidence with which to substantiate the historical existence of Christ, who appears to be a composite figure derived from the myths of Tammuz, Mithra and the Celtic deity Esus. Even though the later Dead Sea Scrolls were written during the 1st century A.D., none of them mention the activities or crucifixion of Christ, which is an unprecedented omission—unless the historical Jesus never existed.

In light of the similarity between numerous passages which occurr in both the Dead Sea Scrolls and the *New Testament,* it is highly probable that the authors of the New Testament (quite possibly members of the Roman oligarchy, such as the Piso family) utilized the scrolls previously written by Covenant Jews as source material for the New Testament. If this is indeed the case, then we must find a credible rationale for the creation and promulgation of Christianity.

With the exception of Judea, peace prevailed for several decades throughout the Roman Empire during the 1st century A.D.. A positive legacy of Roman occupation was that the 40,000 miles of highway spanning the Roman Empire were well policed; in addition, marauding pirates were swept from the Mediterranean, thus enabling commerce to freely flourish.

The growing political unrest in Judea, fomented by Zadokite and other Covenant sects "zealous for the Law," was a political thorn in the side of Imperial Rome, however. Another region causing political concern was Britain. Ever since the reign of Julius Caesar, Rome had cast covetous eyes on Britain, not for its fertile land, but for its fabled treasure of gold and silver artifacts. The high cost of maintaining the large Roman army necessary for maintaining peace within the Empire, prompted Caesar to devise a ploy for seizing control of the Celtic gold. The Celts not only loved to adorn their bodies with gold jewelery, but also had a penchant for hurling their finest examples of the goldsmith's art into rivers and lakes, as offerings to their pantheon of deities!

Just as the Templars aquired their political clout by combining religion with banking and mercantile practices, so the Druids became the overlords of the Celtic commonwealth through their control and regulation of the gold trade. This trade was administered by the Druids through a network of religio-commercial centers. Gold mined in the Wicklow mountains of Ireland, was shipped across the Irish Sea to the Welsh island of Anglesea, which was a druidic center, then transported along a well-defined trade route across England to the continent. Druidic temples were established along this gold route for regulation of the gold trade, as well as for religious purposes.

In order to avoid religious unrest, the Romans usually exhibited tolerance toward the religions of the various ethnic peoples within the Roman Empire, provided that the local religion did not conflict with emperor worship. Accordingly, Rome did not proscribe the Celtic religion. In order for Rome to usurp control of the commerce in gold, however, it became necessary to destroy the Druidic priesthood, which was headquartered in Britain.

Julius Caesar launched two unsuccessful invasion attempts against Britain in 55 and 54 B.C.; these abortive attempts did, however, result in a successful trading relationship being established between the Roman Republic and the Celtic kingdom of south eastern England.

Another invasion attempt was initiated in 43 A.D. by the Claudian General Aulus Plautius. Accompanied by four divisions of battle hardened and well-equipped troops, Plautius landed on the southern coast of England near Porchester. Only a few years earlier, a terrible natural disaster befell the region when the lowlands south of Porchester, known as the Trisanton Estuary, sank beneath the waves, drowning most of the local Leman clan. The only land remaining above sea level became what is now known as the Isle of Wight.

Except for minor skirmishes, Plautius' army was unopposed by the romanized Southern English Celts, but was denied access to the gold trade route by the ferocious opposition meted out by the inter tribal Celtic army of the Silures and Ordovices.

Desperate for new sources of revenue, the profligate Emperor Nero later appointed the brilliant commander Suetonius Paulinus to the task of vanquishing the aggressive army of British Celts. Fresh from his victory over the Moors, Suetonius realized that the most practical way of negating Druidic clout was by interrupting their regulation of the gold trade. He concluded that this could be accomplished by seizing control of the Druidic command center at Anglesea—the commencement of the gold route.

Arriving in Angelsea in 60 A.D. with an armed flotilla and two legions, Suetonius quickly routed the Celtic defenders, putting hapless Druids to the sword and destroying the sacred groves used for worship. His victory was short-lived. Prasutagus, king of the Iceni clan, who inhabited south-eastern England, died in 59 B.C.; Catus, who was Nero's procurator, attempted to seize the deceased monarch's estate. This very rapacious and silly act was resisted by Prasutagus's widow Queen Voada, better known by her romanized name Boadicea. As punishment for attempting to protect her rightful estate, the Celtic queen was seized by Roman troops, flogged and her daughters raped. Seeking vengeance, Boadicea and her army ferociously destroyed the Roman Ninth Legion, but eventually were routed by Suetonius and his remaining three legions.

The crushing defeat suffered by
ized resistance by the British Celt
a proscribed entity. Peace now p
access to the the lucrative gold
order to maintain political sta'
both Britain and the Contine..
gion. This new religion would have to ᴜᴄ
replete with a non-Druidic priesthood which waᴖ

At that time, Judaism was spreading northwards aɴᴄ
European countries. In order to quell the possible spread of Jewish ..
itancy fomented by diaspora Jews, the new religion would have to
falsely discredit the Jews, by accusing them of a particularly heinous act.
Human sacrifices were sometimes offered to their deities by the Celts; in
times of crisis, members of the Druidic priesthood sometimes would
volunteer to be the sacrificial victim.[13]

The Celts accordingly would readily accept the fabricated legend of a
Christian deity who permitted himself to be sacrificed, in order to expi-
ate the sins of humanity. Like his Christian counterpart, the Celtic sky-
god Esus (formerly known in Celtic times as Hesus, until his name was
changed by the Christian priesthood for obvious reasons) was the son
of a deity (Lugh) who was associated with wood. Esus comprised a Holy
Trinity in conjunction with Taranis and Teutates, which is demonstrative of the Celtic love of triads. In addition, the Celtic use of the cross as
a religious solar symbol predated its adoption by Christianity. The
Celtic belief in an afterlife and a Supreme Being, also rendered
Christianity as an alternative religion deemed acceptable to the Celts.

In 54 B.C., Julius Caesar wrote: "The Druids make the immortality of
the soul the basis of all their teaching, holding it to be the principal
incentive and reason for a virtuous life." [14] Perhaps the most telling
comparison between the Celtic religion and Christianity, flowed from
the pen of the bardic Prince Taliesan (500-540 A.D.) when he wrote:

182

was a new thing in Asia, but there never was a time when
of Britain never held its doctrine."

thor suggests that in order to synthesize a religion which
and acceptance with the Celts, a faction of the Roman oligarchy
d doctrinal tenets from the Celtic myth of Esus, supplementing it
h the myths surrounding Tammuz, Mithra, the Babylonian dogma
ppertaining to the Keys of Heaven, and the messianic writings of the
Judaic Covenant sects.

Believing in the maxim that the pen is mightier than the sword, the
European oligarchy for centuries has employed the services of an inner
circle of writers, for the purpose of modifying the belief structure of the
masses, whenever it was deemed necessary. In order to boost their own
egos, some of these inner circle writers make tongue in cheek references
in their works to Mithraism and the true authorship of the New
Testament. Thus Hermann Hesse, an inner circle writer, whose primary
Illuminati task was to condition the German youth into acceptance of a
new mind set, as a precursor to the establishment of Nazism and the
Hitler Youth Movement, wrote the book *Demian*. In it he mentions the
sun god Mithra, and also names one of the principal charcters
Pistorius—an odd name if one is unaware of its origins.

The name "Pistorius" is derived from the latin word *pistor*, meaning
"one who grinds", i.e. a miller or baker. Another derivative of *pistor* is
the name *Piso*, which was the name of one of the most politically powerful Roman families, at the time of the Jewish revolt.

The Illuminati families who wield the real power behind any throne,
usually maintain such a low profile that they remain virtually unknown
to the general public. The family of Calpurnius Piso was no exception.
Claiming descent from Numa Pomilius, the successor to the Romulus
who co-founded Rome, Gaius Lucius Calpurnius Piso, to give him his
full name, was married to the great grand-daughter of Herod the Great.
Piso is believed to have been the author of the first version of the *Gospel
of Mark,* called *Ur Marcus,* circa 60 B.C.. Piso and his friend, the author

Seneca, were forced to commit suicide after their attempt to assassinate Nero failed.

After the failure of the attempted coup, Piso's son Arrius was appointed Governor of Syria, which gave him command of the Roman legions in Judea. After the assassination of Nero by one of his own slaves, Piso assisted Titus in the siege of Jerusalem, and helped him sack the Jerusalem Temple in 70 A.D..

This act would have afforded him the opportunity to aquire some of the sectarian manuscripts during the sacking of the Temple (spies probably would have been infiltrated into the various Covenant sects by the Temple priesthood, in order to seize scrolls which were of a polemic nature).

Since the advent of Mithraism, the Virgin Birth myth has been adopted by various religious cults, so it became incumbent for the Pisos to continue the tradition. The New Testament nativity myth appears to be a synthesis of the Mandean and Buhddistic nativity fables. Even today, the Mandean Baptist sect hold that Elizabeth, the wife of the priest Zechariah, gave birth in a miraculous manner. Mother and child subsequently flee to escape an infanticide ordered by King Herod. Not surprisingly perhaps, there is no historical evidence suggesting that Herod ever perpetrated such a dastardly crime.

Not to be outdone in the tall story department, evangelistic Buddhists descended upon Babylon circa 500 B.C. and promulgated the following myth concerning the life of Buddha: after a virgin birth, Buddha and his parents flee to a foreign land in order to escape an infanticide ordered by King Bimbasara. At the age of twelve, Buddha astounds the priests with his religious knowledge. He later becomes involved in an incident at a well, then undergoes temptation and transfiguration at the age of thirty.

As we have seen, the purported death and resurrection of Christ was, for all intents and purposes, identical with that of the Babylonian deity Tammuz, who purportedly was crucified, his body subsequently

disappearing from his burial cave three days later. It was perfectly natural for the Pisos to incorporate the Tammuz myth into their story of
Christ, for it provides a supernatural mystique, without which no new
religious cult can survive for very long.

It is in the *Epistles of Saint Paul* that we find Mithraism—that martial
religion of imperialism, most blatantly displayed. In chapter after chapter, we find allusions to the fiery Sun God's luminosity: "The Lord Jesus
shall be revealed from heaven with his mighty angels in flaming fire." In
a similar vein, *1 Timothy* states: "The blessed and only Potentate, the
King of kings and Lord of lords: who only hath immortality, dwelling in
the light which no man can approach to...."

To those unconversant with Mithraism, it would appear that the
Pauline Epistles formed the nucleus of a totally new religion, later to
become known as Christianity. But this is only illusiory, for as we have
observed, Mithra—the fellow in the Phrygian cap, had simply reap-
peared in yet another of his numerous disguises. It would appear that
the Pisos based their mythical figure Paul, upon the life and teachings of
Appolonius of Tyana, who was also known as Paulus in Rome. He purportedly was a native of Tarsus who died on the island of Patmos. His
travels in Asia undoubtedly would have brought him in contact with the
story of Chrishna.

Thus, by forming an amalgam of diverse solar deity myths (Esus,
Mithra, Chrishna, Tammuz, etc.) the Piso family were able to package
wine of a very old vintage in a new bottle. It was this very fusion of
ancient solar myths, with anti Judaic overtones, that gave Christianity
its widespread appeal among the Gentile population of the western
world.

Shortly prior to his bizarre death in the Israeli desert, Bishop Pike of
California questioned how Christ could have been crowned with
thorns, when Pike found no evidence of suitable thornbushes ever having been indigenous to the environs of Jerusalem, even in biblical times.
The good Bishop suggested that the crown was, in actuality, a local

species of palm leaf, which possessed a row of seven long thorns along its spine. When wrapped around a person's head with the thorns radiating outwardly, the leaf would simulate the crown of Mithra, the thorns representing the seven solar rays, as on the Statue of Liberty.

One could equally wonder how Peter was able to hear a cock crow thrice, when so severe was the Jewish law that it was a capital offence to keep chickens within Jerusalem, or in the neighboring villages, lest they escape and foul the Temple. This particular biblical passage undoubtedly was an inside joke, written for the benefit of the Mithraic initiates within the Piso circle, for novitiates of the Mithraic priesthood studied at an academy situated on the banks of the River Gallus, in Turkey; the latin word for "cock" is "gallus."

The above examples are illustrative of the manner in which the Piso family, purportedly assisted by their friend, the writer Tacitus, were able to incorporate several layers of interpretation into the Gospels. Despite being unsupportable in matters of historical fact, and lacking in chronological consistency, it is undoubtedly this multi level interpretive format, with its suggestion of Mithraic mysteries, that enables the Gospels to maintain their continuing popularity among both theologians and the undiscerning and credulous Christian masses.

The historical origins and subsequent spread of Christianity are shrouded by the mists of time. We only have the questionable claims made by members of the early Christian Church hierarchy, writing after the fact, that Christianity originated in the Holy Land, prior to its diffusion in adjacent Mediterranean countries.

If the life of Christ as depicted in the *New Testament,* had been a reality, we would have expected historians living in that era to have recorded such tumultuous events. How strange then, that the life, teachings and subsequent crucifixion of such a prominent and newsworthy figure went unrecorded, even by Philo of Alexanria, who wrote until at least 40 A.D., and had mentioned Pilate in relation to another matter.

It is almost certain that Flavius Josephus was the non-de-plûme of a member of the Piso family, for the autobiographical account of Josephus' life totally lacks credibility. The chronology of his sojurn as an Essene belies his knowledge of the novitiate period required prior to becoming a full fledged Essene. His account of his actions against Roman troops is even more implausible. Not noted for their compassion against their enemies, Josephus would have us believe that he was captured after pouring boiling oil and fenugreek upon the heads of Roman soldiers during the siege of Jopata, yet was permitted to live comfortably in Rome afterwards! Equally improbable, he claimed that he was permitted to write Jewish history and marry his descendants into the Roman aristocracy. The obvious reason for the creation of the fictitious Josephus was to provide corroboration for the Jesus fable.

Piso's friends, the writers Tacitus and Pliny, also made reference to Christ. Christian readers may point out that the historian Suetonius (a.k.a. Titus Antonius) also referred to Christ, not surprisingly, his mother was Claudia, the daughter of Arrius Piso.

The trial and subsequent crucifixion of Christ are scarcely believable when one delves deeply into the *New Testament* account. According to the bible, Jesus was charged with blasphemy for claiming to the Sanhedrin that he was the annointed King of the Jews, not the Son of God, as many Christians misperceive. Since the Roman Emperor was regarded as a deity (the Son of Jupiter) it was only the Emperor who possessed the authority, within the jurisdiction of Rome, to nominate anyone for the post of ruler, which is why Pilate had to order Christ's crucifixion.

The biblical claim that Pontius Pilate acquiesced to the demand of the Jewish mob that Jesus be crucified is absurd. Pilate, in his capacity as the representative of the Roman Emperor, was noted for his cruelty; so much so, in fact, that he was removed from his post and exiled to Vienne in 36 A.D., for using excessive cruelty in quelling a protest demonstration by Samaritans.

If the Bible is a divinely-inspired work, as ill-informed or corrupt theologians would have us believe, why is the chronology of Christ's purported arrest and subsequent trial not credible? We are given to believe that between the fourth and eleventh hours of the morning, Christ was arrested, interrogated in Annas' residence, followed by another interrogation at the house of Caiaphas, tried by the Sanhedrin, interrogated three times by Pilate, taken to Herod Antipas, flogged and finally sentenced!

The Romans were noted for maintaining archival records for tax purposes, yet there is no historical record in Roman archives of the trial and crucifixion of Christ, nor of any record of the town of Nazareth ever having existed 2,000 years ago. As Albert Scheiwtzer succinctly stated: "The Jesus of Nazareth who came forward publicly as the Messiah, who preached the ethic of the Kingdom of God, who founded the Kingdom of Heaven upon earth, and died to give His word its final consecration, never had any existence. He is a figure designed by nationalism, endowed with life by liberalism, and clothed by modern theology in a historical garb....This image has not been destroyed from without, it has fallen to pieces, cleft and disintegrated by the concrete historical problems which came to the surface one after the other...."

During the writing of the *New Testament*, the Pisos well may have been influenced by a passage in Plato's *Republic:* "It was essential to destroy his good name....Hence he must be stripped of every-thing....whipped, tortured, imprisoned, nailed to a cross, or torn to pieces."

During its formative years, the Christian hierarchy perpetrated numerous apochryphal works in an attempt to provide false corrobora-tion for the Jesus myth. A typical forgery appeared in the 4th century A.D., entitled *Acta Pilati* (Acts of Pilate). A later type of forgery was the notorius *Shroud of Turin,* which purported to be the burial shroud of Christ, and came into the possession of the de Charnay family in the 14th. Century (de Charnay was a french Templar). What theologians are reluctant to point out is that the 14th century A.D. Bishop of Troyes publicly admitted that the Shroud had been created by a local artist.

Of possible significance is that Troyes was a major Templar stronghold. To make the Shroud, the artist may have sculpted a bas-relief of a human figure (a bas-relief is a low-profile sculpture, providing a flattened frontal appearance). Diluted urine (or a mixture of myrrh and aloes) applied over the prominent areas ofthe fabric draped sculpture, then subjected to heat, would provide a negative image on the fabric. Such a technique would eliminate brush marks, as also would be the case if pigment or dried blood were to be blown onto the cloth. This type of technique would also explain why the pigment only occurs on the upper surface of the Turin Shroud, whose weave is uncharacteristic of Holy Land fabrics from the biblical era.

A great deal of confusion has arisen in the minds of many members of the New Age fraternity concerning several scriptural texts written during the 1st and 2nd centuries A.D. These texts, frequently of a gnostic nature, create the impression among the laity that they are historical accounts of events in the lives of Jesus Christ and his disciples. In reality, such texts are apocryphal, i.e. they are *imaginary* accounts. Typical works of this genre are *The Acts of Peter and the Twelve Apostles,* and *The Revelation of Peter*, both of which are part of the textual cache discovered in 1946 near the Egyptian hamlet of Nag Hammadi, which is located on the bank of the Nile, some sixty miles downstream from Luxor. The location where the texts were discovered is near the site of a monastery constructed in the 4th century A.D. By Saint Pachomius. As we have observed, Saint Peter, the Keeper of the Keys to the Kingdom of Heaven, was merely an apocryphal creation of the Babylonian priesthood.

Theologians would have us believe that during the Ist century A.D., Christianity spread at a rapid rate to neighboring countries from its Holy Land roots. This is scarcely credible if the Christian Church was founded and initially under the direction of semi illiterate disciples, who obviously would have been incapable of establishing a sophisticated centralized administration.

Many history books claim that the Augustine mission introduced Christianity to Britain in 596 A.D., but this is a fallacious claim, the mission only attempted to thrust acceptance of the Papacy onto a Celtic populace, who had already embraced Christianity.

The early British historian Gildas, writing in 520 A.D., stated that Christianity was introduced into Britain during the last year of the reign of Emperor Tiberius (38 A.D.) only five years after the supposed crucifixion of Christ. [15] According to Bishop Usher: "The British National Church was founded A.D.36, 160 years before heathen Rome confessed Christianity." [16] Sabellius claimed in 250 A.D.: "....the first nation that proclaimed it as their religion and called it Christian, after the name of Christ, was Britain." Rather surprisingly, even the Catholic theologian Robert Parsons states: "The Christian religion began in Britain." [17]

Since the foregoing suggests that the Roman oligarchy created, then introduced Christianity to the British in order to supplant the Celtic religion, it is not unreasonable to expect that British converts to the new religion would attempt, in turn, to introduce Christianity to foreign lands. This did in fact occur, the first evangelical target being none other than Rome itself! It is a matter of record that the first Christian church to be established in Rome, was under the direction of Bishop Linus, a member of the British oligarchy.

The circumstances surrounding the establishment of this first British operated church in Rome, were sufficiently unusual as to question whether it was the result of a political accommodation between the Celtic oligarchy of Britain and Rome. At the period when the Roman general Aulus Plautius invaded Britain in 43 A.D., Southern England was ruled by the Archdruid Aviragus, while his cousin Caradoc, known to the Romans as Caractacus, was the monarch of the Welsh Silurian nation. Caractacus then became the Pendragon (commander in chief) of the combined Welsh and English armies. After many bloody battles with the Romans, Caractacus was finally defeated at the Battle of Clune in 52 A.D., due to a bizarre incident.

Winning this particular battle was deemed so crucial to Rome that Emperor Claudius himself arrived, replete with two additional legions and a number of elephants. Claudius had been an object of derision prior to becoming Emperor, due to his physical deformities, but proved to be a very capable administrator and personally directed the Roman forces at the Battle of Clune. The offensive odor of the elephants panicked the horses of the Celtic charioteers during the battle; the scythes attached to the axles of the British chariots created a terrible carnage, as the fear crazed beasts stampeded back into the Celtic ranks.

At the same moment, the hapless Celtic army was ambushed from the rear by members of the treacherous Coraniaid tribe of Celts, who had entered into a clandestine alliance with the Romans.

King Aviragus escaped and later wreaked havoc upon the Coraniaid, but Caractacus was captured and taken to Rome. It was customary in those times for monarchs who had suffered defeat at the hands of the Roman troops, to be publicly humiliated before the Roman citizenry, then executed. Curiously, this cruel fate did not befall Caractacus, even though he had been the largest thorn in the side of the Roman military for several years. Instead, he appeared before the Roman Senate and made an extremely eloquent speech in Latin, after which he was embraced by the Empress Agrippa. Caractacus and his royal Silurian family were permitted to reside in Rome at a palatial villa, and provided with a staff of four hundred servants. This sumptuous estate became known as the Palatium Britannicum.

Even more curious were the marriages entered into between members of the British and Roman oligarchical families: King Aviragus married Venus Julia, the daughter of Emperor Claudius, during a truce period which had been declared between the British Celts and Rome.

During the same truce, Gladys, the sister of Caractacus, became the wife of arch-enemy and Roman commander-in-chief Aulus Plautius! [18]

Gladys subsequently assumed the Romanized name Pomponia Graecina Plautius, and was mentioned by Tacitus in his *Annals*. [19] The British Celts frequently were depicted by Roman writers as woad-painted savages, a claim refuted by the fact that the Britain of the 1st. Century A.D. possessed more than fifty cities and numerous colleges. Gladys, a brilliant scholar, wrote several works of prose and poetry in Latin, Greek and her native Cymric language, and became a prominent member of the Roman intelligentsia.

Among those residing in Rome at the Palatium Britannicum were Caractacus' grandfather Lyr Lladiaith (Shakespeare's King Lear) Prince Linus and the princesses Eurgain and Gladys, the son and daughters of Caractacus. Eurgain later became a missionary, and was honored as the first female Christian saint in Britain. [20]

Gladys, who was born in 36 A.D., became a favorite of Emperor Claudius, who adopted her and renamed her Claudia; following in the footsteps of her aunt and namesake, Gladys also became renowned in Rome as a great beauty and scholar. Extolling her beauty and fine intellect, the Roman writer Martial wrote: "Since Claudia, wife of Pudens, comes from the blue set Britains, how is it that she has won the hearts of the Latin people?" [21]

The Pudens referred to by Martial was a politically-powerful member of the Roman Senate; his marriage to Gladys occurred in 53 A.D., which is surprising when one considers that Aviragus was still engaging the Romans at the time. After their marriage, the Pudens took up residence with the Silurian royal family at the Palatium Britannicum, which became the first house of Christian worship in Rome, with Pastor Hermas officiating.

According to Cardinal Baronius, who was the former curator of the Vatican Library: "It is delivered to us by the firm tradition of our forefathers that the house Pudens was the the first....and that there the

Christians assembling formed the Church, and that of all of our churches the oldest is that which is called after the name Pudens." [22]

Caractacus' son Linus, was appointed the first Bishop of Rome, as is evidenced by: "Concerning those Bishops who have been ordained in our lifetime, we make known to you that they are these....Linus, brother of Claudia." [23] Clemens Romanus, the second Bishop of Rome, confirms the fact: "Sanctissimus Linus, Frater Claudas." [24] A similar confirmation was made by Iranaeus (180 A.D.). [25]

In view of the foregoing, it would appear that Christianity was created by Rome, not only to discredit, and therefore halt, the spread of militant Judaism, but also to negate the political power of the Druidic priesthood, in order to seize control of the lucrative British gold enterprise. The founding of the first Christian Church in Rome by the family of Caractacus, undoubtedly gave a tremendous boost to the early growth of Christianity. This rapid diffusion of the new Christian cult, in conjunction with popularity of the Silurian royal family among the Roman Intelligentsia, must have generated alarm among the Roman oligarchy. This alarm would have been intensified after Gladys married into the politically-powerful Pudens family, for this newly-created power base was clearly a case of the Celtic tail wagging the Imperial Roman dog.

The author postulated that it was the growing political clout of the new Christian cult under the leadership of Caractacus' royal offspring, which initiated a wave of anti Christian persecutions toward the end of the 1st entury A.D.. Linus, the son of Caractacus, had the dubious honor of not only becoming the first Bishop of the Christian Church of Rome, but also its first Christian martyr. Although Gladys died a natural death in 97 A.D., her husband Rufus Pudens and her four children were all executed during the second and third waves of anti-Christian persecutions.

How ironic it is that every year, thousands of Christian tourists flock to Rome to gaze in awe at the splendors of the Vatican, yet ignore the remains of the Palatium Britannicum, where the great drama of the founding of the first Christian Church, by a Celtic royal family unfolded. Shortly after the martyrdom of Praxedes, the youngest daughter of Gladys Pudens, a memorial plaque was inscribed on the palace wall, which is still legible today. When translated into English, the inscription states: "In this sacred and most ancient of churches....formerly the house of Sanctus Pudens, the Senator, repose the remains of three thousand blessed martyrs which Pudentiana and Praxedes, virgins of Christ, with their own hands interred."

It is a tragedy that the hierarchy of the Christian Church takes great pains to insure that newly discovered religious data are not revealed to the lay public, in order that the *New Testament* history and false dogma remain static. A case in point was the British television documentary *"Jesus: the Evidence,"* which religious lobbyists attempted to suppress before filming even commenced. Theologians doubtless will scoff at the material presented in this chapter, even though it is documented historical data, which is more than can be said for the historically unverified *New Testament* narrative which they vociferously defend.

Shortly after the death of the Pudens, a bewildering plethora of Christian cults emerged—the Manicheans, Gnostics, Ebionites, etc.. None of them played a major pivotal role in changing the face of Christianity, due primarily to a lack of a centralized governing authority. That dubious distinction must be accorded to Emperor Constantine, who ruled over the Roman Empire from 312 A.D. to 337 A.D..

According to popular tradition, Constantine converted to the Christian faith after perceiving a vision of a luminous cross which was suspended in the sky. In actuality, Constantine did not undergo a religious conversion, but merely modified the Christian religion, in order to bring it into conformity with the Sol Invictus (Mithraic) solar cult into which he had recently been initiated.

Constantine was accustomed to seeing the cross used as a symbol, for as an ancient Phoenician and Celtic religious solar symbol, it predated Christianity and was emblazoned on British coins following the adoption of Christianity as the national religion of Britain, during the 2nd century A.D..

Moreover, contrary to a popular misconception, Constantine was not a Roman, but a Briton, born in England of a Celtic mother (Queen Helen, daughter of King Coel of nursery rhyme fame) and Emperor Constantius, who was of Trojan descent. Constantine's mother became known as "Helen of the Cross," after allegedly founding the first cathedral at Tréves. Cardinal Baronius wrote: "The man must be mad who, in the face of universal antiquity, refuses to believe that Constantine and his mother were Britons," [26] In a similar manner, Pope Urban claimed: "Christ showed to Constantine the Briton, the victory of the cross for his sceptre." [27]

The Roman Empire under Constantine attained its greatest territorial dominion ever. Constantine realized that achieving peace and stability in an empire comprised of nations which collectively, embraced many disparate religious doctrines, was an impossible task unless a unifying religious belief structure were to be implemented. His political philosophy is exemplified in his statement: "We call God to witness, the Saviour of all men, that in assuming the government we are influenced solely by these two considerations: the uniting of the empire in one faith, and the restoration of peace to a world rent to pieces by the insanity of religious persecution."

With the political insight worthy of a Machievelli, Constantine selected as his unifying religion, not the Christianity of the Pudens family, but rather the religion of that old master of many disguises—Mithra, this time in the guise of the Sol Invictus cult. This was a masterful ploy, for the monotheistic sun god incorporated the major attributes of all the other deities that were worshipped at that time, within the confines of the empire, and accordingly offended nobody.

Just as the Jews had incorporated thinly disguised elements of Mithraism into Judaism, after the Babylonian exile, so Constantine, aided by his close associate Eusebius (who wrote a treatise on the art of lying for the promotion of Christianity) created Christianity as we know it today.This occurred after Constantine presided over the Council of Nicea in 325 A.D.. There is a parallel with the Rabbinical Judaism of today, which incorporates Pharasaic doctrines and is not a comprehensive reflection of earlier Judaistic dogma.

Mithraism, with its emphasis on the appocalypse, Judgemnt Day, resurrection, baptismal rites, symbolic meals of bread and wine, together with the promise of a messianic return, comprises a major corpus of the *New Testament*. In this manner, Christianity underwent a transmutation in order to become the state religion of Constantine's empire. In keeping with its solar overtones, Sunday became the day of rest by edict of Constantine, who also decreed that the alleged birthday of Christ be moved from the traditional January 6th., to the most important day in the Sol Invictus cult: December 25th.—the rebirth of the sun. Very significantly, even though the Dead Sea Scrolls verify the antiquity of the *Old Testament*, no copies of the *New Testament* predate the reign of Constantine.

The Gnostics, who began their activities during the 2nd. Century A.D., did not exalt Mary, the purported mother of Jesus, but instead focussed upon Sophia as the divine feminine deity. Goddess worship remained popular throughout the empire during this particular era, being especially prevalent at Ephesus, where the local goddess was the black virgin Diana of the Ephesians. It therefore comes as no surprise that it was at the Council of Ephesus in 431 A.D., that Cyril of Alexandria, the psychopath who was responsible for the assassination of the brilliant neo-platonic scholar Hypatia, proposed that Mary be declared Mother of God ((*Theotokos*). The name "Mary" is a derivative of the Hebrew *marah*, meaning "bitter sea." The Babylonian goddess Tiamat also was associated with bitter waters. This is also why the church fathers accorded Mary the liturgical title "Stilla Maris" *(Myrrh of the Sea)* which later was revised to "Stella Maris" *(Star of the Sea)*. Thus was Mary elevated from humble Jewish mother to Mother of God. [28]

The results of a survey published in 1971 indicated that many young Christian priests did not believe in a historical Jesus Christ. Being a devout Christian at that time, the survey so incensed the author that he decided to write a book which verified the historical life of Jesus. After several months of in-depth research into comparative religions, the author was mortified to find that he had metaphorically painted himself into a corner and that the supposed life of Jesus was merely a fable. If Christianity was largely composed of false dogma, was it possible that the same held for the *Old Testament* and, horror of horrors, even secular history and science? What you are reading, dear reader, is the result of three decades of painstaking research conducted by the author.

What became self evident as the author progressed with his research into religious history, is that the Bible, together with religion in general, is a most insidious and effective form of mind control. Maintaining a very large segment of the global populace in a state of religious bondage, primarily has been accomplished through the employment of one of the greatest evils that has afflicted humankind throughout recorded history—authoritarianism.

It is imperative that we do not confuse authority with authoritarianism. Authority appears to be a basic component, together with power and hierarchy, of the fundamental structure of both nature (as in a bee colony) and society. Only when these components are used in an unethical manner do they result in authoritarianism. A woman is not a harbinger of evil when she uses the power bestowed by beauty in order to attract a suitable mate; likewise, assigning authority to a person who has attained special skills—the conductor of a symphony orchestra or a surgeon, is not an evil act. Creating a religion based upon false dogma, then threatening the gullible masses that they will not be admitted to heaven unless they have implicit faith in the ideology promulgated by the heirarchical priesthood, is authoritarianism at its worst.

One of the most insidious aspects of the Bible is the authoritarian edict to "turn the other cheek" and that "the meek shall inherit the earth." In view of the fact that the priestly hierarchies of both Judaism and Christianity are beholden to their Illuminati overlords, it is not surprising that such passages should appear in the Bible, in order to implant the subliminal message into the psyche of the masses that they meekly acquiesce to the dictates of the hierarchy of the New World Order, and that they refrain from attempting a militant insurrection against their hierarchical overlords. Turning the other cheek simply empowers one's adversary to create even more authoritarian mayhem. A typical example occurred during the Vietnam war. In order for the Illuminati to determine whether it was possible for a dictatorship to totally depopulate every city and town in a nation, without encountering undue militant resistance from the populace, America conducted a covert Kissinger/Jesuit orchestrated bombing assault on Cambodia, killing 600,000 Cambodians in the process (since the end of W.W.II, America has bombed some twenty nations). The Illuminati controlled Pol Pot regime then forcibly evicted the citizens of the Cambodian cities and villages, assigning them to agricultural work camps in order to create an agrarian national economy, and embarked on a genocidal campaign involving the murder of half of the nation's citizenry. So complete was the societal disintegration, that while an indifferent American public looked the other way, grass grew in the streets of Cambodia's cities.

Not only was this an example of authoritarianism at its worst, it is also a graphic example of the manner in which the Cambodian populace had been conditioned by Buddhism to embrace pacifism, thus negating the ability to defend themselves. Had the Cambodians formed partisan groups and waged a deadly guerrilla campaign against not only their Pol Pot authoritarian oppressors, but also against America for bombing them, instead of turning the other cheek, many Cambodian lives would have been spared.

Today, when weapons of almost unimaginable destructive power, all too often are under the control of bureaucrats and military leaders of very questionable stability and sobriety, it appears to Christians of all denominations, that events "predicted" in the *Book of Revelation* are rapidly coming to pass, when in reality, the truth of the matter is that the Illuminati and its military puppets are deliberately adopting the apocalyptic scenario as described in *Revelation,* including implementation of the infamous "Mark of the Beast."

Chapter 10

REVELATION REVEALED

"Secrets of wisdom are hidden by a variety of methods. Some are hidden under characters and symbols, others hide the secrets in a third manner by their method of writing with consonants only like the Hebrews, Chaldeans, Arabians and as the Greeks do....Fourthly, the obscuring is produced by intermixing various kinds of letters....Fifthly, authors hide their secrets by means of special letters devised by their own ingenuity and will, and different from those which are anywhere in use...."

Roger Bacon: "De Secretus Operibus."

The *Book of Revelation,* in all probability, was written by Julius Piso as a diatribe against his Roman oligarchical relatives, after his grandson was passed over as a successor to Emperor Hadrian. Instead, Antoninus, the son of Julius' sister Claudia, was nominated.

If the *Book of Revelation* primarily was written as an esoteric vehicle intended for the castigation of his relatives, the question to be addressed is: which group of esotericists was Piso attempting to influence through his diatribe? Admittedly, being related to both the Roman oligarchy and the former Herodian ruler of Judea, meant that Julius Piso was conversant with the Rites of Mithra. *Revelation* is, indeed, awash with Mithraic terminology. The fact remains however, that *Revelation* undoubtedly was targetted for a gnostic audience!

Gnosticism is a devolution of the esoteric knowledge transmitted in antiquity by the Phoenicians and other survivors of the Noahic flood, and largely became an amalgam of Mithraism and occultism. Stongly militaristic in nature, Mithraism placed great emphasis on the solar force, which was held to be masculine, and was assigned the numerological correspondence of 666. Similarly, gnostic adepts also embraced the solar belief structure, but stressed that it should be balanced by the earth force, which was claimed to be feminine in character, and was assigned the number 1080.

In the author's view, gnosticism contains a nucleus of esoteric knowledge, surrounded by an amorphous mass of nebulous mumbo jumbo, similar to that found in the higher degrees of Freemasonry and Illuminism.

After the fall of the Masada fortress in 73 A.D., a large segment of the remaining Covenant community, i.e. Essenes, Zadokites etc., settled in Ephesus. The city possessed a port that was rivaled only by Alexandria, due to its location at the mouth of the River Cayster. Some historians claim that several members of the Piso family lived for a time at Ephesus, as also may be deduced from the writings of Pliny. It is therefore possible that Julius Piso became aquainted with gnosticism in that city.

With the quelling of the Jewish uprising in 70 A.D., in which Julius Piso's father played a major role, Judea became a wasteland; the Herodian nobility emigrated to Rome, the quisling Sadducean priests had been put to the sword by the zealots, and the Pharisees preached pacifism and changed their appellation to rabbis. Since it was Julius Piso's apparent objective to expose his relative's newly-created religion which we know as Christianity, for the fraud that it certainly was, it would be logical for him to direct his literary work toward the various gnostic sects who had evolved from the desert communities of Judea. The members of these gnostic sects were the only Jews who were sufficiently millitant to oppose the new authoritarian religion known as Christianity.

That the principal author of the *Book of Revelation* was conversant with the gnostic doctrine, is evidenced by his use of the religious form of numerology known as gemmatria. He also incorporated into his work a curious literary device that was employed solely by gnostic writers: diametrically opposed dualities are highlighted through the selection of words possessing the same number of letters and even the same word shapes (in Greek). Thus the "bride" is opposed by the "harlot," likewise the "beast" is contrasted with the "lamb." The gnostics used this literary technique in order to add a heightened dimension to the written word, as a means of conveying to the reader that these apparent dualities are merely illusions. At an archetypal level, they are merely the material manifestation of universal forces which control the growth and decay of civilizations.

Another gnostic literary device used in *Revelation* is the application of gemmatraic multiples, such as the interrelationship between the "beast" (666) and " Jesus the annointed one" (2368) both being multiples of 37. The word "beast" occurrs thirty seven times in *Revelation.*

The main corpus of *Revelation* comprises two sections: the visions (Ch. 4 through 11) and Ch. 12 through 19, which are more polished, and probably were written by a literary aide to Julius Piso. Chapters 4 through 11 are in keeping with the tradition of the Jewish prophets in that they refer to the vision of a throne, an apocalyptic term of dominion. There are no recorded instances of throne visions occurring in Christian literature.

The chapters abound with references to Mithraism, the bestial symbology, the seven spirits, the crowns and the overall impression of brilliant light. Moreover, we are warned that these creatures are full of eyes, an expression dating back to antiquity, meaning the secret police of the Mithraists. This is probably a warning to the gnostics to be aware of mithraistic agents.

We are told in Chapter 5 that a lamb has seven horns. This could well be a mistranslation, for the Hebrew word for "horn" (*queren*) meaning "power," is very similar to the word for shining rays (*qaran*) which is very fitting for a description of a sun god.

The scroll described in Chapter 5 is very significant, for it was fastened with seven seals. This was a very specific type of Jewish document known as a *get Mequssar*, a bill of divorce. The bride and harlot symbology of *Revelation* supports this hypothesis, the writer urging the Jews to divorce solar worship and marry the New Jerusalem, with its balanced solar and earth forces. In addition to the solar worship that was prevalent among the Covenant sectarians, there are contemporary accounts stating that other Jews adopted solar worship during the 1st century A.D., in order to further their financial and political ambitions. The writing format of Chapter 5 is typically Jewish, and is similar to *Jeremiah 3: 8*, where Yahwey divorces Israel.

At the breaking of the first seal, a white horse appears. This is a somewhat ambiguous translation, for the word "white" in Greek (*leucos*) must be qualified to really mean "white," e.g. "white as snow," otherwise it usually means "gray." There is a possibility that a gray horse would signify an antichrist, disguised as a spiritual being.

The pair of scales associated with the breaking of the third seal is not symbolic of justice, but is an implication of famine, for the "quart of wheat for a denarius" referred to in the text, was many times the normal price, a denarius being the average daily wage. The voice commanding that the oil and wine not be injured (Ch. 6: 6) could be alluding to the edict issued by the Piso family friend Titus, during the siege of Jerusalem (66—70 A.D.) that olive groves and vineyards were to be protected. However, it is more likely that the reference is to the plundering of the Temple by a Jewish mob during the siege, the mob drinking the wine used in the rites of the Feast of Oil and Wine. This was a sacrilege which Titus (and probably the Piso family) considered warranting the destruction of the city.

We see a return to the divorce of Jerusalem in Chapter 10, where a person is told to swallow the scroll which would taste sweet, but would be bitter to the stomach. This meant that the sins of the Jews (spiritual adultery) would be sweet, but the consequences would be bitter. The text clearly is based upon a Jewish ritual, whereby a women accused of adultery, was obliged to eat a parchments scroll that had been soaked in bitter herbs, and bore a curse written by a priest. The passage bears a resemblance to *Numbers 5: 12—31.*

The second half of *Revelation* deals primarily with the judgement of the faithless Jerusalem (the harlot) and the creation of the New Jerusalem. The revelation appears to be very confused, for it begins (Chapter 12) with a reference to the sun god, the dragon being the night (in Egypt the seven-headed dragon represented chaos and darkness) and equated the dragon with Satan.

Forty miles to the north of the city of Ephesus lay the city of Smyrna. The author of the prophecy to Smyrna clearly reveals his non-Jewish background when he refers to the "synagogue of Satan," for the *Revelation* author clearly did not realize that in the *Book of Job,* the Satan was the rank of a deity, not the name of a person, who was regarded as a tester of humanity and a servant of God (*Job* predates all other biblical texts, and is believed to be an Arabian work). The passage probably was prompted because the Jews attained political power in Smyrna, and were opposed to Mithraism.

It is interesting to note that the description of a woman "....clothed with the sun, and the moon under her feet," bears a similarity to the Targum on *Song of Songs,* Ch. 6: 8) which describes the Hasmonean rebels "as being as beautiful as the moon and their good deeds as the sun." The woman appears to represent the gnostics, with their knowledge of the zodiac, while the dragon's diadem identifies the creature as the High Priesthood, the antithesis of Yahwey.

The birth pangs referred to were a traditional way of symbolizing the dawning of a new era. Chapter 12: 10—11, is totally alien to the literary style, and undoubtedly is a later Christian interpolation.

The reference to the beast with a fatal head wound, from which it miraculously recovers, probably refers to the Roman Empire and Arrius Piso's friend Vespasian. Vespasian was obliged to flee for his life after incurring the wrath of Nero, following the aborted assassination attempt on Nero's life. Vespasian later regained political favor, and together with his son Titus, quelled the Jewish revolt. As we saw in the previous chapter, the writer "Josephus" appears to have been a pseudo-nym of Arrius Piso. "Josephus" informs us that the Roman Empire mar-velled at the manner in which Vespasian accomplished his political comeback.

The "hail like hundredweights" released by the seventh angel in Chapter 16, also undoubtedly refers to Vespasian and his son, during the siege of Jerusalem. Roman catapults hurled very heavy white boul-ders on the beleagured Jewish defenders, who were able to dodge tham because of thier conspicuous brightness (the Romans later wised up and began painting their ammunition black).

We are told in Chapter 16 that the River Euphrates dried up and the sea turned to blood. The former could be a recollection of the Babylonian captivity, for Herodotus stated that Cyrus drained the Euphrates as he went to conquer Babylon. The sea is most likely an allu-sion to Lake Gennesareth, also known as the Sea of Galilee; this had been the site of a very bloody naval battle between Roman and Jewish vessels. At the conclusion of the battle, the carnage had been so great, according to "Josephus" that the entire lake was red with blood.

There has been much speculation concerning the location of the fabled Armageddon, the supposed site of the final global battle. Perhaps the key to this mystery is provided in *Isaiah 14: 13,* in which the mountain where the deities meet is called *Har Mo-ed* (the mountain of meeting). Armageddon is possibly a Greek corruption of *Har Moed,* and coulf be Mount Hermon, the source of the Jordan.

The remainder of *Revelation* progressively degenerates into pure Mithraism, until it culminates with the Lake of Fire, which is a mithraic term for Hades. The millenium is a rehash of a very ancient legend which pervades most religions. The Hinus believed that Vishnu, who incarnated in mortal form as Chrishna, is to return again at the completion of the great zodiacal year, in the month of Scorpio. He is supposed to return in the form of a warrior, riding a white horse and wielding a flaming scimitar. At his approach, the sun and moon will be darkened, the earth will tremble, and the stars shall fall.

Similarly, the Buddhists believe that Buddha will return to restore order. It was an ancient Persian belief that Zoroaster would return in order to usher in a millenium of peace; until this time, the earth would be subjected to endless wars and famine. At the second coming, the wicked would be purified with fire. It similarly was the belief of the Scandinavians of antiquity, that great calamities would afflict the world in the latter days, after which the Great Serpent would be chained and Odin would then reign supreme. Last but not least, the Celts believed that their redeemer Brian Boroihme, would return to inaugurate a millenium of peace.

Many theologians believe that the first three chapters of *Revelation* are an interpolation, added at a much later date, presumably by the mithraistic controllers of the Christian Church. This deception would have been perpetrated in order to smear the Gnostics, for the seven communities referred to were the last bastions of the Gnostic Church. It should be noted that although many translations of *Revelation* address the prophecies to seven churches, the original Greek text uses the word *"eklesia,"* which really means "community". This is reinforced by the prophecy to Smyrna, were the word *"sunagogue"* (synagogue) is specifically used when referring to a church.

After the fall of the Masada fortress, the Covenant sects were forced to disband, and some settled in Ephesus. It is understandable that the Mithraist author who wrote the first three chapters of *Revelation* should have been angered at the attitude of the Ephesus community, for "Josephus" informs us that its Jewish citizenry were exempt from military service, whereas mithraists always supported militarism.

Additional evidence that this particular interpolation author was a Mithraist occurrs in the passage attacking the Nikolaitans, who were one of the esoteric pillars of the early Christian Church. They were violently opposed to mithraistic doctrines. In addition to being prolific writers of esoteric works, the Nikolaitans specialized in conducting exorcism rites.

Theologians claim that the reference to the crown of life *(Ch. 2: 10)* was inspired by Aristides, who compared the city to the crown of Ariadne, but in view of the blatantly mithraic overtones in the opening chapters of *Revelation,* this is possibly a reference to the seven-rayed crown of Mithra, identical to that which adorns the Stature of Liberty.

After a mithraic novice had undergone twelve initiatory tests in a cave, he underwent an initiation ceremony which remained unchanged for centuries. He was baptized by immersion in water, the sign of the cross being made upon his forehead. The rite of the taurobolium followed, in which the novice was sprinkled with the blood of a newly-slaughtered bull, the blood symbolizing life. This rite clearly inspired the Piso family at a much later date to create the biblical phrase "sprinkled with the blood of Jesus." The final rite, prior to partaking of a symbolic meal of bread and wine, in the company of twelve Mithraic initiates, consisted of being offered a crown. The novice was obliged to refuse acceptance of the crown, stating: "My crown belongs to Mithra," thereby symbolizing the placing of Mithra the sun god above all else. Reference to the importance of one's crown occurs in Ch. 3: 11.

It is in the address to the community at Pergamum however, that the author leaves absolutely no doubt that he is an initiate of Mithra. The clue lies in the phrase "I will give him the hidden manna; also, I shall give him a white stone; and upon the white stone is written a new name, which no one knows except the recipient." Biblical scholars claim that the white stone was a *tessara,* which was used as a voting ballot, or an admission ticket, but such tessaras bore no secret inscription. And how do we account for the manna? The problem is resolved when we become aware that following initiation, the new soldier of Mithra was given manna (probably honey) and also a white stone bearing an inscribed name that was only revealed to the initiate.

The message toThyatira opens with a reference to "The Son of God." The appellation "Son of God" appears nowhere else in the Bible—the synoptic gospels only mentioning the "Son of Man." The title "Son of God" traditionally has been associated with Mithra, the intermediary between the Creator and humankind.

The sentence closes with a description of eyes like a flame of fire, which is very fitting for a sun god. The message ends with an assurance that the faithful will be given the Morning Star. In an oration, Emperor Julian, who was a purist Mithraist, and also the author of the *Hymn to Mithra,* associated the Morning Star with the privilege of sovereignty. Although the *Revelation* passage is too brief to be conclusive, it is suggestive that the interpolative author of the first three chapters was familiar with the Julian oration, and therefore lived after the 4th century A.D..

The address to Sardis makes reference to the seven spirits, who were the seven Amshaspands—the seven subordinate deities, of who Mithra was the chief. Two archaeological finds at Sardis were a small stone inscribed with Mithraic symbols (human, bird and animal effigies) and the portrait of a crowned priest. The crown was surmounted by twelve other crowned figures, signifying the twelve Mithraic initiates partaking of the eucharistic meal.

The key to undersanding the message to the community at Laodicea lies in the fact that the city was in Phrygia. Considerable debate has centered around the phrase "amen the faithful and true witness." Although the root *"amen"* means "trustworthy," some scholars feel that it was derived from a midrash text referring to Amon the Sun God.

Since Amon was a sun god, we should note that Phrygia was a center of Mithraism, the Phrygian forebear of Mithra being Attys, who was worshipped by the Phrygians as "The only begotten son." Attys was represented in murals as a man nailed to a stake, tethered at the foot of which was a lamb. The 3rd century church father Lanctantius, said of Attys, known to the Jews as Tammuz: "He was a mortal man according to the flesh, wise in miraculous works; but, being arrested by an armed force by command of the Chaldean judges, he suffered a death made bitter with nails and stakes."

Revelation is perhaps best known for the number of the Beast. Many attempts have been made to associate the Beast with emperors, popes and Hitler, but none of these really comply with the 666 format without a great deal of manipulation.

Scholars appear to have overlooked the fact that the principal author of *Revelation* was well versed in gnosticism, and was writing in a format familiar only to gnostics. The cryptic number of the beast would therefore require to be analyzed in a manner in keeping with gnostic thought.

The Spanish monk Beatus, wrote a strange manuscript in which he stated: "This is wisdom: he who has understanding, let him count the number of the Beast. For it is the number of a man, that is, of Christ, whose name the beast takes for itself." Beatus probably arrived at this startling conclusion by applying gemmatria to the entire phrase: "and his number is six hundred, three score and six," which totals 2368—the gemmatraic numerical equivalent of Jesus Christ.

The author reinforces this theme three more times in the same chapter by use of the phrase: "the image of the beast," which has the gemmatraic equivalent of 2260, as does "the Son of Man," which occurrs in the following chapter of *Revelation*.

Although this comparison appears strange and unsettling to those of a Christian background, it should be noted that the 666 solar force represents the masculine, generative force, the initiator of materialistic, instead of spiritual activity. Nations are animated by the power and justice of their leaders; when unrestrained, the 666 force is a director of tyrannical governments and the procreator of a society obsessed with violence, world power and material gain, as is presently exemplified by the United States. When correctly fused with the earth force, the 666 energy assists in building a society possessing balance, vigor and spirituality. It should be noted that some of the magnificent Gothic Cathedrals of Europe incorporate the Magic Square of the Sun into their architecture; in such a magic square, each line of numerals totals 666.

It is worth noting that in the Babylonian Mysteries, the mighty ruler Nimrod was worshipped as *Saturn*, the hidden god, who could only be known after initiation into the Mysteries, which presumably is why the *Litany of the Mass* of the Catholic Church contains the phrase: "God hidden, and my Saviour, have mercy upon us." "Saturn" was written "*Stür.*" in the language of the Babylonians, which gematraically equates to 666.

The action of the Piso family in glorifying the solar force, was the antitheses of gnostic belief. The author of *Revelation* possibly provides us with a cryptic clue to the mythical deity who misdirects the application of the solar force, when he states" "Here is wisdom necessary," for the Hebrew word for wisdom *(hokmah)* the initial letter of which *(heth)* has the numerical equivalent of eight under the kabbalistic system of the gnostics. This is also the corresponding number of Cybele, the Queen of Heaven, who also was known as Isis and Ashtoreth. The latter, according to legend, was banished from heaven and cast into hell. The *Old Testament* prophets repeatedly admonished the Jews for worshipping her.[1]

It was a tradition in biblical times for initiates of Mithra to be tat-
tooed, either on the forehead or wrist, with the sign of the cross; during
the short reign of Emperor Julian (361—363) it was impossible to conduct trade in Rome, unless one bore the mark of Mithra.[2]

It is a sad reflection upon religious organizations that the passage in
the *Book of Revelation* Chapter 21, regarding the dimensions of the New
Jerusalem, is of such little concern to the majority of those professing
the Christian faith, for it tells us a great deal about the ideology of its
author.

The New Jerusalem was a term which originated with the Montanist
sect, who believed that the mythical city would miraculously descend
from heaven, and alight near the Turkish town of Pepuza. Mention of
the New Jerusalem in *Revelation,* reveals the deep esoteric background
of its author. He appears to have been indoctrinated into Montanism,
for the stated dimensions of the fabled city are very meaningful when
one applies the science of geomancy to them. Also of importance is the
emphasis placed in *Revelation* on the waters flowing beneath the New
Jerusalem; all ancient temples which possessed cosmic associations,
such as the Hieropolis and Stonehenge, were constructed over complex
networks of underground streams. Similarly, it was customary, even in
medieval times, to construct Christian churches with the baptismal font
located directly over a blind spring (a spring which does not reach the
surface of the ground).[3]

The founder of the sect, Montanus, and his two seers Priscilla and
Maximilla, were the originators of Pentecostalism (enlightenment
through the descent of the spirit). The Montanists believed that the
descent of the New Jerusalem would herald the birth of a new spiritual
millenium. They attracted a very large following during the formative
years of Christianity, but later incurred the wrath of the Catholic
Church, for questioning the Vatican's false claim of divinely appointed
rule. According to the *Encyclopedia Britannica,* the Montanists used hal-
lucenogenic drugs, and were known as the Illuminati.[4]

Montanus was a contemporary of Julius Piso; Saint Jerome claims that Montanus was a former priest of the ecstatic cult of the mother goddess Cybele, whose consort was Attys, the Phrygian name for Mithra.

In the present era, those curious figures known as magic squares are regarded as mere mathematical curiosities, yet in ancient times, important buildings were constructed with the principal dimensions corresponding to the numbers depicted in magic squares. These magic squares were assigned astronomical names, such as the Magic Square of the Sun and the Magic Square of Mars; the Gothic cathedral at Lichfield, England, incorporates in its architecture the latter magic square. This fact should be of importance to Bible students, for the dimensions of the New Jerusalem, as depicted in the *Book of Revelation,* correspond to the Magic Square of the Sun, whose individual lines of numbers, vertically, horizontally and diagonally, total 666. In other words, magic squares are sacred numerical canons, which enable us to construct buildings which possess the capability of establishing resonance with the cosmos.

As C.A. Browne commented in his book *"Magic Squares and Cubes:"* "When Plato's advice is followed and the mutual relationships between our sciences are understood we may perchance find this clue, and having found it be surprised to discover as great a simplicity underlying the whole fabric of natural phenomenma as exists in the construction of a magic square."

In Laws 656, Plato attributes the stability of the Egyptian civilization to their use of a cosmological canon of numbers. Not surprisingly perhaps, the dimensions of the New Jerusalem, as stated in *Revelation,* enables the construction of that ancient yonic figure known as the *Vesica Pisces.* As the 19th. Century writer Dr. Oliver commented: "This curious figure Vesicus Pisces possessed an unbounded influence in the details of sacred architecture; and it constituted the great and enduring secret of our ancient brethren. The plans of our religious buildings were determined by its use; and the proportions of length and height were dependent upon it alone." 5

Our brief analysis of the *Book of Revelation* clearly reveals that its author was not only conversant with the ceremonial rites of Mithra, but also was well versed in the esoteric canon of numbers, which had been transmitted down through the ages by initates of the Mystery School network. This implies that the author, presumably Julius Piso, was an initiate of Rome's most prestigious Mystery School—the Royal Institute of Architects, whose best-known member in the 1st. Century A.D. was Marcus Vitruvius Pollio, who was noted for his use of sacred geometry, as well as his study of harmonious human proportions. How paradoxically disquieting it is that Christian Fundamentalists revere the *Book of Revelation,* yet insinuate that students of esoteric science are following in Satan's footsteps.

Readers are advised to overlook the fact that the author of *Revelation* attempts to infuse new life into the ancient and puerile Brahmanic myth concerning the messianic second coming, and the baiting of the evangelical hook by promising eternal salvation via the rapture. Despite such false dogma, the *Book of Revelation* is still a work of great importance to us, due to its commentary regarding the mark of the Beast, the emphasis upon the Mithraic number 666 and the descent of the New Jerusalem.

Christianity, in keeping with most religions, is an authoritarian political device which is intended for the subjugation and polarization of a large segment of humanity, through the dissemination of fear and false dogma. We have only to consider the millions of hapless victims who have died at the hands of religious inquisitors, whose only "crime" had been to have owned property coveted by a very rapacious and psychotic priesthood, or the numerous wars fought for the glory of a bloodthirsty god, to realize the hypocracy generated by Judaism and Christianity through the centuries (at least Islam requires that neither women, children nor living trees be harmed by its devotees during wartime).

Establishment historians conveniently overlook the machinations of the Jesuits and their Black Pope behind major political upheavals, e.g. the Black Pope Lorenzo Ricci, who employed the precepts of the ancient Chinese military strategist Sun-tzu in order to initiate and orchestrate the American Revolution, for the purpose of impeding the growth of the Protestant dominated British Empire. How many Protestants would remain freemasons if they were aware that the "unknown superior" to whom their Grand Master reported, was the Black Pope? Much of the American populace would be startled to discover that when President George Washington assigned Jesuit educated Congressman Daniel Carroll to select land on which to build the nation's capital city, Carroll selected a property listed in the property records as "Rome"—now known as the District of Columbia!

The Illuminati controlled newsmedia currently takes great pains to avoid mention of the sado-masochistic Jesuit secret societety known as *Opus Dei,* even though it is one of the most powerful and influential financial institutions of the present era. This secret society was founded in 1928 in Spain by Josemaria Escriva, best known for his mercurial temper and his addiction to self flagellation; unmarried members are required to wear a spiked chain known as a *Cilice,* around the upper thigh for two hours every day, and to whip themselves thirty-three strokes per week. Initiates are prohibited from informing family members of their involvement in this very pernicious sado-masochistic society, which orders its members not to display photographs of loved ones. The cult is so highly regarded by Pope John Paul II that he has granted the cult the status of personal prelature, thus making Opus Dei answerable solely to its own prelate (the pope's personal spokesperson is a member, as are persons formerly involved in the Vatican Bank scandal. Especially disturbing are the allegations that former FBI director Louis

Freeh and two current members of the U.S. Supreme Court are members of Opus Dei (Freeh's son purportedly attends an Opus Dei school).

In concluding this chapter, perhaps it is timely to reflect upon the fact that even though most churches and synogogues throughout the western world contain well-appointed catering facilities, their doors almost invariably remain closed to the multitudes of homeless and ill-nourished people, who are to be found on the streets of any metropolis. Unless the Christian and Jewish religious sects are prepared to delve deeply into their copius coffers, and offer sustenance and compassion to the homeless, they surely must remain the religions of the damned.

It is not the intent of the author to foment antagonism toward any present day religious institution, but rather to foster a move toward transforming them into bastions of spiritual enlightenment and good fellowship. Until this occurrs, we are surely destined to continue the endless cycles of war and peace fostered by the Illuminati for the personal agrandizement of its members.

CHAPTER 11

▼

WHO WAS KING ARTHUR?

"At length he came to an island named after him Britannia,
dwelt there and filled it with his descendants."

Nennius—British Chronicles.

The reader will recall that the seafaring exploits of the Phoenicians were discussed previously in Chapter 4. The subject is briefly being reiterated, in order to clarify a widely-held misperception concerning the origins of the British. Earlier in this book, for the purposes of convention, it was implied that the early Britons were Celts, but this is incorrect, even though the British were part of the Celtic Commonwealth. Sadly, Christian Fundamentalists have been conditioned to believe that the term *"British"* was derived from the Hebrew words *"B'rith,"* meaning "covenant," and *"Ysh,"* meaning "man."

The Christian Fundamentalists and Mormons claim that the British are the descendants of the lost tribes of Israel, primarily the tribe of Dan. According to the Fundamentalists, the first Israelites to settle in Britain were Princess Tea Tephi and her retinue, circa 1250 B.C.. As was stated previously in this book, the Danites were also known as the Sea Peoples, who "dwelt on ships," according to the Bible, and lived in Pho enician territory. This almost certainly implies that they were Phoenicians, not Israelites.

The fact that the British clearly are the descendants of Phoenician colonists, as exemplified by inscriptions on ancient British monoliths, is not the only obfuscated facet of early British history.[1] The truth behind the legend of King Arthur also has been obscured, both by political expediency and also with the passage of time. Are the stories of his exploits and his final mysterious boat trip to Avalon true? Or is it all merely a romantic fable?

Arthur purportedly was born circa 475 A.D.. At the time of his birth, Rome had withdrawn its four occupying legions and the eastern half of Britain was under Anglo-Saxon rule. Early British history was not committed to writing, but followed an oral tradition whereby trained bards meticulously transmitted historical event by word of mouth, and history was not committed to writing until several centuries had elapsed. Unfortunately, key manuscripts such as the *Northern Annals,* which disappeared in the 13th. Century, are no longer available to us. Consequently, the two remaining principal sources of the Arthurian legend are the *Histories of the Kings of Britain,* and *Chronicles of Scotland,* by the medieval historians Geoffrey of Monmouth and Hector Boece, respectively.

Significantly, Geoffrey's epic incorporates *"Merlin's Book of Prophecy,"* which includes the passage: "The island shall be called Britain from the name of Brutus...." thus corroborating the above remarks by the writer Nennius concerning King Brutus the Phoenician.

Subsequent writers and troubadors have romanticized these works until today, the popular image, especially in the movies, is of a band of knights in shining armor, salleying forth from a stone castle to fight dragons and rescue damsels in distress. In reality, Arthur would have lived at a time prior to the construction of stone fortresses in Britain, and would have worn leather armor. The association with dragons probably stems from the fact that the Saint George and the dragon fable originated in King Brutus's homeland of Phoenicia.

Geoffrey locates the locale of the Arthurian battles in the vicinity of Camelot Dun, now called Winchester; this presents a chronological problem, since that region of southern Britain was already occupied and settled by the Anglo Saxons by the time of Arthur's alleged birth.

Some historians assert that the battles were fought in Cornwall, which in that era was a larger region than at present, but this is problematical since the Anglo-Saxons did not claim Cornwall, thus eliminating the potential for armed conflict. After conducting exhaustive research, philologist Professor Norma Lorre Goodrich has concluded that King Arthur was a Romano-Briton who fought his battles in the border country between England and Scotland. She suggests that the mortally-wounded monarch was taken across the sea to Avalon, which she postulates is Saint Patrick's Isle, located in the stormy Irish Sea. This small island was indeed used in antiquity as a necropolis.[2]

The majority of medieval manuscript references to King Arthur's chief residence, known as Camelot, located it at the northern English city of Caerleon—now known as Carlisle. Admittedly, Gerald of Wales (c.1147–1223) claimed that the south-western English town of Glastonbury was the fabled Camelot, and that the grave of Arthur and his Queen were opened there in 1191, but there is no record of armed conflict between Arthur's knights and the Anglo-Saxons in the Glastonbury region. A lead cross was recovered from the grave bearing a text in debased uncials; this type of font was not in use until after Arthur's lifetime. When investigating the patterns of the past, it is wise to follow the money trail, for Gerald was under the patronage of the Benedictine Abbot of Glastonbury; making the spurious claim that Arthur was buried there would have not only have been good for the lucrative pilgrim trade, but would also discredit his rival Geoffrey of Monmouth, who was an Augustinian.

The exemplary research effort of Professor Goodrich leaves little doubt that a British ruler named Arthur fought a series of battles in the border country of northern England, during the 6th century A.D..

It is understandable that the story of Arthur still would be known today, in the border country of northern England, where a local ruler fought his battles during the 6th. Century, but why would the exploits of a local chieftan, whose ineffectual battles fought in a remote region were not even mentioned in the *Anglo-Saxon Chronicles,* attain such heroic proportions not only in southern England, but also throughout western Europe?

Something is clearly amiss with the Arthurian epic as presented by the medievalist historians. Bearing in mind that these events were only committed to writing many centuries after they had occurred, the author suggests that the medieval writers confused the activities of two different rulers who lived some four centuries apart. As a result, the King Arthur of legend is, in actuality, a composite of the 6th century border chieftan named Arthur and Caractacus (Caradoc) of the first century of the present era.

As we saw in the previous chapter, Caractacus was a person of very high ideals, who was held in high esteem by his Roman captors and, together with his daughters, became the toast of Roman society. Moreover, Caractacus bore the tribal appellation *Arwiragus* (Arthur) derived from the British *Arto,* meaning "bear". According to both Geoffrey of Monmouth and Hector Boece, Arwiragus became famous not only in Rome, but also throughout Europe.

Caractacus' father Cybelline married twice, Caractacus being the offspring of the second marriage. Cymbelline's first marriage was to an Alban princess, who bore three children. One of them (Clarine) who married the Ban of Benwick, gave birth to a son, the fabled Lancelot.

The claim made by Geoffrey of Monmouth that the Arthurian battles were fought in the vicinity of Camelot Dun (the former name for Winchester, in southern England) would not be correct for an Arthur living in the 6th century A.D., whose battles were fought in the north, but would substantially be in conformance with the known military campaigns of Caractacus during the 1st Century A.D.. Apart from some skirmishes in Wales in 51 A.D., Caractacus' major battles were all fought in southern England.[3]

The legendary Lady of the Lake may well have been Anna (the purported sister of Caractacus) who was married to Aaron Rheged. He bore the appellation *"Lychlyn,"* meaning "lake," thus possibly making Anna the Lady of the Lake who gave Arthur (Caractacus) the sword Excalibur. As we have seen, the Phoenicians established colonies in Britain at an earlier historical period. Excalibur therefore may represent the Phoenician Sun Cross. This frequently adopted the form on Hittite seals of a human arm holding an upright ankh, symbolizing divine victory. The myth concerning Arthur withdrawing the sword from the stone may likewise be symbolic of the separation of the inner spiritual light (represented by the sword) from the rock (indicative of the material world).[4]

An Arthurian narrative would not be complete without mention of the enigmatic Merlin, who has been transformed (particularly by ill informed New Age writers) from a mortal into a fabled wizard, replete with pointed hat and magic wand.

Professor Goodrich has postulated that he was Dubricious, who was born circa 450 A.D. and was appointed Archbishop of Carlisle; this would place him in the same geographic region and time period as the Arthur who fought in the border country of northern England. According to Geoffrey of Monmouth's *"The Prophecy of Merlin,"* he was a contemporary of King Vortigern, who ascended the throne circa 425 A.D..

In all probability there were a number of Merlins spanning several centuries, for the term "Merlin" is an agnomen, a title, not the name of a person, just as *The Book of Job* emphasizes that the Satan is the title of a deity who sat at the right hand of Yahwey.

Merlin is the ancient Cornish name for a blackbird, which suggests that the person who was appointed the Merlin was associated with the druidic order known as the *Black Man* during the time of Caractacus, in the 1st century A.D.. It was a very great honor to be appointed to the position of the Black Man, for the successful candidate had to be extremely adept in the esoteric sciences, especially in the art of rain-making. The fact that Merlin is best remembered for his seemingly occult powers rather than for evangelical prowess, implies that Geoffrey may have confused the Black Man of the 1st century A.D. with a major Christian evangelist who lived several centuries later. The Black Man may well have been transformed into the Black Knight of the medieval Grail romances.

Sadly, what we perceive as history is all too frequently a distorted image of historical events, presented in a manner that justifies the actions of the victors.[5] Such appears to be the case with the Arthurian epic, where important historical data appears to have been destroyed or suppressed, in order to enhance the political clout of the unpopular British monarch King Henry II (1133-1189).

Unfortunately for the lay reader, the perception of this monarch which we have been given by present day medievalists, has been deter-mined primarily by the cultural and spiritual idiosyncracies of the historians in question.[6] Thus to a historian with a Thomist outlook, the primary feature of Henry II reign was his replacement of the traditional feudal system of government with administrative kingship.[7] To a British commoner living in the 12th. Century A.D. however, Henry's principal characteristic was his ruthless lust for power.

Hailing from Anjou, the French center of occultism, Henry II was the first English Plantagenet monarch. After peremptorily declaring himself Lord of Scotland and Wales (the prosperous Scottish wool trade with the Continent doubtlessly providing an incentive) Henry's zeal for power led him to order the murder of the querulous Thomas Becket, Archbisop of Canterbury, then proceeded to conquer Ireland in 1171.[8]

A mentally unbalanced individual (for a time he went naked in public and chewed straw) Henry became alarmed upon learning of an ancient prophecy which claimed that King Arthur did not die, but would return again. This prompted the unpopular monarch to have what he claimed was Arthur's grave at Glastonbury opened, thus "proving" to the super-stitious populace that Arthur really was dead, and could not return to lead a rebellion.

The Arthurian legend became the confused amalgam of fact and fable that we have today, largely due to Henry's disinterest in his wife, Eleanor of Aquitaine, who left him and returned to her very extensive French domains. One of her daughters, Marie de Champagne, commis-sioned Chrétien de Troyes to write an Arthurian romance. Since adul-tery was a favorite pastime at Marie's court, Chrétien, who specialized in writing lurid tales involving rape and mayhem in general, created a fantasy in which Queen Guinevere commits adultery with Lancelot. Chrétien probably added factual Scottish history to his romantic fable, for he had access to at least one manuscript from Beauvais Abbey, in France, whose monks were instrumental in reorganizing the adminis-trative structure during the 12th century.

The Arthurian epic presents us with a paradox: on the one hand it depicts a fearless leader who displayed great vision and very high ideals; on the other hand it spawned the concept of the despotic Round Table of the present era.[9]

The Arthur/Caractacus of the 1st century A.D. undoubtedly realized that the druidic priesthood had been unable to inspire and unify the British with a spiritual zeal. It is why he probably attempted to accom-plish this task through his promotion of Christianity. The early British form of Christianity is exalted throughout the Arthurian literary corpus (there is no historical evidence that Joseph of Arimathea ever founded the first British Church at Glastonbury, as is claimed by numerous writ-ers; the *Welsh Triads* claim that Christianity was introduced to Britain in 37 A.D. by Illid, who founded a church at Inys-witryn, now known as the Isle of Wight. The church's administration allegedly was transferred to Glastonbury in 63 A.D.).

Even though the ravages of time has severely distorted the Arthurian legend, we are still bestowed with the legacy of a magnificent individual, a righter of wrongs, who triumphed in the face of extreme adversity and even today, still grips our imagination.

CHAPTER 12

▼

THE TEMPLARS—SAINTS OR SINNERS?

"Since many Templars now disport themselves on this side of the sea, riding their gray horses or taking their ease in the shade and admiring their own fair locks; since they so often set a bad example to the world; since they are so outrageously proud that one can hardly look them in the face: tell me, Batard, why the Pope continues to tolerate them; tell me why he permits them to misuse the riches which were offered them for God's service on dishonorable and even criminal ends."

Rostan Berenguier, circa 1306 A.D..

Jerusalem in the 12th century A.D., was the veritable hub of the known world to Jew and Gentile alike, for it was in this ancient city that Solomon purportedly built his Temple on Mount Moriah, and where the Church of the Holy Sepulchre housed a vessel which provided inspiration for the writers of the Grail romances.[1] King Solomon's Temple was constructed in the 10th century B.C, for the alleged purpose of housing the Ark of the Covenant, and was destroyed by the Babylonians in 575 B.C..

Unfortunately for humankind in general, an Arab mosque known formally as the Mosque of Omar and colloquially as the Dome of the Rock, was built on what is incorrectly believed to have been the site of the Temple, an act which not only resulted in bloodshed during the Crusades, but may occur again in the very near future. Fundamentalist Jewish and Christian fanatics operating under the control of the *Quator Coronati* masonic research lodge, have declared their intent to destroy the Dome of the Rock and the adjacent Al Aqsa mosque, and rebuild the Temple. If their insane plan is implemented, it will certainly precipitate a Holy War involving the global powers—a W.W.III scenario devised long ago by the Illuminati hierarchy, who thrive on genocide and chaos.

A wind of change swept through Europe during the 11th century A.D.. Prior to that era, most European nobles were lawless, rapacious thugs, who devoted much of their time to murder and mayhem, in order to swell the family coffers, and accordingly were regarded with disdain by the various religious orders of Christendom. It became evident to the Christian hierarchy that by persuading knights of noble status to lead a series of religious crusades, with the intent of wresting control of the Holy Land from Muslim hands, Europe would not only rid itself of its licentious knightly nobles for several years, but there was a distinct possibility that some of the spoils of war might find their way into the papal treasury.

The 11th century wind of change brought not only the Norman Conquest of England, which resulted in a high degree of political unification throughout much of western Europe, but also a religious zeal among the general population that was directed by the church fathers against the Muslim rulers of Palestine. This virulent outbreak of religious fanaticism resulted in the First Crusade, which in turn led to the capture of Jerusalem in 1099 A.D., and the formation of the chivalric Most Venerable Military and Hospitaller Order of Saint John of

Jerusalem. This order was founded by Godfrey de Bouillon ostensibly for the purposes of establishing hospices, guarding the Church of the Holy Sepulchre and making Palestinian roads safe for pilgrims.

Like many Christian endeavors which are conducted in the name of God, the appalling bloodlust displayed by the members of the First Crusade during the storming of Jerusalem, fills one with revulsion. According to the Koran, Allah led Muhammed to the site of the Dome of the Rock; Jerusalem accordingly is the third holiest city of Islam, after Mecca and Medina. In an orgy of bloodletting, the crusaders burned alive Jews who had sought sanctuary in their synagogue, and spent a week massacring Muslims, including many who had taken refuge within the Al Aqsa mosque.

Commenting on the bestial nature of the typical crusader, Saint Bernard of Clairvaux noted that: "It is really convenient that you will find very few men in the vast multitude which throngs the Holy Land who have not been unbelieving scoundrels, sacreligious plunderers, homicides, perjurers, adulterers, whose departure from Europe is certainly a double benefit, seeing that people in Europe are glad to see the back of them, and the people to whose assistance they are going to the Holy Land are delighted to see them! It is certainly beneficial to those who live on both sides of the sea, since they protect one side and desist from molesting the other!"[2]

One outcome of the crusades which largely has been overlooked, is the imprint that it has left on today's banking establishment. The transportation of soldiers and supplies overland to the Holy Land represented a major logistical problem for the military planners of the crusades. The situation proved to be a major economical boon for the Italian mechant fleets and shipbuilders of Genoa, Pisa and Venice however, who transported not only the soldiers, horses and materiel for the crusades, but also the thousands of pilgrims, who were caught up in the religious fervor of the times. Exploiting this new source of wealth to the fullest, the merchants aquired exclusive trading rights, including exemptions from custom duties in the now Christianized seaports of the Levant; on the return trip, the ships transported lucrative cargoes such as spices, which commanded high prices in the European marketplace.

The trade was even more enhanced after Constantinople, the richest city in the world at the time, was plundered during the 2nd crusade of 1204 A.D.. Funding for this largely maritime venture was provided by the banking institutions known as the *fondi,* which were owned by the noble families of Venice and Genoa; this sudden influx of major capital catapulted these rapacious families into rarified realms of political influence, the effects of which are still very much in evidence today.

In 1582 for instance, a cabal of Venetian oligarchic banking families created a political strategic planning group known as the *Giovanni,* whose principal objective was the creation of wars by means of a divide and conquer policy. Among the group's participants was the Servite monk Paolo Sarpi. One of the most famous and controversial European figures of his time, Sarpi exerted great influence over King James 1st, and the Rosicrucian pederast Sir Francis Bacon. Sarpi was one of the major architects of the Protestant Reformation and the Thirty Year's War. The Genoese and Venetian banking nobility (e.g. Horatio Pallavincini) were instrumental in the establishment of the notorius pseudo-religious intelligence cult known as the *Society of Jesus* (the Jesuits).

It was in the aftermath of the genocidal 1st crusade that a small band of French knights rode into Jerusalem in 1119, and were permitted by King Baldwin 1st. of Jerusalem to establish their command post in a portion of the Al Aqsa mosque, on the Temple Mount. Under the leadership of French nobleman Hugh de Payens, the group called themselves the Order of the Poor Knights of Christ, and claimed that they intended to police the road travelled by pilgrims between the port of Jaffa and Jerusalem. Since the knightly group supposedly only totalled nine in number, this was an odd claim, since the much larger Hospitaller Order already had been patrolling the same road for several years. In addition, the knights seldom left their headquarters during the first seven years of their Jerusalem sojourn.

Clearly the knights had a very covert agenda that had nothing to do with patrolling the highways. Perhaps this explains why Hugh de Payens made at least two prior visits to Jerusalem, accompanied by the Count of Champagne. Recently, a team of Israeli archaeologists discovered that the knights had dug an exploratory tunnel in the Temple Mount.[3] The knights clearly were searching for something, but what?

Prior to the second sacking of the Temple in 70 A.D., the Temple was not only a place of worship; it also was a major center of commerce, where thousands of sacrificial animals were bought and sold, the monetary proceeds from such transactions greatly adding to the Temple treasury. Just as the Temple treasures had been safely hidden prior to the Babylonian destruction of the first Temple, as stated in an earlier chapter, so it is probable that the Jewish priesthood took steps to hide the Temple artifacts and much of its gold before the Romans stormed the Temple.[4]

In addition, the knights were almost certainly searching for the Ark of the Covenant, which had purportedly reposed in the first Temple prior to the Temple's destruction, after which it had mysteriously disappeared. There is no record of it being taken as booty by the conquering Babylonians, but an Ethiopian text written in the 13th century A.D. called the *Kebra Nagast* (Glory of Kings) claimed that the Ark of the Covenant had surreptitiously been removed from the Temple by Menelik, the alleged son of the Queen of Sheba and King Solomon. According to the text, the Ark eventually arrived in Ethiopia, where, according to local tradition, it resides today in the city of Axum. This story is patently false. The Ethiopian Ark is a fake—the true Ark of the Covenant (which does not contain the Ten Commandments) resides at an Illuminati underground facility at Karnak, in Egypt, surrounded by water. It should be noted that there is no historical evidence that King

Solomon ever existed, the biblical story of his life almost certainly being an apocryphal fabrication of the Levites.

Although most knights of that period were at best only semi-literate, one of the knights at the Temple Mount was André de Montbard. In all probability, his nephew, Saint Bernard of Clairvaux, had instructed the knights to search for hidden documents, in addition to other Temple artifacts. Of not inconsiderable significance is the fact that all the founding knights in the order hailed from the French province of Champagne, where the city of Troyes was shortly to become a focal point for Templar related activities.

It was at the church-convened Council of Troyes in 1128 A.D., that Saint Bernard secured authorization for the Poor Knights of the Temple to become a religious militia. This was a radical innovation for that era in which the affairs of state were sharply delineated between the Church of Rome, whose members were forbidden to shed blood, and the nobility, who were not adverse to murder and mayhem if it resulted in an opportunity to enlarge their estates. Caught in between the two factions were the European monarchs, who considered it their divine right to rule.

The action of the Council in making the fledgling Templar Order an arm of the Papacy, fitted into Saint Bernard's goal of creating a theocratic New World Order. In an effort to forestall any criticism from clerics concerning the proposed amalgam of religiosity and killing, Saint Bernard hypocritically commented: "The soldier of Christ kills safely; he dies more safely. He serves his own interest in dying, and Christ's interest in killing!" Not to be outdone by the politically-powerful Saint Bernard, the inappropriately named Pope Innocent II, in his papal bull *Omne datum optimum,* claimed that a dead Templar whose hands were stained with the blood of an unbeliever, would attain eternal life.

Having been declared a religious order, the Templars were now permitted to wear a white mantle emblazoned with a red cross. In contrast to the impoverished nature of the Templar Order during the first seven years of its existence, it suddenly aquired not only widespread recognition and acceptance in Catholic Europe, but also became the recipient of financial donations and large estates, provided by various monarchs and noble families throughout Christendom.

The sudden influx of great wealth, largely due to the public relations capability and political clout of Saint Bernard, necessitated the creation of a large administrative system, not only for the recruitment of knights, but also for handling the transfer of supplies and currency to the Templars in the Holy Land.

The Templar Order was run on feudal lines, with knights predominantly recruited from the lower echelons of the aristocratic warrior families. The knights were the only Templars who were permitted to wear the white mantles, the remainder, who managed the numerous estates, or were foot soldiers, wore either black or brown mantles. As the size of the Templar administration and its monetary wealth grew, it pioneered practices such as the issuance of letters of credit, which are the foundation of the modern banking system. Its temples and preceptories were so secure that the royal treasury of France was deposited in the Order's Parisian Temple. They also were appointed tithe and tax collectors for the papacy and various monarchs respectively.

The Templars maintained cordial relationships with several of Europe's monarchs and princes; Aymeric de St. Maur, the Templar Grand Master of England was King John's closest advisor, who persuaded the reluctant monarch to sign the Magna Carta. What academia has never revealed to history students, as far as the author has been able to determine, is that in 1203, King John, in his capacity as Crown Corporation Sole of England, assigned England and her dominions, *in perpetuity* to the Vatican Corporation Sole. In return, the Pope, in his role of Vicar of Christ, assigned the Crown Corporation Sole of England, the right to administrate England and her dominions, in perpetuity, on behalf of the Vatican Corporation Sole. This is why Federal trials in America are held under British Admiralty (Military) Law, not

Common Law, signified by the gold fringe bordering the United States flags displayed in Federal institutions. As previously stated, even the District of Columbia is built on a parcel of land formerly named Rome.

With some of their newly found wealth, the Templars constructed numerous fortresses throughout Europe and the Holy Land; the Hospitallers who, like the Templars, had converted from a purely charitable to a militaristic religious order, followed suit. Hospitaller castles incorporated the latest European defensive architecture, as exemplified by their Syrian fortress at Krak (to which several major Nazis fled at the conclusion of W.W.II) but the Templars, who frequently fraternized with their Muslim enemies, built castles with a pronounced Muslim architectural influence, e.g. Chastel Pélerin, erected near the Holy Land city of Athlit.

The crusaders received a severe setback in 1144 A.D., when the Christian principality of Edessa surrendered to a Muslim army under the command of Imad ad-Din Zangi, the Atabeg of Aleppo and Mosul. Two years later, Zangi was assassinated by one of his own servants, who was of Frankish descent. That night, Mahmoud, a son of Zangi, removed his father's signet ring and placed it on his own finger, in the process dedicating his life to the unification of Islamic nations.[6] He bore the appellation Nuram ad Din (the Light of the Faith). Unlike the Christian Crusaders, most of whom were illiterate, murderous thugs, the Muslim warrior was not only expected to conduct his fighting in accordance with the precepts of Islamic law, but also was expected to be a scholar. Nuram ad Din was no exception to the rule: he was accompanied in his travels by learned Sufis, and lived frugally, thereby abiding with the Islamic concept of equality for all members of society.

Nuram ad Din won the respect of the Muslim commoners for his adherence to Islamic principles, and was appointed Sultan after declaring a *Jihad*. The *Jihad* was waged not against Christianity itself, for Muslims had become tolerant of other religions by that time, but against the Crusaders, for the Koran forbids Muslims to strike the first blow *(2:191)* but adds that persecution is worse than killing, and accordingly must be curtailed.

Nuram ad Din appointed a young Kurdish man by the name of Yusuf to be Vizier of Egypt in 1169 A.D.. The thirty-one year old Yusuf was a slightly-built man with a dazzling smile and a sensitive nature, who had an abhorrence of war. Reluctant to live in Egypt, which was politically unstable, Yusef, through no effort of his own, suddenly found himself ensconced in the Vizier's palace, clothed in the traditional Vizier's regalia of gold and white turban, scarlet-lined tunic and jewelled sword. Disregarding the luxurious palace ambience, Yusef personally adopted the frugal lifestyle expected of a Muslim ruler, engaging in religious study and distributing large sums of money to the poor. Fearless in the campaign against the Crusaders, he was always in the thick of the battle, which helped achieve a unified sense of purpose among his troops, according to his biographer Baha ad Din.

Nur ad Din died of a heart attack in 1174 A.D., and Yusaf became Sultan with the title Salah ad-Din ((the Righteousness of the Faith). By this time his fearless and wise leadership of the Muslim *Jihad* had earned him respect among the Crusaders, who called him Saladin; in addition, he was revered by the Muslims for his compassion and accessibility to his subjects.

Many European Crusaders and pilgrims settled in the Holy Land at the conclusion of the 1st Crusade. Gradually they came to the realization that the rhetoric issuing from the papacy concerning the barbarous Muslim infidels was false and malicious propaganda, calculated to incite ill-informed Europeans for the purpose of making religious war. In peacefully co-existing with Muslim neighbors, they observed that Muslims were far more culturally advanced than they were, and also practiced tolerance toward citizens of other religious faiths. Most European immigrants in the Holy Land adopted many Muslim cultural influences after establishing friendly relationships with their Eastern neighbors; upon learning that the Koran forbids a Muslim from striking the first blow, Europeans felt secure in their new surroundings, and many lost their Christian religious zeal and became doves. Some of the doves were Christian barons, who had been born in the Holy land and had inherited fiefdoms, which had been created in the aftermath of the 1st Crusade.

These particular barons believed that the Kingdom of Jerusalem could not withstand a major conflict with Saladin's superior military forces, and accordingly felt that a peace treaty was called for. This political philosophy created a schism with fanatical baronial hawks newly arrived from Europe. To make matters worse, the belligerant newcomers hated the Greek Orthodox and Armenian members of the Eastern Christian Churches of Byzantium even more than they disliked the Muslims.

The worst of the hawkish knights was the cruelly belligerant Reynaud of Antioch, who had arrived in the Holy land in 1147 A.D.. After toruring the Byzantine Patriarch of Antioch, Reynaud attacked the island of Cyprus, which was under Byzantine rule at the time. After allowing his troops to massacre thousands of hapless men, women and children in an orgy of genocidal religious fanaticism, Reynaud ordered all the Greek monks (whom he regarded as Christian heretics) arrested and their noses severed.

Fearful of the ever increasing strength of Saladin's army, Baldwin, the King of Jerusalem, who was dying of leprosy, requested a truce with Saladin in 1177 A.D.. The Sultan had no alternative but to agree, for the Koran stipulates that since war is repellant, Muslims must agree to a truce if it is requested by the adversary, provided that the truce terms are not detrimental to the Muslims.

The beligerant Reynaud had no intention of obeying the truce, however. In 1181, he conducted a series of raids against Muslim camel trains, followed by an assault on several Red Sea ports, in which he was defeated by an Egyptian army led by Saladin's brother.[5] Most of his troops were killed, but Reynaud escaped.

Reynaud's impetuous action compelled Saladin to launch another *Jihad*, but the Christian doves managed to secure another truce, which lasted three years, until Reynaud attacked yet another caravan that was carrying pilgrims to Mecca. This was an act of incredible political folly, for among the pilgrims was Saladin's sister.

Saladin led an army into Galilee, leaving half of his troops camped near the lake, Saladin attacked and occupied the city of Tiberias with the other half. A Templar army led by Guy, the King of Jerusalem, marched eastward, intending to defeat Saladin's army. Marching across the sun baked hills of Galilee in the stifling heat of a Palestinian summer, clad in armor, would be an extremely arduous feat; in this instance it became a living nightmare, for all the wells along the route had dried up. To their horror, the exhausted Templars, suffering from acute dehydration, found that the Muslim troops were camped between them and the Sea of Galilee. The Templars had no alternative but to camp for the night near the hill known as the Horns of Hattin. Without water, their plight worsened when Saladin's soldiers set large fires which enveloped the Templars in smoke.

During the night, the Muslim army encircled the Templar encampment and attacked the thirst-crazed Templars at dawn. Very few Templars escaped the carnage, and the King of Jerusalem and the religious extremist Reynaud were taken captive. Reynaud was executed for his treachury, but Saladin magnanimously released the king.

Salidin's *Jihad* occurred at a period when the concepts of chivalry and courtly love had become well-established in western Europe; there were even times when chivalry manifested itself during the *Jihad*. Such an event occurred when Saladin was besieging the Hospitaller castle in the Transjordan known as Krak des Chevaliers. While the Muslims were using their catapaults to bombard the castle walls with giant rocks, a royal wedding was taking place inside. In an act of chivalry, the Christian wedding party brought some of the wedding food to Saladin, who returned the courtesy by ordering his troops not to bombard the wing of the castle in which the newly-married couple were to spend their wedding night!

Now that the Christian army had been destroyed, Saladin entered Jerusalem in October, 1187 A.D., where it remained under Muslim jurisdiction for the next eight centuries. Unlike the previous capture of the city by the Templars, who had mercilessly slaughtered all the Jewish and Muslim residents, and expelled all Greek and Byzantine Christians, Saladin expelled the European Christians, but permitted Christians of other ethnicities, and the Jews, to re-enter the city and co-exist peaceably with the Muslims.[6]

The fall of Jerusalem prompted a papal call for a 3rd Crusade. Whipped into a religious frenzy by ecclesiastical rhetoric, several English cities conducted pogroms against Jewish residents, as the Crusaders began to muster. The crusading army set sail for the Holy Land in the Spring of 1191, led jointly by King Phillipe of France and King Richard the Lionheart of Britain, the favorite son of Eleanor of Aquitaine. In addition to being a capable soldier, Richard also was a troubador, a talent fostered by his mother.

The city of Acre fell to the Christians after a lengthy siege, and the French monarch returned home. Feeling that his prisoners of war constituted a logistical problem, Richard had 2,700 Muslim men women and children killed.

The Crusaders proceeded down the coast, capturing several towns on the way. Both military leaders respected each other's military capabilities: upon seeing Richard's horse felled in battle, Saladin immediately sent his own groom into the fray with two more horses for Richard; when the English king fell ill, Saladin sent his own physician and gifts of fruit. When both opposing armies became deadlocked, a five year treaty was entered into, in which Jerusalem remained under Muslim control, but European pilgrims were permitted to worship there. Richard returned to Europe, and Saladin died the following year.

With peace restored in the Holy Land, passion for the *Jihad* waned rapidly as the Muslim world encountered new political problems: fanatical Berbers destabilized Morocco, and Seljuk Turks invaded the Middle East, in the process replacing the free thinking spirit so characteristic of Arab academia, with dogmatic conservatism.

In Europe however, Pope Innocent III was planning the 4th. Crusade, with transportation costs to be brokered by the blind Doge of Venice, Enrico Dandolo. The original target of the Crusade was to be Egypt, to be used as an operational base for launching the liberation of the Holy Land. The wily Dandolo however, persuaded the Pope to attack Constantinople, the Christian capital of Byzantium.

Such a nefarious scheme would not only be favorable for Venetian trade, but also would put the Eastern Christian Church under papal control. The magnificent city of Constantinople succumbed after ten days of fighting. In one of the most malevolent incidents in the annals of Christianity, the victorious Crusaders and their Venetian compatriots, engaged in a three-day rampage, looting, killing women and children in the streets, and even raping nuns in their convents. Thus the Crusaders shamefully violated the admonition of Saint Augustine that it is criminal for Christians to fight one another.

While the 2nd Crusade was waging its bloody carnage to the glory of Christ in the Holy Land, missionaries from eastern Europe were spreading a new form of Christianity throughout southern France. Calling themselves *Cathari* (Pure Ones) they preached a dualistic doctrine somewhat similar to Gnosticism and Manicheanism, claiming that the world had been created by an evil being with whom God constantly battled. Unlike other heretical Christian sects in northern France, such as the Waldensians, who were merely a disorganized group who had taken a vow of poverty and preached to commoners, the Cathars of southern France had a centralized administratice structure based at Albi. Avowed pacifists, who lived frugally, the Cathars found religious acceptance across all strata of society, including the nobility. They accordingly were regarded as a dire threat to the papacy, particularly since they permitted women to be admitted to their priesthood.

The 4th Crusade, led by the Abbot of Citeaux, got underway in 1209 A.D.. In actuality, it was a French civil war. After the city of Béziers had surrendered, the Crusaders inquired of the Abbot how they were to distinguish between captured Catholics and Cathars. The Abbot relied: "Kill them all, God will know his own." Acting upon the psychopathic Abbot's advice, the Crusaders massacred every citizen. At the conclusion of the Crusade, the dreaded inquisition began at Toulose; at the former Cathar stronghold of Montségur, two hundred men, women and children were burned at the stake in a single day. Only a handful of Cathars survived the Catholic genocide, which lasted almost twenty years, the few who escaped from France seeking refuge in Germany, Italy, Liguria and Sicily.

The evangelical success of the Cathars prompted Rome to attempt the conversion of Muslims to Christianity. The preacher James of Vitry, was accordingly sent to the Holy Land and duly appointed Bishop of Acre. He was shocked to find Christians and Muslims coexisting peacefully together and trading profitably with the Venetians; even worse, Christian knights were having affairs with Muslim women. A 5th Crusade was therefore convened to put a stop to such behavior. Once more, stalemate was reached between the two armies. Tired of war, the Sultan offered Cardinal Pelagius, the papal legate, unprecedented terms: he would return Jerusalem, Central Palestine and Galilee to the Christians, provided that the Crusaders returned to Europe.[7] The papal clout in Europe was increasingly rapidly, thanks to the inquisition, so Pelagius, egged on by the Templars, foolishly declined the offer and set sail in an invasion fleet of 630 ships for Egypt.[8]

Upon arriving in Egypt, the Crusaders marched toward Cairo, but failed to notice that the Nile was rising, until the sodden ground forced their retreat. Muslim troops promptly demolished levees, stranding the beleagured Christian forces on a mudbank.[9] Facing certain anhilation, the Crusaders reluctantly agreed to an eight year truce and headed home.

During the 5th Crusade, word reached the Sultan regarding a powerful young monarch—Frederick II, Emperor of Germany and Sicily, who had wrested control of the Order of Teutonic Knights away from the Pope. Needing additional information about this mysterious figure, the Sultan dispatched a learned emir to Sicily on a fact-finding mission. The emir reported back that in contrast with most other European rulers, who could scarcely write their names, Frederick was fluent in nine languages, including Arabic, had studied jurisprudence, mathematics and philosophy, corresponded with Muslim scholars, and even owned the first giraffe in Europe! Moreover, many of his senior staff were Muslims, which is not surprising since he had been raised in Palermo, among wealthy Muslims and Greeks. Upon hearing the good news, it was self-evident to the Sultan that he should send a gift of animals for Frederick's fine menagerie, and commence correspondence with him, which he did.

After a very amicable correspondence, in which both men realised that neither wanted a war over control of Jerusalem, the Sultan invited Frederick to the Holy Land. Together, they conspired to effect a treaty without the shedding of blood. This was accomplished by both parties announcing that there would be a long and bloody conflict if a treaty was not entered into immediately. Senior officials on both sides fell for the ruse, and a ten year truce was declared without any loss of life, with Jerusalem reverting to Christian control, but with access to Muslim pilgrims. How ironic that during the era of the Crusades, more than a century of wanton killing for religion's sake had elapsed before a Christian ruler had the sense to employ diplomacy instead of belligerence.

At the conclusion of the truce, crusading fervor returned, and religious warfare in the Holy Land dragged on until the ill-conceived last Crusade, led by King Louis IX of France, was soundly defeated at Acre in 1291 A.D.. After that time, no Templar ever set foot in the Holy Land again, even though there were several aborted attempts to launch new Crusades during the following two centuries.

Upon fleeing the Holy land, both the Templars and the Hospitallers went to the island of Crete, the Templars remaining there for only a short period, before dispersing to their various temples and preceptories in Europe. During the ensuing centuries, the Hospitallers migrated to various islands, including Malta, which they ruled until defeated by Napoleon in 1789. Today they are known as the Sovereign and Military Order of Malta, headquartered in an enclave on the Via Condotti in Rome, which is recognized as a sovereign state. The Order is regarded as a charitable organization by the media and those who believe in the tooth fairy. Since many of its leading members have been prominent in Nazi and Fascist political circles, we will conduct an in depth examination of this bizarre quasi-secret order, in a later chapter of this book.

The Templars did not fare as well after their return to Europe. King Philip IV of France had the Templars arrested in 1307, and the Order was officially dissolved five years later. Many of the Templars, including their Grand Master Jaques de Molay, were executed, title to the Templar estates being transferred to their bitter rivals, the Hospitallers.

Some writers have claimed that attempted seizure of the Templar's vast wealth was the sole reason for Philip's actions, but other factors probably also influenced his decision. To medieval clerics such as Otto, the Bishop of Freising, the Templars were fighting in the Holy Land against the heathen Muslims by the just judgement of God. It was unacceptable for such members of the Christian Church (who probably had never met a Muslim) to think that a military religious order such as the Templars could be capable of losing one battle after another. To the medieval priesthood, Muhammad had been a servant of Satan, as is graphically depicted by Dante in his *Divine Comedy*. It was patently obvious to such ill-informed men of the cloth that God would not allow the Templars to have been so decisively defeated and driven out of Jerusalem, unless they had committed grievous sins.

Emotionally ill equipped to handle the loss of the Holy Land, the clergy vented their wrath upon the Templars, accusing them of the sins of pride and avarice. Having grown from a small band of impoverished knights into an international banking behemoth, the Order fell easy prey to such charges. With papal exemption from usury laws, the Templars were charging up to 60% interest on their loans. They particularly incurred the anger of bishops, who found that whenever they had closed a church for religious infractions, the Templars would send one of their own preachers into the offending parish, in order to conduct church business for a fee. King Philip probably was influenced by such allegations, since he regarded himself as an intermediary between the secular state and the Church.

If greed were the sole motive for Philip's actions, he simply could have ordered the arrest of French Templars, and seized their main treasury, which was located at their Paris temple. Instead, he attempted to arrange the arrest of all Templars throughout Christendom. Another probable factor motivating the monarch, was the denial by the Templars of his request of a merger between the Templar and Hospitaller Orders, which he probably initiated as a ploy to inhibit the ever increasing political and financial Templar clout.[10]

A curious charge made during the subsequent Templar trial was that they worshipped a demonistic entity named Baphomet. Some historians have equated this name with Mahomet, but the biblical scholar Hugh Schonfield points out: "Baphomet" coverts to "Sophia" when the ancient Hebrew code known as the *Atbash Cipher* is applied to it, and "Sophia" is the Greek word symbolizing the principle of "Wisdom".[11] Not surprisingly, according to the Inquisition records, the Templars were in possession of a casket which was surmounted by a women's head wrought in gilded silver.

This suggests that the Templars possessed arcane knowledge similar to that of the Gnostics, who claimed that Wisdom was captured by material powers and forced to prostitute herself, as represented by Mary

Magdalene in the New Testament (the town of Magdala was a center of occultism). Similarly, followers of Simon Magus worshipped Athena as the Goddess of Wisdom; to the Syrians she was Astarte, in Egypt she also was the Queen of Heaven, Isis, and back in the Babylonian era she had been deified as Inanna, who had been mistreated at the seven gates to the lower world.

Some of the Templars evaded arrest and fled to other countries, including Austria, where they laid the foundation for the Austro Hungarian Empire, and Portugal, where they changed the name of the Order to *"Knights of Christ."* Several Portuguese monarchs subsequently became their Grand Master, including Prince Henry the Navigator. The large Templar fleet of naval and merchant vessels mysteriously disappeared at the time of Philip's purge, and were never heard from again. In all probability, the fleet sailed up the west coast of Ireland, in order to evade English naval patrols, and were given sanctuary in Scotland by King Robert Bruce. Many current noble families of Britain are of the Bruce bloodline, e.g. The Marlbroughs.

Some of the Templar naval ships may well have been converted to privateers, commencing the custom of flying the skull and crossbones, for some Templars appear to have been buried with their skull atop crossed leg bones; King Robert Bruce purportedly was buried in the same manner, and the pirate flag is also associated with the masonic degree known as Knights Templar. This bizarre burial practice suggests that the Templars well may have perpetuated the oracular head tradition, which can be traced back among various cults for millennia.

One of the most momentous battles ever to be fought on British soil occurred in 1314 A.D., at Bannockburn, Scotland. The flames of a Scottish revolt initiated by William Wallace against King Edward 1st of England, had been dampened in 1305 with the grisly execution of Wallace in London, but newly-crowned King Robert Bruce of Scotland revived the struggle for Scottish independence. The English army was led by King Edward 2nd, the effete son of Edward 1st, who had died in 1307, three months before the mass arrest of the French Templars.

The battle should have been a resounding defeat for the poorly equipped Scots, who possessed few cavalry and were outnumbered at least three to one. At the height of the battle, a new contingent, replete with flying banners, entered the fray on the side of the Scots, causing the English to flee the battlefield in panic, hotly pursued by axe wielding Scots. Some accounts claim that the new force was comprised of peasants and camp followers, but this is highly improbable, for the battle hardened English knights would be unlikely to panic at the sight of yokels lacking in discipline and military skills.

It is more likely that the new contingent who entered the field of battle on horseback, was composed of Templars who had been given sanctuary by Robert Bruce. Acknowledged to have been the finest fighting force in Christendom, and readily recognizable by their black and white banners, the sudden shock of seeing mounted Templar knights charging furiously toward them, would have been the one thing capable of instilling fear in the English knights. By changing the probable outcome of the battle, the Templars enabled Scotland to remain an independent nation for most of the next three centuries.

One of the Scottish knights who fought at Bannockburn was William de St. Clair; in 1330 A.D. he was killed in Spain. St.Clair's tombstone at Rosslyn Chapel, near Edinburgh, displays a chalice, which is a symbol denoting the grave of a Templar. According to his descendant Andrew Sinclair, some of the refugee Templars took their treasure to the St. Clair castle in Scotland.[12] One of the refugees may have been Huges de Chalons, who was known to have escaped arrest and was the nephew of the Paris Templar treasurer.

Following the Battle of Bannockburn, King Robert Bruce merged what remained of the Templar Order with the various noble Orders of Scotland, and appointed himself Sovereign Master of all Scottish Orders and Guilds. Disputes between the lodges of the various Orders were settled at the court of the Grand Master, located at Kilwinning. When the Grand Lodge of Scotland was created three centuries later, its Mother Lodge was also located at Kilwinning. In this manner, Robert Bruce became the spiritual creator of Freemasonry, and the Bruce dynasty has cast its ominous shadow over political affairs ever since. The 8th Earl of Elgin, Jame Bruce, was the architect of the first Chinese opium war, and various family relatives have directed nefarious City of London banking and political machinations even to the present era.

Even though this chapter does not make particularly interesting reading, there are important lessons to be learned from it. We have seen that contrary to Christian belief structure, the Koran does not advocate killing in the name of religion, in fact it only tolerates the taking of human life as an extreme defensive measure. Since tolerance is a cornerstone of Islamic ideology, the violent and intolerant acts of some present day Muslim Fundamentalist groups (often as a cover for narcotics operations which are directed by high-level western Illuminists) violates Islamic ethics. We also observed how Emperor Frederick secured a decade of peace for the Holy Land through communication with the adversary, instead of displaying the belligerent attitude of his crusading predecessors. Lastly, it appears that Freemasonry, with its attendant secret rites and practices, is at the root of much of the genocide afflicting the world today, and could not function if its inner workings were to be subjected to public scrutiny. Freemasonry appears to have evolved from Templar activities; had the latter not been driven underground during the purge by King Philip of France, Freemasonry in its present covert form, together with its controlling secret societies such as the Club of the Isles and the "Unkown Superior" to whom the Grand Masters of both Protestant and Catholic Masonic Orders report (the Jesuit Superior General) may never have been spawned.

At the same time period which gave rise to the Templar Order, revolutionary architectural design concepts were being applied to the creation of the world's most audacious and spectacular buildings—the Gothic Cathedrals of Europe. It is not a coincidence that the previously-mentioned Saint Bernard of Clairvaux was the principal mover and shaker behind both ventures. This raises the question as to the various possible pathways by which the sacred geometry which is at the core of Gothic architecture, was transmitted to Saint Bernard and his esoteric Mystery School known as the *Fraters Solomonis:* Did the Templars discover ancient Jewish scrolls, was it from the Comacine Masters of Italy, or was it via those masters of telepathy, the Kwajaghan, and their associates, the Sarmoun—two extremely secret Afghani sects (and scourge of the Jesuits and western members of the thirteen Illuminati bloodlines) who emerge to influence the course of history periodically? Unfortunately, the answer justifies a book in its own right.

CHAPTER 13

▼

MIND CONTROL:
THE ULTIMATE EVIL

"In my reading of history, I recall no instance where a government perished because of the abscence of a secret service force, but many there are that perished as a result of the spy system. If Anglo-Saxon civilization stands for anything, it is for a government where the humblest of citizens is safeguarded against the secret activities of the executive of the government."
                    U.S. Congressperson Sherly (1908).

As previous chapters in this book have demonstrated, Judaism and Christianity clearly were developed, not for the spiritual uplifting of humankind, but rather, through the promulgation of false dogma, for the control of the minds of the masses. Tragically, in their striving to comprehend unsolvable biblical mysteries, which were concocted by power hungry priesthoods, Jews and Christians alike are in denial concerning ghastly acts perpetrated to the glory of the Creator. A rational person views rape, pillage and murder with abhorrence, yet adherents of the Christian and Jewish faiths elect to overlook the purported command of

Moses, in which the apocryphal psychopath orders the slaughter of all the Midianite women and male children, and the rape of virgin girls.

A person who conforms to the tenets and false dogma of a religious doctrine that elects to ignore the murderous activities which the Bible attributes to Moses, is suggestive of an irrational mindset, for a spiritually oriented person does not conform without considering why he or she is conforming.

Modern religious behavior modification evolved from the teachings and practices of American evangelist and Professor of Theology at Oberlin College, E. Grandison Finney (1792—1875).

When Finney commenced his ministry, his sermons were delivered in a calm manner, with little emotion and designed to appeal to the intellect of the congregation. Unfortunately for the good shepherd, large numbers of his flock abandoned his church, never to return.

Realizing that he had to find a way to attract and maintain an enthusiastic congregation, Finney discovered, after a period of experimentation, that if normal brain function is disturbed through major fear, anger, shock or emotion, heightened suggestibility and impaired judgement occurr temporarily. This facilitates the implanting of a new belief structure.

Instead of appealing to the intellect, Finney began to deliver sermons replete with copius amounts of fire and brimstone, and spoken in a loud, emotion-filled manner. Realizing that Finney had discovered a technique that turned previously rational people into mindless robots, other pastors adopted Finney's evangelical method, which became known as the Boston Movement, the foundation of the Christian Fundamentalist Church. This is exemplified today in the hysterical rantings and ravings of television evangelists, who are more intent upon making a buck than in saving souls.

Manipulating the minds of an unwitting church congregation by means of this insidious form of mind control is, in the author's opinion, an act of the most despicable evil.

During the Jesus Movement of the 1960's, Finney's mind control system was used very successfully by the Children of God religious cult. In his book *Battle for the Mind*, author and Tavistock Institute mind control psychiatrist William Sargent, stated that a favorite recruiting ploy of Children of God proselytizers, was to approach a group of teenagers and focus on the one who expressed the most opposition to religion. The hostile victim would be provoked into an uncontrollable rage. In order to prevent a neural overload, the mind of the unfortunate victim rejected the previously held religious belief structure, replacing it with the ideology implanted by the victim's Children of God tormentors. According to Sargent, this insidious mind control technique enabled Children of God missionaries to make fanatical converts out of atheists in only fifteen minutes.

Founded by David Berg, the Children of God had established communities in sixty countries by the end of the 1970's. Former cult members claim that church members practised pedophilia. One British newspaper reported that children of the cult's members exhibited visual evidence of rectal excoriation, and that pre-pubescent girls had torn hymens and flayed vulvae.[2]

Berg's pamphlets promoted pedophilia and sex between children, while another pamphlet displayed a photograph of a Children of God nurse engaged in oral sex with a young boy.[3] A prosecution witness and former cult member alleged that Children of God girls were expected to lure men into having affairs with them, in order to recruit new members; this practice was known within the Children of God movement as "flirty fishing." Berg promoted not only pedophilia, but also racism, proclaiming that "I'm a racist because God is!'

Joyanne Treadwell Berg, the grand-daughter of the cult's founder, alleges that she was made to have sex with important government officials, and had "…met Presidents from around the world." If this claim is valid, it would imply that possibly she could have been used as a "Black Widow." This is an Illuminati term for mind controlled sex slaves (frequently pre-pubescent children) who are used for the entrapment of high-level dignitaries, many of whom are pedophiles. One of Berg's own daughters claimed that her father had an incestuous relationship with her and her sisters.[4]

Remarkably, the Children of God organization has withstood several prosecutorial attempts, including one in 1974 brought by the New York Attorney General's Office, which accused the cult of incest, rape and kidnapping. Incredibly, the case was dropped by order of the Attorney General, who made the amazing claim that the cult was protected from prosecution by the First Amendment! Could it be that the cult is protected by very powerful figures? Former Chilean dictator Pinochet and Libya's Muammar al Qaddafi, allegedly have connections with this organization, whose choir even performed for President George Bush Sr. at the White House.

In 1991, movie actor River Phoenix revealed that as a child, he had been forced to have sex. This was during the period when his father served as an Archbishop of the Children of God Church. Because the actor had not aquired celebrity status at that time, his comments were largely unreported by the newsmedia.

Some 170 children were taken into protective custody in 1993, after a police raid on an Argentinian compound of the Children of God cult. The police claimed that the children had been sexually abused by church members; cocaine and pornographic videotapes had been siezed in a previous raid. Not surprisingly perhaps, no charges were brought against church members.[5]

State Chief Inspector Rebollo, who led the 1993 raid, claimed to have found evidence that the Children of God Church was being funded by a global cabal of influential people.

By the time of Argentinian raid on the Children of God compound, River Phoenix had become a well known movie star. A few weeks after the raid, River Phoenix died from a purported drug overdose; his body bore no evidence of needle marks. Since he died on Halloween night, was his death accidental, as claimed—or was it a ritual murder conducted in order to prevent him from disclosing what he knew about the Children of God organization and their financial benefactors.

Since the Argentinian raid, the Church has undergone restructuring and has changed its name to the Family of Love. It disavows that its adult members engaged in sex with minors; it also claims that it terminated its practice of "flirty fishing" in 1987, which implies that this outrageously corrupt practice did, infact, take place in previous years.

Since religious brainwashing is only one facet of the Illuminati's goal to eventually achieve a totally mind-controlled global populace, a brief overview of the history of mind control is presented in order to aquaint the reader with the principal conspiratorial persons and subversive organizations who have participated in this evil undertaking.

In "*The Island of Dr. Moreau,* by H.G. Wells, the evil geneticist states: "Its not simply the outward form of an animal I can change. The physiology, the chemical rhythm of the creature, may also be made to undergo an enduring modification...."[6]

The novel was based upon a real life geneticist of the same name, who promoted the use of hashish among members of the Rothschild literary circle in Paris, during the mid 19th century.[7] Moreau administered large doses of narcotics to unsuspecting mental patients, and *advocated the use of hashish in order to increase suggestibility during the training of assassins.* The Jesuit associated Moreau researched the use of narcotics for mind control purposes by ancient cultures, e.g. the evil priesthood of the Royal Court of the Dragon, in Egypt.[8]

While Dr. Moreau was studying the drug-induced psychosis of hapless mental patients in France, Lewis Cass Payseur, the grandson of King Louis XVI of France, was creating a vast financial empire in America. Unwilling to be in the limelight, Payseur employed John D. Rockefeller, Andrew Carnegie, J.P. Morgan and Cornelius Vanderbilt to act as presidents of his numerous companies, paying them five percent of the corporate profits.

John D. Rockefeller's brother William was appointed president of Standard Oil. In 1911, William Rockefeller hired a high-level British Intelligence operative named Claude Dansey. Dansey converted the U.S. Army Intelligence Service into a subsidiary of the British Secret Service. A loyal supporter of Dansey was General Marlborough Churchill, a relative of Winston Churchill. General Churchill became director of the U.S. Military Intelligence.

After the conclusion of the very bloody W.W.I, General Churchill created the "Black Chamber," a New York espionage group serving the needs of the U.S. Army and also anglophile New York financiers. A short time later, Churchill became director of the Josiah Macy, Jr, Foundation. The foundation owned a medical center that was to play a pivotal role in the development of mind control techniques, on behalf of the Illuminati.

Sound, in keeping with all other forces of nature, is not biased toward the production of beneficial or destructive forces. The ancient Chinese were well aware of this, realizing that music compositions exert significant transendental influences upon humankind, and hence upon the planet. The Chinese believed that musical tones were but one physical manifestation of an inaudible superphysical sound, which governed the cosmos. Depending upon the combination of musical notes, rhythms and instrumentation, music possessed the ability to either enhance the spirituality, or the darker side of humanity.

The metaphysical aspects of music is too vast a subject to be dealt with here; it has only been referred to because during the 1920's, British Intelligence acquired control of a behavioral sciences laboratory in Frankfurt, Germany. Like the ancient Chinese, the lab researchers had concluded that the psychological profile of large segments of the population could be modified through the particular form of music to which they were subjected.

These German researchers relocated to America during the 1930's, founding the Radio Research Institute at Princeton University. Their efforts were coordinated with the Columbia Broadcasting System, whose chief executive officer was career intelligence operative William Paley. Today, the entertainment media is dominated by a few transnational corporations, thereby rendering it easy to control the types of music to which nations are subjected.[9]

The central coordinating body responsible for the oversight of the global mind control network is the London based Tavistock Institute. Founded as a clinic in 1922 to serve the psychological warfare requirements of the British military, its first director was Brigadier General John Rawlings Rees. In keeping with the previously mentioned W. Grandison Finney, Rees and his staff realized that by means of repeated psychological shocks, or stressful events, entire populations could be psychologically controlled. This is achievable by providing a controlled psychological environment.

Rees's objective was to develop a vast network of psychiatrists, who would create a society; "...where it is possible for people of every social group to have treatment when they need it, *even when they do not wish it, without it being necessary to invoke the law.*" [Emphasis added].

For all practical purposes, Rees controlled the British military during W.W.II by virtue of his position as head of the Army Psychiatric Directorate. Rees was able to infiltrate his staff into every British army unit and even into the Allied Command itself. In this manner, Rees's network, which he termed his "invisible college," eventually was able to infiltrate, then control, the North Atlantic Treaty Organization (NATO). As the war wound down, Tavistock personnel acquired control of the World Federation of Mental Health.

Paralleling the development of Tavistock mind control research, was the evolution of the eugenics movement (racial purity). This research was initiated at London's Galton Laboratory. In the 1920's, the Rockefeller Foundation funded the Kaiser Wilhelm Institute for Psychiatry in Munich, which was directed by Ernst Rudin. Initial funding in 1925 was $2.5 million, with additional funding provided by the

Harriman family, the Warburgs and the British Crown. The Nazi Dr. Rudin was appointed president of the global Eugenics Federation in 1932.[10] Hitler came to power in 1933 and delegated Rudin to direct the Racial Hygiene Society, which advocated sterilization or death of the "racially impure." Rudin's staff drew up a sterilization law which was based on statuary law from the Commonwealth of Virginia.

Not all of this revolting eugenics research was conducted in Germany. Dr. Nolan Lewis, director of the New York Psychiatric Institute, undertook fourteen research projects into the nature of schizophrenia (dementia praecox). He was assisted in this work by Nazi psychiatrist and Rudin protegé Franz Kallmann, who ironically had been forced to leave Germany after being determined to be part Jewish. Kallmann had proposed the forced sterilization of even *healthy relatives of schizophrenics.*

This American schizophrenia research was funded by the Supreme Council of the Scottish Rite of Freemasonry, whose Grand Master was the Duke of Connaught. Dr. Kallmann conducted a study of more than a thousand cases of schizophrenia. His report referred to schizophrenics as: "…the lowest type of criminal offenders," and was used as a pretext for the Nazis to execute mental patients.

Mind control technology took a giant leap forwards after Dr. Joseph Mengele was appointed medical commandant of the Auschwitz concentration camp in 1943. Infants selected for mind control programming were subjected to intense trauma in order to induce the mind to split into several thousand alter personalities. Such trauma (even at the present time) consists variously of sexual abuse, limb dislocation, electroshock, prolonged solitary confinement, enforced consumption of one's own excrement and enforced observation of executions.

Mengele, who was a high-level Illuminatus, specialized in mind control research involving twins. Frequently, trauma was induced in one twin by forcing he or she to watch the other twin being flayed or burned alive. After the mind had disassociated into multiple alter personalities,

169 alters would be individually programmed for specific tasks, e.g. to be a sex slave for Illuminati pedophiles, a drug courier, or an assassin.

Each alter personality was given an access code. For reference purposes, the programmer then drew a 13 x13 grid, each square denoting one specific programmed alter personality. Each programmed multiple was implanted with thirteen such grids; interspersed between the grids were alters who were programmed to act as gate keepers, thus rendering it extremely difficult for a deprogrammer to access the next grid level.

At the conclusion of W.W.II, Mengele was brought to America under the Operation Paperclip program, where he directed mind control programming at such diverse locations as China Lake Naval Weapons Facility, Fort Irwin and the Mendocino State Mental Institution—the latter facility was involved in the programming of black foster children destined for Jonestown. Mind control victims who were intended to function as intelligence couriers were subjected to a surgical operation known as brain stem scarring, which enabled specific alters to possess a photographic memory. It should be noted that the front alter personality was always programmed to be totally oblivious of the other alters, which were kept compartmentalized until required to perform a specific task. The front alter was never programmed to possess a photographic memory. The author has spoken to mind-control survivors who had been programmed as infants by Mengele at the China Lake Naval facility; without prompting, they individually mentioned being shackled around the neck. As an example of governmental collusion in the matter of mind-control, Mengele frequently used a passport bearing his true identity when travelling to Paraguay, or when visiting relatives in Germany (who owned a manufacturing company).

To render deprogramming exceedingly difficult, alters are sometimes programmed using a web consisting of the Greek alphabet, divided into three groups of letters. Nursery rhymes and fairy tales, e.g. The *Wizard of Oz* and *Alice Through the Looking Glass,* are frequently used in the programming of young children. Castle themes are also used—important alters being implanted in imaginary dungeons, guarded by a dungeon-master alter personality.

Mind controlled individuals are programmed to exhibit intense loyalty to their programmer. A well-programmed victim only begins to recover memories after the death of the programmer. If the programming begins to break down, alter personalities known as "cutters" are automatically actuated, causing the victim to slash their arms or fingers; this inhibits further memories of the programming.

Victims are programmed to respond to reinforcing triggers encoded in specific newspapers, television programs and commercials. The American television show *"Millenium"* was filled with such subliminal triggers, mainly of a numerical nature (the triggers on each three consecutive shows added up to 666).

When planning future global strategy, the Illuminati heirarchy studies the outcome of a game of Enochian Chess, which involves four players who are influenced by beings not of this world. Psychic energy is generated by the Illuminati Mother Goddess during the chess game, in order to facilitate the physical manifestation of these reptilian entities. Mengele (who also went under the names of Greenbaum and David) was one of the players in this bizarre game, together with another major programmer who posed as "Dr. Black."

While Mengele was conducting his gruesome mind control experiments at Auschwitz, Montague Norman resigned his position as Managing Director of the Bank of England, and formed the National Association for Mental Health. In 1948, this organization convened a meeting of the world's leading mental health specialists; at this convention the World Federation for Mental Health was created. Not surprisingly, the person elected President was none other than Tavistock Institute's John Rawlings Rees.

Montague Norman's New York associate Clarence G. Michalis, was appointed board chairman of the Macy Foundation, which in turn became a major funding source for Tavistock's activities in America.

At the conclusion of W.W.II, Tavistock began to establish a global network of psychiatric research centers, in order to influence the ideologies of mass populations. This subversive network, which was funded primarily by the Rockefeller Foundation together with large corporations, included such establishments as the Stanford Research Institute, the Center for Research in Group Dynamics and the United States Office of Naval Research. 1966 saw the creation of the Science Policy Research Unit at Sussex University, in England. This institution, which acquired several Tavistock staff members, became a major force in the development of social manipulation techniques, and has engaged in classified contract studies on behalf of NATO.

President Kennedy incurred the wrath of the Tavistock Institute in 1963, when he ignored their counsel to permit NATO to engage in the psychological manipulation of domestic populations in NATO countries. It was probably this act, in conjunction with his plans to Federalize the privately-owned Federal Reserve Board and also to terminate the Vietnam War (thus ending the genocide of Buhddhists), which prompted the Illuminati and their Jesuit lackeys to order his assassination.[11]

It was the JFK space program that sounded the economic death knell for the western nations. Until that time, the geopolitical clout primarily had been derived from the profits of the opium trade and industrial growth. In 1963, NASA placed a contract with the Tavistock Institute to determine the effects of the fledgling aerospace industry on western society. Tavistock found that the space program had so ignited the imagination of the public, that the western world was in danger of becoming a technological society, replete with many free thinkers. If allowed to continue, this would cause the Illuminati to lose its dominance over the populace.

So alarmed were the Illuminati by the NASA report that they convened a meeting in Deauville, France, called the *Conference on Transatlantic Technological Imbalance and Collaboration*. In attendance were U.S. State Department planner Dr. Zbigniew Brzezinsky and Dr. Aurelio Peccei, chairman of a major NATO think tank.

The conference concluded that in order for the Illuminati movers and shakers to continue their dominion over the masses, the populace of western nations must be brainwashed into accepting the de industrialization of their respective countries. De-industrialization accordingly was accomplished by culturally-shocking the masses into accepting the formation of vast authoritarian environmental agencies staffed with parasitic bureaucrats.[12] This effort was initiated by having the newsmedia alarm the public by drawing to their attention Rachel Carson's book on environmental pollution called *Silent Spring*. The book drew heavily for its information on the environmental research of Dutch scientist Dr. C.J. Briejer, whom the author had the pleasure of meeting on several occasions three decades ago, in the Pacific Northwest.

Admittedly, some antipollution legislation is necessary, but the mountains of nebulous paper and attendant draconian penalties issuing forth from environmental agencies, has thrust the western world into a nearly insolvent post industrial era. Most of the global pollution arising from transportation and industry could be readily eradicated through the implementation of proven "free energy" devices, while polluted rivers can be cleansed through the application of the technology developed many years ago by the brilliant Austrian, Victor Schauberger. Not surisingly, corrupt environmental bureaucrats have repeatedly blocked the implementation of such technology, for fear of losing political clout.[12]

The Deauville conference spawned books both by Brzezinski and Peccei: *Technetronic Era* and *The Chasm Ahead*, respectively. In calling for the establishment of a post industrial dictatorship, Brzezinski wrote: "….new forms of social control may be needed to limit the indiscriminate exercise by individuals of their new powers." He went on to suggest bio-chemical means to control the populace and stated: "It will soon be possible to assert almost continuous surveillance over every citizen and to maintain up-to-date complete files…" In view of such arrogant and inflammatory phrases, the author suggests that it is timely for loyal American partisans and military flag officers to place this wretched punk in the dock and charge him with high treason.

In his later book *Between Two Ages*, the fellow called for the establishment of a global government, and, in the manner of a thug operating a protection racket, indicated what the global elite (implying the Illuminati, who refer to themselves as the Olympians—an oxymoron if ever there was one) would do to punish the masses if they resisted. This included geophysical warfare and satellites which emitted a frequency (presumably 12 Hertz) capable of initiating mass epilepsy as the satellite passed overhead. Instead of charging this miserable apology for a human being with treason, Illuminati puppet President Jimmy Carter appointed him to a presidential cabinet position. Perhaps Brzezinski and the rest of his ilk should recall what happened to Mussolini following his capture by outraged Italian partisans.[13]

Similarly, Peccei's book called for the establishment of a global government, employing "global planning" and "crises management." Pandering to the Illuminati dragons, Peccei wrote: "Man invented the story of the bad dragon, but if there ever was a bad dragon on earth, it is man himself…". No, Mr. Peccei, it is the avaricious, adrenalchrome-lusting, bad dragons that you have elected to serve, which have prevented humanity throughout recorded history from creating a global social order based upon good fellowship and freedom from war.

The major outcome of the Deauville conference was the founding of the Club of Rome in 1968, under the direction of Peccei. In keeping with Henry Kissinger's National Security Council's notorious Policy Directive 200, the club called for a massive global population reduction by means of famine, plague and controlled nuclear warfare. Already we are observing the results of the implementation of this evil policy directive in Africa, where millions of innocent Africans have died from the genetically engineered AIDS virus.

The club's first report was *"The Limits to Growth."* It claimed that scientific research was an infeasible method for attaining material progress, stating that the only way was to permit a global government to control the allocation of resources. The report falsely claimed that nuclear fusion was infeasible as an energy system, ignoring the fact that both Philo Farnsworth and Bogdan Maglich had both developed feasible fusion systems (nuclear fusion energy systems have been suppressed because they do not provide fissionable radioactive by-products required by the military for the production of nuclear weapons).

Since its inception, the Club of Rome, on behalf of the Illuminati and the Tavistock Institute, has established a vast global network of national chapters, which wield influence over policy makers. Under the influence of the Club of Rome, NATO has evolved from being "a bastion against communism" into a social control apparatus. It functions in an Hegelian manner by creating an insurgency involving genocidal activity. Responding to demands made by members of the global populace, a NATO "peace keeping" force then quells the uprising and permanently remains in that country. Often, mind controlled members of the U.S. Delta Force are an integral part of the insurgency group, since they are conditioned to kill in a dispassionate manner. It should be noted that the genocidal United Nations operations in Bosnia were under the direction of Lord David Owen, a psychiatrist and long time executive of the Tavistock Institute.[14]

Bilderberger and NATO supporter U.S. Senator Claiborne Pell, has advocated NATO becoming an overseer of global environmentalism. Not surprisingly, he is a Club of Rome member.

In its quest to promote its subversive goals of de-industrialization and controlled disintegration of the global economy, the Club of Rome convened the 1976 *Re-shaping the International Order* (RIO) conference, which attacked Americans as being greedy. This was followed in 1977 by a diatribe against industrialization and a call for limits to industrial growth.

What the above narrative depicts, is an organized attempt by treasonous Illuminati front organizations to brain wash the global populace into accepting the destruction of national sovereignty, in preparation for the implementation of a totalitarian world government. This is being accomplished by means of massive social engineering programs.

The New Age movement was created during the 19th century, as a ploy by the Illuminati to obfuscate a true understanding of ætheric energy (known to physicists as the neutrino sea) for those who have learned to harness it can wield considerable power. The New Age movement greatly expanded as a result of the psychological warfare efforts of the Tavistock applied psychology American think-tank known as the Stanford Research Institute.

The Institute published an internal report in 1974 which revealed that environmentalist, New Age and various religious organizations are, in actuality, all part of a unified planned social engineering conspiracy. Six years later, at the request of the Institute's director, Dr. Willis Harmon, key elements of the in house report were published in book form as *The Aquarian Conspiracy,* by Harmon protegé Marilyn Ferguson. The last thing that the Illuminati desires is a populace which thinks for itself—something most New Agers fail to do, relying instead on the books and lectures promulgated by disinformers and kooks. The recent New Age emphasis on angels, for instance, has only occurred because New Agers have failed to determine the origins of the angel myth.[15]

It was necessary to digress from the subject of religious mind control in this narrative, in order to present the sheer magnitude of the ongoing social engineering (global brain washing) project of the Illuminati. Returning now to the subject of religious mind control, de-industrialization propaganda was promoted through the founding in 1975 of the *Inter Religious Peace Colloquim* (IRPC) in Bellagio, Italy. Its board of directors included Club of Rome members the Jesuit William

Ryan and liberation theology proponent Peter Henriot (liberation theology is a Jesuit doctrine originated by Cardinal Robert Bellarmine in
the 17th century. Bellarmine held that the populace was entitled to
appoint or to depose monarchs; Bellarmine's writings formed the basis
of the American *Declaration of Independence,* which is not surprising,
since the American Revolution was orchestrated by the Black Pope,
Lorenzo Ricci, in order to diminish Protestant clout).Several of its
Islamic theoreticians later became major players in the Ayatollah
Khomeini's ascension to power (in keeping with his father, Khomeini
was an asset of British Intelligence).

In order to divert public attention away from science and toward
zero growth ideology, the IRPC has played a major role in the promotion of religious fundamentalism, with its emphasis upon the 19th century mind control techniques of evangelist Grandison Finney, and also
in the area of religious cults.

Many religious cults are merely fronts for mind-control or occult
activities. Such cults are structured in the form of concentric circles, the
outer circles being restricted to conventional religious doctrines, the
members of which serve as a front for the occult or satanic rituals that
are conducted by core members (lay Mormons, for instance, are
unaware of the importance that the Mormon heirarchy places upon
solar rites performed in honor of *Kolob,* their name for the central sun).

A typical cult of this nature has been the *Process Church for the Final
Judgment.* Founded during the 1960's in Britain by Church of
Scientology initiates Mary Anne and Robert DeGrimston, the cult
opened branches in Mexico and America, recruiting mainly from centers of counterculture, such as Haight-Ashbury and Hollywood.

According to author Maury Terry, Process church members were
heavily involved in human sacrifice, drug-trafficking and kiddieporn.
The "Son of Sam" and the Charlie Manson murders were both linked to
the Process Church (Manson wrote articles for the Church's magazine).
David Berkovitz, the supposed lone Son of Sam killer, joined the

Process Church in 1975. Interestingly, the Process Church's attorney was member John Markham. Markham later was hired by U.S. Attorney William Weld (the Weld family made its fortune in the opium trade). Weld invested money in the counterculture tabloid *Real Paper,* which published a major article on the Process Church.

At the time that the Son of Sam killings commenced, the Process Church changed its name to the *Foundation Faith of the Millenium.* Since cult member Markham was a prosecutorial member of the U.S. Justice Department, is it any wonder that satanic cult murderers are seldom prosecuted?

Until the base was recently closed, U.S. Naval Intelligence used to train Marine Corps Satanists at the El Toro Marine Base in Southern California, in techniques for infiltrating civilian police departments after completion of military service, for the purpose of establishing covert satanic cells. The satanic police officers then provide protection against arrest for Satanists engaged in ritual murder. Such an operation is currently occuring in Orange County, California, in which a satanic cult preys upon attractive single women frequenting local cocktail lounges (which are managed by cult members) by spiking their drinks with Rohypnol. The drugged victim is then taken to an upscale residential development, replete with an underground tunnel system, in the city of Tustin, where the victim is then programmed to be a sex slave. The High Priestess of this particular cult is a Youth Corrections Officer, whose cult name is "The Empress." Upon completion of programming, narcotics are planted in the mind controlled victim's car, so that police officers who are cult members are able to make an arrest. Following incarceration, the hapless victim is used as a sex slave by prison guards who are members of the same evil cult. A "Christian" fellowship also has links to this cult.This particular low-level cult performs minor tasks on behalf of the Illuminati High Council of the United States, which is headquartered in Orange County.

Another national satanic church in America poses as a New Age Catholic Church with Celtic overtones. In actuality, it is heavily involved in child pornography and ritual orgies at its inner circle. It is not known whether or not the Church engages in mind control programming, which is highly probable since some of the congregation are known to be programmed multiples.

Perhaps the most insidious cultic threat to the political stability of the western world, emanates from five interconnected Asian religious cults: the Unification Church (the Moonies), Aum Shinrykyo, Soka Gakkai, Agon shu and the Sukyo Mahikari. Collectively, these five cults are known to the intelligance community as the *Black Hand.*

The American CIA was completely caught off guard in 1961, when a group of South Korean junior army officers staged a successful coup, which installed Park Chung Hee as President. In order to improve its surveillance of South Korean politics, the CIA assigned one of its top operatives—E. Howard Hunt (whose case officer was broadcaster and author William F. Buckley) to create the Unification Church as a front for CIA surveillance activities. The initial task of organizing the newly-founded church fell to one of the coup leaders, Kim Chong Pil, who had been appointed director of the Korean CIA. The person selected to front the church was the Reverend Sun Myung Moon, who later was accused in a lengthy U.S. Congressional report of bank fraud, illegal kickbacks and the illegal sale of arms. Moon also has been accused of entering into ritual sexual "initiations" with young female converts.

A 1977 Congressional report alleged that the Church's primary interest was not religious, but in actuality was an attempt to gain political power and influence. This is evidenced by the Unification Church's creation of the *Washington Times* newspaper, under the editorship of Rothschild relative Arnaud de Borgrave. President George H. Bush has claimed that this particular newspaper is the first thing he reads in the morning. Moon, who has advocated lying for the promotion of his Church, also has stated in a television show that the media is an instrument to be used in the battle for the minds of individuals: "So, in this war, all weapons will be mobilized, political means, economic means and propagandist means, and basically trying to take over the person's mind."

Moon has put these chilling words into practice by founding the *World Media Association,* as a means of exerting journalistic influence. In consequence, American syndicated columnist Jack Anderson became chairman of the executive commitee of Moon's Diplomat Bank. Prominent politicians have been lavishly entertained by attractive young female members of the Unification Church.

Ironically, although the Unification Church was established by the CIA as an intelligence front for the purpose of monitoring Korean political activities, it has become a case of the tail wagging the dog, with Moon becoming the guest of then Vice President George Bush (a former director of the CIA) at President Reagan's inauguration. This very dangerous situation has arisen because despite its Korean origins, one of Moon's principal funders has been Japan's Ryoichi Sasakawa, self-proclaimed as "The world's richest Fascist."

In addition to being one of Japan's wealthiest persons, Sasakawa also is one of the most powerful of the Japanese power brokers. After founding a Japanese Fascist party, Sasakawa assisted in 1939 in the creation of the Japanese-German-Italian alliance, and also established the fascist Japanese Black Shirt organization.

In keeping with Sasakawa, another ultra-nationalist Japanese supporter of Moon is Brigadier General Yoshio Kodama, who made an immense fortune by looting Chinese diamonds, precious metals and weapons during W.W.II, according to U.S. Army Counterintelligence records.

Moon, Sasakawa and Kodama created the *Asian People's Anti-Communist League* during the phony "Cold War" (concocted by Winston Churchill) as a front for the global unification of Fascists. This subversive organization later spawned the *World Anti Communist*

League, under the direction of Major General Jack Singlaub, which comprises a network of Nazis, Fascists and Latin-American death-squad personnel, encompassing almost one hundred nations. It is head-quartered in the American offices of the *Freedom Center,* another Unification Church enterprise.

Significantly, both Sasakawa and Kodama are prominent members of Japan's Liberal Democratic Party, which is the most powerful political organization in Asia. This particular political party appears to be the glue which bonds the individual fingers of the Black Hand together. Until his death, the political king maker of the party was Shin Kanemaru, who was linked to the Unification Church as well as to the Aum Shinrykyo cult.

According to a Tass news agency report dated February 25th, 2000, the Aum cult owns a security company in Russia known as *"Aum Protect,"* which allegedly is headed by high-ranking Aum monks and former KGB operatives.

The late evening of May 28th, 1993, was extremely memorable for many residents of Western Australia, as a large fireball travelling in a north-easterly direction, passed overhead and culminated over the horizon in a brilliant flash of bluish white light, followed by an earth-quake which measured 3.9 on the Richter scale. Sightings of similar anomalous fireballs were to follow in subsequent years, in various countries, sometimes causing electrical generating facilities to go off line; unlike the typical paths of meteors, these curious objects tended to possess trajectories which were parallel with the earth's curvature.

Thanks to the sterling investigative efforts of geophysicist Harry Mason, who resides in Western Australia, much has been learned about these mysterious events, despite the customary disinformation promul-gated by government agencies.

The "ground zero" where the first earthquake occurred in the aftermath of the 1993 fireball sighting, was located at the vast Banjawarn sheep sta-tion, a 500,000 acre arid tract located some 400 miles north-east of Perth.

Curiously, thirty five days prior to the first fireball event, the Banjawarn property had been purchased by the Aum Shinrikyo cult! The title deed to the property named Aum founder Asahara and a Japanese born Australian citizen named Yasuko Shimada.

Ms. Shimada exemplifies another interlink between the Aum and Mahikari cults, for she had been a Mahikari activist for more than a decade, prior to becoming a prominent member of the Aum cult.

Could these mysterious fireballs be of terrestrial origin? The trajectory of many of these Australian fireball sightings suggests that this is so. According to observers of the first fireball, it was initially sighted approaching the Australian coast from a south-southwesterly direction. This suggests that it may have emanated from the coastal region of Antarctica known as Enderby Land. Most significantly, this particular region is the location of two Japanese research stations.

The visual appearance of the fireballs suggests that they were plasmoids, that had been created and guided along their flightpath by means of a very large electro magnetic device known as a Magnifying Transmitter. Developed more than a century ago by that towering intellect of electrical engineering Nikola Tesla, this type of transmitter harnesses the virtually limitless store of electrical energy that accumulates in the earth's crust, and uses it to transmit an incredibly powerful longitudinally-pulsed wave of energy. Tesla's phenomenal invention is a double-edged sword: the device is capable of delivering enormous quantities of non-polluting electrical energy for peaceful applications; however, in various military modes, it is able to create massive earthquakes thousands of miles distant from the transmitter, or flashfreeze the unsuspecting citizens of a target city. In a defensive mode, the device is capable of creating an electromagnetic hemispherical canopy charged with millions of volts of electricity over a city, causing the destruction of in-coming missiles.

In 1991, Japan and Russia entered into a covert technology alliance, for the express purpose of advancing the state-of-the-art of the Tesla geophysical warfare superweapons, which make nuclear warfare pale in comparison. A Japanese/Russian University was established in Moscow under the alliance, staffed by scientists from both countries. Chillingly, the university is administrated by senior members of the Aum Shinrkio cult.

A covert geophysical warfare research center was established in Japan at the Kobe Iron and Steel Corporation. A few weeks after the Aum Shinrikyo science minister claimed on a Tokyo radio broadcast that a foreign power would shortly destroy Kobe with a geophysically-engineered earthquake, the devastating Kobe earthquake did, in fact, occur. Since it is highly unlikely that either Japan, Russia or Korea would elect to destroy one of their key geophysical warfare laboratories by this heinous act, suspicion must fall on the United States as the most probable perpetrator, since it is known that America has similar Tesla systems, such as the unit located at the Office of Naval Research facility at Squim, in Washington State. Such devices emit an electromagnetic signature when operating, which is why the Tesla Magnifying Transmitter at Squim is known to have been operational at the precise moment that Mount Saint Helens exploded. It is possible that the Mount Saint Helens eruption was a test, in order to verify that such highly destructive technology could be used at a later date on behalf of the Illuminati, in order to destroy much of the West Coast of America by means of tsunamis thousands of feet in height, in conjunction with the engineered eruption of volcanoes in the Pacific Northwest, as a depopulation measure. This evil enterprise would be in accordance with the Club of Rome's diabolical machinations. Such horrific events could occur as early as the Spring of 2002.

Eyewitnesses claim that blue plasma was observed emanating from the roof of the Murrah Federal Building in Oklahoma City, in 1995, a few seconds prior to the blast which killed many people. In addition, computers in nearby buildings had their electrical circuits destroyed, suggestive that a Tesla Magnifying Transmitter was used to generate an electromagnetic pulsed shockwave, which momentarily raised the building off its foundations. The impact caused by the structure falling back to earth would have been sufficient to detonate charges of unstable explosive (e.g. mercury fulminate) which allegedly had been placed in the building adjacent to structural columns. It is a matter of record that rescue workers had to evacuate the wrecked building four times on the day of the explosion, after the discovery of explosives which had failed to detonate. In addition, witnesses claim that the FBI had ordered a larger crater in the structure's foundations to be filled with cement only three hours after the blast. Why? Rescue workers claim that they were interrupted in their search for survivors by FBI officials, while the latter retrieved important papers. Were these papers the ones purportedly stored there by fired FBI director William Webster, who was pursuing an investigation involving the alleged illegal use of the Children Defense Fund as a drug money laundering vehicle?

Shortly after the catastrophic Kobe earthquake, the Aum Shinrykyo science minister who had accurately predicted the quake warning over the airwaves, was killed by a North Korean assassin. This event was followed by the deadly gas attack in the Tokyo subway system, for which the Aum cult was blamed. Since the intelligence community has evidence which suggests that the Aum cult was not involved in the incident, nor that the chemical warfare agent used by the terrorists was Sarin, as claimed by the media, it would appear that the Aum cult was framed. This may be because the Aum science minister's radio broadcast had attracted too much attention to the cult's scientific research activities. By discrediting the cult, the media's attention has been misdirected away from the other four fingers of the Black Hand. As was previously mentioned, it was the Mahikari cult member Yasuko Shimada who was instrumental in acquiring the Banjawarn sheep station in Australia, on behalf of the Aum Shinrykyo organization, presumably so that the Aum cult could monitor the trajectory of the Australian fireball plasmoids. In order to assume a lower public profile, the Aum cult has changed its name to *Aleph.*

It is imperative that we address the question as to why Russia wanted to form a scientific alliance with Japan, for the purpose of developing second generation Tesla superweapons; why not form the alliance with America for instance? The answer lies in the mergers and acquisitions frenzy which plagued the major industrial corporations of the western nations during the 1980's.

This insidious practice often entailed not merely the hostile takeover of a corporation, but also the stripping of company assets, including employee pension funds. Even in the case of corporations which successfully fought off corporate raiders, the company was left so financially depleted that much of its key labor force had to be laid off. In consequence, it has been virtually impossible for western corporations to establish the ten year plans that are usually necessary for the development and production implementation of sophisticated items such as computer chips, for instance. To make matters worse, western nations have embraced the post industrial society ideology, by having industrial products manufactured by third world nations.

In contrast to this economic lunacy, Japan has avoided the corporate takeover mania that has destroyed the industrial base which made America a dominant global power. This has enabled Japan to maintain the long term plans necessary for the development and production of extremely complex 100 megabit computer chips, which is something western nations are unable to accomplish. At the commencement of a nuclear war, it is imperative for an aggressor to destroy the opposing nation's nuclear missiles, before they can be launched in retaliation. This entails scoring a virtually direct hit on the opponent's underground missile silos—something which can not be accomplished unless the incoming missile has a guidance system which incorporates 100 megabit computer chips. Since Japan is the only nation with the production capability to manufacture chips of such complexity, this has placed Japan in the enviable position of deciding whether the computer chips are sold to Russia or America, thus permitting Japan to hold the nuclear balance of power.

Unfortunately for the NATO countries, it is known that Japan has provided Russia with the 100 megabit computer chips, in return for receiving Tesla superweapon technology. Such a trade could be payback for the manner in which Japan was forced into W.W.II by Rockefeller political intrigue. In addition, Japan is quite cognizant of the fact that Russia and China, gravely concerned about British and American plans to establish a global hegemony, clearly intend to forestall this conspiracy by launching a nuclear first strike on America, to be followed by an invasion (possibly as early as 2004). Japan hopes that the demise of America will ultimately pave the way for the Japanese oligarchy to establish their own global hegemony, the latter being the primary reason for the creation of the Black Hand organization.

Another major political figure in the Japanese Liberal Democratic Party is ultra-nationalist Shintaro Ishihara, who happens to have been a major sponsor of the Aum cult, and also has links to the Mahikari cult. The Sukyo Mahikari cult was founded in 1978 by Oshienushisama, the adopted daughter of the late Lt. Colonel Yoshikazu Okada. Okada was a former member of the Japanese Imperial Guard, who had participated in the infamous Rape of Nanking in 1937.

A fervent believer in the divinity of the Japanese Emperor, whom Okada claimed was the reincarnation of the former ruler of the world, prior to the biblical flood, Okada was a rabid racist who despised those of the Jewish faith. After being ousted from a Shinto-oriented religious group for alleged sexual improprieties and displaying an interest in ritual magic, Okada founded a religious cult which he named Sekai Mahikari Bunmei Kyodan (SMBK) and promoted the concept of healing through the use of a healing force projected through the hands.

In order to further his aim of establishing a global hegemony on behalf of his Emperor, Okada clearly designed his religious cult to be appealing to people of many religious beliefs, through the simple ploy of falsely associating biblical figures with Japan. Thus, Okada claimed that Moses visited Japan and that Christ was buried there! This is blatantly false dogma, as archaeological data presented in this book demonstrated that the biblical figures of Christ and Moses were clearly apochryphal.

His adopted daughter lost a bitterly contested court battle over leadership of the cult, following Okada's death in 1974, and accordingly founded the Sukyo Mahikari religious cult, which now has extensive branches throughout the world. Since all the cult's property is in her name, she has become one of Japan's wealthiest individuals.

The Mahikari has been termed "dangerous" by a Belgian parliamentary commission, and has been under investigation by Australian Federal Police for ties to the Aum Shinrkyo cult, in addition to allegations of behavior modification of its members. According to an article by Norman Abjorensen in the *Australia/Israel Review,* "Sukyo Mahikari has, behind a facade of benign spiritual enlightenment, a doctrine based on world domination and veneration for the Emperor of Japan."

In keeping with the other fingers of the Black Hand, the Sukyo Mahikari religious cult possesses an outer shell comprised of gullible religious converts, which occludes an inner core of members, such as the previously mentioned Ms. Shimada, who clearly are linked to the geophysical warfare developmental efforts of the Black Hand. Just as the notorius *I Am* New Age movement was ordered disbanded by the United States Government during W.W.II for subersion, after it was discovered that it had been covertly controlled by Nazis, as a means for the establishment of a fifth column in foreign countries, so the Sukyo Mahikari makes an ideal vehicle for the infiltration of foreign governmental agencies, as exemplified by the cult's alleged infiltration of members into the Belgian police force.

The inner core of the Black Hand clearly embraces Emperor worship and the establishment of a Japanese global political hegemony. A female relative of the present Japanese Emperor recently wrote disparagingly about the western branches of the Illuminati, shortly after she had interviewed the heads of state of various western nations. This is not surprising since the various regional Illuminati factions all wish to have the greatest slice of the global pie for themselves, after the planned Illuminati totalitarian global government has been established circa 2010. The Japanese Imperial Family is a very old established faction of the Illuminati, whose members are known to still participate in rituals held in conjunction with Illuminists of western Illuminati bloodline families. It is therefore understandable that the Japanese faction would wish to be the dominant group, especially since Japan is one of the portions of Atlantis that was not submerged in the biblical flood, according to Illuminati historians.

The author believes that the Illuminati controlled Tavistock Institute, together with its vast global network of social engineering think tanks, has sown the seeds of its self destruction; in other words, the entire Illuminati structure will implode. This will be initiated through the religious mind control activities of its "friendly enemies"—Russia and its geophysical warfare ally, the Black Hand.

To comprehend the political overtones behind this probable event, it is necessary to briefly review Russian history. In 988 A.D., Prince Vladimir of Kievan Rus, the offspring of Prince Svyatoslav and the daughter of a Khazar Rabbi, adopted the Eastern Orthodox branch of Christianity.

From that time on, Russia fell under the feudal control of a few aristocratic landowners, who created a secret society known as the Holy Brotherhood. In the 19th century, as previously stated, the Illuminati created the New Age movement as a disinformation ploy, primarily in order to misdirect attention away from meaningful research into the nature of ætheric energy. A secondary intent was the subversion of western culture, the latter being successfully accomplished during the 20th century by the Tavistock cabal.

New Age disinformation initially was effected through the creation of the Theosophical Society, whose founding members, including

Russian born Helena Blavatsky, were initiates of various Illuminati secret sub-groups, including the satanic Order of Luxor. The Theosophical Society developed from Abbé Dom Pernetty's *Avignon Society*, which created a ritual known as the Rite of the Illuminati, circa 1760. Benedict Chastanier, a founding member of the Avignon Society, relocated to England and created the *Order of Illuminated Theosophists* in 1767, which changed its name to the Theosophical Society in 1784. Another occult lodge—the *Rite of Swedenborg*, was an offshoot of this latter organization.

Among its members were Colonel Olcott and Charles Southeran, both of whom founded, in conjunction with Blavatsky, the Theosophical Society of today. In her private correspondence with her sister, Blavatsky revealed that her "Ascended Masters" were, in actuality, merely nicknames that she had assigned to wealthy masonic patrons of the Theosophical Society, and displayed outrage against phony psychics who were claiming to channel these non existent beings.[17]

Prominently associated with the Theosophical Society during its formative years was Russian military attaché Count Muraviev-Amursky, who was an intelligence operative of Count Alexander Ignatiev, whose family were long-time controllers of the military arm of the Okrana, Russia's pre-revolutionary intelligence service. The Okrana was headquartered within the Saint Petersburg Ecclesiastical Academy, which was an arm of the Russian Orthodox Church.

After the 1917 Russian Revolution, Soviet influence infiltrated into various Theosophical and Ordo Templi Orientis (OTO) lodges in Europe, including the Vienese Blue Lodge of Theosophy, with which both Carl Jung and Sigmund Freud were associated. The Carl Jung Foundation allegedly has been linked to mind control cultic activities.

Carl Jung was a major figure in the on-going struggle by the Illuminati social engineers to control the minds of humanity. He devoted much time to developing ways to change the mindset of the masses "…which gave us the Renaissance." Jung lectured at the *Children of the Sun* at Ascona, Italy, a learning center for Illuminati offspring. He provided a safehouse for Lenin and Trotsky there. Jung lectured to Mary Mellon, who later founded the *Bollingen Center* in America; this particular center spawned several cults.

Jung was not only an influential advisor to Nazi sympathizer and CIA director Allen Dulles, he also instructed Alice Bailey and her 33rd Degree husband Foster. Bailey founded the Lucifer Publishing Company, which later changed its name to the *Lucis Trust*, for obvious reasons. Her book *Education in the New Age*, outlined a social engineering program which later was adopted by the Club of Rome. In it she wrote: "….the science of eugenics will grow."[18]

The Lucis Trust is a major New Age command center for the Illuminati, as evidenced by its sponsors, who have included John D. Rockefeller; former U.S. Defense Secretary Robert McNamara; former World Bank President and Masonic Grand Master Henry Clausen; Thomas Watson, former U.S. Ambassador to Russia and IBM President; and the late Canon West, Dean of New York's Cathedral of Saint John the Divine and Protocol Officer to Queen Elizabeth II.[19]

The Lucis Trust operates a network of New Age groups known as *"Triangles;"* the author has personally observed a Triangles coordinator telephone the CIA and report personal details regarding group members.

Jung's Russian connection extended beyond providing sanctuary to Trotsky and Lenin (Lenin studied for the priesthood, and was initiated into a satanic cult on the Isle of Capri, Italy). Jung's assistant at Ascona was Olga Froebe Kapteyn, the grand daughter of Russian founding member of the Theosophical Society, Prince Kropotkin. It was she who initiated the current Earth Mother Goddess fad so enamoured by New Agers.

A United Nations conference was held in Brussels in 1976 to celebrate the UN's *"Year of the Woman."* Out of the conference emerged another UN organization named the *"Women's International Collectives* (WICCE). This organization publishes a journal called *Isis,* and is involved in the coordination of feminine Wicca groups. It interfaces with the Russian controlled *Women's International League for Peace and Freedom,* in Geneva; it is also associated in America with the *Revolutionary Communist Party.* The latter organization was involved in precursor activities which culminated in the last Los Angeles riot, which was a carefully orchestrated event directed by elements associated with the United States Government—not a spontaneous act.

The above comments would suggest that Russia is a willing co-conspirator in the Illuminati's global social engineering project, but in actuality, a hidden agenda may be involved. This is because in 1982, a mysterious organization was founded in Russia. Known as Pamyat (memory) and intensely nationalistic, its leaders believe that Russians have a spiritual destiny to rule the world, and that Moscow will become the new global religious center, succeeding Rome and Constantinople.

Pamyat cannot be readily dismissed as yet another New Age kook organization, even though it emphasizes Planet Earth worship, for it has been under the direction of Russian Intelligence and military officials, such as the late General Aleksei Yepishev, director of the *Main Political Directorate* (MPD) of the Soviet Army and Navy. Yepishev was a close associate of KGB chief Yuri Andropov.[20] Pamyat recruits many members from numerous societies sponsored by the Russian military, e.g. the *Rossiya Society,* founded by Marshall Vasili Chuikov, which boasts more than ten million members.

Pamyat was the brainchild of rabid anti-Zionist and Fascist ideologue Valeri Yemelyanov, who was associated with the Institute of Oriental Studies, a think-tank whose gnostic research was used by Russian Intelligence to create cults in foreign nations.

According to Yemelyanov, who promoted the fraudulent *"Protocols of the Elders of Zion"* (almost certainly a Jesuit fabrication) the Russian Orthodox Church was a Jewish plot for the purpose of supplanting paganism. As a result of his public rantings, Russian Jews have been persecuted and some murdered. Yemelyanov himself murdered his wife with an axe in 1980, but was not prosecuted due to KGB intervention. Instead, he was institutionalized until 1987.

Pamyat's intent is well defined in its manifesto, which states: "International Zionism and Freemasonry have removed their visor and gone openly on the offensive against the last remaining islets of spirituality and national conciousness. Three years ago, Pamyat began ringing the alarm bell."

Since Pamyat exerts such a powerful influence on the Russian military, its manifesto should be taken very seriously, particularly since both Gorbachev and Yeltsin are admirers of Pamyat. It should be noted that in his 1987 address to the Russian Politburo, Gorbachev (who faked his own overthrow) stated that in the next few years, Russians would hear much mention of *Perestroika*. Such talk, he said, was to be ignored, since it was merely a ploy to lull foolish Americans into disarming. Ironically, not only has the treasonous American Government sold Gorbachev a portion of the San Francisco military Presideo for the princely sum of one dollar, as a site for his draconian global environmental organization, but he is also on the commitee that determines which U.S. military bases are to be closed!

The Nixon administration purportedly entered into a secret treaty with the Soviets on behalf of the Illuminati, whereby Russia would launch a limited nuclear first strike on several American cities, shortly prior to commencement of W.W.III, for the purpose of population reduction. With the aid of the Russian military, Pamyat, with its demands for a return to a pagan form of religion is, in effect, conducting what amounts to a brainwashing of the Russian public. Even though Russia currently is awash with money derived from petroleum exports, much of this money has been witheld from the private sector, in order to fool the Russian public into concluding that capitalism does not work, thus prompting a demand by the majority of economically deprived Russians for a return to a more authoritarian form of government. In consequence of recent Russian polls, General Alexander Lebed summed up the attitude of the Russian public when he stated: "Democracy in Russia is completely impossible. Most Russians don't care whether they are ruled by the Fascists or Communists or even Martians, as long as they are able to buy six kinds of sausage in the stores and lots of cheap vodka. What's wrong with a military dictator?"

The author believes that Russia is perpetrating a grand strategic deception, whereby Russia and China will invade America and Western Europe in a bid to destroy the western arm of the Illuminati, then establish a global government incorporating a gold backed currency and ruled by Russian and Chinese Illuminati bloodlines. Japan will then be destroyed as payback for the Rape of Nanking.

If such an extreme scenario does not occur, a new global religion will replace existing religions as part of the New World Order. In a remote area of Colorado, in Crestone County, a compound has been established in order to create the Illuminati new global religion. Staffed by representatives of various religions—each group having its separate living quarters, other residents allegedly include rebirthers, a group of midwives known as "Emissaries of Light," and various religious celebrities. Shape-shifting reptilians purportedly have been observed there, according to an informant of the author's, who has worked undercover at the compound, and mind control activities allegedly are practiced. The operation is purportedly under the direction of billionaire and former British Intelligence operative Maurice Strong, and is allegedly Rockefeller funded. Strong allegedly is also active among the Japanese Black Hand Illuminati factions who are associated with the Japanese Emperor.

In conclusion, it is worth remembering that Aldous Huxley, the MK Ultra operative who played a major role in introducing LSD to the public, in order to create the rock counterculture of the 1960's, wrote *"Brave New World."* The purpose of the novel primarily was to enlighten teenaged members of Illuminati families about the intended lifestyle of the mind controlled masses, after a totalitarian New World Order had been accomplished.

The novel described how the global populace would be mind controlled by means of narcotics. It is therefore fitting to quote from a 1967 report written by two MK-Ultra mind control researchers, Dr. Wayne Evans, director of the U.S. Army Military Stress Laboratory, and eugenics advocate and psychiatrist Nathan Kline: "….The present breadth of drug use may be almost trivial when we compare it to the possible numbers of chemical substances that will be available for the control of selective aspects of man's life in the year 2000." Happy New Year!

CHAPTER 14

▼

McCarthyism

All that is necessary for the forces of evil to win in the world is for enough good men to do nothing.

Edmund Burke

This particular chapter is being written on the day that American novelist Ring Lardner died, which is synchronistic since Lardner was imprisoned for refusing to name purported communists, during the notorius McCarthy Congressional Hearings of 1950. The newsmedia would have us believe that the congressional hearings which were chaired by Senator Joseph McCarthy, were held for the express purpose of exposing American citizens who were believed to be communist subversive elements.

In actuality, the McCarthy hearings mainly targeted members of the Hollywood movie community who merely were communist sympathizers—not subversives intent on the overthrow of the United States Government. Only a few of those targetted, e.g. Hollywood journalist Cedric Belfrage and movie producer Boris Morros, were identified in the Venona intercepts as KGB agents. Even to this very day, victims of

McCarthyism, many of whom were denied employment in the movie industry in the aftermath of the hearings for several years, apparently are unaware that the sole purpose of the congressional hearings was to misdirect the attention of the newsmedia and the judicial branch of government away from a powerful faction within the Russian intelligence system known as the *"Trust."*

In order to comprehend why such a political charade was perpetrated, and why McCarthy was chosen to chair the hearings, we must first examine the origins of the subversive organization known as the Trust, which even at the present time, exerts a major influence upon global affairs.

Constantinople, the capital of the mighty Byzantine Empire, which had been founded by the half English Constantine, was known as the Second Rome after the fall of the Roman Empire. One of the most heavily fortified cities in the world, Constantinople became besieged in 1453 A.D. by the army of Sultan Mehmed II, who was the ruler of the Turkish Ottoman Empire. The city's defense force of 10,000 troops was no match for the more than 100,000 Turkish invaders. After fifty days, the enormous Turkish cannons successfully breached the city walls; using trumpets to distract the defenders, the Sultan's troops stormed into the city, but were repelled with heavy losses. After several more attempts, troops from the Sultan's ships, which had been blockading the city's sea defenses, stormed ashore to reinforce the besieging army, which then was able to capture the city. And so ended the Byzantine Empire—but only in name.

The fall of Constantinople had been orchestrated by the oligarchic banking families of Venice, who had controlled the economy of Europe since the 9th century A.D., due to its geopolitical location between eastern and western trading blocs. In order to provide credit between Constantinople and Britain, and all trading centers in between, noble Venetian families had created specialized banking institutions, thus enabling Venice to play a pivotal role in European politics. The

Venetians had provided the Sultan with artillery and mercenaries. After the conquest, the Sultan awarded the Venetians large tracts of land in Byzantine Greece, where the Paleologues were the most prominent family, and also provided them with authority over the Ottoman intelligence service.[1]

The deposed Emperor, Constantine Paleologue, found sanctuary in Rome. In 1472, his daughter Zoe changed her name to Sophia, and married Ivan III of Russia. Sophia successfully persuaded her new husband to adopt the Byzantine title of Caesar (Czar in Muscovite Russia) and the Byzantine imperial ideology of totalitarian rule.[2]

Prince Vladimir (972—1015) was a disenchanted man. Rape and pillage no longer excited the Russian barbarian; the 200 concubines he kept at Berestof, nor the 300 at Vychegorod, nor even the 3,000, give or take a few, who were maintained at Bielgorod for his exclusive pleasure, made him contented any more. Poor Vladimir eventually concluded that what was lacking in his life was a religion capable of uplifting his soul.

Atop the precipitous sandy cliffs of his capital city of Kiev, overlooking the Dnieper River, Vladimir ordered the construction of a statue of the Slavic deity Perun, which bore a silver head and a beard of gold. Sacrificing a Varangian father and son at the base of the idol did nothing for the barbarian's soul. Not to be defeated in his religious quest, Vladimir dispatched ambassadors to various nations, with orders to report back on religions deemed capable of fulfilling the prince's spiritual needs.

Evaluating the various reports, Vladimir disliked the notion of circumcision, and so rejected Judaism. Islam fared no better since it forbade the consumption of alchohol—a Russian national pastime. Catholicism he considered lacking in ceremonial majesty. The reports that he received from the ambassadors who had returned from Constantinople however, left him amazed. They had been awestruck by the glorious religious ceremonies of the Eastern Orthodox Church, which were attended by the Emperor and his Court, and the opulence of the sacerdotal vestments worn by the High Priest. This obviously was the preferred religion for a Russian barbarian prince.

To become a member of the Eastern Christian Church necessitated that Prince Vladimir undergo baptism. This presented a problem, for the proud Russian barbarian found it unacceptable to humble himself before the Byzantine Emperor. Answering to no one, Vladimir resolved the thorny problem simply by capturing several Greek Byzantine priests (together with the requisite sacred relics of course) who conducted the baptismal rite on the prince in the captured Byzantine city of Cherson. Returning to his capital city of Kiev, Prince Vladimir ordered the statue of the deity Perun to be flogged, then dispatched to a watery grave in the River Dnieper, much to the consternation of the superstitious towns-folk, who were promptly ordered into the frigid river for a mass baptism. Vladimir now was a spiritually contented individual, according to the historian Nestor and, rather remarkably, eventually attained sainthood.

Prior to his religious conversion, Prince Vladimir, like his predecessors, was merely a tribal leader, not a sovereign ruler. Vladimir's conversion to Byzantine Christianity gradually transformed Russia, for his captive Greek priests introduced not only their Byzantine religion, but also Byzantine governmental doctrine. No longer were his soldiers free to quit whenever they elected to do so, for now they were part of an imperial standing army, whose commander-in-chief had become a majestic sovereign overlord, with power bequeathed him from God. Unlike other Slavic nations such as Poland, who became satrapies of the Roman Church, with its lack of separation between religious and secular matters, Vladimir, in fortuitously receiving Christianity from Byzantium, where the Eastern Christian Church leaders refrained from intruding into governmental matters, was free to govern without clerical interference. And thus Russia became a Christian nation.

As was mentioned previously, the overthrow of the Byzantine Empire was perpetrated with assistance from the Venetian banking oligarchy. Soon after Ivan III had married Zoe, he was pursuaded by the Venetian Senate to declare Moscow the Third Rome, as a successor to Rome and Constantinople. This ideology was later popularized by the 16th century Russian Orthodox priest Philotheos of Pskov.

A major reform of what was now the Russian Orthodox Church occurred in 1654, when the Church Patriarch Nikon, concerned over errors made by priests several centuries earlier, during the course of translating Byzantine religious texts into Old Slavic, prompted him to adopt the texts and practices of the Greek Orthodox Church as they existed in 1652, the year he was elected Patriarch.

The Patriarch's religious reforms sent shockwaves throughout Russia. Led by Archpriest Avvakum Petrovich, millions of Russians who preferred the earlier religious format, rose in opposition, initially in the more remote peasant regions of Russia, then later in Moscow. A series of church councils endorsed the reformation, and Avvakum, together with other leading dissenters, were executed.

The dissenters became known as the *"Raskolniki"* (Old Believers). Possessed of a "blood and soil" national ideology, the Raskolniki were resistant to change in both religious and secular matters. In later years they were to oppose the reforms of Peter the Great, who attempted to westernize Russia, and also Czar Alezander II, who had threatened Britain to refrain from interceding in the American Civil War. A major Raskolniki ideologue of the 19th century was the writer Fyodor Dostoevsky. It cannot be overemphasized that Raskolniki influence in Russian affairs of state is not a thing of the past, for its overtones of Byzantine Imperialism still exerts a very powerful influence among Russian political leaders, civil and military, and also in the hierarchy of the Russian Imperial Church. All of these factions are intent upon establishing Moscow as the Third Rome, by force, if necessary. The ultra nationalistic Russian organization Pamyat is simply a new bottle for this very old wine.

Until the disintegration of the Soviet Union, both the ruling Nomenklatura of the Soviet Communist Party and the great military strategist Marshall Ogarkov, embraced the Byzantine oligarchical social order of the Raskolniki. At the present time, as was stated in the previous chapter, Russia is conspiring to effect a grand deception by creating the illusion that it has become a second class global power. In actuality, at the apparent dissolution of the Soviet Union, the Raskolnik power structure simply transferred much of Russia's wealth, together with many of its ruling members, overseas, leaving second level bureaucrats such as Yeltsin and Vladimir Putin to front for the real Russian covert power structure, with its attendant Byzantine oriented totalitarian "blood and soil" ideology. This is typified by the fact that during the year prior to becoming the purported Russian head of state, Vladimir Putin undertook five clandestine trips to the Spanish estate of Russian power broker and multi billionaire Boris Borezovsky.[3]

Much has been written in conspiracy oriented books concerning the funding for the Russian Revolution by Illuminist members of the City of London and Wall Street financial houses, but little has been said regarding the role of the same Venetian oligarchic banking families who inspired Czar Ivan III in his attempt to create Moscow as the Third Rome.

It was a Venetian-Swiss-Austrian intelligence network under the direction of Venetian diplomat Volpi di Misurata, that persuaded the German Foreign Office to provide funding and a safe passage for the former Russian Jesuit seminary student and satanist Lenin, to covertly re-enter Russia from his exile in Switzerland, for the purpose of igniting the Bolshevik revolution. Volpi's principal spy was Alexander Israel Helphand, a Russian Jew who was born in Odessa, on the Black Sea. Helphand, code named "Parvus," was paid a very large sum of money by the British oligarchy to oversee the assassination of Archduke Ferdinand, the infamous event which initiated W.W.I.

After the Russian Revolution had become a reality, Lenin's dreaded secret police agency known as the Cheka, was under the direction of spymaster Felix Dzerzhinski, a beady-eyed, gnomelike Polish activist, who had spent many hard years in the jails of Czar Nicholas II. It was through the relationship between Dzerzhinski, Volpi and Helphand that the intelligence organization called the *"Trust"* was spawned.[4]

The Trust was (and still is) an intelligence cabal and command center which operates on behalf of certain Illuminati oligarchic parties in Russia and also in various western nations. In its formative years, it also included high-level members of the Czarist secret police agency known as the Okhrana.

During the 1930's, Stalin became alarmed at the manner in which western oligarchical members of the Trust were looting the Soviet Union of its natural resources and grain production, which consequently created a schism within the Trust. The schism was finally healed with the death of Stalin, who, like Franklin D.Roosevelt, died under mysterious circumstances.

The oligarchic members of the Trust, through their influence on global geopolitics, have generated vast fortunes for themselves at the expense of the masses. This is particularly so through their creation of the phony Cold War, whose principal architect was Sir Winston Churchill. This cold war period financially benefited the corrupt military industrial complex. It was precisely to misdirect attention away from the political machinations of the Trust that the McCarthy Congressional Hearings were held.

Senator Joseph McCarthy's political handler was Father Edmund Walsh, the Jesuit Regent of the Georgetown University Foreign Service School. Here it should be noted that the *Society of Jesus* (popularly known as the Jesuits) was created by Ignatius Loyola in 1540 A.D. as an intelligence agency, under the patronage of the Contarinis, a Venetian noble family involved in banking. Prior to escaping from his incarceration on the island of Saint Helena, Napoleon noted that first and foremost, the Jesuits are a *military* order.

The Jesuit's organization is structured along Freemasonic lines and has a long history of involvement in political affairs of state. These affairs include orchestrating the American Revolution, whose perpetrators, acting on behalf of the Jesuit Superior General Lorenzo Ricci, included the 3rd Earl of Bute (advisor to King George III) the Jesuit professor John Carroll and his cousin Charles. Even the first colonial flag selected by a Flag Commitee headed by General George Washington and Ben Franklin, was the house flag of the Jesuit controlled East India Company, which consisted of a Union Jack and thirteen stripes. The Jesuits also were very much involved in the assassination of Presidents Abraham Lincoln and John Kennedy, the latter having incurred the wrath of the Jesuit Superior General and his American asset Cardinal Spellman, for intending to halt the Vietnam War, thus preventing the genocide of many Vietnamese Buddhists— Buddhism being anathema to the Jesuits (as are all non Catholic religions).

In the aftermath of the bloody Russian Revolution of 1917, it was only natural for western powers to infiltrate intelligence operatives into the Soviet Union, in order to effectively monitor the internal political power struggles. Many of these spies were members of the International Red cross, in order to gain easy access into the fledgling Soviet Union. In a similar manner, the Vatican sent Father Walsh to Russia in 1922, to become head of a Papal Relief Mission. Despite the enmity which exists between the Vatican hierarchy and the Jesuits (the Jesuit headquarters are at the Piazza del Gesu, in Rome, hence the letter "G" in the masonic logo) selecting Walsh for the task made good strategic sense, for Russia had provided sanctuary for the Jesuits after Pope Innocent had outlawed the Jesuit Order in 1773. While in Russia, the Jesuits created schools and also performed social work until they left Russia after Pope

Innocent was assassinated. They then founded the University of Louvain. At the university, they developed a plan for a Holy Alliance, which later became an integral part of the New World Order. Walsh was known to have been involved with this Louvain Jesuit network. Perhaps at this point in our narrative it is well to point out that in the overall global scheme of things, the various masonic Grand Masters— Protestant, Jewish and Catholic, all report to an "Unknown Superior," who is the Jesuit Superior General, also known as the Black Pope. The Black Pope in turn reports to the head of the Illuminati, who is known by his codename of Pin d'Ar (note that Hilary Clinton held her press conference announcing her senatorial candidacy, at Pindar's Corner).

Helphand (Parvus) who was one of the instigators of the Russian revolution, also was one of the early architects of the Soviet intelligence service known as the Cheka. In addition, he was the mentor of Trotsky, who attained a position of prominence within the Trust, due to his promotion of the concept of initiating revolution on a global scale. During the period of Walsh's sojurn in Moscow, the Raskolnik Bukharin, another Parvus protegé, joined the Trust and became the Soviet dictator, until ousted by Stalin for allowing the looting of Soviet agricultural products.

It was during the 1920's that Father Walsh became a member of the Trust. After Stalin severed contact with the Trust and purged its Bolshevik members, Walsh began an association with Karl Haushofer, head of the German Geopolitical Institute. It was Haushofer who conceived the Nazi *"Lebensraum"* (living room) policy, which Hitler used as a pretext to invade Czechoslovakia. Haushofer was the mentor of Deputy Reichsfuehrer Rudolph Hess. Hess was a member of the Communist International Conference that was held in 1920; he was accompanied at the conference by Soviet asset and anthroposophist Rudolf Steiner, who also was a member of the Ordo Templi Orientis cult. Interestingly, Father Walsh later was appointed to head a prosecutorial team that was delegated to interrogate Karl Haushofer at the

Nuremburg War Crimes Tribunal after the capitulation of Nazi Germany. Walsh's lack of an intensive interrogation of Haushofer presumably was for the purpose of suppressing any inadvertent disclosures by Haushofer regarding the Trust.

The schism within the Trust that was initiated by Stalin, prompted western Trust members to launch an anti communist campaign within the United States, in an attempt to pressure the Soviets into restoring a pro-Trust faction within the Soviet power structure. According to the late American journalist Drew Pearson, it was Father Walsh who sold Senator Joe McCarthy on the plan to hold Congressional hearings into alleged subversive communist activities. Pearson's allegation later was substantiated in the writings of McCarthy counsel Roy Cohn, and Father Walsh's protegé, the Illuminati apologist Professor Carrol Quigley, of the Jesuit controlled Georgetown University, in his book *Tragedy and Hope*.[6]

Since the Trust, in keeping with most subversive happenings in the world, essentially has been an Illuminati activity, directed as usual by their lackeys the Jesuits, it is advisable to note that the Jesuits invariably incorporate into their convoluted stategies the precepts, or articles, of that ancient Chinese military strategist Sun-tzu. Being cognizant of Sun-tzu's thirteen precepts, as outlined in his written work known as *The Art of War*, makes it easier to track the evil machinations of the Jesuits.

The rationale for Father Walsh to select Senator McCarthy as head Congressional inquisitor of the hapless Hollywood communist sympathizers was obvious: McCarthy, who was scheduled to begin preparations for his 1952 re-election campaign, had several major skeletons in his closet. As a Nazi sympathizer, McCarthy had been associated with Frau Hede Messing, a leading member of a Nazi spy ring, which had connections to the Trust and also to Soviet spy-master M.N. Roy. It was apparently Hede-Messing who persuaded McCarthy to intercede on behalf of Nazi S.S. Officers who had received death sentences by the

Nuremburg Tribunal for their involvement in the infamous Malmedy massacre, in which American prisoners of war were shot in cold blood. The senator also had taken a $10,000 bribe from a construction company that was under congressional investigation. McCarthy also was a known associate of the German Communist Party member Rudolf Aschenauer.

McCarthy initially was linked to Father Walsh through Roy Cohn, a homosexual member of McCarthy's staff who later died of Aids. Both the *Las Vegas Sun* newspaper and an FBI report claimed that McCarthy was a closet homosexual, suggestive that the senator may have been blackmailed by the Soviets, particularly since another FBI report alleged that there was a conspiracy instigated by Jesuit intelligence asset Cardinal Spellman and the late Joseph Kennedy to undermine the Eisenhower administration for the purpose of installing Senator McCarthy as President of the United States.[7]

It was on February 9th, 1950, that Senator McCarthy gave his infamous speech at Wheeling, West Virginia, which misdirected the attention of the media away from the Trust conspirators, and also allowed McCarthy's numerous skeletons to remain undisturbed in their closet. The Senator's congressional hearings, which had struck fear into the hearts of Hollywood's communist sympathizers, met their Waterloo when the counsel for the army (Welch) made his memorable "Have you no shame?" speech at the Army-McCarthy hearings.

By then the damage had been done however. Truly subversive Soviet elements, who had successfully penetrated Wall Street, were more firmly entrenched than ever, and McCarthyites had attained high positions within the American intelligence community. Sadly, the "communist behind every bush" mentality that was fostered among the American populace by the McCarthy Hearings, served to fan the flames of the phony cold war, which had been created by the military industrial complex.[8]

It was McCarthyism hysteria which sealed the fate of nuclear physicists Ethel and Julius Rosenberg. Regardless of whether or not they were guilty of passing nuclear secrets to the Soviets, the McCarthy Hearings undoubtedly influenced the trial outcome and their subsequent executions. Hypocritically, key nuclear secrets, together with much of the American stockpile of fissionable nuclear materials, covertly had been flown to Russia in 1943, from a military airfield in Montana (Gore Field) under the direction of Truman aide Harry Hopkins, allegedly at the instigation of the Rockefeller family.

In conclusion, the data presented in this chapter is indicative that Communism did not commence with the satanist Karl Marx, as is popularly believed, but has been an integral part of the Raskolnik ideology for centuries, with its emphasis on authoritarian state control of the masses. The fact that the hidden power structure behind the current Russian grand deception appears to be mainly composed of Raskolnik ideologues, does not bode well for America and Western Europe, especially since Russia has established covert strategic alliances with China and Japan, for the express purpose of embarking upon the military destruction of Western nations. Obviously, the situation presents a clear and present danger, especially when the treasonous President Clinton has provided China with advanced military technology and equipment, including propulsion systems for cruise missiles and a prototype hand-held chemical fusion weapon, the latter having been illegally sold to China at an auction held at the Redstone Arsenal, the bill of sale being written up as "used furniture." [9]

Perhaps the optimum way to avert armed conflict in the present situation is to attempt to modify the mindset of the Russian, Chinese and Japanese public, so that they no longer adhere to their present nationalistic cultural paradigms which hold that they are a master race (e.g. the Japanese contemptuously refer to the Chinese as "garlic eaters"). The belief structure of political and military leaders has largely been determined since childhood by their overlords; to make matters worse, interracial communication between the masses has until recently been quite limited, hence it is sometimes difficult to comprehend the social mores of other nationalities, particularly if separated by vast geographical distances.

Fortunately, a paradigm shift occurred through the commercialization of the internet, which has facilitated the dissemination of a vast amount of knowledge on a global scale. No longer does public opinion have to be shaped by corrupt political spinmeisters doing the bidding of their Illuminati overlords. For the first time in recorded history, we the people have an opportunity to disseminate the truth concerning political events through the internet, to members of the public in far off lands.

In this manner, public opinion can be shaped from the bottom up, for a change, hopefully influencing political and military leaders in the process. If we avail ourselves of this international form of communication, we the people have an excellent opportunity to attune interracially, and through sheer weight of numbers, refuse to fight wars fought for the self aggrandisement of the Illuminati. If we fail in this endeavor, then with certitude we will have sown the seeds of our own destruction.

CHAPTER 15

▼

FLYING SAUCERS FROM PLANET EARTH

"Truth will ultimately prevail where there is pains taken to bring it to light."

George Washington.

The principal focus of most UFO-oriented literature is that UFO's are solely the creation of extra terrestrial beings, which is utter nonsense; very little has been published concerning anti gravitic craft of terrestrial origin.

This sorry state of affairs is probably due to disinformation promulgated at the instigation of Illuminati "One World" controllers, in order to conceal the reality of terrestrially constructed flying saucers from the general public. Presumably this is because the military-industrial complex has derived its global political clout through its control of energy sources, in addition to the accumulation of vast wealth derived from the sale of weaponry and fossil derived fuel to opposing factions, during protracted and controlled major wars. In consequence, public knowledge regarding flying saucers and other types of anti gravitic craft which have been developed by humans, has been suppressed for the following reasons:

a)   Antigravitic craft such as flying saucers, utilize propulsion systems which possess free energy characteristics (i.e. they develop far more energy than they consume, unlike conventional internal combustion engines, whose efficiency is less than one hundred percent). Consequently, adoption of this propulsion technology for such applications as electrical generating facilities, automobiles and other transportation systems, would drastically reduce the the consumption of fossil fuels. At the present time, it is easy for the Illuminati overlords to control the mobility of the public, if deemed necessary, simply by curtailing the supply of fossil fuels, as was evidenced during the 1973 contrived energy crisis. Naturally, this would be impossible if public transportation was not dependent upon fossil fuels.

b)   The utilization of such craft for military purposes would drastically curtail the duration of major wars, thus reducing the profits of the military/industrial complex.

In America, UFO matters and promulgation of relevant disinformation, are under the direction of the National Reconassance Office, which has the authority to order retaliation against hostile UFO's (public domain footage downloaded during a transmission from a space shuttle, graphically shows a UFO taking evasive action in order to avoid being hit by a laser weapon fired from earth). A scalar beam weapon that was developed under Project Sealight and tested at the Port Hueneme Naval Facility in California, has now been installed on certain naval vessels for the purpose of destroying UFO's deemed hostile. Major resonsibility for the security of covert subterranean flying saucer bases in American is undertaken by the Defense Industrial Security Command (DISC) which delegated lesser security tasks to the notorius privately owned Wackenhut Corporation.

The DISC is a super-secret intelligence agency that was created in order to protect the interests of the military/industrial complex, and is fronted by the U.S. Office of Naval Intelligence. Early members of DISC were high-level Nazis who were covertly brought to America under the Operation Paperclip program. Lee Harvey Oswald, Clay Shaw and novelist Ian Fleming were all members of DISC; the DISC cabal played a major role in the assassinations of President Kennedy and Martin Luther King.

During the 19th century, one of the most influential public figures in global politics was the previously mentioned Lord Bulwer Lytton. An exponent of the Isis Cult, Lytton created a very efficient terrorist network along ethnic lines, on behalf of the British oligarchy, which is still operational today, directing the activities of many terrorist groups worldwide, in conjunction with the elite Special Air Services (SAS) division of the British military. Lytton also revitalized the almost defunct Sicillian Mafia, under the direction of Guiseppi Mazzini, who was the Grand Master of the Italian branch of the Scottish Rite Masonic Order. One of Lord Lytton's proteges was Karl Haushofer, who founded the Vril Society in Germany after reading Lytton's novel *"Vril: The Power of the Coming Race."* Vril is a term for ætheric energy, and was symbolized by the lightning insignia on Nazi S.S. uniforms.

Lytton was the principal overlord of the Illuminati global opium trade; opium grown in India was sold to China, the resultant profits being used to purchase cotton plantations in America. African slaves to work the plantations were transported in ships financed by the Church of England (hypocritically, the first slave ship operating on the West African coast was the good ship *Jesus*; existing records of Lloyd's insurance company reveal that the Church of England was recompensed for slaves that were thrown overboard whenever water supplies ran low). Cotton grown in America was shipped to England, where it was woven into cloth for export to India, where it was traded in exchange for opium. The corrupt New England families who managed the American end of this global enterprise, later became the American Establishment (e.g. The Cabots, Welds, Roosevelts, Spellmans, etc.). It was the vast profits generated by this still on going narco enterprise, that enabled the various secret societies spawned by Lord Lytton to finance the development of terrestrially constructed flying saucers.[1]

Today, the United States branch of this illicit venture is composed of the military/ industrial intelligence complex, and is known as the *Black Rose Society;* it was co-founded by George Bush Sr., when he was director of the CIA. The Black Rose name was derived from the Illuminati custom of presenting twelve black roses and one white one to an Illuminati associated person slated for assassination.

The Industrial Revolution was an event not exactly in accordance with the traditional Illuminati ideology of preventing the upward mobility of the masses, for the advent of the Industrial Age enabled inventors and entrepreneurs of modest financial means, to rise above their allotted social station in life. In an attempt to inhibit technological advances (for a well informed populace is difficult to subjugate) the Illuminati established scientific institutions such as Britain's Royal Society, which was founded by the pederast Sir Francis Bacon, for the purpose of suppressing advanced technology.

A typical example was the invention of a steam engine by the French inventor Denis Papin in 1690. The Royal Society refused Papin's request for payment of fifteen guineas, in order to oversee the development of an advanced version of his steam engine, designed specifically for powering a boat. In this manner, the society was able to delay the advancement of steam power for fifty years, until Newcomen constructed an inferior version of one of Papin's earliest designs. At the present time, universities suppress the technological breakthroughs in electrical engineering which were discovered more than a century ago by inventive geniuses such as d'Arsonval and Tesla, in order to prevent the commercial implementation of so-called free energy devices. Similarly, Maxwell's theory of electromagnetism, which incorporated the relationship between magnetism and gravity, and accordingly was a true unified field theory, was harshly edited after his death by a scientific clique consisting of physicists Oliver Heavyside and Heinrich Hertz and chemist Willard Gibbs, who removed the gravitational component from Maxwell's posthumously-published work, thus rendering it badly flawed (present physics of electromagnetic theory incorrectly do not allow for hyperspatial domains to exist).

At the present time, science students are taught that the positive proton charge at the nucleus of an atom is balanced exactly by the negatively charged electrons orbiting around the nucleus of the atom. This is a deliberate falsehood perpetrated in order to complicate the development of anti gravitic craft by privately-owned organizations. While studying the hydrogen atom, the Dutch physicist Hendrik Lorentz (1833-1928) discovered that atoms possess a very slight net positive charge, which is responsible for the effect we perceive as gravity. Lorentz postulated that by increasing the negative electron charge, the gravity of an atom's nuclear positive mass would be cancelled. Lorentz also determined that the forces encountered by a body within an electromagnetic field (termed the Lorentz Force) is 2×10^{40} power greater than the gravitational interaction. Armed with this information, Lorentz's friend Nikola Tesla, published his *Dynamic Theory of Gravity* in 1897. Tesla later applied to the Swiss Patent Office for patent coverage of an anti gravitic craft. This was during the era when one of the patent examiners employed there was Albert Einstein.

Although the patent was rejected, Tesla purportedly went ahead and constructed a prototype anti gravitic craft. The machine was rectangular in shape and powered by one of his magnifying transmitters, which discharged powerful pulses of negatively charged high-voltage electricity from one end of the transmitting coil.

Another simple way to accomplish anti gravitic propulsion is by means of tri-polar electromagnets, which are energized by high amperage free-energy power units. While a regular dipole magnet (i.e. a bar magnet with a north pole at one end and a south pole at the other end) will try to reverse its direction when subjected to a magnetic field of similar polarity, a tripolar electromagnet will maintain its orientation, because it tends to behave in the manner of a unipolar magnet. Thus a flying saucer powered by two tripolar magnets, one oriented horizontally and the other vertically, will be propelled rapidly along the earth's magnetic lines of force, provided that there is a disparity between the field strength of the inner and outer poles of the tripolar magnets.

Disturbed by Tesla's command of free energy and anti gravity technology, Tesla's financial backer Louis Cass Payseur, ordered his front man J.P.Morgan, to withraw his financial support. This act financially ruined Tesla through the initiation of false foreclosure proceedings.[2]

The toast of New York's café society during the first decade of the 20th century, Tesla was a nightly visitor to Delmonicos Restaurant, where actress Sarah Bernhart was his frequent dinner guest; another added impetus for Morgan's financial withdrawl was the amorous advances made toward Tesla by Morgan's daughter. The manservant previously loaned Tesla by Morgan was, in reality, an industrial spy who, in collusion with one of Tesla's staff, a German engineer named Fritz Lowenstein, stole Tesla's anti gravity secrets and assigned them to various Illuminati secret societies, both in Britain and America.

Tesla was such a meticulous researcher that he frequently modified and rewrote his daily research notes many times, before he was satisfied with them. Being a frugal man, Tesla's laboratory janitor began taking Tesla's discarded notes home with him for the purpose of using the unmarked rear face of each page as note paper. Upon being advised by a friend that any technical notes written by Tesla were far too precious to discard or scribble upon, the janitor compiled the pages into a very large manual.. The manual later came into possession of an electrical engineer who observed that some of the lab notes appertained to a free energy device. The device consisted of two sealed tubes filled with a multiplicity of chemical elements.When connected in series, the device generated electrical energy. After a period of experimentation, the engineer succeeded in replicating Tesla's device and subsequently licensed the system to NASA. One of the units currently is providing electrical power in the new Space Station. Although the author has not seen an actual unit, he has been shown a photograph of the system by the person who has been engaged in providing developmental funding for this particular engineer.

It has long been rumored that certain of the secret societies created by Lytton's protegés, were developing anti gravitic craft, nuclear weapons and time travel devices as early as the late 19th century. This well may have been the case, for one of the masterminds behind Cecil Rhodes' plan for the establishment of a totalitarian global government, was the despicably evil writer H.G.Wells. Wells was a member of London's *Coefficients Club,* which consisted of leading members of the British aristocracy, such as Lord Milner, who provided much of the funding for the Russian Revolution, Lord Robert Cecil, whose Jesuit-influenced family has controlled British Intelligence since the era of Queen Elizabeth 1st, and Beatrice Webb, founder of the Fabian Socialists and one of the principal architects of the Nazi Party. The major goal of this geopolitical fraternity was the creation of a fascist New World Order, to be ruled from the City of London by an Anglo Saxon elite, as a successor to the failing British Empire.

In describing the ruthless manner in which he felt that the intended dictatorship should be administrated, Wells wrote: "The men of the New Republic will not be squeamish either in facing or inflicting death....They will hold that a certain portion of the population exists only on sufferance out of pity and patience, and on the understanding that they do not propagate, and I do not foresee any reason to suppose that they will hesitate to kill when that sufferance is abused."

It was the Coefficients who arranged for Alexander Helphand (Parvus) mentioned in the previous chapter, to mastermind the assassination of Archduke Ferdinand in Sarajevo, for the purpose of fomenting W.W.I, in order to prevent the creation of a proposed industrial alliance between Russia, France and Germany. Such an alliance would have severely undermined the commercial strength of the British Empire.

As stated in a previous chapter, when Wells wrote *The Island of Dr. Moreau,* he was writing about a real-life person of that name, who experimented with genetic engineering in the 19th century. In writing *The Time Machine,* Wells similarly may have based his story upon such an existing device, for at a later date, his political co-conspirators Aleister Crowley and Ian Fleming were known to have visited Montauk, located at Long Island, New York, where covert mind control, satanic rituals involving human sacrifice, and an astral travel program known as *Project Lazarus,* were conducted. Wells' protegés Aldous Huxley and Gregory Bateson, later were to become major players in the establishment of the drug counterculture, conducted as part of the Tavistock Institute's MK-Ultra mind control program.

Aldhous Huxley was a member of a fascist occult group active in the post W.W.I era, that was the counterpart of Germany's *Thule Society;* known as the *Children of the Sun,* the cult included such members as George Orwell, who wrote the book *1984* as a primer for the teenaged offspring of Illuminists, spy Guy Burgess, the wife of Lord Louis Mountbatten, and novelist Jessica Mitford and her sisters, one of whom was a mistress of Hitler.

The ambience of the *Café Schopenhaur* was as friendly and inviting as the aroma of freshly brewed coffee which pervaded the dining room, that particular morning in Vienna, in 1917. The air was filled with the lively conversation of the restaurant's regular patrons, who had stopped by for their mid morning coffee. Seated at one of the tables were a young woman and four men, who were destined to change the course of history.

The woman, Maria Ortisch, had become a magnet to the four men because of her exceptional psychic abilities.The four men were geopolitician Karl Haushofer, who was the founder of the Vril Society,

Baron Sebottendorf, the racist Grand Master of the Bavarian Chapter of the *Germanen Orden* and initiate of the *Order of the Rose Garland*, fighter pilot Lothar Weitz, and the aristocrat Granette Gannotte, who recently had been initiated into a neo Templar Order.

These five people were meeting to discuss the possibility of creating a new esoteric cult for the purpose of establishing a dominant force in global politics. The group was well aware that the tides of W.W.I were about to change, now that America was entering the war. As Baron Sebottendorf had stated previously: "A vast organization, of monstrous proportions, intends to bend to its will the civilized world. The religious institutions have been so gravely weakened that they are not even capable of pulling themselves together, let alone putting up a united front. If spiritual leaders do not come forth in the west, chaos may bring down everything into the abyss. In this kind of danger, the Moslem Brotherhood recalled that tradition had it that there was a time, in Europe, when men possessed ultimate knowledge. These men were initiates of the *Order of Teutonic Knights,* who had acquired their esoteric knowledge from the highest levels of the Sufis."

"It is a tragedy for humankind" the Baron continued, "that the Papacy destroyed this enlightened Order and extinguished the flame of knowledge and wisdom. The Western nations are the raw materials of our history; we must therefore free the world from the chaos of its historical past and fashion these nations into something more noble." And so the five individuals resolved to create a new secret society which would incorporate the finest aspects of the old esoteric Orders.

On a sunny August day the following year, the small group met again at Baron Sebottendorf's request and inaugurated the secret society, whose principle objective would be the search for new esoteric knowledge, which would enable Germany to take the helm of a New World Order. It was decided to name the cult the *Thule Gesellschaft,* after the capital city of the mythical island known as Hyperborea, whose inhabitants supposedly possessed technology far in advance of the Atlanteans.

The fledgling cult also decided to adopt two emblems: one being a swastika with two lances, the other being the Black Sun, an ancient Sumerian emblem signifying the primary source of all cosmic energy. It was also decided on that fateful day that the society's salutation would be *"Seig Heil."* It was in this manner that the newly founded Thule Cult became the driving force behind the Germanen Orden and the latter's ally, Anton Drexler's *German Workers' Party.*

On a chilly November day in 1919, a select group of disgruntled members from the Thule and Vril secret societies, met at a rustic hunting lodge in the Bavarian Alps. Conspicuously absent were Karl Haushofer and Baron Sebottendorf. Both men had taken control of Anton Drexler's German Workers' Party and had renamed it the *National Socialist Workers' Party.* It was their overly pre-occupation with racial purity that eventually sounded alarm bells in the small group, who had decided to covertly meet at the hunting lodge for the purpose of restructuring the Vril Society as a platform for the pursuance of esoteric knowledge, without the presence of Haushofer or Sebottendorf.

Among those in attendance were Maria Ortisch, who had brought along another female psychic—eighteen year old Segrun, and the distinguished scientist Dr. Walter Schumann. A few month's earlier, Maria Ortisch had begun channeling messages supposedly emanating from a planet near the star Aldebaran, in the constellation of Taurus. Some of the messages were in the Sumerian language, while others were in the form of a code known to the Knights Templar. Amazingly, the channeled information provided instructions for the construction of a time machine!

In 1922, the restructured Vril Society had completed construction of their prototype time machine, at the Messerschmidt factory in Wolfsburg, under the direction of Dr. Schumann (he later was to become renowned for his work concerning planetary resonance). To the group's surprise, as the time machine, which incorporated a large rotating disc, was being tested, it suddenly began to display anti-gravitic characteristics.

Realizing that an anti gravity craft possibly could be developed by incorporating the time machine technology into a saucer shaped craft, the Vril Society procured appropriate private funding and built a prototype flying saucer, which flew for the first time in 1929, piloted by a very experienced female test pilot. Designated *Rund Flugzeug,* the design was improved over the next decade, and by 1939, later variants attained speeds of Mach 2.6—a speed not equalled by conventional aircraft until after the conclusion of W.W.II.

Shortly after the conclusion of W.W.I, members of London's Coefficients Club became alarmed when a German political faction once again began a move to form an industrial alliance between Germany, France and Russia. Britain previously had countered a similar threat to the British Empire in 1905, by paying the Venetian-controlled agent provocateur Alexander Helphand (Parvus) to create an ethnic insurrection in the Russian oilfields at Baku, using one of Lord Lytton's Islamic terrorist groups, who staged a riot which set the Russian oilfields ablaze. This act forced the resignation of Russia's brilliant Foreign Minister Count Witte, the driving force behind the proposed alliance. To counter the present threat, the Coefficients, together with fellow travellers Winston Churchill, Albert Einstein and the Venetian nobleman Count Coudenhove-Kalerghi, founded the Jesuit dominated Pan European Union, a Fascist organization which remains one of the most powerful political secret societies even at the present time, with membership drawn from the various branches of the *Hospitaler Order.* Its economic arm is the Mont Pelerin Society, a very dominant force in global monetarism.[3]

The principal objective of the Pan European Union was to create the Nazi Party as a totalitarian entity, and use it to force Germany into a war with Russia, thus negating any possibility of a multi national industrial alliance (the Illuminati heirarchy often permits in-fighting within its ranks, presumably because it generates great wealth for a privileged few and also because the cult thrives on the creation of chaos, fear and the suffering of the masses).

Until the creation of the Pan European Union, Adolf Hitler (probably the illegitimate descendant of Salomon Rothschild) and the National Socialists had primarily been funded by Henry Ford, but the newly formed Pan European Union would soon take over that role, with assistance of their Wall Street Anglophile cronies. Necessary funds for the establishment of the Nazi Party were obtained by Brown Brothers, Harriman. The CEO of the British-owned Brown Brothers was Montague Norman, who also was the managing director of the privately-owned Bank of England. The Harriman family, who later were to acquaint Hitler with the insidious ideology of eugenics, had made their fortune through co-ownership of the Rockefeller funded Remington Company, which had manufactured most of the munitions for the American war effort during W.W.I.

The bagman for this wretched cabal of merchants of death was Senator Prescott Bush, the father of George Bush Sr. and the CEO of the merger between Brown Brothers and the Harriman Company. Prescott Bush also was the CEO of the Upper Silesian Coalfields Company of Poland, which provided much of the coal and iron for the Nazi armaments build-up. Dismayed at seeing the nation's coal and iron ore resources being exported to Germany, the Polish government applied a stiff tariff. An outraged Hitler retaliated by ordering the invasion of Poland.

In addition to providing funding for the establishment of the Nazi Party, it also was necessary to provide massive amounts of financial capital for the development and production of Nazi military armaments. This was accomplished by having three American Nazi members of the German-American Bund, Helen and E. Clifton Barton and Hector Echevarria, all residents of New York, form a private corporation known as the *Internal Revenue and Tax Audit Service,* with offices at 15,

Dover Green Street, Delaware, which was incorporated on July 11th., 1933. Its incorporation papers revealed that the corporation intended to monopolize the collection of all Federal taxes on behalf of the Federal Reserve Board—also a private corporation. In 1936, in order to adopt a lower public profile, the corporation disenfranchised itself, and adopted a new company name: the *Internal Revenue Service.*

Taxes unlawfully collected by this treasonous organization, were conduited to the Nazis by Prescott Bush on behalf of the Illuminati bankers. During the 1930's, the IRS gave tax exemptions to Nazi sympathizers, and harassed loyal Americans who opposed Hitler's nefarious plans. Thus the IRS, aided and abetted by treasonous members of the American judicial branch of government, enabled the Nazis to create and manufacture weapons for the purpose of killing American military personnel during the W.W.II conflict. The Bureau of Internal Revenue, created in 1862 for the purpose of collecting excise taxes, was disbanded in 1953, thereby allowing the IRS—a private company created by Nazis, free reign to impose its deceptive and illegal practices upon an unsuspecting American public.

During the early formative phase of the Nazi Party in the 1930's, a brilliant Austrian gentleman by the name of Victor Schauberger was conducting exhaustive research appertaining to vortex technology. A former forester, responsible for the stewardship of some of Austria's primeval forests, Schauberger had noticed that when trout were disturbed, they invariably fled upstream. This suggested to Schauberger that the fish were able to derive energy from the fast flowing mountain streams; moreover, when Schauberger had warm water poured into the stream some yards ahead of the trout, the fish were unable to make headway. The observant forester concluded that vortices formed when fast moving cold water flowed around rocks, produced an energy which he termed diamagnetic energy. Schauberger subsequently learned that such vortices incorporate into their physical form, so-called sacred geometry, based upon the Fibonacci mathematical series. Continuing his research, Schauberger eventually developed a turbine which possessed a rotor containing a series of interconnecting annular cavities which progressively diminished in size as they approached the rotor's periphery. When rotated at high speed, air passing through the rotor formed toroidal vortices and torsion fields, prior to emerging from the rotor's periphery at very high speed. Air passing through the rotor was able to tap the zero point energy of the cosmos, resulting in a massive output of free energy from the device. A Vienna fabrication company constructed a prototype turbine for Schauberger which contained a copper housing some two meters in diameter, in the form of a typical flying saucer. The unit was secured to the factory floor by means of six high-tensile steel bolts, which had been grouted into the concrete floor. Ignoring Schauberger's demand that the unit not be tested until he was present, the impatient factory management ran the unit prior to the inventor's arrival at the facility. To their utter amazement, the craft tore itself free from its anchor bolts, rapidly rose in the air and crashed into the factory roof!

Upon hearing of Schauberger's amazing flying saucer, Himmler, the head of the Nazi dreaded S.S., sent for Schauberger and offered him the choice of either designing a full sized flying saucer for the Nazis, or being hanged. Assigned an engineering staff at the Mauthausen Concentration Camp, Schauberger designed a large flying saucer; at least one manned prototype of this craft was constructed and flew successfully prior to the German surrender.

In the spring of 1941, the Nazi military commissioned Luftwaffe Flugkapitan Rudolph Schriever to develop a 1/5 th scale working prototype of a saucer-shaped fighter code named *Kugelblitz* (Ball Lightning). Funding for the project was no problem, since major American companies, such as General Motors and Standard Oil, retained their substantial stock holdings in I.G. Farben throughout W.W.II, and reinvested their profits in other German companies producing items for the Nazi war machine. Similarly, the British Royal Family, who owned the rights to a process for making high-octane aviation fuel, continued licensing the process to Germany throughout the war. While bombs rained down on Britain, royalties were being paid by the Nazis into the treasonous Royal Family's Swiss bank account. Schriever's scale model was successfully flown during the Summer of 1942; Schriever was subsequently despatched to Prague in order to oversee the construction of a full-sized Kugelblitz. This was to be constructed in the nearby BMW plant.

Some writers claim that this full sized craft flew in 1942, but this is incorrect; engineering drawings mysteriously disappeared and key components never arrived on schedule. Consequently, hovering tests did not commence until January 1944. Poor visibility delayed further testing, and by the time that the weather had improved sufficiently, Hitler ordered the saucer destroyed, lest it fell into the hands of advancing Soviet troops.

After the war, Schriever resided at Bremerhaven until his death in 1950. It was RSHA intelligence operatives of the S.S. who stole the Kugelblitz plans and delayed its construction, so that Heinrich Himmler could covertly produce a fleet of saucers at another facility. Presumably Himmler intended to use the craft as a bargaining chip with the allies if Germany lost the war, just as he apparently arranged the murder of Rudolf Hess, and sent a look alike to Britain in an ill fated attempt to negotiate a peace treaty and depose Hitler.[4] Heinrich Himmler, whose father had been a tutor to the Jesuit controlled House of Wittlesbach—controllers of Bavaria for seven hundred years, created the S.S. structurally along the lines of the Jesuit Order. Himmler appeared to have been unaware that the saucer technology of the Vril Society was far in advance of Schriever's efforts.

Himmler assigned the task of constructing a duplicate of the Schriever craft to Dr. Ernst Miethe, who built the craft at an underground facility at Kahla, in Thuringia. With a diameter of more than one hundred feet, the disc had a central cabin surrounded by a multiplicity of fan blades; it was powered by three Heinkel-Ohain turbines.

The prototype craft attained a speed in excess of 1000 m.p.h. on its initial test flight.

The December 14th, 1944 edition of the *New York Times* reported that Allied bomber crews flying over Germany, sometimes were intercepted by luminous spheres, which darted away rapidly to a safe distance when fired upon. Termed *"Foo Fighters"* by the Allies, these were pilotless, spherical, jet-propelled anti-gravitic craft, that were designed by the Germans to function as interceptors. Assigned the appellation *"Feurball,"* the craft possessed a porous skin, behind which was a thin aluminum secondary skin, which carried an electrical charge. A bullet passing through both skins completed an electrical circuit, which in turn caused the craft to change direction and take evasive action. The glow that surrounded the craft was caused by ionized exhaust gases, which formed a boundary layer around the craft. Construction of the craft was under the direction of General Hans Kammler, the cold-blooded developer of the Auschwitz concentration camp.[5]   Another interesting early German flying saucer was designed by Heinrich Fleissner, a native of Augsburg. The saucer, thirty meters in diameter, was powered by a multiplicity of small ramjets, which were fed a mixture of hydrogen and oxygen, although powdered coal dust could also be used as a fuel. The craft was constructed by the E 4 Division of the S.S.. Gyroscopes prevented the spherical cockpit from rotating in flight, while the periphery of the disc rotated around it; top speed of the saucer was 6,500 m.p.h.. After the conclusion of the war, Fleissner (without remuneration) was forced to assign the design rights to his successful craft to a United States company headquartered in Los Angeles (presumably a front company for an intelligence agency) who patented it in 1954.[6]

A major administrative flaw of the Nazis was that various Nazi military organizations were permitted to conduct their own research programs, without liason to a central coordinating body. Consequently, raw materials and engineering components ordered by one development group would be apprehended en route by another organization, for subsequent use on a totally different project.

Due to this lack of an oversight commitee, the Vril Society's central core group, known as the *Black Sun,* created Division E4 of the S.S. for the purpose of covertly developing their own anti-gravitic craft. Having successfully designed and flown their own unmanned 16 ft. diameter saucer designated RFZ 22 in 1934, which possessed a magnetic impulse directional system, the Black Sun group went on to develop the very successful RFZ 25, which was test flown in 1939 and later became known as the Haunabu 1. It incorporated an electromagnetic propulsion system purportedly designed by Hans Kohler, although Dr. Schumann may well have been involved. The very large Haunabu 2 flew in 1942 and was equipped with a prototype beam weapon; an even larger craft with a diameter of approximately 400 ft. also was designed. The Black Sun also designed a large cigar-shaped mother ship which accommodated several smaller saucers. Known as the *Andromeda,* a similar craft was observed and photographed by the crew of an American airliner over Central America after the war. This craft probably was constructed at an underground base known to exist in the Andes Mountains, which was created by Nazis who fled Germany. In 1943, the Vril Society held a secret meeting in the Baltic region, purportedly to discuss a proposed flight to the home planet of their allegedly Aldebaranian extraterrestrial associates.

Having created and funded the Nazi Party as a ploy to prevent the formation of a transnational industrial alliance, Hitler's Illuminati overlords expected him to be a loyal puppet and support their plan which called for Germany to only attack Russia. Hitler however, possessed a diametrically opposed agenda, which incorporated the best aspects of socialism together with strong nationalistic overtones. He made a tactical error however, in following the recommendation of the Rockefeller family to invade Western European countries.

The Rockefellers had a hidden agenda for issuing the recommendation: prior to W.W.II, the British had refused to allow the Rockefeller's Standard Oil employees to enter British controlled Arabia for the purpose of developing the Rockefeller owned vast oil deposits. Anticipating that Britain inevitably would be drawn into a war with Germany, the Rockefellers promised to supply the Nazi war effort with the necessary petroleum from their Venezuelan oilfileds, in the expectation that Germany would defeat Britain in such a conflict. Suffering defeat at Dunkirk, the British were forced to promise the Rockefellers access to their Arabian oil deposits at the conclusion of the war, provided that the Venezuelan oil shipments to the Nazis were terminated. After the conclusion of hostilities, American troops constructed the Rockefeller's Arabian oilfields at American taxpayer's expense.

Nazi war preparations also included contingency plans, in order to insure continuance of the Third Reich in the event of Germany losing the war. One of the continuity plans called for the colonization of Antarctica. In 1937, a covert German expeditionary force under the direction of Kapitan Ritscher, claimed a vast tract of Northern Antarctica larger than Germany itself. Named Nue Schwabenland, the region possesses many ice free warm water lakes. At the commencement of W.W.II, Nazi cabinet minister Joachim von Ribbentrop stated: "In accordance with Germany's long range political strategy, we have taken into firm possession the Antarctic area, called Nue Schwabenland, to ensure a safe retreat in case of necessity."

Many Nazi submarine convoys were rumored to have delivered supplies to a large underground facility in Antarctica; lending credence to the rumor, the newspaper *France Soir* reported that the Icelandic whaler *Juliana* was intercepted by a large U boat, almost eighteen months after the cessation of European hostilities.

A meeting was convened at the Maison Rouge Hotel in Strasbourg in August 1944; in attendance were leading members of the German military/industrial complex, who decided that a major portion of the national treasury should be secreted abroad, to enable the Third Reich to covertly continue in absentia after the surrender of Germany. The author has been informed by a confidante of the late Fillipino President, Ferdinand Marcos, that the latter was the custodian of a major portion of the Nazi treasury. Much of this gold bullion (looted from countries conquered by the Nazis) has been recovered by a neo-Nazi CIA rogue element working in conjunction with surviving remnants of the Abwehr Nazi military intelligence organization that was under the direction of the Hitler loathing Admiral Canaris (probably a neo-Teutonic Knight). This German cabal received sanctuary in America after the war under Operation Paperclip, and became founding members of the CIA. Marcos also was the custodian of a vast treasure consisting of gold and diamonds, which had been looted by the Japanese and deposited at 172 separate Fiillipino locations. Not to be outdone, the Vatican still has in its possession gold bullion obtained from the Nazi controlled Croation Treasury.

By repeatedly providing Hitler with disinformation and also withholding information crucial to the Nazi war effort, Canaris probably contributed more than any other person on either side to the defeat of Nazi Germany. It was Canaris who dissuaded Hitler from seizing Gibraltar. One of Hitler's greatest blunders, occupation of the British held Gibraltar would have given the Nazis control of the Mediterranean and probably altered the outcome of the war in favor of Germany.

The claim that Hitler committed suicide at his Berlin bunker is apocryphal. Hitler's dental records had been removed prior to his alleged death; identification had been made by means of a sketch of dental records which had been drawn from memory by a dental assistant. Moreover, the bloodstains found in Hitler's bunker were not of his bloodtype, and probably came from Hitler's double, Paul Bartholdy, or Hitler's look alike chauffeur. Hitler purportedly committed suicide at the bunker on April 30th, 1945, at 3:30 p.m., yet eyewitnessess allegedly saw him alive at the nearby Templehof airport an hour later in the company of Eva Braun. It is known that a secret tunnel connected the bunker and the airport, and it is strongly rumored that Hitler was flown by Flugkapitan Peter Baumgart in a twin engined turbojet Arado 234 aircraft, to an awaiting submarine in Norway, which is believed to have taken him to Spain.[7]

As previously stated, many small children who had been the victims of the Illuminati's Monarch trauma based mind-control program, were programed at the China Lake Naval Weapons Facility in California by the infamous Dr. Joseph Mengele. Some of these mind controlled survivors report seeing Mengele at China Lake in the company of Eva Braun and a senile Adolf Hitler.

Credence to the claim that the Nazis established an Antarctica base replete with some of their flying saucers, is provided by the fact that Admiral Byrd headed a "scientific" expedition, which departed Norfolk, Virginia, on December 2nd, 1946, bound for Antarctica. Instead of the usual civillian scientific personnel and non-military vessels customarily employed for such polar expeditions, this expeditionary force consisted of three battle groups, consisting of thirteen naval ships, including a submarine, a destroyer, the aircraft carrier *Phillipine Sea,* four thousand troops and supplies for an eight month stay. A contingent of Norwegian, Soviet and British personnel also were present in a support capacity.

Instead of remaining in Antarctica for the allotted time period, Byrd quickly cancelled the expedition after losing several aircraft. In an interview with journalist Lee Van Atta, Byrd stated that in the event of a new war, the United States would be attacked by flying objects possessing the capability of flying pole to pole at stupendous speeds. Whether the admiral was referring to missiles or flying saucers remains speculative. Upon arriving back in America, Byrd was immediately hospitalized, possibly because he had disclosed too much sensitive information.

During W.W.II, the Harriman and Bush families steadily increased their dominance over the United States intelligence community. Since both families had played a major role in the establishment of the Nazi Party, and were profiting very handsomely by covertly doing business with Germany via neutral countries during W.W.II, as was revealed during the *Trading with the Enemy* congressional hearings, it was only natural that they would recruit key Nazi intelligence operatives and scientists at the conclusion of the war, as a nucleus for the secret government which they unlawfully were in the process of establishing.

As the Third Reich was rapidly disintegrating, OSS director Allen Dulles secretly arranged for nearly 300 of the *Belarus Brigade*—an amalgamation of Nazi and White Russian troops, who were fighting the Soviets in Byelorussia, to be brought to America and given key positions in governmental and intelligence circles. Dulles also provided Hitler's spymaster Reinhard Gehlen with $200 million, provided by the Rockefeller and Mellon families, in order to bring 350 of Gehlen's spies to America. These spies became founding members of the CIA, together with members of Admiral Canaris' Abwehr military intelligence organization.

Another key Nazi spirited into the United States was Hitler aide Fritz Kraemer, the mentor of Dr. Henry Kissinger and General Al Haig. Kraemer was hired by the Pentagon, and later founded the American chapter of the infamous Round Table. At the cessation of hostilities in Europe, one of the most wanted war criminals in Romania was Nicolae Malaxa, a member of the Nazi Iron Guard. The evil Malaxa's entry into America was facilitated by Richard "I am not a crook" Nixon, who arranged for the United States Congress to pass a special citizenship bill for Malaxa. Malaxa deposited $200 million in a New York bank, then resided in Nixon's hometown of Whittier, California, for more than a decade, prior to emigrating, like many Nazi criminals, to Argentina.

According to a British Intelligence report declassifed in 1956, the British discovered a vast underground Nazi flying saucer facility located in the Hartz Mountains of Bavaria, six months after the end of hostilites in Europe. The report stated that six freight train loads of flying saucer hardware and technical documents were removed and shipped to Britain. In all probability, the shipment went to the Boscombe Down experimental base in Southern England, where UFO sightings became a fairly regular occurrence. It is believed that much of the later British flying saucer development was transferred to an underground facility in a remote region of British Columbia, Canada. It is hinted in certain intelligence circles that by 1970, Britain had numerous pilotless anti-gravity craft, possibly a development of the Nazi RFZ 2 craft.

When western governments began to envelop the development of terrestrially designed flying saucers in a cloak of secrecy, it was decided to promulgate a disinformation agenda by claiming that UFO's, if they existed at all, were of extraterrstrial origin, since humans lack the technological ability to create such advanced craft. This is, of course, utter nonsense (in 1999, due to prior commitments, the author declined an invitation from one of Japan's ruling families to participate in the design of a very large flying saucer, to be developed with private funding).

This ruse was relatively straightforward to implement, since it has been known since the early 1930's that by means of directed energy devices tuned to a wavelength of 2.33 feet, or a higher harmonic thereof, it is possible to subliminally program an individual to hear voices inside of their head. At a specific harmonic, the transmitted command is not perceived by the concious mind—only by the subconcious, thereby rendering it a simple matter to implant the suggestion, while the subject is in the sleep state, that they have been the victim of an alien abduction. A variant of the system has been installed in satellites, in order to instill the belief in psychically sensitive people that they are in communication with the Ashtar Space Command.

A false screen memory frequently is implanted in the subconcious of mind controlled victims, in order to create the impression of an alien abduction scenario. This is accomplished by placing a helmet over the head of the subject. Attached to the helmet are numerous solenoids which are tuned to a frequency of 3.8 Hertz; computer generated graphics of an extra-terrestrial abduction are fed into the solenoids, in order to implant a false abduction memory into the mind of the hapless victim. Such victims are often programmed during infancy while attending daycare centers which are operated by intelligence personnel, and are programmed as "sleepers," to be activated years later to shoot high school classmates, or to participate in major civil unrest as a pretext for the declaration of a state of national emergency. The name of this particular mind-control program is *"Operation Greenstar"* and is part of the Illuminati's Janus end-times project. A paricularly insidious aspect of this particular form of programming is that the victim will undergo a very convincing, albeit imaginary, abduction scenario, if hypnotically regressed.

Many leading authors and lecturers who pontificate about situations involving flying saucers and extraterrestrial beings, belong to an organization known as the *"Aviary."* This is a very subversive organization created by the intelligence community in order to disseminate misinformation concerning UFO's and E.T.'s. Much of the funding for this operation is provided by the Human Ecology Fund, a conduit for the financing of mind control activities. This is a graphic example of why you, dear reader, should conduct your own research, instead of relying upon "experts."

Implants have been removed from some supposed victims of alien abductions. Invariably, UFO lecturers claim that such implants are the work of extraterrestrials, yet in actuality, the typical implant recovered is one of the various types developed by such companies as Motorola or IBM. One insidious implant commonly found contains a lithium battery, which is recharged by fluctuations in body temperature. This model was frequently implanted into the back of the hand of American soldiers during the Vietnam War, in order to stimulate adrenaline flow. When implanted in the third eye area of the forehead, it also causes young girls to undergo immediate menopause. This particular type is currently being implanted into young girls in Third World countries by Illuminati personnel, as part of a mass sterilization program.

A more recent development is a liquid crystal implant, which is intravenously inserted—convenient for covert introduction by means of flu vaccinations, etc.. Another diabolical implant consists of powerful microscopic bioprocessors, which are manufactured from synthetic protein, and are attached to either neurotropic or dermotropic viruses. Such pathogens migrate to specific regions of the human body, transporting the attached implants with them. Other mind control implants are of the dental type, which are judiciously installed by dentists under contract with various intelligence agencies. This latter type of implant was invented by the late Dr. A. Puharich, who also conducted a mind control experiment in which a group of unsuspecting victims believed that they were in communication with a group of highly evolved astral beings known as the *"Nine."* Several million gullible New Agers have been duped by the nefarious Puharich and his accomplices, into believing in the existence of the Nine. Puharich died after falling down a flight of stairs; while not insinuating that Humpty Dumpty was pushed, this could have been the case with Puharich, who was becoming a political loose cannon.

The ultimate goal of Illuminati sub-groups such as the Tavistock Institute and the Black Rose Society, in conducting such massive mind control activity, in addition to the creation of Manchurian Candidates such as the Columbine High School shooters is, of course, the creation of a very compliant public. In view of the fact that a widespread segment of the public has been unwittingly subjected to the insertion of implants, it seems ludicrous that extraterrestrials would travel vast distances across the universe, in order to insert an implant up someone's nose, when all that would be necessary for the purpose of controlling a large segment of humanity by extraterrestrials, would be to utilize the implants known to have been already inserted by various Federal agencies.

This could be accomplished through the simple expediency of super-imposing an A.M. signal onto a local F.M. Radio frequency (such implants are often actuated by means of satellite downlinks). Control of an implanted person is enhanced if the person is a good hypnotic subject, which is why a certain intelligence agency purchased a controlling interest in a national chain of aversion therapy clinics, in order to identify such psychically gifted potential mind-control subjects. Military mind control programmers have been identified as board members of an American "commercial" remote viewing school. Mind control programming is more readily accomplished if the subject is under the influence of methamphetamine or ketamine.

Some terrestrially developed anti gravitic craft possess a multiplicity of miniature video cameras on the craft's upper surface, and a corresponding number of miniature television monitors on the lower surface. When flying on starry nights, the video cameras film the overhead stars and project their images onto the television monitors on the underside of the craft, thus creating the illusion of an absence of a craft. Conversely, Operation Bluebeam was initiated in order to develop holographic equipment capable of simulating an attack by gigantic mother-ships.

In order to dissuade the public into thinking for themselves, Lord Lytton used his protegé Helena Blavatsky to claim that she was in communication with 'Ascended Masters," with the implication that they would do the thinking for humanity. In a similar manner, intelligence agencies beholden to the Illuminati, via such lackeys as the Jesuits and the Knights of Malta, have deceived the majority of UFO afficionados into believing that all UFO's are of extraterrestrial origin, in order to conceal the reality of humanly created flying saucers. This ploy is easily accomplished by infiltrating intelligence contract operatives into the various UFO cults. Thus, the United States Naval Intelligence funded George Adamski, and even provided him with a diplomatic passport, in order to convey the impression that he had been contacted by

Venusians. Adamski previously had tried to publish a science fiction novel containing a similar scenario, except that the central figure was Christ, not a Venusian.

It is a common practice for intelligence agencies to be involved with very dark secret occult societies, as is evidenced by former CIA director George Bush Sr.'s initiation into the A.U.V. cult while still in prep school. Bush later was inducted into Yale's Skull and Bones Society, which is under the direction of Britain's very satanic Wessex Lodge, an Illuminati sub-group. Adamski's UFO encounters purportedly were witnessed by Ric Williamson, the founder of the *Ancient Amythestine Order;* two other members of Williamson's occult order were electrical engineers Karl Hunrath and Wilbur Wilkinsin. Hunrath and Wilkinsin rented a small aircraft, stating that they were flying to a desert rendezvous with extraterrestrials. They were never seen again; a search of Wilkinsin's home later revealed an interior wall covered with occult symbols.

Most ufologists ignore the peculiar relationship between occult symbols and the names of supposed extraterrestrials, such as Billy Meir's Semjase and Adamski's Orthon. Among the symbols found on a wall in Wilkinsin's home were some belonging to a code of the sinister Royal Arch Masonic Order. For many centuries, secret societies have transmitted key information by means of secret ciphers, in order to maintain political power, and also for the concealment of arcane knowledge from the eyes of the profane.

After the Royal Arch cipher received public exposure in the 19th century, a revised cipher was created in 1904 by British Intelligence operative and Golden Dawn initiate Aleister Crowley. Crowley claimed that the cipher was revealed to him by an alien entity named Aiwass, whose description closely resembles that of the proverbial Men in Black. Here one must keep an open mind. Although the field of UFO research has been heavily infiltrated by intelligence personnel and charlatans, the related energy grid research of Captain Bruce Cathie stands above reproach. In a private conversation with the author some three decades ago in the Pacific Northwest, Captain Cathie stated that he had been kept under surveillance at an airport by two swarthy beings, whose features were somewhat uncharacteristic of regular humans.

The significance of Aleister Crowley's cipher is that when it is applied to the names of several purportedly channeled extraterrestrials, including Crowley's *Aiwass,* there is a correspondence with the numeral eleven, e.g., alleged contactee Truman Bethrum's alien *Aura Raynes* and George van Tassel's *Ashtar.* Prior to his mysterious dissappearance, Hunrath began calling himself *Firkon,* which also has the numerological value of eleven under Crowluy's cipher.

In view of the fact that Illuminati satanic rituals, attended by real extraterrestrials and involving human sacrifice, have been observed at various covert underground facilities, including Area 51 and Montauk, it is perhaps not surprising that there is a curious relationship between occult secret societies and notable names in early UFO lore. Charles Stanfield Jones assumed leadership of both Crowley's occult order and the Ordo Templi Orientis. Meade Layne, who wrote about flying discs prior to the celebrated alleged sightings of intelligence operative Kenneth Arnold in the Pacific Northwest, was a student of Jones, and also was a member of the sado-masochistically oriented Golden Dawn offspring, the *Society of the Inner Light.*

Layne was associated with *"Frater Damon,"* who was the Primate of the *Qabalistic Alchemist Church.* Curiously, this church was the American subsidiary of the Brish occult society known as the *Ordo Argentium Astrum,* which employed Crowley's cipher. The previously mentioned Ric Williamson was an associate of Guy Ballard, the founder of the *I Am* movement, which was ordered disbanded in W.W.II by the United States Government, because of its pro Nazi stance. And let us not forget that Aleister Crowley, accompanied by British Intelligence operative and novelist Ian Fleming, once visited Montauk, in New York State, for occultic purposes.

It would appear from the above, that either some notable UFO contactees have been in communication with alien intelligences, who are oriented toward Crowley's unsavory occult doctrine, or, more likely, that occultists with ties to various intelligence agencies, have been promulgating disinformation to the public concerning UFO's.

At the conclusion of W.W.II, U.S. Naval Intelligence assigned Lt. Commander L. Ron Hubbard and Jack Parsons to infiltrate the *Ordo Templi Orientis* at a control level. Hubbard later founded the Scientology organization; prior to blowing himself up, Parsons became a founding member of the Jet Propulsion Laboratory, and also High Priest of the *Ordo Templi Orientis Agape Lodge,* taking the "Oath of the Anti-Christ" in 1949. Curiously, he also was the business partner of Kenneth Arnold, who made history with his alleged sighting of UFO's over Mount Rainier in 1947. Another associate of Hubbard was Paul Twitchell, founder of the controversial *Eckankar* cult.[9]

During the latter phase of W.W.II, United States intelligence personnel primarily were focussed upon the Japanese sphere of influence. In consequence, America was not in a position to avail itself of German flying saucer technology after the Nazi surrender; instead, they were forced to settle for German rocket technology gleaned from the Peenemunde facility. The British, on the other hand, who covertly had been monitoring the German flying saucer program since 1941, knew precisely where to apprehend high technology saucer projects and key scientists, such as Dr. Ernst Westermann, who was an authority of the Feurball anti-gravitic craft, and consequently acquired the bulk of the German scientific technology.

This coup probably was attributable to British Intelligence having established a dummy corporation in Vichy France during the war. Known as *Omnium Societé Francais des Produits Synthétiques,* the company was able to establish a dialogue with Nazi scientists who were working on advanced technology projects. Major items of advanced German technology obtained by the British in this manner were Hans

Kohler's flying saucer propulsion system, and the sintered porous metal skin research that was utilized on the Feurball. Britain had commenced metallic porous skin research during W.W.II, in an effort to reduce the boundary layer drag on aircraft wings. It was soon discovered that the technology was not very effective when used on conventional aircraft, but performed extremely well on discoidal craft.

Shortly after the cessation of hostilities in Europe, British scientist and aviation spokesperson Sir Ben Lockspiser, leaked word to the press that the British military currently were testing a craft with a speed capability of 4,500 m.p.h.; this was at a time when the world's fastest jet aitcraft could barely attain a speed of 600 m.p.h.. Not long after this curious announcement, UFO's were sighted which were enveloped by a shimmering light; this is a characteristic of a porousskinned craft. This phenomenon is created by sunlight being reflected off the boundary layer of air, as it flows through the surface of the porous metal skin— not by the effect of ionized air, which is a characteristic of many types of non porous skinned flying saucers.

Iranian businessman Chassin Fali felt a powerful suction when he approached the upper surface of a flying saucer, which had landed near his Teheran home in 1954, presumably because the craft possessed a porous skin. Another characteristic of porous-skinned flying discs is that they ingest nearby clouds and expel the water vapor in the form of a con-trail; such an event occurred over Pasadena, California, on January 3rd, 1956.

One member of the American intelligence community who did, in fact, scour Germany for advanced technology projects at the conclusion of hostilities, was Laurance Rockefeller. Ever since that time, the shadowy figure of Laurence Rockefeller has covertly been directing the activities of so called ufologists, who peddle the "all UFO's, implants and abductions are the work of extraterrestrials" rhetoric. A typical Rockefeller effort in this field has been an attempt to persuade scientists engaged in anti-gravity research, at covert facilities such as Nevada's

Area 51, to violate their oath of secrecy and go public with their information—an act rendering such an individual susceptible to a lengthy term in a Federal prison.

As American involvement in the development of anti-gravitic craft grew after W.W.II, it became necessary to construct underground facilities in order to maintain secrecy. As previously mentioned in this chapter, the overall security of covert facilities belonging to the military/industrial complex, is usually under the direction of the Defense Industrial Security Command, which in turn contracts local security activities to the Wackenhut Corporation. Many UFO buffs wrongly assume that this particular corporation is merely a company which engages in routine security duties; in actuality, there is a very dark side to the Wackenhut Corporation.

Founded in 1954 by former FBI agent George Wackenhut, who resides at Coral Gables, Florida, in a castle replete with a moat, the company initially specialized in private investigations; it also compiled dossiers on private citizens, primarily civil rights activists and ant war protesters, who were attempting to create a better world for humanity. These dossiers were sold to interested parties. By 1966, this wretched company had more than four million names on file. In order to circumvent the Pinkerton Law, which deems it unlawful for private investigators to accept Federal contracts, Wackenhut created a subsidiary company, whose sole function is the supply of security guards to both Federal and private establishments.

Severe legislation passed by the United States Congress in the aftermath of the Watergate scandal, curtailed many of the illegal acts previously committed by various American intelligence agencies. In consequence, many "black" intelligence operations, such as the supply of weapons to Third World dictatorships, were offered to Wackenhut. In return, the company was rewarded with lucrative contracts to guard such covert facilities as Area 51. Wackenhut vice president and former intelligence operative, Bruce Bermans, who had been assigned to the

CIA's Mexico City station, formed Wackenhut's Special Projects Division in 1981. This division became involved with former CIA operative John Nichol's covert subterranean facility at the Cabazon Indian Reservation near Indio, California. The alleged purpose of the facility was the manufacture of chemical and biological weapons for Eden Pastora's narco smuggliong contras. Investigative journalist Danny Casolaro, died under very mysterious circumstances while investigating both satanic ritual abuse involving congressional members, and also the activities at the Cabazon reservation.

Products used in the manufacture of weapons which are unavailable to Iraq and Libya through legitimate channels, have a tendency to disappear from American companies which are guarded by Wackenhut. A typical case involved the Product Ingredient Company of Boca Raton, Florida; a major stockholder in the company was Iraqi businessman Ihsan Barbouti, the designer of a chemical weapons manufacturing plant in Libya. The Product Ingredient Company manufactures a cherry food flavoring.

The company resisted Barbouti's efforts to have its proprietary manufacturing technology licensed to one of Barbouti's European plants. Shortly thereafter, 2,000 gallons of ferric cyanide, a by-product of the cherry flavoring process, were stolen from the facility, security for which was provided by Wackenhut. It is a matter of record that prior to the theft, Barbouti was introduced to Wackenhut by General Secorde, who appears to be associated with the Black Rose Society linked to George Bush, Sr.. The significance of this episode is that ferric cyanide is a precursor chemical which is used in the manufacture of hydrogen cyanide, a substance with the capability of penetrating gas masks and protective clothing. This deadly substance was used by Saddam Hussein in his war against Iran.[10]

One of the most vociferous proponents of the notion that there is no evidence supportive of the existence of flying saucers, was the late Carl Sagan. For positive evidence proving the existence of anti gravitic craft, the myopic Sagan had to look no further than the large pilotless discoidal craft that were developed and flown in England by Professor John Searle. Developed solely with very limited private funding, Searle's team have constructed saucer shaped craft as large as forty feet in diameter, which have been filmed in flight by BBC and ITV camera crews.

Some writers have published technical papers which claim that the anti gravitic propulsion unit which powers Searle's craft consists of a segmented rotor containing embeded magnets. This is incorrect. In actuality, Searle's propulsion unit consists of three stationary laminated annular rings, around which a multiplicity of rollers travel. The rollers and rings are composed of sintered rare earth metals, aluminum and nylon. The resultant composite units are imprinted with pulsed a.c. and d.c. current prior to use. In operation, the self-starting rollers collect and concentrate electrons from the cosmos, as they roll around the stationary laminated rings. The amplified electrical charge is successively transferred to the outer rings, where it is collected as electricity by means of induction coils. Since the rollers are held in suspension between adjacent rings, there is nothing in the device to cause wear. Unlike conventional electrical generators, which create high temperatures and burn out when overloaded, the Searle device becomes very cold, and behaves as a superconductor, generating many megawatts of electrical power. When sufficiently electrically loaded, the craft degravitates, surrounding itself with a luminous halo of ionized air molecules.

Professor Searle's craft appears to function in accordance with Schappeler's theory of "glowing magnetism." Sadly, Searle received a jail sentence from a kangaroo court, for using a miniature version of his power plant to provide electricity for his home. This electrical home power unit measured eighteen inches in diameter by four inches deep.

There is a very esoteric secret behind the Searle propulsion system: the units are only capable of tapping the limitless energy which pervades the cosmos, if the blend of rare earths contained in the rings and rollers are compounded in proportions determined by specific magic squares (numerical tables in which the rows of numbers total the same horizontally, vertically and diagonally). Magic squares appear to be a fundamental building block of the universe, together with the Fibonacci mathematical series.

Much of the success of the German flying saucer program is due to the foresight of its directors in constructing the craft in vast underground facilities, secure from prying eyes and possible bomb damage. Present flying saucer facilities in America are constructed underground, by means of gigantic nuclear powered tunnel boring machines (e.g. U.S. Patent 3, 693, 731) which are capable of producing six miles of tunnel, fifty feet in diameter, per day. Some of these subterranean facilities, including one at Area 51, are at depths of 11,500 feet, and are interconnected by high-speed subway systems, sometimes thousands of miles in length.

It is unwise to assume that any creature which resembles the typical gray alien is, of necessity, an extraterrestrial being, for the creation of similar humanoid lifeforms is not beyond the capability of human technology, and is indeed, currently being conducted at covert facilities, according to conversations that the author has had with people who have observed them, at facilities such as China Lake Naval Weapons Facility, Seal Beach Naval Weapons Depot and at Area 51.

This advanced technology is made possible by virtue of the fact that the bioenergetic Meissner field which surrounds each DNA strand, contains encoded genetic information which is in a dynamic state (which is why New Agers should use extreme caution when using large crystals for healing purposes). It is therefore possible to electronically download genetic information from a donor and encode it by means of ultra high frequency equipment, into a totally biologically dissimilar recipient. The offspring would possess the biological characteristics of both subjects, thus rendering it feasible to electronically cross a human with a reptile.

Although such experimentation is covertly conducted for obvious reasons, Chinese scientist Dr. Tsian Kanchen has published results of similar experiments, in which he successfully electronically crossed a goat with a rabbit. Such experiments may account for the recent animal attacks by a creature known as the *Chupacabra*. Significantly, the first alleged sightings of the creature, described as being between three and six feet in height, with red eyes and winglets, occurred in Puerto Rico, a country long rumored to be the site of American covert biological experimentation. A similar creature, which escaped after receiving a gunshot wound from a police officer in the Puerto Rican town of Canovanas, left bloodstains. An analysis of the blood revealed that the albumin/globulin ratio did not correspond to that of any known animal species, suggestive that the creature may have been the result of high technology genetic experimentation. Curiously, attendees of Illuminati rituals have described to the author, the presence at these functions of reptilians, some of whom possess winglets. Since the chupacabras purportedly possess winglets, they may therefore possess reptilian genes.

In conversations with the author, the former Mother Godess of the Illuminati, Arizona Wilder, has described how she was sent to Russia as a child for training in psychic development and remote viewing. She subsequently was taken to Area 51 and other covert military facilities for the purpose of telepathically communicating with extraterrestrials, and also with genetically engineered humanoids, some of whom possessed dolphin genes. She also described small child like human replicas purportedly referred to by scientific staff as "chemical children," and claimed that vivisection experiments were performed on humanoids without the aid of anesthetics. Her left arm bears the scars where she burned off a laser encoded Area 51 identification tatoo with a cigarette (the author is aware of another mind control survivor who has a similar intact tatoo). Her story has been corroborated by another high level mind control survivor, who also had worked at similar covert military facilities, in conversations with the author. The author has received a sample of a yellowish green slime that purportedly was secreted by a reptilian creature in a Canadian residence. When the author independently inquired of the former Mother Goddess and another mind control survivor whether they had ever seen a yellowish green slime, they both unhesitatingly stated that they had seen it excreted from the chests of reptillians during Illuminati rituals. Both also stated that they had seen reptilians expectorate a similar slime.

Most flying saucer information in the public domain is unfortunately false, thanks to disinformation groups such as the Aviary. One of the most blatant disinformers was the late Lt. Colonel Philip Corso. Shortly prior to his death, Corso claimed that the transistor and fiber optics technology was reverse engineered from the Roswell crash of a wedge shaped anti-gravitic craft in 1947 (purportedly shot down with a 12 Hertz infra-sonic cannon that had been captured from the Nazis). Corso's claim is patently false. In actuality, Alexander Graham Bell was experimenting with fiber optics technology in the late 19th century; the transistor was invented by Dr. Henry Moray in 1922, for use in his free energy device. He was refused a patent for his invention, which incorporated high purity germanium. Moray's transistor drawings and notes were given to a university on a confidential basis, and mysteriously ended up in Bell Labs—the same company which was subsequently awarded a patent for the invention of the transistor. To add insult to injury, the patent attorney who wrote the Bell Labs patent application was the same person who had written Moray's transistor patent application several years earlier! Another solid state device which pre-dated the Roswell crash, was an unique combination radio frequency detector, rectifier and amplifier developed by the American inventor Dr. Palmer Craig in 1925, which harnessed sufficient electricity from the cosmos to power a conventional tube radio.

Why would Colonel Corso disseminate such blatant misinformation, unwittingly accepted by the very gullible UFO fraternity? In all probability, Corso was attempting to misdirect public attention away from the technological breakthroughs of those pioneers of free energy systems, who had elected to develop their inventions outside of the academic and military/industrial complex sphere of influence. The technology developed by such pioneers, who include Tesla, Schauberger and Moray, is still of immense value to the military/industrial complex, a cabal very reluctant to see such free energy systems commercialized.

The reason for suppressing such free energy inventions is obvious: in W.W.II, the American public, unaware that the Nazi Party had been the creation of British and American financial groups, were requested to donate their spare car tires to the government, purportedly for conversion into chemicals that were required for the war effort. In actuality, the tires were placed in large piles and burned. The reason for destroying the tires was to restrict the mobility of the American public. During the Eisenhower administration, a national freeway construction program was commenced in America, not for the benefit of the public, but to facilitate the movement of military vehicles in the event of public unrest. At the present time, a major public uprising could be quelled by simply cutting off the supply of gasoline, thus restricting the mobility of the activists—a feat rendered very difficult if cars were powered by free energy devices which required no fuel.

Near the end of W.W.II, when the collapse of Nazi Germany was inevitable, German industrialists, in order to ensure the continuity of the Third Reich after the war, established some 700 corporations in various nations, one hunderd of them being in the United States. Nazi propaganda fronts were established in these countries, using a crusade against communism as a cover. One of the chief propagandists was Dr. Walter Becher, the former editor of a Nazi propaganda newspaper which called for the purging of Jewish broadcasters. After the war, perhaps not surprisingly, Becher collaborated with Senator Joe McCarthy, and received letters of support from several senators, including Albert Gore, the father of Vice President Gore, Strom Thurmond, and Prescott Bush, the father of President George W. Bush.

The Nazi propagandists held an anti communist conference in Mexico City in 1957. The conference spawned an organization known as Liberty Lobby, under the direction of Willis Carto, whose mentor, Francis Yockey, had been jailed as a Nazi sympathizer during W.W.II. Curiously, the steering committee of Liberty Lobby included such people as Lt. Colonel Philip Corso and Major General Charles Willoughby.

Every December 7th, American television viewers are subjected to images of the Japanese attack on Pearl Harbor, clearly an attempt to stimulate anti-Japanese hostility. Sadly, the viewers are not informed that Japan was provoked into launching the attack by the Rockefeller family and its flunkies within the Roosevelt cabinet. Fearful that Japan might invade Russia, securing the Rockefeller's Soviet lumber and oil interests in the process, the Rockefeller's successfully persuaded China to terminate its supply of oil to Japan. The provocation was amplified on July 25th, 1941, when President Franklin D. Roosevelt froze all Japanese assets in the United States. Upon conclusion of the Atlantic Conference held the following month, Winston Churchill noted "the astonishing depth of Roosevelt's intense desire for war."

At the time of the Pearl Harbor attack, one half of the entire American bomber fleet was in the Phillipines as part of General Douglas MacArthur's Far Eastern Command. Since the Japanese task force had to sail past the Phillipines en route to Japan, after wreaking havoc at Pearl Harbor, the opportunity was afforded for MacArthur to order his bombers to launch a counterattack. Instead, he locked himself in his room and refused to see his air commander General Brereton. Even when MacArthur's radar detected a large number of aircraft from the Japanese task force approaching his airfield, his head of intelligence, none other than Major General Charles Willoughby, ordered the bombers grounded. As a result of the treasonous activities of MacArthur and Willoughby, the American bomber fleet was destroyed, a far worse military strategic disaster than the sinking of very aged naval vessels at Pearl Harbor. In actuality "Willoughby" was top Nazi spy and

Knight of Malta, Adolph Wiedenbach, born in Heidelberg, Germany, and friend of Henry Kissinger's mentor Fritz Kraemer. Wiedenbach's intelligence aide was Lt. Colonel Philip Corso.

Hopefully the day will dawn when the American public becomes sufficiently aware of the nation's true history, that December 7th will be commemorated for the infamy of President Franklin D. Roosevelt and his political and military subordinates, rather than for fostering hatred for a nation who retaliated against American aggression.

The alien craft that crashed at Roswell, New Mexico, in 1947, had symbiotic characteristics, i.e.its flight controls were actuated by the pilot's thoughts. However, the pilot's hands had to have been in contact with a control pad in order to fly the craft. In contrast, a more advanced antigravitic craft was under construction in the high desert of Southern California at the time of the Roswell incident. Designed by Otis Carr, who was a protégé of Nikola Tesla, the craft was truly symbiotic, for the craft went wherever the pilot wished it, without the necessity of touching a control pad, as was the case with the Roswell alien craft. During a test flight performed on behalf of the military, the pilot flew a triangular course, stopping at the end of each leg for fifteen minutes. Upon completion of of the flight, only four minutes of real time purportedly had elapsed. Needless to say, the craft was immediately classified; today, the civilian pilot who flew the craft resides in Nevada. In order to misdirect the attention of the UFO community, a cover story was disseminated which claimed that Otis Carr was a fraud—something which invariably occurs whenever someone invents a successful free energy device.

The various antigravity craft which have been developed by humankind, not by extraterrestrials, provides a clear indication that free-energy propulsion systems can be utilized very effectively for the production of very inexpensive electrical power. We can learn a very valuable lesson from the Lakota Indians of North America, who derisively refer to Caucasians as *"spider people,"* due to our habit of enmeshing each continent with a web of electrical transmission lines. Lakota folklore predicts that this tendency will eventually cause the planet to be consumed by fire. The planetary natural energy grid consists not only of straight ley lines, but also includes regional networks of ætheric energy, which meander threadlike over the earth's surface. These energy networks impart a major influence on the routing of underground streams and also on the geologic structure of an area. In addition, they influence weather patterns and the conciousness of all life forms in each respective region. Architects of ancient megalithic structures and Gothic Cathedrals knew how to harness this subtle energy, in order to elevate human conciousness to a higher spiritual level.[11]

Through the act of constructing railroads and overhead electrical transmission lines which traverse entire continents, we have totally disrupted the natural flow of these ætheric energy networks, thus destroying regional energy boundaries. Our present hopelessly inefficient and expensive centralized generating facilities derive much of their vast profit, not from the sale of electricity, but from the sale of multi billion dollar bond issues, which are used for the financing of grandiose expansion schemes. Flying saucer propulsion systems develop prodigious outputs of electrical energy. Small commercial versions of such non-polluting units could provide very low cost electrical power to individual homes and commercial facilities, without disrupting the natural ætheric energy flow of our beautiful planet.

Such a suggestion is, of course, anathema to the Illuminati controlled public utility companies, and their bloated bureaucracies. Could this be the real reason why Illuminati political puppets repeatedly deny the existence of terrestrially developed flying saucers?

CHAPTER 16

———————▼———————

YES, VIRGINIA, THERE ARE EXTRATERRESTRIALS

At every crossway on the road that leads to the future, tradition has placed against each of us, ten thousand men to guard the past.

Maeterlink

The subject of UFO sightings and related phenomena, presents an enigmatic puzzle rendered even more difficult to solve due to voluminous amounts of misinformation poured forth by numerous writers and lecturers, who lack the necessary scientific skills for a rational analysis of the matter. There is a marked tendency among such people only to find that which they seek, in the process ignoring relevant data which is not in conformance with their belief structure. Sadly, only ufologists who promote the big lie that the entire UFO phenomenon is the work of extraterrestrial beings receive frequent invitations to appear on national UFO lecture circuits. Mr. William Lyne, one of the very few writers who has anything meaningful to say regarding UFO related matters, has presented very lucid information regarding terrestrially-constructed antigravitic craft. Although very well versed on the subject of such craft, Lyne receives very few invitations to lecture at national UFO symposiums. One wonders whether this is due to a case of myopic vision on the part of event organizers, or could it possibly be that they were warned not to invite him "in the interests of national security"?[1]

As a direct result of being recipients of such misleading information, a large segment of the UFO fraternity has adopted a false and rigid mindset, which maintains that all UFO contactee and abduction phenomena must be a form of extraterrestrial activity. To confound matters even further, some lecturers insist that all recovered crashed UFO's must be of extraterrestrial origin, because they are fabricated from metal of a non-crystalline nature, which is too hard to cut with normal cutting tools—a technology that they claim is not possessed by human metallurgists. For the record, the process known as splat cooling, in which molten metal is deposited upon a cryogenically cooled surface, results in a non crystalline product. Similarly, when aluminum is compressed at temperatures approaching absolute zero, the metal attains a hardness exceeding that of a diamond.[2] This latter process, which was developed in Germany in the 1930's, has remained a closely guarded secret, in all probability because when liquid hydrogen is subjected to the same process, it results in a bomb possessing a detonating force comparable to that of a nuclear weapon—a technology known to Iraqi scientists.[3]

If we see an object resembling a freight train travelling along the railroad, it is logical to assume that it is indeed a physical construct of terrestrial origin. Similarly it is reasonable to conclude that a glowing cigar shaped object observed in deep space is also a physical construct, possibly the German-designed Andromeda mother-ship, or the product of an extraterrestrial civilization. It is not logical however, to assume that an object of similar appearance detected in our atmosphere must be of extraterrestrial origin, for such a luminous object would, in all probability, be a gorgon. Gorgons are naturally occurring luminous plasmoids of earthly origin, often replete with rapidly changing colored lights. Gorgons can attain lengths of up to one half mile and travel at supersonic speeds; they are induced by zones of terrestrial geopathic stress, which are generated by seismic movements along faultlines, and have absolutely nothing to do with E.T.'s.

Even though some NASA photographs of the Lunar and Martian terrain exhibit evidence of artificial structures, it does not necessarily imply that they are the result of extraterrestrial activity, for they well could be the creation of an advanced terrestrial alien race. There are many alleged eyewitness reports concerning encounters with alien races who reside within our planet's subterranean regions. Giant humanoids purportedly were observed in the Hal Saflini catacombs in Malta during the 1930's; the lower extremities of the catacombs were closed after a party of schoolchildren and their guide disappeared.[4] More than thirty vast tunnel complexes and underground cities of great antiquity have been discovered near the Turkish town of Derinkuya.[5]

A very ancient tunnel complex exists beneath Los Angeles; according to Hopi Indian legend, this habitat was occupied by a reptilian race some 5,000 years ago. In 1933, G. Warren Shufelt, a Los Angeles mining engineer, apparently detected what he perceived to be a labyrinth of subterranean tunnels beneath Los Angeles, while prospecting for precious metals with a radio-detection unit of his own invention.

Shufelt was informed by an Hopi Indian Chief that the tunnel system, which extends out under Santa Monica Bay, was constructed by a reptilian race, which previously had occupied an ancient city off the California coast. A cataclysmic earthquake submerged the city, but some survivors established an underground city beneath what is now Los Angeles, in order to escape a disastrous meteor shower about which they had been foretold. The reptilians eventually perished when toxic gas from the meteor shower entered the tunnel system, according to the Hopi Chief. Activity involving the Office of Naval Intelligence—an agency long involved in Satanic rituals, occurred in the tunnel system during the 1950's. Some very dark masonic rituals are occasionally held in the tunnel system at the present time. Evidence of a possible submerged ancient city off the Los Angeles coast is in the form of an ancient submerged artificial structure, possibly a temple, which was discovered with the aid of an underwater television camera during the past decade, by a marine geologist.

Flying saucers are occasionally sighted diving beneath the ocean off Seal Beach, which is situated in Southern California, south of Los Angeles. During interviews conducted by the author, the former Illuminati Mother Goddess, Arizona Wilder, and a person with a high security clearance, both mentioned the existence of a large underground facility beneath the Seal Beach Naval Weapons Depot. According to the Mother Goddess, flying saucers enter the facility through a submerged tunnel which extends out for some distance under the ocean. Interestingly, the Mother Goddess has informed the author that she had been taken to the Seal Beach facility, where her trauma based mind control programming had been reinforced by a very sadistic high ranking naval officer, who took delight in dislocating her fingers. The author subsequently has learned from an informant associated with the Illuminati High Council of the United States that this officer, whom the Mother Goddess had named, does in fact still work at the Seal Beach Depot, and currently resides at Newport Beach. Not far from the naval facility is an aircraft manufacturing plant, where new flying saucers have been observed in a high security area.

Anthroposophist and Ordo Templi Orientis member, the late Rudolph Steiner, stated that "certain circles" desire to keep the public ignorant of the existence of subterranean races.[6] Steiner's claim is given credence by the fact that the Smithsonian Institution has never publicly revealed details of an archaeological exploration that it conducted in 1909, of the subterranean city located adjacent to the Grand Canyon. Discovered by G.E. Kincaid, the city could accommodate 50,000 persons; mummified bodies found at the site were of Oriental or possibly Egyptian origin, according to the expedition's leader, Professor S.A. Jordan. The numerous recovered artifacts included copper implements as hard as steel. Had it not been for two articles which fortuitously appeared in a local newspaper at the time of Kincaid's discovery, the public would still be unaware of this momentous event.[7]

A pilot who accompanied Admiral Byrd on one of his polar flights during the 1920's, claimed that Byrd's aircraft landed near a terrestrially based flying saucer and that Byrd communicated with the occupants of the strange craft. Perhaps this is the reason why Byrd's polar flights have been shrouded in mystery, for one of the most shadowy figures orchestrating the cover up of UFO reality has been Lloyd V. Berkner, who accompanied Byrd on his polar expeditions. Berkner was appointed to the super secret Majority Agency for Joint Intelligence (MAJIC) which is the real MJ-12, during the Eisenhower administration, and was a member of the Robertson Panel in 1953; the panel was formed for the purpose of debunking the existence of UFO's and was funded by the CIA. It would appear that a major objective of the International Geophysical Year (1957-58) was to explore further the subterranean bases of terrestrial alien races and their UFO's, particularly in the polar regions. Not surprisingly, the International Geophysical Year was the brainchild of none other than Lloyd V. Berkner! [8]

Sedona, Arizona, is blessed with not only magnificent natural beauty, but also with four very powerful ætheric energy vortices. Sadly, the area is infested with very satanic cults, who use the ætheric energy of the vortices to enhance the effect of their rituals. Occupying part of Boynton Canyon, which is revered by the local Yapapai Indian tribal members for the power of its vortex, is the Enchantment Resort. There have been numerous claims of sightings of black helicopters, UFO's and reptilians in the vicinity of the canyon in recent years, together with rumors of the existence of ancient subterranean tunnels beneath the expensive resort and the nearby Secret Mountain wilderness area.

A modicum of credulity to these claims is provided by the fact that people hiking on public trails in the vicinity of the canyon have, on occasion, been turned back by surly black-uniformed military personnel armed with automatic weapons. Although the Enchantment Resort is still open to the public, it was purchased by the United States Government approximately six years ago over the objections of the owner. Although it is quite common for covert government agencies to rent entire floors of hotels on a permanent basis, (e.g. some key Area 51 employees have permanent accommodation at a specific Las Vegas Casino) it appeared to the author that the government must have a very important reason for purchasing a commercial resort in such a rural area. Upon checking through his intelligence sources, the author learned that the resort in question was purchased on behalf of MAJIC.

Satanic rituals involving human sacrifice have been observed at other covert military facilities in the past, such as Area 51 and Montauk, both of which are associated with the MAJIC organization. In all probability, Boynton Canyon's powerful vortex and the possible existence of a portal into other astral realms were the reason why a federal organization should elect to acquire a commercial enterprise, such as the Enchantment Resort. Suspicions would have been aroused had the government barred the public from the resort; however, the ability to conduct nefarious covert deeds under the noses of unsuspecting resort guests, provides a beautiful cover (the author is aware of two vacation-related facilities in Southern California where Illuminati rituals occur). It accordingly makes one wonder what goes on *beneath* the Enchantment Resort.

If technologically advanced alien races have been co-existing with us for milleniums within the subterranean regions of our planet, this well may be the reason that Western governments, with media assistance, have made a concerted effort to generate a public mindset that if UFO's exist at all, they incorporate a technology so far beyond human capabilities that they must be of extraterrestrial origin.[9] The global ruling elite, purportedly intends to establish totalitarian rule over the American populace, to be accomplished through the implementation of a National State of Emergency. In order to accomplish such a task, it is necessary to instill fear of a possible threat in the minds of the general public. This was succinctly stated by Dr. Henry Kissinger when he addressed a Bilderberg meeting at Evian-les-Bains, France, in 1991: "Today America would be outraged if United Nations troops entered Los Angeles to restore order; tomorrow they will be grateful! This is especially true if they were told that there were an outside threat from beyond, whether real or promulgated, that threatened our very existence. It is then that all peoples of the world will plead to deliver them from this evil. The one thing that every man fears is the unknown. When presented with this scenario, individual rights will be willingly relinquished for the guarantee of their well being granted to them by the World Government."

Dr. Kissinger's chilling words are reflected in the current genre of very dark movie and television plots, revolving around invasion of our planet by malevolent extraterrestrials. Since the 1950's, there has been a concerted effort by various federal agencies, to promulgate disinformation concerning the true nature of purported UFO contactee and abduction phenomena. This disinformation has been perpetrated not only to conceal the reality of terrestrial alien beings, especially reptilians, who apparently have co-existed with us for millenia, but also to obfuscate the fact that man made UFO's were operational prior to W.W.II. Such disinformation also supports a major recommendation of the Iron Mountain Report. This report was written in 1963 by an allegedly federally commissioned think tank, that was assigned to propose a course of federal action in the event that global peace broke out.[10]

The commitee reported that a federal goverment would undoubtedly collapse in such a peaceful environment, unless the public was conditioned to fear a real, or imaginary threat, which is why the Cold War myth was created, even though much of the Soviet military hardware was funded by the United States during this period, with money conduited through the United States Export/Import Bank.[11] In addition to fabricating the Cold War hoax, the Iron Mountain committee also recommended that the public be instilled with the threat of a possible invasion by extraterrestrials

The current abundance of movies and television shows depicting aggressive extraterrestrials, is not only supportive of the Iron Mountain ideology, but may be part of an on-going effort by the global oligarchy to generate a sufficient public awareness of a possible extraterrestrial invasion threat, that it will be easy for the "secret government" to declare a state of national emergency using an invasion by E.T.'s as a pretext, if phony "terrorist attacks" covertly staged by treasonous elements within and without the United States Government fail to accomplish the task.

UFO investigator and lecturer Norio Hayakawa claims that the oligarchy has developed a duplicitous plan known as *"Project Panic."* Under this plan, very high-technology equipment would be used in order to create the optical illusion of an invasion by UFO's, as a pretext for declaring a State of National Emergency. Credence is lent to Mr. Hayakawa's claim, by a purported eyewitness to an apparent test of the device in question. On a radio talk show hosted by Anthony J. Hilder, the eyewitness stated that one night in 1992, accompanied by two friends, he was on a mountain which overlooked the secret Nevada facility known as Area 51. Suddenly, he experienced a subterranean low rumbling sound that rolled across the valley. This immediately was followed by a very brilliant light in the sky, which he likened to a supernova. Multiple glowing discs then emerged from the first object and performed geometric patterns in the sky; one of his companions photographed the phenomenon, which gave the appearance of flying saucers departing a mother ship.

The subterranean rumbling sound provides us with a major clue as to how the phenomenon was achieved: the entire effect almost certainly involved the detonation of an opto-explosive device.[12] This type of device consists of a very low-yield nuclear explosive, which is doped with low-atomic number metal elements, and detonated in an underground chamber. The outlet from the chamber consists of a labyrinth of tunnels which absorb the blast and nuclear debris. What remains of the explosion consists of a stream of highly energized photons in the form of a beam of incredibly bright atomic light. The beam is focused by means of disposable mirrors and is used to pump a laser to unimaginable levels of luminosity, in order to stage the ultimate light show.

The subject of UFO contactee and abduction phenomena is far more complex than the typical writer or lecturer on UFO-related matters would have us believe. A major point invariably ignored by such ill-informed persons is that a major component of UFO-oriented abduction and contactee phenomena is the presence of a powerful electromagnetic field.[13] The nature of the phenomena tends to be dependent upon whether or not the electromagnetic field which initiates the event is very powerful, or weak and non-turbulent.[14] Be that as it may, the resultant phenomenon exhibits an electromagnetic field that is sufficiently strong as to modify the percipient's brain chemistry. How the phenomenon is perceived is largely dependent upon the changes in the neurochemistry of the percipient, due to the presence of of the electromagnetic field. These changes in brain chemistry have been studied intensively by members of the infamous CIA funded MK-ULTRA and Project Monarch mind control programs; many scientists are currently engaged in studying the UFO related phenomena, including electromagnetic field experiments in which human subjects perceive, under controlled laboratory conditions, what they believe to be typical gray aliens.

Specific electromagnetic frequencies and wavelengths stimulate the production of various hallucinatory associated chemicals, such as pinoline, and can result in anomalous activity and perceptual changes through neuronal kindling in specific regions of the brain, e.g. the temporal lobes. Even the phenomenon of being in love is dependent upon the brain producing phenylethylamine—a chemical which diminishes one's ability to discriminate effectively, hence the expression "love is blind." This particular chemical is also present in chocolate and possibly explains why some women marry convicted serial killers. Production of this chemical is sustained by the release of endorphins; romance dies when these chemicals are no longer produced by the brain.

Perceptual effects noted in purported alien abduction cases are missing time, clicking or buzzing sounds, sexual feelings or sulphurous odor. These phenomena are typical results arising from contact with intense electromagnetic fields, and are caused by neurochemical changes in the following regions of the brain:

Missing time: caused by electromagnetic stimulation of the reticular portion of the mid-brain, at frequencies between 100 and 1500 Hertz;

Buzzing noise or sulphurous odor: internally produced in the limbic region of the brain;

Clicking: known as the Page Effect, this is due to changes in magnetic flux;

Sexual feelings: induced in the septal region of the brain by electromagnetic frequencies of 30–40 Hertz;

Hallucinations: in 1930, Professor Cazamalli discovered that electromagnetic frequencies of 500 Megahertz induced hallucinatory phenomena.[15]

A classic close encounter occurred in 1974 near the English town of Aveley, where the author once worked. A married couple and their three children were heading home in their car after dark, one evening, when they observed a blue irridescent light in the sky. After travelling for several miles with the light following them, they turned a corner in the road and were engulfed in a very dense fogbank, which emitted a green phosphorescent glow. Simultaneously, the headlights failed and smoke issued from the car radio. The occupants felt a tingling sensation and could hear no extraneous sounds. After the mist cleared, the car occupants drove home and were unable to account for three hours of missing time; moreover, all occupants of the car apparently maintained the same posture without moving, throughout the entire missing time period.

This type of phenomena typically has nothing to do with extraterrestrial activity, but everything to do with a combination of geopathic stress and electromagnetic energy radiated from a man made source, such as high voltage power lines.

It is significant that the highway was adjacent to overhead high-voltage power lines in the area where the green fog was encountered. The intense electromagnetic fields generated by such high voltage sometimes results in the formation of a fluorescent green mist, particularly if occurring at a frequency in the region of 10,000 Hertz; the green fluorescent effect is due to ionization of noble gases (e.g. Argon) in the atmosphere.

Distributed throughout the human body are nerve centers called proprioreceptors, which inform the brain about body posture and muscular condition. This electrical activity results in considerable sensory noise within the brain. The car occupants clearly entered into a state of electroanaesthesia during the missing time period; this has the effect of attenuating internally-derived sensory noise. Electroanaesthesia occurs when the brain is subjected to external frequencies ranging between 100-1500 Hertz. The fact that the victims maintained the same frozen postures during the entire period of missing time, is indicative that their brain neurotransmitters sustained an electrical overload, resulting in a temporary muscular immobilization known as akinesia.

It should be noted that electrical pylons divide the electrical flow wherever there is a change in the direction of the overhead power lines. This directional change causes a portion of the electrical energy to flow down the pylon and along the ground, thereby generating a localized turbulent electromagnetic field. In the present case, the power lines took an abrupt directional change in the area where the green mist occurred.

Electro convulsive therapy employs a jolt of electricity in order to reorganize the patient's bio-electrical and chemical functions. The subjection of the human brain to intense external electromagnetic fields exerts a similar effect, resulting in a cathartic modification of one's mental and physical processes, such as chemical hypersensitivity, heightened E.S.P. and adjustments in spiritual values. In the above case, four members of the family developed an aversion to meat, and the husband underwent a mental breakdown.[16]

The above phenomena have been duplicated under controlled conditions by various scientists, including some associated with CIA funded mind-control projects, and are explainable by conventional physics. However, the light observed in the sky during the Aveley episode presents a far more complex situation. Even though physical UFO's emit intense electromagnetic fields, which causes the ionized air surrounding the craft to glow, another type of glowing aerial phenomena possessing the capability of travelling at high speeds, frequently has been observed.

This type adopts either the form of the previously described cigar shaped gorgon, or a ball of light resembling ball lightning, and ranging in size from a few inches to one hundred feet in diameter. These glowing forms, which are sometimes saucer shaped, tend to slowly meander near the ground, then depart at supersonic speed toward the horizon, apparently attracted to water towers (water is a rich source of ætheric energy) or to microwave transmitting towers. These luminous objects often display a multiplicity of colored lights, which rotate around the periphery of the sphere; they sometimes project light beams which expand and contract in length, unlike conventional light beams, which merely dissipate with distance.

This type of glowing object is created by the enormous piezo-electrical charges that are generated by rock movement along seismic fault lines. An additional source of electricical energy is derived from a petro voltaic effect. This effect is virtually unknown to civilian scientists, presumably because the fifty years of research into this phenomenon has covertly been conducted by the United States Office of Naval Research. It appears that rock formations absorb gravity waves and broad band radio frequencies which appear to emanate from binary stars, or possibly quasars. Rocks selectively detect and convert some of these frequencies and transmit them in the form of electricity—a phenomenon that the energy cartel would prefer to remain unknown to the public.[17]

These various electrical charges cause pockets of air entrapped below ground to become ionized. If the ionized air escapes into the atmosphere through a fissure in the rock, it emerges from the ground in the form of a glowing plasma, encapsulated within a sheath of water vapor. The surface tension of the water enables the plasma to maintain its form, which may be either cigar shaped in the case of a gorgon, or more commonly, a sphere. Occasionally the plasmoid is saucer shaped. The plasmoid emits a powerful electromagnetic energy field, which sometimes causes light refracted from the sheath of water vapor, to create an optical effect known as *Heillingenschein,* in which the plasmoid appears to have a shiny metallic surface. These various forms of plasmoid, sometimes referred to as earthlights, contain no voltage, merely pure current and plasma within a water vapor sheath. Any object entrapped within a plasmoid implodes and apparently dematerializes, presumably by warping the space-time continuum.[18]

The powerful radiation emitted by earthlights not only causes burning of the skin, but also alters the brain chemistry of any nearby percipients. Conciousness appears to be a field effect, possibly of the morphic resonance variety as postulated by Rupert Sheldrake.[19] The electromagnetic field emitted by earthlights appears to entrain both the earthlight and the percipient in a conciousness field, thus providing the earthlight with a form of quasi-intelligence; this would account for the strange interaction that frequently occurs between earthlights and observers.[20] Humanoid figures have been seen to emerge from earthlights, communicate telepathically with the percipient, then dematerialize. During such an encounter, the electromagnetic field desensitizes the concious mind, allowing the subconcious mind of the observer to assume a dominant role, and actually create the semi-physical construct of a humanoid from the components of the electromagnetic spectrum. This anomaly illustrates the awesome creative capabilities of the human unconcious mind, when not under the constraints normally imposed upon it by the concious mind, and is evidenced graphically by the materialization of physical objects by psychics, while in a state of altered conciousness.[21] Lacking the apparent capability of handling fine detail, the subconcious mind tends to create such humanoid figures in a simplistic manner, omitting many facial details and invariably clothing them in one piece jumpsuits, without fastenings.[22]

This type of anomaly requires that the electromagnetic field be operating at a relatively low frequency. However, if there is an interaction between two or more microwave signals operating in the gigahertz range, but only a few cycles apart in frequency, the combined resultant frequency will be in the extra low frequency range, and consequently is capable of interacting with earth energies, resulting in the formation of plasmoidal lights.

Plasmoidal lights and poltergeist activity were a rare occurrence prior to W.W.II; until that time, electromagnetic energy in the environment was at a low level. In the present era however, we have become immersed in a veritable sea of ever changing electromagnetic waveforms, which emanate from microwave transmitters, television stations, satellites, radar and telephones. These various waveforms sometimes interact to create electromagnetic "hotspots" consisting of powerful standing waves. It is at such hotspots that paranormal events occurr, particularly if the standing waves are in the vicinity of a seismically active fault zone.

Paranormal phenomena can be created under controlled laboratory conditions, by operating Tesla coils and radio frequency equipment simultaneously in a confined area. Such studies have been conducted in Toronto by John Huchison, in which plasma balls were created, common objects levitated or flew through the air, and other objects fractured catasrophically. Of great significance is the fact that non metallic wooden and plastic objects levitated in Huchison's laboratory, a phenomenon which transcends the known laws of physics. Anomalous heating effects were also noted, in which metal objects and concrete became white hot without burning adjacent wooden surfaces. This latter phenomenon may help to provide a rational explanation for instances of spontaneous human combustion.

Many ufologists hold the belief that UFO abduction scenarios are always the work of extraterrestrials, who either wish to interbreed with humans or save us from destroying Planet Earth. A major problem with this premise is that most abduction details only emerge under hypnotic regression, the percipient's prior knowledge of the event usually only consisting of a feeling that something unusual occurred while in the sleep state, or after discovering scratches, bruises or clawmarks on their bodies. If this planet is regularly being visited by numerous E.T.'s from many diverse regions of the universe, we must question why we were not inundated with abduction accounts prior to the advent of the 1950's.

When Cortez and his bloody-minded conquistadors landed in the New World, the hapless natives succumbed not only to superior weaponry, but also to the deadly European diseases to which they had no resistance. During the Appollo lunar missions, great precautionary steps were taken to ensure that the astronauts did not contaminate the earth with any lunar pathogens. One wonders therefore, why any extraterrestrial being would be so foolhardy as to engage in sexual encounters with humans. The claim that a cross breeding program is in progress is equally ludicrous, since a technologically advanced race could readily improve their stock by means of recombinant engineering techniques; we must also question why an advanced race of beings would elect to dilute their gene pool with purportedly inferior human genes.

As stated previously, federal agencies have concealed the fact that terrestrially constructed flying saucers exist.[23] A similar cover-up surrounds the animal mutilation mystery. If this evil act is the work of extraterrestrials, as many ufologists claim, why are so many of the carcasses found to be daubed with fluorescent paint, which is invisible in daylight? Is it not more rational to surmise that the mutilations are associated with chemical warfare research?

Development of a new chemical warfare agent wouild necessitate the determination of its residual longevity in plant growth, and effects of ingestion. Target cattle could be daubed with fluorescent dye prior to spraying the grazing area with a very diluted form of the chemical agent. After a suitable time period has elapsed, the target animal is identified at night be means of the fluorescent patch on its back, tranquilized, then hoisted aboard a so called silent helicopter of the type used by the National Security agency, or a man made antigravitic craft. A powerful light beam projected down the winch cable as the animal is hoisted aboard an unlit craft, would create the illusion that the creature was being levitated by means of a tractor beam (the author has seen actual tractor beam equipment, a replica of a German design from the 1930's).

Aboard the craft, the animal would be drained of blood, then the organs removed by means of a portable laser scalpel of the type developed by the USAF Phillips Laboratory, for use by special forces personnel. The output wavelength of this scalpel is variable, in order to provide different tissue interactions. It is used as a scalpel and also for blood coagulation and wound closing. The carcass can then be lowered in a different area of the pasture, thus leaving no footprints in the vicinity.

Notably, some of the first animal mutilations occurred near the chemical warfare lab near Dulce, but not until after development of the laser.

Promulgation of stories that E.T.'s are engaged in the construction of major underground flying saucer bases in America, lend a convenient cover story for the M.X. missile program, which required the construction of tunnels several hundred miles in length, in addition to subterranean cities (Project Noah's Ark) and underground facilities owned by various transnational corporations. Several prominent persons in the UFO fraternity who have had involvement with intelligence agencies, have disclosed lurid tales concerning an underground facility which is located on the Jicarilla Indian Reservation near Dulce, New Mexico. These persons fail to mention that this facility, officially known as D6, accommodates a Wackenhut/Stormont Laboratories consortium, which allegedly is used for the manufacture of chemical and biological weapons. The codename for this nefarious undertaking is *Project Yellow Lodge.*[24] There is, however, another subterranean base near the D6 facility, where horrific genetic engineering experiments involving E.T.'s purportedly occurrs. The Wackenhut /Stormont consortium also purportedly owns a facility at Hercules, California which manufactures ethnically selective bioweapons. Disturbingly, allegations have been made that this consortium has had involvement with the Japanese Yakuza criminal organization, MI6 biowarfare specialist the late Sir Dennis Kendall, and alleged Rockefeller and Bush family business partner Osama bin Laden.

Some highly publicized contactee accounts are particularly suspicious, e.g. UFO photographs presented by George Adamski (who was involved with U.S. Naval Intelligence) bear a striking resemblance to the early German flying saucers that were equipped with inflatable hemispherical landing gear.[25] Prior to his alleged UFO experiences, Adamski, who possessed a diplomatic passport, was involved with scientists from the Point Loma Naval Electronics Laboratory in San Diego, and from a similar facility in Pasadena.

In order to direct the flow of disinformation among the UFO community, key members of the MK-ULTRA and Monarch mind control programs, were assigned to establish a UFO disinformation group which became known among the intelligence community as the Aviary. As was mentioned in the previous chapter, several of the most prominent authors and lecturers on UFO-related matters, are known to be Aviary members.[26] When members of federal agencies retire, they customarily remain close-mouthed regarding matters of national security; violation of a sworn oath of secrecy incurs at the very least a loss of pension, or being subjected to Electronic Dissolution of Memory (EDOM). One should accordingly exercise caution in the presence of "former" federal employees, who accept speaking engagements of the UFO lecture circuit, particularly if they promote a One World agenda, are known members of a secret society, or attempt to coerce scientists who are engaged in covert projects to violate their secrecy oaths. Such wretched people are frequently used not only for the purpose of disseminating disinformation, but also to gather intelligence on members of the UFO community. These very personable characters are known to the intelligence community as "friendly aunts and uncles."

Many mind control victims have been programmed with a screen memory *(Operation Greenstar)* as was stated in the previous chapter, in order to create a false abduction belief. However the typical abduction scenario which does not involve a mind control element, quite frequently is an incredibly complex grand illusion involving what Carl Jung termed *Psychoidal Energies.* Jung hypothesized that these archetypal entities are beings of pure energy, who possess intelligence and coexist with us. Their atomic structure appears to operate at extremely high rates of frequency, thus normally rendering them invisible to us.[27]

Unlike earthlights, which manifest only in areas of intense interactive electromagnetic fields, archetypes only appear to be able to lower their frequency rate and intrude into our realm of physical reality at periods when the earth's magnetic field is in a quiescent state. During the day, the solar wind, which consists of electrically-charged particles, creates a great deal of electromagnetic turbulence as it interacts with the earth's magnetic field, but at night the field becomes relatively stable, which helps to explain why abduction events are most prevalent after dark. The earth's magnetic field is most stable during total eclipses. This is a period when native tribes held their most important ceremonies, presumably in order to facilitate the physical materialization of archetypal psychoidal energies, apparently for the purpose of communication with the tribal shaman. In all cases, the magnetic field must be in compliance with certain conditions, in order for the entities to be able to physically materialize.[28]

When such a being materializes, the magnetite crystals in the percipient's brain orient themselves to the biofield of the entity in question, which results in an alteration of ionic flow in the percipient's brain. This modifies the output of neurotransmitters and causes the percipient to experience temporal lobe lability, an engineered altered state of conciousness. As the archetypal entity materializes, the local electromagnetic field interacts with the Meissner biofield of the percipient, thus enabling the archetype to extract information from the percipient's mind and adopt any physical form which is socially, or culturally acceptable to the subconcious mind of the percipient. Thus archetypal entities have appeared as fairies or elves to peasants, as the Madonna, angels or Christ to Christians, and most recently as extraterrestrials. In short, archetypyal entities assume a physical form that is in compliance with the cultural idiosyncracies of the percipients, presumably the reason why gray aliens were not observed, or reported, in previous eras.[29]

The first public description of a gray alien apparently was given by electronics manufacturer Paul Bennevitz, after allegedly becoming a victim of mind manipulation perpetrated by federal operatives.[30] Due to widespread media exposure since that time, gray "aliens" have become a standard archetypal form of physical manifestation. This is not to imply that humanoids possessing the physical appearance of gray entities may not exist on other planets, or at covert governmental facilities on earth, only that the gray entities described in abduction scenarios are frequently not what they claim to be, as exemplified by the fact that grays have been known to materialize accompanied by entities who possess the form of the percipient's deceased relatives.[31]

Some high-level survivors of mind control programming, who were taught how to communicate telepathically with gray aliens at covert facilities, have informed the author that the grays are a product of genetic engineering. Africa is a vast continent which has experienced numerous flying saucer crashes. These have gone unreported other than by author David Icke. Mr. Credo Mutwa is the Sanusi (head shaman and historian) of the Zulu Nation. Thanks to Mr. Icke, it was the author's great privilege to meet the very erudite Mr. Mutwa, who stated that he has seen the very tough outer covering of a dead gray alien cut open. Inside, according to the Sanusi, was a small dead reptilian.

During a typical encounter with the archetypal form of entity, the biofields of archetype and percipient merge, enabling the minds of both the entity and the "abductee" to phase in and out of our physical world and into what we term the spirit, or astral world. Native American shamans have warned that there are two types of archetypal entity: highly-evolved spiritual beings and a deceptive type, the latter deluding the percipient by forcefully conducting bogus medical examinations, or disseminating misinformation. This is the type of entity which usually seems to manifest in UFO abduction scenarios. Spiritually oriented archetypes on the other hand, frequently provide healing therapy to the percipient when appropriate

If the percipient is awake at the time of the encounter, the deceptive type of entity occasionally will attempt to dupe the victim into becoming involved in a project that invariably results in disastrous consequences. Such entities have exerted a profound psychological effect upon their victims, and have altered the course of history by fomenting wars and changing the nature of religion. Such a paranormal event replete with calamitous consequences was the manifestations at Fatima, in Portugal, in 1917. Three children, Lucia, Jacinta and Francisco, received several visits from a madonna-like apparition, who was visible only to them. An estimated crowd of 70,000 persons were present at the final visitation, which occurred shortly after a rainstorm.

Many published reports of the incident, claimed that the sun began to rotate and approach the earth in a series of wild gyrations. The fact that several observatories reported no unusual solar disturbances in the vicinity that particular day, strongly suggests that what was observed at Fatima was something else, particularly since heavy cloud cover occluded the region at the time; a more factual report came from an English eyewitness to the phenomenon, who stated that the rotating aerial object was a disc "the color of stainless steel."32

It would appear that the entire event was staged by the duplicitous type of archetypal entity. After initially promising the children that they would not be harmed, the entity later informed Jacinta and Francisco that she would return shortly to take them to heaven, but that Lucia would continue to live; this prediction suggests that the entity was implicated in orchestrating the entire scenario. Jacinta and Francisco contracted a deadly pathogen and died painful deaths shortly after the event, thereby negating the entity's promise that the children woud not be harmed. It would appear that many of the multitude observing the final visitation of the entity at Fatima became infected with the deadly pathogen known as *"the Spanish Lady,"* which was a recombination of genes from two different strains of influenza. It was the recombination of the two genes which made the pathogen unrecognizable to the immune system, thus creating a pandemic which eventually killed more than twenty million people, a figure greater than that resulting from the Black Death of the Middle Ages.

In most instances, "abductees" are in a sleep state when encountered by archetypal entities, and only relate details regarding the presence of E.T.'s during hypnotic regression. Unfortunately, research conducted at

Belgrade University by Dejan Racovic demonstrated that an interaction between the Meissner biofield of the hypnotist and that of the person under hypnosis occurs. This biofield interaction functions as a carrier wave, thereby facilitating an informational flow from the subconcious mind of the hypnotist to that of the subject. If the hypnotist has a mindset which believes that all abduction scenarios are the work of E.T.'s, a preconceived image of a typical abduction event, replete with the obligatory medical experimentation or sexual encounter, is transferred from the subconcious mind of the hypnotist to the mind of the hypnotic subject, thereby making the unwitting subject believe that the imagined event actually happened to them personally.

Another hypnotic regression problem arises from the fact that if a person, while in a normal waking state, momentarily glances at the text of a book, the textual data is encoded in the subconcious mind of the percipient, who then forgets the event on a concious level; this is known as cryptoamnesia. Persons undergoing hypnotic past life regression have recalled verifiable events which occurred in a foreign country many centuries ago. When asked while still under hypnosis to state their informational sources, the subjects responded that they had momentarily glanced at a page in a history book several years previously.

Cryptoamnesia could well account for false screen memories if an "abductee" previously had forgotten about events portrayed in an UFO related book or movie. Hypnotists who fail to elicit the informational sources in regression cases clearly are not competent to practice their craft. Many well meaning abductee support groups engage in the practice of hypnotic regression; this can prove disastrous to mind-controlled subjects who have been programmed with an abduction type of screen memory. Such victims invariably are programmed with defensive alter-personalities, who intensify the level of programming in the event that the victim is subjected to hypnotic regression.

Curiously, archetypal entities frequently materialize through glass or crystal, sometimes even through a television screen, implying that various forms of silica may function as a materialization portal.[33] It was this type of entity that the prestigious cosmologist Sir Fred Hoyle obviously had in mind, when he stated at a London press conference in 1971, that human beings are simply pawns in a scenario being played out by aliens from another universe, one which possesses five dimensions. Hoyle claimed that these beings have learned to transcend the time barriers which restrict us, and are free from the encumbrance of needing a physical body. They have pervaded our earthly realm for aeons, according to Hoyle, and probably have controlled the evolution of the human race.

Before we judge the trickster type of archetypal entity too harshly, for their seemingly callous and irresponsible actions, perhaps we should question whether such entities are attempting to persuade us to attune to our higher selves (the super concious) for answers, instead of expecting the Creator, extraterrestrials, or discarnate entities to solve our problems for us. It is perhaps well to realize that the cosmos is pervaded by an energy and intelligence continuum, into which we can attune for advanced information, without seeking the channeled help of discarnate entities, real or imagined.

During the 1970's, the author was heavily involved in conducting exorcisms. What soon became readily apparent, was that not all situations where psychic phenomena was occurring simply involved discarnate humans. Occasionally, reptilian lifeforms also materialized. Interestingly, high-level survivors of Illuminati trauma based mind control programs have described satanic rituals in which they were programmed to participate. At the rituals, well known global movers and shakers, together with members of European and Asian nobility, shapeshifted into reptilian form.

Bizarre as such a claim may appear, the author has had graphic descriptions of such shapeshifting described by several former Illuminati survivors. A previous chapter mentioned that the former Illuminati Mother Goddess, Arizona Wilder, had provided the author with a sketch of a well-known New Age writer, as she claimed he appeared at Illuminati rituals after shape-shifting into reptilian form. The description and color of his ceremonial robe matched the description of the same person given by a Montauk survivor to author David Icke. Many of the statements made to the author by Ms. Wilder appeared outrageous, but have been verified by members of the intelligence community and other high-level mind-control survivors. Be that as it may, the notion that creatures possessing a normal human physical appearance have the ability to transform into not just reptilians, but into actual dragons, is patently absurd to most people. However, before we dismiss such claims as utter nonsense, let us consider a single celled marine creature known to marine biologists as "the cell from hell." This bizarre creature has been named *pfiesteria piscicida,* and is a phytoplankton, many varieties of which pervade our coastal waters and estuaries (one variety causes the toxic red tides).

It was in 1995 that residents of North Carolina began to experience severe neurological problems, after wading or swimming in local rivers. Concurrently, literally billions of fish in North Carolina estuaries and rivers began developing horrible ebola-like lesions and dying. Thanks to Dr. JoAnn Burkholder, a limnologist at North Carolina State University, the source of the problem was traced to pfiesteria, which may be a genetically engineered strain of phytoplankton. When no fish are present, the pfiesteria, which is able to live in both rivers and coastal marine waters, adopts the physical form of a plankton, relying upon photosynthesis for its energy needs. Whenever a fish approaches however, this peculiar creature immediately grows two long flagella, thus enabling it to propel itself toward the fish.

Approaching its prey, the pfiesteria ejects a deadly toxin; the toxin affects the central nervous system of the hapless fish, causing it to swim in circles, while ebola-like lesions erupt on its skin. Amazingly, the pfiesteria shapeshifts again, growing a trunk-like peduncle, with which it attaches itself to the lesion, from which it extracts nutrients. It follows that if a single celled creature has the ability to rapidly shapeshift, then a highly-evolved entity from another astral realm, should have no difficulty in modifying the multiplicity of waveforms comprising its physical body, for the purpose of transforming from a human to a reptilian form. Perhaps this is the reason that the Illuminati hierarchy refer to themselves as *"Olympians."*

Ever since the book *"The Sirius Mystery,"* by Robert Temple, was published in 1976, a plethora of channelers have claimed that we are being visited by aliens from the Sirius star system, a notion probably stimulated by Temple's hypothesis that knowledge of the Sirius system purportedly displayed by members of the Dogon tribe of West Africa, is attributable to contact with beings from the Sirius system some five millenia ago.[34] Since the publication of his book, Afrocentrist writers such as Adams, Van Sertima, etc., have also promoted Mr. Temple's premise. Adams wrote: "The Dogon knew of the white dwarf companion star of Sirius."[35] Unfortunately,Temple apparently obtained his information concerning the Dogon folklore from the writings of French anthropologist Marcel Griaule, who began studying the Dogon people in 1931. According to Griaule, the Dogon hold a ceremony which is associated with the brightest star in the heavens—Sirius A, which is claimed by Griaule to be known among the Dogon as *sigu tolo,* he further alleged that the Dogon also were cognizant of the companion star, a white dwarf (Sirius B) which they called *po tolo.*

Since Sirius B is not visible to the naked eye, reasoned Temple, the Dogon's knowledge of it must have derived from a visitation by inhabitants of the Sirius star system, some time in the distant past.

The problem with this hypothesis is that Griaule was not conversant with the Dogon language, and had to obtain his information via an interpreter from a single informant. Tribal Africans are extremely polite, and go to great lengths to avoid a verbal dispute, which also is a characteristic of the Japanese. Griaule almost certainly was aware of Sirius B, since its discovery was a newsworthy event at that time, and probably read too much into the statements of his Dogon informant. Be that as it may, Belgian anthropologist Walter van Beek, who spent eleven years among the Dogon and could speak their language, discovered that although the Dogon were naturally acquanted with Sirius A due to its brightness, "Knowledge of the stars is not important either in daily life or in ritual. The position of the sun and the phases of the moon are more pertinent for Dogon reckoning. No Dogon outside the circle of Griaule's informants had ever heard of sigu tolo or po tolo…."[36] Jacky Boujou, who studied the Dogon for a decade, concurs with van Beek and the Dogon penchant for harmony: "I am struck by the degree to which van Beek's analysis coincides with those I have gradually arrived at….I would underline the obvious desire of the Dogon for collective harmony and consensus that is striking to the participant observer." [37] In fairness to Mr. Temple, despite the credibility problem concerning Sirius B, his book is well worth reading for the valuable information concerning early African culture.

Since electromagnetic fields exert a profound influence on the nature of the abduction phenomenon, it behooves us to take a cursory look at a potentially major emitter of electromagnetic radiation, the High Frequency Active Auroral Program (HAARP). A subscale prototype of the HAARP system has been constructed and operated at Gakona, Alaska, by Arco Power Technologies, on behalf of E. Systems, a major defense contractor.

Considerable alarm has been voiced in certain sections of the media about the project, primarily due to claims made by Dr. Bernard Eastlund in patents which he assigned to Arco, a company which owns substantial petroleum and natural gas fields in Alaska. Eastlund's proposed system would project high frequency radio waves into the lower regions of the ionosphere (the interface betweeen the earth's atmosphere and deep space). By means of electron cyclotron resonance, the radio waves would heat an area of the ionosphere several miles in diameter, thereby densifying the ionospheric plasma sufficiently for the generation of extra-low frequency (ELF) waves.

Various journalists of the New Age genre are alarmed that claimed uses for the HAARP system include tomography (detection of subterranean cavities) weather modification, destruction of aircraft, and widespread disruption of radio communications. These writers and lecturers appear to have lacked practical experience in the design and fabrication of Tesla related technology; in consequence, they have failed to question whether the Eastlund patents could ever manifest in a feasible system, since they merely encompass conventional wave radio technology, not the longitudinally pulsed scalar wave technology developed by Nikola Tesla.

The Eastlund patents require that the transmitted radio waves be helically-entrained along geomagnetic lines of force; in order to accomplish this effectively, the transmitter would require a location nearer the earth's magnetic north pole than Gakona. In addition, ELF waves are several thousand miles in length, thereby rendering their use inadmissable for the purpose of tomography, a task more suitable for the Mossbauer gamma ray beam systems currently employed in orbiting satellites. Moreover, conventional ELF waves are much too long to be effectively focussed, rendering them unsuitable for controlled geophysical warfare applications.

Because Dr. Eastlund made several patent references to the Tesla Magnifying Transmitter, journalists have assumed that the Eastlund patents and the HAARP protype at Gakona incorporate Tesla technology. Nothing could be further from the truth. Tesla charged the primary circuit of his device with high voltage pulsed D.C. electricity. Because the pulses were of extremely short duration, in the nanosecond range, current reversal was eliminated. The rapid oscillations imparted a severe stress (torsion field) upon the surrounding ætheric continuum, causing a rupturing of the dipole tachyons emanating from the sun. Many of these dipoles are split when they encounter the earth's geomagnetic field, which enables the positron portion of the dipole to assist in plant photosynthesis. The negative portion of the dipole, containing an electron, is absorbed by the earth's crust, which consequently has become a vast accumulator of electricity that increases at a rate of approximately four exajoules per year (one exajoule has the energy equivalent of 125 million barrels of petroleum. Because of the ultra-rapid D.C. pulses emanating from the primary circuit of Tesla's Magnifying Transmitter, the system was able to harness a massive inflow of electrical energy either from the atmosphere, or by tapping into the vast electrical storehouse in the earth's crust. In this manner, a very small electrical input resulted in a tremendously amplified output, which is why the corrupt energy cartel has suppressed Tesla's magnificent technology for the past century (a Tesla power unit for an automobile would be approximately the size of this book, excluding the electric motor powered by it, and a very small rechargeable starter battery.

Unlike conventional radio, which employs tranverse waves and is so inefficient it should never have been commercialized, the Tesla system discharged longitudinally pulsed scalar waves which were not influenced by electrostatic interference, could be readily focussed, and at high frequencies, were not life-threatening.[38]

Since the New World Order oligarchy maintains its dominance over the masses through its control over information disseminated by the newsmedia, energy and precious metals, it is understandable why Dr. Tesla's amazing technology has been so heavily suppressed during the past century. However, one has to question why ARCO did not upgrade the existing ionospheric heater located at Arecibo, Puerto Rico. This gigantic facility transmits microwaves, thus rendering it a far more efficient ionospheric heater than the Eastlund system. If a new system was deemed necessary, possibly to fulfill the requirements of a congressional "pork" bill, why did it not incorporate the Gyrotron type of high energy microwave generator, instead of the less efficient Eastlund system?

In view of the above, is it not possible that the HAARP prototype at Gakona was constructed for a purpose vastly different from the objectives stated in the Eastlund patents? This postulated agenda is clarified when we consider that in 1990, U.S. Senator Ted Stevens procured federal funding for the purpose of exploring the feasibility of harnessing the energy in the auroral electrojet, a prodigious stream of electrical energy that circulates around the north magnetic pole. The electrojet is formed through the interaction of the solar wind and the earth's magnetic lines of force. For several decades, pulsed waves emanating from radios located near the arctic circle, have occasionally modulated the auroral electrojet, resulting in auroral streamers charged with electrical energy descending to the ground.

Gakona is an ideal location for tapping into the auroral electrojet; moreover, the HAARP prototype incorporates a large array of crossed dipole antennae. High frequency radio waves transmitted from this antenna array would spiral upwards into the electrojet like a corkscrew. If the radio signals were to be pulsed at the appropriate resonant frequency, the auroral electrojet would respond by discharging auroral electrical streamers into the HAARP unit. HAARP would require a massive electrical receiving system in order to accommodate the mind boggling inflow of electrical energy, amounting to many gigawatts of electrical energy; such a receiver just happens to have been incorporated into the HAARP prototype. Deceptively termed a Faraday Cage reflector by the media, it is in the form of extremely thick copper mesh which is mounted beneath the antenna array, far more copper than would be necessary for protection of the staff. Encompassing an area of twelve acres, the copper mesh at Gakona is an ideal receiver for accommodating such an horrendous electrical bombardment from space. The popular claim that HAARP is an offensive weapon, is belied by the fact that such a large exposed static facility would be extremely vulnerable to sabotage, especially since public visitations are permitted. By issuing public relations releases concerning HAARP, the government is able to misdirect public attention away from a much more covert high technology facility at Camp Newingham, on the Alaskan coast near the Yupik Indian reservation.

It would appear therefore, that HAARP was conceived in order to fulfill a future electrical energy need, the Eastlund patents merely being used as a convenient cover story. In order to comprehend the significance of this deception, it is necessary to briefly delve into the geopolitical importance of petroleum. For several decades, most of the United Staes energy requirements have been derived from Middle Eastern petroleum deposits, in fact, Saudi Arabia supplies more than 60 % of the current global oil consumption. Contrary to the mindset of deluded environmentalists, petroleum is a readily renewable commodity, a fact that the Illuminati movers and shakers would like to remain a big secret.[39]

In 1973, the Middle Eastern member nations of OPEC were coerced by the global oligarchy into demanding exorbitant price increases for their oil. In return for their windfall profits and a not inconsiderable supply of pre pubescent kidnapped American children destined for Saudi brothels, the OPEC nations naively agreed to the oligarchic bankers holding the OPEC oil profits in the form of thirty year Certificates of Deposit.[40] Unbeknown to the Arabs, the bankers promptly transferred the ever accumulating oil profits into bank holding companies, then loaned the money to profligate third world governments; these governments in turn put up their natural resources as collateral. It has become apparent to the Saudi government that the oligarchic bankers intend to collapse their holding companies, foreclosing on the third world debtor clients in the process. This ploy will permit the bankers to acquire ownership of the vast natural resources that the debtor nations had submitted as collateral, and leave the parent banks free from any obligation to repay the principal owing on the C.D.'s held by the OPEC members.

Realizing that they had been swindled by the oligarchic bankers and noting the rising anti American resentment among Islamic fundamentalists, fomented by Zbigniew Brzezinski's *"Arc of Crisis"* policy, the Saudi Royal Family attempted to minimize the American military presence in their country. President George Bush countered by falsely claiming that Iraqi tanks were massing on the Kuwaiti border (satellite photographs revealed no Iraqi tanks, nor tank tracks) in an attempt to frighten the Saudis into permitting a massive American military build up in Saudi Arabia. Bush business partner Saddam Hussein was then given the green light by U.S. State Department official April Glaspie to invade Kuwait. Despite his rhetoric against Hussein, President Bush provided no support for the Iraqi opposition groups. In the aftermath of the bloody war, Saddam Hussein emerged with enhanced political clout, his opposition groups were crushed, at least half a million Iraqi women and children have died as a direct result of the destruction of the Iraqi infrastructure and depleted uranium dust, more than two hundred thousand American Gulf War veterans have contracted the Gulf War syndrome, and the Bush family were awarded Kuwaiti reconstruction contracts worth billions of dollars. The other winners of this evil war besides Saddam Hussein and the Bush family (major stockholders of the Carlyle Group of weapons manufacturing companies) were the Jesuits—principal Illuminati henchmen. Just as the Jesuits orchestrated the Vietnam war in order to kill Buddhists, so we see the shadowy hand of the Jesuits behind the Gulf War genocide of women and children, for the purpose of limiting the growth of their religious rival—Islam.

Two decades ago, the Soviets discovered vast oil deposits under Chechnya and the Caspian Sea, sufficient to meet global needs for centuries. The Soviets planned to ship the oil up the River Danube, then via a short pipeline through Kosovo to the Mediteranean. The Chinese thwarted this plan by sending armed Albanian guerrilas into Kosovo. Needing an alternative route, the Soviets then invaded Afghanistan with the aim of constructing a pipeline through Afghanistan to a Pakistani port. President George Bush, Sr. countered this move by creating the Afghani Mujahideen freedom fighters, in 1984, Bush engaged the services of Osama bin Laden for the purpose of constructing a maze of tunnels, in order to protect the Mujahideen from Soviet bombs. After defeating the Soviets, Bush refused to agree to Mujahideen royalty demands for allowing the flow of Caspian Sea oil through a pipleline to be owned by the Unocal corporation, and created the oppressive Taliban government, which forced a Mujahideen withrawl to Northern Afghanistan, where they formed the Northern Alliance, which controls the production of much of the world's opium.

When the Taliban in turn demanded pipeline royalties deemed excessive, Osama bin Laden—a business asset of both the Bush and Rockefeller families, with substantial stock ownership in corporations ranging from Bioport, the only American corporation licensed to produce anthrax vaccine, to Fox Television, was used as a focal point for anti Islamic propaganda fomented by a controlled western newsmedia.

The author expects an escalation of terrorism within the borders of America, perpetrated on behalf of the Illuminati by elements associated with the United States Government. These heinous acts will be blamed on Islamic fundamentalist terrorist goups (twenty two of which are headquartered in Britain, as part of the Illuminati plan to destroy nation-states). An inflamed and unquestioning American public will then willingly support a war on terrorism, to be waged by the United States military against Third World nations deemed hostile (and useful to the energy cartel) by very corrupt and malleable United States politicians. In the process, gullible Americans will willingly surrender their hard-earned civil rights in order to be "protected" by the very neo-Nazi elements who created the situation in the first place.The author suspects that the principal nations to be targeted by United States military forces will be nations rich in natural resources, such as the Phillipines, where the London-deployed *Abu Sayef* terrorist group is being used to thwart commencement of the Filipino portion of the proposed inter-Asian transportation corridor.   Implementation of this particular transportation corridor (in which the author had been invited to participate) would have included the construction of new townships and industrial centers. Such a plan would have drastically enhanced the quality of life for impoverished Filipinos, which in turn would have resulted in a loss of Jesuit clout in the Phillipines. Just as we saw the covert hand of the Jesuits orchestrating the Vietnam War, in order to inflict genocide upon a predominantly Buddhist populace, so may we expect to see the Jesuit Superior General use the NATO military muscle to wage war upon the hapless non-Catholic segment of the Filipino community. As this phony war against terrorism escalates, the author surmises that Jewish Fundamentalists, funded by wealthy Christian Fundamentalists who are under the control of London's Quator Coronati Masonic Lodge, will blow up the Dome of the Rock in Jerusalem; this in turn will be the pretext for a Middle East nuclear war involving "dirty" nuclear weapons, which will render the Arabian oil-fields too radioactive to be operational for decades.

Such a geopolitical scenario would create a major financial crisis in many nations, initiating a major power shift among global oligarchical powers. The establishment of several HAARP facilities at this juncture, would fulfill America's electrical energy requirements. This is the horrific scenario that the author believes is currently being perpetrated by the American establishment, in order to create a global hegemony. However, it is likely that this insanity will be countered by a nuclear first strike on the United States launched by a coalition of China, Japan, Russia and India, initiated on a day when solar flares will temporarily "blind" American surveillance satellites. The attack will probably be followed by a Chinese occupation force.

A UFO related topic currently receiving considerable attention is the mysterious appearance of crop circles. In actuality, reports of crop circles date back to at least the Middle Ages, but until the last two decades, such circles have adopted the form of simple swirl patterns, and quite possibly are the result of intense electrical discharges from zones of geopathic stress, or even "whistler" related phenomena.[41]

Very elaborate crop circles have made their appearance during the past decade; admittedly, many of these are hoaxes perpetrated by vandals, but the remainder cannot be duplicated simply by trampling the grain stalks. Principal characteristics of authentic crop circles are:

The stalks are bent at a growth node, not broken, with nodal cellular expansion.

Crop circles emit microwave energy.

Radioactive isotopes of Bismuth 105 and Ytrium 88 are evident in the crop circle soil, which emits high levels of radiation.

Seeds taken from crop circles reveal evidence of DNA modification.

Dead animals found in the circles have been carbonized.

A high frequency sound or clicking noise is sometimes heard in newly formed circles.

Plasma spheres have sometimes been observed at the time that the circle was   formed.

Some UFO writers and lecturers who lack a scientific background, claim that humans lack the technology to create such complex crop circles. For the record, the basic crop circle characteristics outlined above are *exactly* the evidential signs that would remain if the crop circle were to be created by means of a low powered gamma ray beam device. Such technology was only implemented into widespread use by the military during the past two decades—the same time period that elaborate crop circles first began to appear.

The swollen nodes of grain stalks are of high moisture content; the high frequency gamma ray beam would cause the moisture in the nodes to convert into super-heated steam, swelling and softening the nodal cells and causing the stalks to bend in the direction swept by the beam. Such beams are capable of creating extremely fine detail; the high frequency clicking sound which is emitted from newly formed circles strongly suggests that the beam systems employed in this duplicitous act incorporate Mossbauer beam technology. The soil within the circle would emit radiation, and any creature unfortunate to be irradiated by the beam, would be carbonized.

In order to add to the illusion that crop circles are the creation of a technologically superior race of extraterrestrials, the Mossbauer beam units probably are mounted in terrestrially manufactured flying saucers. Of possible significance is the fact that the majority of the elaborate crop circles first began appearing in the vicinity of Stonehenge, in southern England. This ancient edifice is located in the same county as Boscombe Down, the Area 51 of Britain, where captured Nazi flying saucers have been flight tested.

Prior to commencing a crop circle, the gamma ray beam would require adjustment for focus and power setting. This could account for the one, or more, small circular depressions usually to be found adjacent to the crop circle. Crop circles made during periods of high humidity would facilitate the formation of luminous plasma spheres, which would tend to meander over the crop-circle location. On rare occasions, eyewitnesses have observed a vertical beam of light emerging from an overcast sky at night, and discovering the next day a new crop circle in the location where the light beam had occurred. Once again, this is what would be expected if the circle had been created by a Mossbauer beam unit. Crop circle buffs who have been camping in locales where crop circles frequently occurr, claim to have discovered a crop circle shortly after thinking about them. This could be because some covert agencies possess equipment capable of reading one's mind, and known to have been installed in so-called silent helicopters which are used by the National Security Agency

Crop-circle devotees who foolishly sleep overnight in crop circles well may contract leukemia in time, if their immune systems function inefficiently, due to the high level of alpha radiation discovered at newly formed crop circle sites. Had very elaborate crop circles been observed prior to the implementation into military aircraft and satellites of Mossbauer beam weaponry, one could rationally assume that crop circles were of extraterrestrial origin. However, the recent advent of sophisticated crop circles strongly suggests a terrestrial source for them;

moreover, the incorporation of sacred geometry may not only be for the purpose of fooling gullible New-Agers into believing that the circles are the work of extraterrestrials. Every geometric shape possesses an aetheric energy field. Typical large crop circle formations will emit powerful aetheric vortices, and therefore may be used for influencing ley lines, the weather, or even human emotions, in the vicinity.

A great deal of federally funded covert research currently is being directed toward the interaction between humans and psychoidal entities. In all probability, the United States Government would not be funding scientific projects of this nature, unless it perceives such paranormal encounters to be a possible threat to the proposed establishment of a totalitarian global government.

Such a threat becomes self evident, when one considers that it is possible to induce the physical materialization of such psychoidal beings, who astrally co-exist with us, under controlled conditions.[42] A temporary merging of the minds of entity and percipient, could elevate remote viewing to new heights, while entraining the melded minds through an orgone powered Heironymous type of psychotronic amplifier, could generate a veritable storm—even in the very depths of the Mount Weather Continuity of Government facility.

As we saw in a previous chapter of this book, New World Order proponent Zbigniew Brzezinski has threatened the American public that if they resisted the surrender of their national sovereignty, the global oligarchy would grind them into submission through the deployment of high technology terror weapons. As a rebuttal to the contumelious Brzezinski's attitude (he is known among geopolitical policy planners as a "bleeder"), perhaps it is timely to conclude this overview of paranormal activities, by informing Brzezinski and his reptilian overlords, that they have, in all probability, foolishly sown the seeds of their own destruction (a wise parasite never attempts to kill the host upon which it feeds). While it is easy for treasonous intelligence agencies to monitor the activities of individuals who belong to organizations who oppose the surrender of national sovereignty, such as militia groups, who are heavily infiltrated by FBI agent provocateurs, it is another matter to develop accurate intelligence data on low-profile persons who are not affiliated with any organization, yet who maintain very covert relationships with kindred souls who are dedicated to the eradication of tyranny.

In all probability, there are several small partisan groups who have aquired sufficient wealth and very high technology weaponry, to cause the global oligarchical structure to collapse like a deck of cards, if necessary, especially if they merge with the ever-growing numbers of patriotic United States flag officers (i.e. Admirals and Generals) who have become very disenchanted with the Bush brothers and their hacks within the realms of the military, Congress, and law enforcemnent. It would require fewer than a dozen such dedicated persons to sever the head of the oligarchical dragon by destroying the global money supply of fractional reserve banking paper; deprived of its ability to pay its fifth column military, law enforcement and intelligence operatives, the New World Order conspiracy would rapidly collapse.[43]

Such a scenario regrettably would result in horrendous loss of life among the global oligarchy and their bureaucratic quislings, but would represent a fitting rebuttal to Brzezinski's ill-conceived threat to the American populace. It is well to remember, however, that we are all karmically responsible for our actions; destructuring the present global regime by means of the above hypothetical scenario, creating much carnage in the process, would be futile unless the perpetrators possess a blueprint for a better world.[44] The actions of most people—even Adolf Hitler, arise from the best of intentions, even if they are diametrically opposed to our own ideology

Unfortunately for us, the global overlords have acquired a collective mindset which is derived from the teachings of the Greek philosopher Heraclitus, who held that the general populace were like irresponsible and apathetic sheep, who had to be dominated and fleeced by an elite minority. The oligarchy also accepts the false premise of the Reverend Malthus, who claimed that the world is overpopulated, hence the on-going effort to reduce the global population by means of geophysical warfare, plague and controlled ethnic wars.[45]

In conclusion, the author believes that the optimum way to resolve a conflict is not through warfare, but by modulating the belief structure of one's enemy until it coincides with your own. It is through meaning-ful dialogue between the global hierarchy and the populace, not war, that will pave the way toward a more civilized planet, for the present turmoil on earth is a mere reflection of a far greater conflict that is cur-rently raging on a non-physical plane—but that is a subject beyond the scope of this book.

CHAPTER 17

▼

THE STRANGE CASE OF
ADOLF EICHMANN

"The Third Reich is the first world power which not only acknowledges but also puts into practice the high principles of the papacy."

Franz von Papen

A primary objective of this book is to persuade readers to emulate Socrates and investigate matters of interest for themselves, instead of placing reliance upon so-called "experts," who frequently have a vested interest in presenting a very biased viewpoint. All too often, media reports of major events are simply too glib, which should raise a red flag to astute readers. Such was the case with the media accounts of the life, arrest, trial and subsequent execution of the prominent Nazi, Adolf Eichmann. Not a single media account inquired as to why Adolf Eichmann was tried and executed as a war criminal, yet the person from whom he had received his orders during the earlier phases of W.W.II was never prosecuted, even though he was living under his real name in the United States at the time of Eichmann's arrest and trial

Many historians have deluded themselves by believing that Adolf Hitler presided over a Third Reich which was a centrally controlled, fully integrated, totalitarian socialist state. In actuality, the Nazi government was an amorphous agglomeration of vested interests, who formed their own spheres of authority; this bureacratic disarray can be attributed to Hitler's tendency of distancing himself from his administrative staff. In consequence, a great deal of miscommunication arose between the Führer and his subordinates, thus negating the possibility of the Nazi bureacracy ever functioning as a monolithic structure.

It was Hitler's ambiguous statements regarding the "Jewish problem" to his Nazi underlings, most of whom were afraid to seek clarification for fear of incurring the dictator's mercurial wrath, which led to Eichmann's rise to prominence within the Nazi regime. Strangely enough, Eichmann did not succumb to anti-Semitic behavior until he became a member of the Nazi Party. In fact, many of his childhood friends were Jews, from whom he acquired the basics of Hewbrew and Yiddish; he even dated a Jewish girl during early adulthood. Born in the German town of Solingen in 1906, Eichmann, because of his familiarity with Jewish traditions, was appointed director of the Jewish Museum, where his principal task was the amassing of data appertaining to Jewish history, in addition to determining the wealth and corporate holdings of German Jews. An exteriorization of Eichmann's lack of self esteem manifested in the manner in which he clicked his heels and sprang to attention, whenever any member of the Nazi heirarchy visited the museum. This ingratiating trait attracted the attention of Heinrich Himler, the satanic Reichsfüher of the S.S., who arranged to have Eichmann become a member of the Reich Security Service (S.D.). At the S.D., Eichmann was assigned to the Zionist Organization desk, where his knowledge of Jewish matters enabled him to write *The Zionist World Organization,* which was published as an S.S. Pamphlet in 1936.

In the pamphlet, Eichmann expressed the fear that the S.S. desire to send all German Jews to Palestine, could culminate in the creation of a Jewish Palestinian state, which might pose a threat to Germany. Here it should be noted that the scenario for Illuminati global domination, as developed by satanist Albert Pike in the 19th century, did in fact, call for the creation of a Jewish state in Palestine, as a precursor to initiating W.W.III. This is why Rothschild Illuminists were instrumental in financing the costs of Russian and German Jews who were desirous of emigrating to Palestine, during the first two decades of the 20th century.[1]

In order to ascertain the probability of the formation of a Jewish state in Palestine, it became incumbent upon the S.D. to penetrate the innermost core of the Zionist movement, a counter espionage and administrative branch of the World Zionist Organization known as the Hagganah. It so happened that an S.D. informant and Nazi Party member named Baron Otto von Bolschwing, had a connection with the Rothschild dynasty and also with a Polish accountant, Feival Polkes, who was in charge of the military self defense organization of the Palestinian Jews. Polkes met with Eichmann at the Traube Restaurant in Berlin in February, 1937. Polkes stated that it was his objective to accelerate the emigration of German Jews to Palestine in the hope that they eventually would outnumber the Palestinian Arabs.

Eichmann reciprocated the visit by meeting Polkes in Cairo later that year. Polkes agreed to become an informant for the Nazis, in return for a monthly stipend of fifteen pounds sterling. This was not a clandestine arrangement between an individual informant and the Third Reich, but a formal, if covert, *alliance* between the Nazis and the Hagganah! In return for information, Eichmann gave the assurance that Germany would pressure Jews wishing to emigrate, that they would be obligated to select Palestine as their new homeland, and not any other country.

Pleased with Eichmann's efforts, Himmler promoted him in 1938, and transferred him to Austria for the purpose of promoting Jewish emigration. A natural organizer, and alarmed at the bureaucratic infighting between State and Nazi Party officials who were involved in Jewish emigration matters, Eichmann, who by now possessed sweeping authoritative powers, decreed that a central administrative bureau would henceforth handle all Jewish emigration matters. And so the Central Office for Jewish Emigration was created, with Eichmann at the helm, of course.

Armed with his recently-bestowed sweeping powers, Eichmann, newly ensconced in a former Rothschild palace in Vienna (the Rothschilds bear the official title of *Guardians of the Vatican Treasury*) ordered the mandatory expulsion of all Austrian Jews; within eighteen months, 150,000 Jews had been forced to emigrate. Unfortunately for Eichmann, the inflammatory rhetoric spewed forth by Julius Streicher's *Der Sturmer* newspaper, which portrayed Jews as "World Enemy No.1," ignited a wave of anti Semitism throughout the Third Reich, spurred on by Propaganda Minister Goebbels rantings, which resulted in a demand for an acceleration in the expulsion of Jews. This could not have come at a worse time for Eichmann, for after an outbreak of bloody altercations between Palestinian Arabs and Jews, the British issued an edict designed to restrict the admission of Jews into Palestine, to a maximum of 75,000 over a five-year period.

In order to thwart the British Mandate, the Hagganah created a Zionist resistance organization, which they designated *Mossad el Aliyah Bet* (Immigration Bureau) under the direction of Hagannah leader Eliahu Golomb. The Mossad proceeded to establish a clandestine network of operatives throughout Europe for the purpose of arranging the smuggling of Jews into Palestine. With much of the Third Reich budget being devoted to its massive military build up, the S.D. lacked the funds necessary to provide financial assistance to impoverished German Jews, who were attempting to flee to Palestine.

The Mossad proved to be the answer to Eichmann's prayers: German Foreign Minister Joachim von Ribbentrop—not the brightest of persons, was opposed to the transportation of German Jews to Palestine; moreover, some countries, including the United States, were erecting political barriers toward Jewish immigration. Consequently, Jewish emigration figures were declining. Fortunately for Eichmann, Mossad representatives Pino Ginzburg and Moshe Aurbach, boldly requested a meeting with Eichmann's superiors in the S.D., which was duly granted.

Incredibly, as a result of the meeting, a covert alliance was established between the S.D. and the Mossad, in which the latter agreed to arrange and finance the shipping of German Jews to Palestine. Such an arrangement had to be kept secret, for it diametrically opposed the edicts of both the official Nazi policy, which was dedicated toward the disintegration of Zionism, and the British, who had established naval patrols off the Palestinian coast, with orders to intercept emigrant ships.Ginzburg relocated to Berlin and supervised the operation, complying with the S.D. proviso that the Palestinian destination of the emigrating Jews be withheld from German Foreign Ministry officials. This duplicitous act serves to dispel the popular myth that the Nazis operated a monolithic totalitarian governmental structure, for here was the S.D., later to become part of the S.S., opposing the edict established by another powerful segment of the Nazi hierarchy.

Much of the coal, iron ore and zinc which fueled the growth of Germany's military muscle during the 1930's, was supplied by Poland's *Upper Silesian Coal and Steel Company,* largely owned by the American company *Brown Brothers, Harriman,* and the *German Steel Trust,* the latter company being under the co-ownership of Baron Fritz Thyssen and Friedrich Flick, both of whom funded Himmler's S.S. with the intent, for all practical purposes, of creating the S.S. as a quasi-private company security force. Dismayed at the manner in which the Polish company's German and American owners were perpetrating the evasion of excise taxes, the Polish government attempted to impose a tariff on the nation's natural resources being exported to Germany. Anxious to provide more "living room" for Germany's growing populace, it was this ill-fated act by the Polish Government which prompted Hitler to order a plan for the Nazi invasion of Poland in September, 1939. It was, of course, necessary to justify such an invasion to the satisfaction of the German populace.

This was accomplished by staging a mock attack on a German customs post near Hochlinden, by S.S. personnel disguised as Polish soldiers, on August 31st, 1939. Due to a communications error, the customs staff were not informed that it was only a mock battle, and opened fire, killing several S.S. "attackers." Meanwhile, other accomplices, also clad in Polish uniforms, and under the command of senior S.D. member Alfred Naujocks, staged a phony raid on a German owned radio station in the Polish town of Gleiwitz, handcuffed the unsuspecting German staff and broadcast inflammatory anti-German statements. These duplicitous actions provided Hitler with the pretext required for the Nazi invasion of Poland the very next day. And thus began W.W.II.

The advent of war was accompanied by the infamous "Final Solution"—the eradication of those deemed undesirable by the hierarchy of the Third Reich; these included not only the Jews, Gypsies and Communists, but also New Agers, the latter for fear that some of them might psychically monitor top secret Nazi meetings.[2]

The Final Solution program initially was a logistical nightmare for those assigned to administrate it, since the more territory conquered by the advancing Nazi hoard, resulted in increased numbers of people to be arrested, and greater distances for them to be shipped to the concentration camps in Germany. Moreover, such a vast and complex undertaking necessitated the utilization of a large labor force, and trains which were also badly needed for the planned invasion of Russia.

Alarmed at the inefficient manner in which the Final Solution program was being handled, Himmler (who had structured the S.S. along Jesuit lines) and his fellow merchants of death, assigned Eichmann to head up the program. Always eager to please his superiors, Eichmann ignored the fact that in his formative years, most of his friends had been

Jews, and dispassionately plunged into the task of developing a stream-lined and more cost effective system for the extermination of Third Reich elements deemed undesirable. For Eichmann, the challenge was merely a numbers game; the fact that he was embarking on one of the largest mass murder projects of the century, meant nothing to him, only operational efficiency mattered.

Eichmann intuitively realized that instead of transporting the hap-less victims hundreds of miles to the concentration camps to await exe-cution, it would be more efficient to form mobile execution squads that would conduct executions in each city which surrendered to the seem-ingly unstoppable Nazi military onslaught. After being informed that his diabolical plan had met with Hitler's approval, Eichmann estab-lished four *Einsatzgruppen,* or mobile execution squads, consisting of several hundred S.S. personnel apiece. Upon arriving at a newly-con-quered city, each group would establish a council of elders, consisting of that particular city's most respected Jews. Each council would be told to provide a list identifying every Jew in the locality, in order to transport them to a safer area. After the Jews had been assembled, they were taken into the secluded countryside and shot. The council of Jewish elders was then summarily executed.[3]

In keeping with that cross dressing criminal J. Edgar Hoover (who falsely denied the existence of organized crime in America) Reinhardt Heydrich kept his political foes in check through the simple expediency of compiling blackmail files devoted to the indiscretions of his party superiors. The devil incarnate, Heyrich was one of the attendees of the Wannsee Conference held on January 20th, 1942, where the Final Solution plan was conceived. Hitler was a great admirer of Heydrich because of the creative planning role which the latter had played in the previously mentioned mock raid on the Gleiwitz radio station, which had initiated W.W.II. Hitler subsequently delegated him to be in charge of the S.D. organization, much to the chagrin of the insecure Himmler, who was jealous of Heydrich's popularity with Hitler even though, like Hitler, Heydrich was suspected of having Jewish blood.

After the capitulation of Czechoslovakia, Heydrich relocated his headquarters to Hradcany Castle, near Prague, for the purpose of conducting a reign of terror against Czech citizens who were attempting to sabotage the Nazi war effort. Conditions became so brutal that the Czech government, exhiled in England, ordered the assassination of Heydrich, who was secretly being groomed to be Hitler's successor, instead of Martin Bormann. On May 27th., 1942, Heyrich was wounded in an assassination attempt by two Czech freedom fighters, one of whom lobbed a handgrenade at Heydrich's limousine, as it slowed to negotiate an acute turn in the road. Heydrich died of his wounds several days later.

Intensely jealous of Heydrich's popularity with Hitler, Himmler had covertly advised the Czech resistance that since Heydrich's limousine customarily was driven at 100 m.p.h. (in order to foil assassination attempts) the only place on the route between Heyrich's castle and his office where the limousine was obligated to slow to a crawl, was at the acute corner where the assassination did, in fact, occur. This treasonous act of Himmler exemplifies the fact that a great weakness in the command structure of the Nazi Party, in keeping with the Illuminati today, was that too many individuals were "friendly enemies," who put their own selfish interests above those of the organization. During the bloody reprisals ordered by Hitler in the aftermath of the assassination of Heydrich, the male inhabitants of the Czech village of Lidice were summarily executed by the S.S. and the village razed to the ground.

Heydrich was superceded as head of the S.D. by Ernst Kaltenbrunner, who had attended the original Final Solution conference, and was eventually hanged at Nuremburg for war crimes. Ironically, the evil Kaltenbrunner had been the co-founder of Interpol, together with Raymond Fosdick, a Rockefeller private secretary.

As for the loyal but utterly ruthless mass murderer Eichmann, he quietly slipped away after hostilities ceased, aided by the *Die Spinne*, the Nazi underground escape network, and settled in Argentina, protected by the Perons. Argentina had become a totalitarian state under the regime of Juan Perón and his corrupt mistress Eva Duarte, thus providing a safe haven for Eichmann, who found employment at the Mercedes-Benz plant, in Buenos Aires. Unsuccessful in extradition proceedings against Eichmann, the Israelis kidnapped him from his residence in 1960 and took him to Israel, where he was convicted and hanged for war crimes in 1962.

In keeping with many individuals in the intelligence community and the military High Command of the present era, Eichmann was a little person, more concerned with ingratiating himself with his corrupt superiors for the purpose of enhancing his personal career, than heeding the dictates of his conscience. Had fate in the form of Baron Otto von Bolschwing not intervened, Eichmann would, in all probability, have remained an obscure, but loyal member of the Third Reich. According to captured S.S. records, it was Bolschwing, working undercover as an importer in Jerusalem in the 1930's, who was pivotal in establishing the secret alliance between the Hagganah and the S.D.. Bolschwing was operating a complex Middle Eastern intelligence operation at the time, on behalf of the S.D., in conjunction with rabid British anti-Semite intelligence operative Jack Kilby, Saudi monarch Ibn Saud and American traitor Allen Dulles (who was covertly involved in arranging funding and the supply of petroleum for the Third Reich, even during the war).

As one of Eichmann's anti-Semitic superiors and mentors in 1936, it was Bolschwing who established the first comprehensive S.S. plan for purging Germany of its Jews. Prior to meeting Bolschwing, Eichmann displayed no traces of anti-Semitism. While not wishing to minimize the role that Eichmann played in overseeing the hideous *Einsatzgruppen* execution teams, Eichmann performed his task dispassionately, without apparent sadism. The same cannot be said for Bolschwing however. In 1941, Bolschwing instigated and oversaw the Bucharest pogrom, in which members of the elite Romanian Iron Guard looted, burned Synagogues and murdered hundreds of Jewish men, women and children, some of whom were sadistically hung on meat hooks and branded as "kosher meat", while others were beheaded and skinned. As was mentioned in a previous chapter of this book, it was another corrupt little person—Richard Nixon, who arranged congressional passage of special legislation, in order to permit the notorius Romanian Iron Guard murderer Nikolai Malaxa, to enter the United States and reside in Nixon's home town.

At the conclusion of W.W.II, the newly created CIA assigned Bolschwing to the Reinhardt Gehlen intelligence organization, precisely because of his Iron Guard activities during the infamous Bucharest pogrom, according to a sworn deposition which he gave to the United States Justice Department in 1979. Bolschwing later became the CEO of a California computer company. Very disturbingly, his protégée, the Austrian national Helene von Damme, became the White House private secretary to President Ronald Reagan, and established the list from which Reagan's cabinet appointees were selected.[4]

The obvious question to be raised is why did the Israelis expend a great deal of effort spanning a decade, to effect the abduction and subsequent execution of Eichmann, while his former Nazi superior, the sadistically inhuman Baron Otto von Bolschwing—the principal architect of the Final Solution, was never arrested and brought to trial by the Israelis?

Since Bolschwing, like the Auschwitz "Angel of Death" Josef Mengele, freely travelled internationally under his own name after W.W.II (the author has interviewed several persons who claimed to have met Mengele in the post war era, including one of his American chauffeurs) there would have been numerous opportunities for the Israeli Mossad to have apprehended the Butcher of Bucharest. The fact that the Mossad appeared to be totally disinterested in arresting Bolschwing, suggests that the Israelis may have had an ulterior motive in apprehending and executing Eichmann. Here, it must be recognized that by embracing socialism, with its attendant economic inefficiencies, the theocratic State of Israel is incapable of remaining solvent without receiving abundant largesse from the international community. In return for such financial aid, the Israelis are obligated to do favors for certain foreign powers, as exemplified by having the Mossad dirty its hands by undertaking "wet work" on behalf of American intelligence agencies.

The show trial and execution of Adolf Eichmann, established a precedent which "legitimized" the kidnapping of a person residing in a foreign country for the purpose of bringing them to trial in another country. The author believes that this was the real reason behind the abduction of Eichmann, who was considered a sacrificial pawn, whereas his Nazi superior Bolschwing was not. This Israeli effort, perpetrated on behalf of the principal Israeli financial benefactor, the United States Government, permitted President George Bush, Sr. to institute sweeping legislation, authorizing extraterritorial interference (kidnapping) in defiance of international law, for the purpose of removing Panamanian dictator and double agent Manuel Noriega from office. This heinous act, involving the death of several thousand innocent Panamanians, many of whom were buried in mass graves, was perpetrated in order to replace Noriega with a Head of State more receptive to the use of Panama as a staging post and money laundering center for the Colombian narco industry. In addition, Eichmann's execution prevented his possibility of informing the Israeli public about the pre-war clandestine interrelationship between the Mossad and the Nazis.[5]

Lest we forget, in the early years of the 20th century, most Orthodox Jews were totally disinterested in relocating to Palestine and creating the nation state of Israel. Had it not been for Bolschwing's forced emigration program, so ably implemented by his protégé Eichmann and the Illuminati controlled Zionists, the Illuminati planned scenario for

W.W.III, which is intended to include a Middle East nuclear conflict, could not take place. In other words, we are obligated to think the unthinkable: Adolf Hitler was a political patsy, elevated into a position of power by subversive Illuminati elements within Britain and Western Europe. These Illuminati elements not only initiated W.W.II, but deliberately prolonged it, not only for the purpose of terminating colonialism, in order to justify the establishment of the United Nations, but also for the creation of the nation state of Israel. The war also enabled the Illuminati to create a balance of power between communist nations and the Western Powers.

These diabolical subversive elements are not difficult to identify, for the unifying bond between them was the Illuminati sub-organization known as the Pan European Union (PEU) which was mentioned in Chapter 14. The PEU was founded in 1923, shortly after publication of the book *Paneuropa,* by Count Richard Coudenhove Kalergi, which called for the establishment of a totalitarian world government, accompanied by national de-industrialization. After becoming acquainted with the book, Baron Louis Rothschild arranged for his banker friend Max Warburg, to provide the initial funding for the establishment of the PEU in 1923. Key members included Lord Robert Cecil (whose family had covertly directed the affairs of British Intelligence on behalf of the Jesuits, since the reign of Queen Elizabeth 1st) Winston Churchill, George Bernard Shaw, H.G. Wells and Hjalmar Schact, the latter becoming Hitler's Finance Minister.

In his book, Kahlergi advocated a zero industrial growth counterculture (which has been successfully implemented in America, thanks to subversive environmental agencies) a rejection of American culture and, in true fascist style: "....only securing the maximum standard of living for those most fit."

Like flies around a dung hill, the worst elements of Europe's aristocracy became devotees of Kalergi's warped and arrogant totalitarian ideology. All that remained for the conspirators to do, in order to usher in a new dark era for the world, was to develop a suitable vehicle. That vehicle was the Nazi Party, and its chauffeur that master of oratory and demagoguery, Adolf Hitler.

Pivotal to the success of the PEU's plan for the creation of the Nazi Party was the Thurn und Taxis dynasty, which originated in Bergamo, in Northern Italy. After emigrating to Belgium, the family established a courier service for the Venetian banking nobility in the 15th century. The family fortunes increased after the Holy Roman Emperor Maximillian 1st granted the family a charter to operate a postal service throughout western and central Europe. The postal service headquarters was located at Frankfurt—the same city where Meyer Rothschild (1743-1812) lived; it was not long before Rothschild was permitted by the Turn und Taxis family to peek at the letters, prior to delivery. In this manner, the wily Rothschild acquired intimate knowledge concerning the financial status of European nobility, and consequently to which families he could discreetly offer his financial services. Since that era, the House of Rothschild has maintained a close political alliance with the Turn und Taxis dynasty, the latter being one of the wealthiest families globally, with vast real estate holdings throughout Europe and Central America.

It was a Turn und Taxis prince who was the driving force behind the creation of the Thule occult group, which was later to spawn the Nazi Party; many family members constituted the heirarchy of the very satanic Nazi S.S.. The Turn und Taxis family seat at Regensburg Castle, in Bavaria, was the site during the Nazi era of hideous satanic blood rituals conducted by the S.S. hierarchy, which were hosted by the late Prince Karl-August Thurn und Taxis, and presided over by Heinrich Himmler.

The PEU comprises two of the four branches of the Hospitaller Order, also known as the Knights of Malta, itself a major Illuminati sub-section. The first of these two branches is called the *Sovereign Military Order of Malta* (SMOM) whose emissaries have diplomatic immunity; it is affiliated with the Jesuit side of the Vatican, and has been the controlling arm of such notorius groups as the *Propaganda II Lodge* and the *Red Brigade.*[6]

Major oligarchic families whose family seats are in other Europe regions and are members of the SMOM, include the Turn und Taxis clan and their intermarried relatives, the Braganza dynasty of Portugal and the Lobkowitz family of Bohemia. These families oversee, or have founded, paramilitary cults such as the *Blue Army of Fatima* (which has 25 million members) and *Tradition Family and Property,* both of which are active in Central America. The Blue Army is particularly active in Brazil; perhaps not surprisingly, it has received patronage from Prince Luis de Orléons e Braganza, the Pretender to the throne of Brazil (the Turn und Taxis family has vast real estate holdings in Brazil). Presiding at a Benedictine seminary at Regensburg is Father Emmeram, a patron of the powerful leftist schismatic Jesuit cult run by Bishop Lefebrvre. Father Emmeram is a prince of the Turn und Taxis dynasty.

The second branch of the hospitallers that was involved in the establishment of the Nazi Party, is known as the *Most Venerable Order of the Hospital of Saint John of Jerusalem* (MVO) and comprises influential aristocratic and oligarchic members from Britain, the British Commonwealth and America. Its members dominate the major banking houses of Britain, Canada and America. The MVO, heavily involved in laundering the profits derived from narco terrorism, also oversees the intelligence networks of the *Johanniterorden,* which are active in the Baltic region.

For evidence that the PEU deliberately prolonged W.W.II (for the purpose of population reduction, and also to insure that the masses would be so sick of war that they would readily accept the creation of the United Nations) we have to look no further than the ill-fated commando raid on the French coastal city of Dieppe, in 1942. Wishing to alleviate the stranglehold that the Nazis had imposed on Russia, American General George Marshall proposed launching an European offensive. The PEU realized that if such an allied invasion of Europe in 1942 proved successful, "this delicious war" as Churchill callously described it, would be drastically shortened.

In order to dissuade General Marshall from implementing his plan, Churchill lured him into agreeing to the launching of a large-scale raid on the city of Dieppe—supposedly to test the German military strength. If successful, Churchill would condone the establishment of a European second front, or so he claimed. And so a Combined Operations Force primarily consisting of three elite Canadian commando units, with occultist Lord Louis Mountbatten as their Commander in Chief, landed on the beach at Dieppe in July, 1942, and into a deadly trap.[7] Only 32 % of the hapless troops made it back to the landing craft which had brought them into this veritable jaws of death, leaving behind six thousand dead, wounded or captured comrades. What General Marshall was unaware of at the time of the raid, was that the treacherous Churchill had ordered a British Intelligence operative from the prestigious "M" Group to notify the German Abwehr (German Military Intelligence under the command of Admiral Wilhelm Canaris) of the impending raid. This ignominious defeat persuaded the unsuspecting Marshall to agree to a North Africa offensive instead, which enabled Britain to protect its Arabian petroleum interests.[8]

The name of Adolf Eichmann is synomymous with that of self proclaimed Nazi hunter Simon Wiesenthal, ever since the publicity seeking Wiesenthal claimed to have been instrumental in the apprehension of Eichmann. It therefore behooves us to conclude this chapter with a brief overview of this legendary "Nazi Hunter," particularly since many of his claims are disturbing, to say the least.

The son of a prosperous sugar wholesaler, Simon Wiesenthal was born in 1908, in the Ukrainian town of Buczacz. Neo-Nazi publications have openly accused Wiesenthal of having been a Nazi informant; be that as it may, it is the comments not only of Jews, but also contradictory statements made by Wiesenthal himself, that the author finds upsetting. It is the claim that he had been interned in no less than five Nazi prisons and twelve internment camps that investigative journalists find so puzzling, a claim which has prompted journalists to conjecture whether he functioned as a Nazi informant. Former Austrian Chancellor Bruno Kreisky—himself a Jew, openly accused Wiesenthal of being just that.

Remarkably, Wiesenthal claims that in one instance, his Nazi captors allowed him to keep two pistols, a strange occurrence considering that civilians discovered to be carrying guns were invariably summarily executed by the Nazis. One is obliged to conjecture therefore, whether his basic story is false, or was he permitted to keep the weapons in order to defend himself aginst prisoners who suspected him of being a Nazi informant? It was customary for the Nazis not only to summarily execute recaptured Jewish escapees, but also to execute innocent victims along with them, as a reprisal measure. In consequence, it was an accepted practice for prisoners assigned to work details outside of the prison camps not to attempt to escape, even when the opportunity arose, for fear of initiating collective reprisals against other prisoners. How strange then, that Wiesenthal claimed in his memoirs that he had escaped, only to be recaptured on several different occasions. On one such occasion, according to Wiesenthal, the recaptured escapees were brought before prison camp commandant S.S. *Hauptsturmfürer* Friedrich Warzok, who ordered the execution of the other 39 ill-fated escapees, yet amazingly ordered Wiesenthal back to his barracks, relieved him of work duties, and doubled his rations! [9]

From one of Wiesenthal's authorized biographies, we are informed that during one of his escapes, he was sheltered in a house by Polish partisans. While there, he made detailed notes and maps in his diary of partisan locations—but only while he was in the bathroom, or alone in the house. Why would Wiesenthal write clandestine information which could lead to the apprehension and execution of many partisans, if the diary fell into Nazi hands? Needless to say, the partisans fled during a house to house search, but Wiesenthal mysteriously remained behind and was captured, together with his diary. Such incidents prompts one to wonder whether Wiesenthal was the heroic partisan he purports to be, or a Nazi informant.

In an interview for the *USA Today* newspaper in 1983, Wiesenthal claimed to have been only one of 34 inmates who survived at the Mauthausen concentration camp, yet according to his autobiography, he claimed that 3,000 victims died *after* being liberated from the camp by American troops in 1945. Evelyn le Cheyne, a former Mauthausen inmate, claimed in her book that there were 64,000 prisoners in the camp at the time of their liberation—a far cry from Wiesenthal's 34 survivors.[10]

Wiesenthal has been denounced in scathing terms by several Jews, including the French Nazi-hunter Beate Klarsfeld and Eli Rosenbaum, of the United States Justice Department. It was Wiesenthal's claim that he was instrumental in the location and arrest of Adolf Eichmann which aroused the ire of Issar Harel, the legendary former head of the Israeli Mossad intelligence organization, who led the team which found and abducted the ill fated Eichmann. According to Harel, "All the information supplied by Wiesenthal before, and in anticipation of the operation was utterly worthless, and sometimes even misleading and of negative value." Harel's remark is not surprising considering that shortly prior to Eichmann's arrest, Wiesenthal was claiming that Eichmann was in Saudi Arabia and Japan, according to the *Jerusalem Post*.[11]

At the very least, Simon Wiesenthal's own words lack veracity. One is accordingly obligated to question why the *Los Angeles Simon Wiesenthal Center* bears his name, an act which suggests that the center is more interested in making a fast buck than in presenting the truth; in fact, both the director of Israel's *Yad Vashem Holocaust Center* and the *Jewish Press* newspaper have accused the center of trivializing the Holocaust.

If the Simon Wiesenthal Center is so concerned about the persecution of Jews, why did its directors refrain from demanding the arrest and trial of the Nazi war criminal Baron von Bolschwing and that insidious disciple of the devil Josef Mengele (who liked to be called David) especially since both mass murderers spent a great deal of time in California and openly travelled internationally using passports issued in their real names? The Center appears to be inordinately concerned with attempting to close down the Internet. Admittedly the Internet provides a platform for neo Nazi ideologues and Christian Fundamentalist anti Semitism, both of which the author abhors, but the Internet is truly a powerful bastion against global totalitarianism.

Is this the real reason why the Los Angeles Simon Wiesenthal Center is so vociferously opposed to freedom of speech on the Internet? Is it conceivably just possible that the principal purpose of the Center is not the furtherance of those who embrace the various forms of Judaism, but rather the suppression of free speech, in order to pave the way for the establishment of a totalitarian Zionist global government, functioning as an arm of the Iluminati? If so, this is high treason perpetrated against the global populace—Jew and Gentile alike. In the event that this is considered a ludicrous question, perhaps the reader should consider the words of Israel's first Prime Minister—Leninist and principal architect of its nuclear weapons program, David ben Gurion (1886–1973) when he chillingly stated that the ultimate goal of Zionism is the establishment of a Zionist global government, enforced by a Zionist directed world military force. Is this the type of world you would wish to live in, dear reader?

EPILOGUE

"May your days be good and long upon this earth."
A line from a Washoe Indian prayer.

It has often been stated that necessity is the mother of invention. This was certainly the case when the imposition of the Stamp act by the British, upon her American colonies, prompted the ne'er-do-well Samuel Adams to write essays of protest. Adams, whose unkempt appearance created the impression that here was a man who slept in his clothes, had been a failure in business. He was, however, possessed of an uncommon gift—he was a great communicator. Had it not been for his fiery essays, which stirred the rascally Founding Fathers into forming the Continental Congress, the American Revolution, so surreptitiously orchestrated by the Jesuit Superior General Lorenzo Ricci (the Black Pope) and his very wealthy American co-conspirators the Carrolls, might never have occurred.

Similarly, most Americans are conversant with the manner in which Paul Revere rallied the populace during his ride west toward Lexington, yet very few Americans appear to have heard of William Dawes. As Boston silversmith and freemason Paul Revere made his famous midnight ride in 1775, for the purpose of alerting various colonial leaders along his route, that the British were coming to arrest smuggler John Hancock and the rumpled Samuel Adams, William Dawes, a tanner by profession, was alerting the townships west of Lexington. The gregarious and well-known Revere so motivated the populace along the thirteen miles of his route, that church bells were rung, and other messengers were dispatched on horseback in order to alert others who lived farther afield.

Due to the efforts of Paul Revere, sufficient Colonial Militias were mustered to soundly defeat the British troops at Concord the next day. And thus Paul Revere rode into history. As for William Dawes, even though his seventeen mile route took him through as many towns as Revere, very few people heeded his warning. The difference was that unlike Dawes, whose name has been written out of the history books, Paul Revere was a born communicator, who possessed the capability of generating a word-of-mouth pandemic during his legendary ride

A direct result of our living in the present information age, is that we have a tendency to tune out the media blitz to which we are subjected almost every waking moment, particularly if the information is at variance with our ingrained beliefs. Occasionally however, we are subjected to information which compels us to act, even though the perceived data persuades us to modify our belief structure. Such was the situation that arose as a result of Paul Revere's midnight ride. Many of the people who received Revere's message had been impoverished Europeans prior to emigrating to the colonies. In America, they had fulfilled their impossible dream of owning land; moreover, taxes were very low, so they were prospering.Yet so powerful were Revere's communication skills that the townsfolk were jolted out of their complacency, and heeded the master communicator's call to arms, even though it possibly might result in their deaths, or at the very least, a radical change in their lifestyles.

Master communicators possess the ability to effect massive change very rapidly. Like a contagious pathogen, the word of mouth communication quickly spreads throughout a nation, and sometimes even transnationally, effecting major change in its wake.

Throughout recorded history, the Illuminati has successfully with-held from humankind, major aspects of history and science, in order to subjugate the masses. As we saw in an earlier chapter of this book, Britain's Royal Society was founded by Illuminists such as Sir Francis Bacon, not for the advancement of science, but for its suppression. Similarly, many academic institutions have withheld from the public, knowledge of major archaeological discoveries, whenever the latter are in conflict with accepted academic dogma. In consequence, historical, political and religious truths have been withheld from the general public in order to perpetuate armed conflict. Similarly, if the presently sup-pressed technology were to be made commercially available, disease, famine and environmental pollution virtually would become eradicated.

The Illuminati and its corrupt lackeys, only constitute approximately one percent of the global population. As previously was presented in this book, the advanced weapons technology and psy-ops capability which exists within the private sector, is more than adequate to perma-nently sever the head of the Illuminati dragon.

But is this the optimum means for releasing humanity from the insufferable Illuminati yoke, which has prevented the creation of a veri-table planetary paradise? Monumental structures, such as the very tallest highrise buildings, are designed to withstand the damage arising from an airliner impact, yet rapidly collapse if the underpinnings are destroyed by strategically-placed shaped charges of explosive; in a simi-lar manner, the Illuminati House of Cards, which is only supported through the dissemination of fear, will collapse if the global populace is made cognizant of the true nature of history, religion and science. This will require the creation of a word-of-mouth pandemic, spread in par-ticular by college students, since their high testosterone levels sustain their activism in causes in which they believe. Unlike previous eras, when national, let alone transnational mass communication was virtu-ally impossible, the present day Internet provides the means by which such a communication pandemic may be accomplished.

This author has devoted some three decades, under somewhat difficult circumstances, to researching and accumulating the data presented
in this book, in the hope that some young contemporary Paul Revere
(or a better attired Samuel Adams) will possess the communication
skills to initiate a word of mouth pandemic, and succeed in collapsing
the Illuminati House of Cards. The author does not profess to be a master communicator, nor even a competent one, but, in the manner of
poet William Carlos Williams' sparrow, he has tried to do his best.

ABOUT THE AUTHOR

Brian Desborough has been a Director of Research and Development for several engineering companies, and has worked in the aerospace, marine and automotive industries. He also has provided consultation to a company engaged in deep space research. Born and raised in Southern England, he currently lives in Southern California, where he is engaged in the development of free energy systems for electrical power and transportation applications.

REFERENCES

CHAPTER 2

1.   Sagan failed to inform the public that George Lawrence had developed a functioning biological communication system suitable for the interception of intelligent interstellar signals. Lawrence informed his patent attorney in 1987 that NASA intended to use biological communication receivers on its proposed Mars missions and space stations.

Sagan was a Fellow of the Committee for the Scientific Investigation of Claims of the Paranormal (CSICOP). This bizarre organization has such a penchant for debunking both the paranormal and the existence of functioning so called "free energy" systems (even the U.S, Department of Energy acknowledges the existence of such proven energy devices) that the author suspects that the organization is a disinformation vehicle which acts in the interests of both the energy cartel and the intelligence community.

CICOP's board of directors is interlocked with an equally strange organization known as the False Memory Syndrome Foundation (FMSF). This latter organization dismisses claims made by mind control survivors and victims of ritual satanic abuse as "false memories."

Not surprisingly, board members of the FMSF have included prominent perpetrators of mind control activities, including the infamous mind control researcher Dr. Jolyon West. Both organizations have had prominent members who have been linked to pedophile activities.

FMSF advisor Dr. Harold Merksey lost his medical license after admitting to allegations of pedophilia, while prominent member Dr. Ralph Unterwager was forced to resign after it was revealed publicly that he had stated in an interview with the Danish pedophile magazine *Paedika,* that he found sex between adults and minors acceptable. Not surprisingly perhaps, CSICOP chairman is Professor Paul Kurz, owner of *Prometheus Books,* which publishes books concerning sexual involvement between adults and minors. A CSICOP Fellow is Professor Vern Bullough, a board member of *Paedika.*

Dr. Sagan repeatedly debunked the existence of flying saucers. Considering his connections with high-level military personnel, it is extremely unlikely that Sagan was not made privy to the existence of the numerous terrestrial and extraterrestrial anti gravitic craft known to exist at various covert subterranean facilities around the world. One also has to wonder why he would elect to be a member of an organization interlocked through prominent members, with the world of pedophilia.

2.   Lawrence's research has been resumed by members of the *Borderland Sciences Research Foundation,* P.O. Box 220, Bayside, California 95524. The Foundation also sells Lawrence's book entitled *"Galactic Life Unveiled."* Borderlands conducts outstanding research, particularly in the field of Tesla's longitudinally pulsed scalar wave technology. Philanthropists should seriously consider donating funds to this very worthwhile institution, which also publishes books on various esoteric subjects.

CHAPTER 3

1.   Portolan is a term meaning "port to port."
2.   Jochmans, J. *Forgotten Ages.* P.O. Box 10703, Rock Hill, South Carolina.
3.   Flem-Ath. 1995. *When the Sky Fell.* Weidenfeld.

4.   Jenny, Hans. *Cymatics, Vol. II*. Macromedia. P.O. Box 279, Epping, New Hampshire.

5.   The publication in 1950 of Dr. Velikovsky's book *"Worlds in Collision,"* resulted in a malevolent and unwarranted attack being unleashed against him by prominent members of academia, led by Dr. Carl Sagan. Many of Velikovsky's predictions, e.g. the composition of the Venusian atmosphere, were vehemently rebutted by Sagan, but subsequently verified by later NASA space missions. Since publication of his book, several younger astronomers have also proposed that Planet Earth has been subjected to catastrophic upheavals initiated by celestial bodies, without giving credit to the trailblazing efforts of Dr. Velikovsky.

Sadly, prominent astronomer Patrick Moore referred to Velikovsky as a charlatan, yet hypocritically praised the book *"The Cosmic Serpent,"* by astronomers Napier and Clube as "revolutionary" and "….an honest effort to link astronomy and paleontology, geology, mythology and even history"—the very reasons for which Moore and the academic mafia crucified Velikovsky! Even more galling is the fact that the basic theory propounded in *The Cosmic Serpent* is that the earth has been devastated in the past by comets, asteroids and meteors, which gave rise to ancient myths. The crowning insult is that the authors cite what is essentially Velikovsky's evidence in support of their own hypothesis! Fortunately, some ethical scholars and scientists are now promoting Dr. Velikovsky's reasearch in several countries.

6.   Like Dr. Velikovsky before him, Dr. Frank was branded a heretic by several leading scientists, for publishing his ice comet hypothesis, until overwhelming supportive space satellite data proved him correct and silenced his detractors.

CHAPTER 4

1.   The statement is typical of Russell's arrogance. A member of the Coefficient's Club, whose members were the driving force behind the

establishment of both Communism and the Nazi Party as precursors to the creation of a totalitarian New World Order, with which to replace a failing British Empire. In *"Impact of Science on Society,"* Russell wrote: "If a Black Death could spread throughout the world once in every generation, survivors could procreate more freely without making the world too full. The state of affairs might be unpleasant, but what of it?"

2.   West, J. A.. 1987. *Serpent in the Sky.* New York: Julian Press.

3.   Bauval, R. And Gilbert, A. 1984. *The Orion Mystery.* London: William Heinemann, Ltd..

4.   Hancock, G. and Bauval, R..1996. *The Message of the Sphinx.* New York: Three Rivers Press.

5.   Despite the hype promulgated by Cayce biographers, some of Cayce's predictions were incorrect, otherwise much of California would be submerged by now. Many predictions were hopelessly vague. Cayce failed to mentally purge himself of false dogma, and consequently appears to have been influenced by his first mentor, the Theosophist Arthur Lammers, who was conversant with Helena Blavatsky's statements regarding Atlantis. Cayce devoted almost a decade in an unsuccessful attempt to locate petroleum deposits by means of his psychic powers.

6.   The Egyptian Cult of Isis is believed in some scholastic circles to have been a mind control cult, involving mind altering substances. Dr. Svetla Balabanova has discoverd the presence of cocaine and nicotine in Egyptian mummies.

7.   West, J.A.. Op cit..

8.   Jochmans, J.. *Forgotten Ages.*

9.   Otomani artifacts comprise part of the Pitt Rivers Museum collection. The Myceneans did not develop a new curvilinear art form, as many historians claim, but simply became middlemen, because of their strategic location on the Otomani trade route, which appears to have extended as far south as Egypt.

10. Hislop, Rev. A. 1916. *The Two Babylons.* New Jersey: Loiseaux Bros..

11. Waddell, L. 1924. *The Phoenician Origins of Britons.* Hawthorne: The Christian Book Club.

12. Petrie, F. *Life of Akhenaten.*

13. Budge, W.. *Osiris and the Egyptian Resurrection.* Dover Publications.

14. The cubit has been incorporated into amazing bioenergetic devices developed by American inventor Mr. Slim Spurling, Ph. (303) 279-8324. When viewed in a subdued light, a tensor energy field readily can be seen with the naked eye.

15. We must not overlook the possibility that the "sarcophagus" was cast from an artificial red granite. An Oregon metalurgist has developed an artificial stone resembling limestone, which raises the possibility that the largest stone blocks used in the construction of the Great Pyramid were cast on site. This would explain their remarkably close fit.

CHAPTER 5

1. Data sources utilized include ethnomusicology, mythology, archaeology, Biblical and Illuminati history.

2. There are two Talmuds, the Babylonian and the Jerusalem. The Jerusalem Talmud is less extensive than the Babylonian version, and was compiled circa 400 A.D. at academies in Ceasaria, Sepphoris and Tiberias. The Babylonian Talmud was written a century later in Babylon by morally bankrupt priests who displayed a penchant for pedophilia. They condoned the rape of infant girls and the sodomizing of young boys, in addition to approving monetary contributions to the priesthood, for: "….money given to a man by a harlot to associate with his dog." Sadly, as a result of a decree issued by Rabbi Hai Gaon, who died 1038 A.D., the disgusting Babylonian Talmud takes precedence over the Jerusalem version, wherever the two are in conflict.

3.   According to Sumerian clay texts, the Anannage (also known as the Annunaki) descended what appears to be Mount Hermon, and established a habitat at Kharsag, prior to migrating to the Mesopotamian region. In all probability, they were technologically advanced human survivors of the Noahic global flood. It should be noted that the Babylonians, who later adopted and modified the Sumerian language, displayed a penchant for deifying notable human beings who had been deceased for several centuries. Accordingly, the Annanage (referred to in the Bible as Nephilim) probably were humans, not extraterrestrial humanoids, as claimed by New Agers.

4.   Genesis 24:1-10

5.   Ibid., 16: 2.

6.   Ibid., 30:3.

7.   Ibid., 31:3.

8.   Ibid., 24:1-10.

9.   Ibid., 12:5.

10.   Ibid,. 23:1.

11.   Rainey, A.. 1991. *Biblical Archaeological Review.* Vol. XVII, No. 6.

12.   Finkelstein, A. and Esse, D.. September, 1988. Ibid..

13.   Numbers 31:8.

14.   Judges 8:24.

15.   Exodus 2:17 and Genesis 37:28-36, respectively.

16.   Genesis 25:2-6.

17.   1 Chronicles 4:12-14.

18.   Samuel 1:27.

19.   Exodus 27:1.

20.   Volcanic ash from the Thera eruption has been discovered in the Negev hill country.

21.   According to the *Harris Papyrus,* two percent of the Egyptian population became temple slaves, but at a date later than that of the purported Exodus period.

22.   Hypolyte, C..1820. *The Dionysian Artificers.* London.

23. Saint Bernard of Clairvaux was the financial driving force behind the creation of the Templars. Bernard had a lifelong fascination with the Black Madonna cult, which was created by the corrupt Babylonian priesthood, in deification of Queen Semiramis, whom they claimed had been immaculately conceived. She also bore the appellation *Semelé* (image) hence the expression in the *Book of Revelation:* "image of the beast." A Greek version of Semiramis was the Immaculate Virgin *Persephone,* who was abducted to Hades and was the Goddess to whom the Eleusinian Mystery cult was dedicated; several Roman Emperors became initiates of the cult. In 501 A.D., what amounted to a corporation of bishops was established by Rome, which for all practical purposes enabled the corporation to function as a separate entity from the rest of the Catholic Church; from that time forth, the event was symbolized by the wearing of the pallium by bishops.

The statue atop the United States Capitol rotunda is popularly known as *"Freedom;"* in actuality, the sculpture is a representation of Persephone, signifying that the United States of America, whose capital is located on a parcel of land formerly known as *"Rome,"* is the property of the *Vatican Corporation Sole* and its commercial subsidiary *Opus Dei.* The personal icon of Pope John-Paul II is the Black Madonna.

24. We must not make the mistake of assuming that the Mosaic Covenant, with its inherent ethos of racial purity, resulted in major strife solely between the Jews and adversary nations, for two other societal groups of the present era have embroiled themselves in political turmoil and bloodshed, in consequence of establishing cultural identities based upon a mythical covenant with God: the Boers of South Africa, and the Protestant populace of Northern Ireland.

So strong was the belief of the Boers, that they were specifically selected by God to form a nation which excluded non-covenantal people (black Africans) they named their holiest day the *"Day of the Covenant."* In the 16th century, Scottish Presbyterians composed a religious covenant based upon the Mosaic predecessor; in 1912, the majority of the male population of Northern Ireland, Protestants of Scottish descent, signed a revised version of the Presbyterian covenant entitled *"Ulster's Solemn League and Covenant,"* which proved to be the catalyst for the creation of the Northern Ireland Government.

Even though the nations of Israel, South Africa and Northern Ireland claim to have democratic forms of government, non-covenantal minorities will never experience equal rights within the confines of their respective national borders, until the insidious covenantal mindset is erradicated. What we have are three contemporary nations who, in their relatively brief existence, have incurred much needless bloodshed through their having adopted cultural identities derived from the fraudulent Mosaic Covenant, with its markedly racist and supremacist overtones.

Tragically, as we have observed, the Old Testament covenants clearly were false dogmas, which were composed and promulgated by the corrupt Levitical priesthood, in order to benefit their self-aggrandizement. Attempting to change the mindset of covenantal societies by means of applied external pressures is ineffective, since they believe that it is their divine task to protect their religious doctrines from the profane. Accordingly, external pressures only serve to reinforce the group solidarity of covenantal peoples. Oddly enough, Jewish interest in the covenant of their ancestors had waned dramatically by the 19th century of the present era, despite the urgings of Napoleon in 1799 for the Jews to return to their biblical homeland. Even though a few Sephardic Jews settled in Palestine during the 18th century, the majority of European Jews, being of Khazar, not Israeli ancestry, remained disinterested in acquiring sovereignty over Palestine despite the creation of the *World Zionist Organization* by British asset Theodor Hertzl in 1897. One would imagine that the founder of a national Jewish organization would be well-versed in Jewish tradition, and zealous for the establishment of a Jewish homeland in Palestine, yet this was not the case. Amazingly, this atheistic Viennese dilettante, who contracted a social disease and displayed a pederastic propensity toward pre-pubescent girls, had little knowledge of Judaism and was unable to speak either Hebrew or Yiddish.

Despite Hertzl's lack of influence among the Jewish intelligentsia, his appeal for the creation of a Jewish State located in a sparsely populated region of the world, attracted the attention of the poorly educated Ashkenazic Jews of Eastern Europe, who were experiencing a wave of anti-Semitism, and in consequence were becoming increasingly dispossessed. Various locations for the homeland were considered, the principal ones being Uganda and Argentina, not Palestine. At the 6th Zionist Congress, Hertzl and a majority of delegates voted in favor of Uganda becoming the favored Jewish homeland. This proposal was soon abandoned when it was discovered that the choicest Ugandan farmland was already occupied by British settlers.

The eventual impetus for the creation of a Jewish homeland in Palestine came in W.W.I, not from Orthodox Jews, who regarded Zionism as a heresy, and were content to remain in their present domicile and patiently await the return of their Messiah, but from two British groups: the Protestants, who believed that a Jewish colonization of Palestine would lead to war, thereby expediting Armageddon, and the Illuminati geopolitical think tank, the Circle of Initiates.

25. Thompson, G..1994. *American Discovery, Our Multi-Cultural Heritage*. Misty Isles Press.

26. Fell, B. 1993. *America, B.C.*.New York: Simon and Schuster.

27. Sept./Oct. 1993. *Ancient America Magazine*.

28. Chaitkin, A..August, 1999. *Executive Intelligence Review*.

29. Feb. 1st. *Richmond Times Dispatch*.

CHAPTER 6

1. Archaeological research has demonstrated that the lives and deeds of David and his son Solomon, as depicted in the Bible, primarily

are apocryphal stories written at a much later date, in order to justify the dominance of the Levites over Judean affairs; hence the reason for King David's name appearing more than a thousand times in the Bible. Such apocryphal tales are a means by which oligarchical powers are able to exert influence over the masses.

That such a devious ploy is effective, is demonstrated by the fact that most tourists visiting Jerusalem believe that the famous landmark known as the Tower of David, was constructed during David's purported reign. In actuality, it was ordered built by King Herod, a millenium later.

CHAPTER 7

1.   According to the *Universal Jewish Encyclopædia*, "....even the Talmud remarks that one should drink so much that he can not distinguish between 'Cursed be Haman' and 'Blessed be Mordechai' (Megillah 7b)."

2.   Mar.1st,1946. *American Hebrew.*

CHAPTER 8

1.   Bickerman, E..1988. *The Jews in the Greek Age.* Massachusetts: Harvard University Press.

2.   1 Maccabees 1: 29-31.

3.   Pliny. 1989. *Natural History.* Massachusetts: Harvard University Press.

4.   2 Chronicles 26: 23.

5.   John 12: 35–36.
       Wars of the Sons of Light Against the Sons of Darkness.

6.   *Manual of Discipline.*
       Corinthians 15: 20—28, 51—57.

7. Ibid. 9: 9—11.

8. *Dead Sea Scroll 4Q 521.*

CHAPTER 9

1. *Dead Sea Scroll 4Q 561.*

2. *Dead Sea Scroll 4Q 318.*

3. Patrick, J. Sept./Oct. 1989. *Biblical Archaeological Review.*

4. Taylor, T. March 1992. *Scientific American.*

5. Proverbs 1: 20-21.

6. Ibid., 8: 22-23.

7. Winston, D. 1979. *The Wisdom of Solomon.* New York: Doubleday.

8. Proverbs 9: 1-2.

9. Winston, op. cit.

10. Chadwick, N.1971. *The Celts.* London: Penguin Books.

11. *Manual of Discipline 10: 17-18.*

12. *War of the Sons of Light Against the Sons of Darkness 14:17.*

13. Ross, A. and Robbins, D. 1989. *The Life and Death of a Druid Prince.* New York: Touchstone Press.

14. *Gallic War.*

15. *De Exidis Brittanæ.*

16. Usher, Bishop. *Brittanicorum Ecclesiarium Antiquitates.*

17. Parsons, R. *The Tree conversions of England.*

18. Tacitus. *Annals 12: 37.*

19. Ibid, 13:32.

20. Prydain, Saint. *Genealogies of the Saints of Britain.*

21. Martial. *Vol. 1V.*

22. Baronius, Cardinal. *Annales Ecclesias.*

23. *The Apostolic Constitutions.*

24. *Epistola ad Corinthios.*

25. *Irenai Opera 3:1.*

26. Baronius, op. cit.

27. Urban, Pope. *Brief Brittania.*

28. There are elements which are common to both the Dead Sea Scrolls and Gnosticism, such as the incorporation of *Wisdom* (Sophia, Achamoth) as a divine being, and the employment of dualism in the form of good versus evil. Evil, as represented in the dualism of India, Plato and the Dead Sea Scrolls, is non-corporeal, whereas the Gnostics regarded the physical world and all material things as evil. In both the Dead Sea scrolls and Gnosticism, Wisdom, in the form of Sophia, has difficulty in influencing the minds of humanity. According to 1 Enoch, 42: "Wisdom went forth to make her dwelling among the children of men, and found no dwelling place."

CHAPTER 10

1.   Jeremiah 7: 18; Judges 2: 13. Ashtoroth epitomized the incorrect use of the 666 solar force, and under the guise of Cybele, was honored on a day now known in the Catholic Church as "Our Lady Day," the Catholic Church still retaining in its rites, the galli originally used in the rites of Cybele.

2.   Our Illuminati overlords tend to re-introduce political scenarios which have worked successfully for them in the past. The scenario which they used in order to establish the Nazi dictatorship, is being repeated, in order to subjugate the American populace, prior to the establishment of a totalitarian government. Even the U.S. Congressional gun-control legislation which was introduced by Senator Norman Dodd, is a virtual copy of the Nazi gun control law that was used to simplify the arrest of German Jews during the 1930's. Dodd's father was a prosecutor at the Nuremburg war-crimes trials. In a similar manner, the Illuminati plans to introduce a global cashless society, in which the masses will be laser encoded with a number, just as the Romans were obligated to be tatooed with the cross, in order to conduct

trade, during the reign of Emperor Julian, who composed a hymn in honor of Mithra.

The Universal Price Code presently used by retailers, is too limited to facilitate the marking of the entire global population. The author speculates that a marking system invented by Dr. Keith Farrell, which utilizes a combination of right angles and lines, will be adopted as the universal marking system.

3.   In earlier centuries, when soldiers spent much of their military careers marching to various battles, they tended to suffer from rheumatism, due to excessive exposure to the elements. They found that their rheumatism was alleviated if they elected to sleep on the spot where a cow was known to have given birth to a calf. Cows instinctively know that if they give birth directly over a blind spring, an easier birth will result. The ætheric radiation emanating from most blind springs is very beneficial to life forms. Old country lanes in Britain tend to meander; this is because they followed the route of underground streams. Sensing the radiation field emanating from the streams, animals being herded tended to follow the route of the stream and not stray. For the same reason, entrances to fields were located over a blind spring whenever possible, thus encouraging animals to intuitively enter the field when being herded.

4.   The basis of ancient religions primarily was solar worship and also the worship of hallucinogenic mushrooms, particularly in the case of the amanita mushroom. Solar worship did not literally entail the worship of the sun, only the acknowledgement of the return of its life sustaining rays, and the lengthening of the days, following the winter solstice. In a similar manner, the present day Prophets of Navoo worship *Kolob,* the intelligence associated with the central sun.

Ever since the Babylonian era, the amanita was prized by the corrupt priesthood for its hallucinogenic properties. The Sumerians believed that the growth of amanita mushrooms was initiated by thunderstorms. This belief was perpetuated in the New Testament by referring to James and John Zebidee as "sons of thunder," the colloquial Sumerian term for the amanita. Similarly, the roots of the first line of the *Lord's Prayer* in the Aramaic language are derived from the Sumerian word for the amanita mushroom.

The hallucinogenic properties of the amanita mushroom were so important to ancient priestly rites, that its hemispherical shape is commemorated in the head-dress that traditionally was worn by Jewish High Priests. Hallucinogenic agents played a key role, together with behavioral modification techniques, during initiation ceremonies held by the Eleusinian Mystery cult, in order to create a malleable initiate.

5.   Magic squares constitute fundamental building blocks of nature, and occur in all forms of physical matter. Without studying magic squares, one cannot comprehend the inner workings of nature. By suppressing the dissemination of such esoteric knowledge, religion has prevented the masses from living in attunement with the cosmos.

CHAPTER 11

1.   Waddell, op. cit..

2.   Goodrich, N. 1984. *King Arthur.* New York: Harper and Rowe.

3.   Whitehead, J. 1993. *Guardians of the Grail.* New York: Harper and Rowe.

4.   The Phoenician symbol for the inner light was the moon surmounted by the sun. This was later transformed in mediæval Britain into a heraldic emblem consisting of three fiery crowns.

5.   A typical example was the 1968 "capture" of the *USS Pueblo* by the North Koreans. In actuality, the ship was deliberately surrendered as part of a covert mission perpetrated by the National Security Agency, whose operatives boarded the vessel. The action enabled the United States to break key Soviet security codes and prevent a possible Sino/Soviet conflict.

6.   Not being content to remain ensconced in the cloistered ivory towers of academia, several of the leading mediævalist scholars of the

20th century, have exerted a far greater influence on global politics that the general public is aware. Harvard's Charles Homer Haskins was not only a senior advisor to President Woodrow Wilson in the creation of the disastrous *League of Nations,* but also was one of the driving forces behind the formation of Czechoslovakia and Yugoslavia.

Similarly, Professor Percy Schramm (1894—1970) a German born mediævalist and Nazi, was appointed official historian of the Wehrmacht, working at Hitler's general headquarters. Narrowly escaping being tried as a war criminal, he wrote a sanitized biography of Hitler in 1963.

A major thorn in the side of the Vatican has been the demands of mediævalist and Thomist, Étienne Gilson (1884—1978) that Catholicism should enter into an integrated embrace with science, philosophy and art. Unfortunately for humankind, the influence of Thomism resulted in Gilson becoming one of the principal architects of the infamous United Nations. He later became one of the drafters of the equally notorius UNESCO plan.

7.   The philosophical and theological system of Saint Thomas Aquinas held that religion should be integrated with Aristotelian science.

8.   Contrary to the popular notion that Thomas Becket was a saintly and very learned man, in actuality he was a University of Paris dropout, who never mastered the ecclesiastical Latin of his time and accordingly was obligated to delegate the writing of official correspondence to others. After being appointed to ecclesiastical orders, Becket hypocritically donned armor and led a feudal campaign in France. Becket lived at the time of the Lateran Councils, which forbade married clerics.

9.   The Round Table was spawned by the core membership of Cecil Rhode's *Circle of Initiates,* with the initial objective being the looting of African precious metal deposits. This objective was later expanded to effect control of major commercial institutions throughout the world,

by means of a global network of Round Tables acting in a fifth column capacity.

Early Round Table members were trained at Oxford and Cambridge Universities, under the direction of Marxist John Ruskin and British Intelligence operative T.H. Green. The principal driving force behind the treasonous American branch of the Round Table, has been Oxford trained Rothschild agent William Yandell Elliot—a mentor of Dr. Henry Kissinger, the latter having been accused by some journalists as working for British Intelligence and London's Royal Institute of International Affairs, under the code name "Bor." A major Round Table objective (largely successful to date) has been the de-industrialization of America, accomplished by means of draconian environmental legislation and promulgation of false environmental dogma, e.g. the damaging of the ozone layer by CFC's.

Round Table spin-off organizations include the Bilderberg Group,the Ditchley Foundation, the Trilateral Commission, the Mont Pelerin Society and the Aspen Institute. Round Table members have been responsible for fomenting all the major armed conflicts of the past century.

CHAPTER 12

1. The *Church of the Holy Sepulchre* contained a short marble column which served as a base for a vessel containing a stone. A second Temple was constructed on the original site 520—515 B.C..

2. *Sermo Exhortatorius ad Milites Templi.* Translation by Partner, P. 1975. *The Murdered Magicians.* Oxford University Press.

3. Meir, Ben-Dov. 1985. *In the Shadow of the Temple: the Discovery of Ancient Jerusalem.* New York: Harper and Rowe.

4. The price of gold fell dramatically in neighboring countries in the aftermath of the destruction of the Temple; this suggests that either

the Romans or the Priesthood dumped a very large quantity of gold onto the international market.

5.   Reynaud's troops portaged collapsible sailboats across the Negev Desert, then sailed down the Gulf of Aqaba and up the Red Sea, in order to pillage the Arab ports.

6.   Unlike medæval Europe, where the Jews were barred from entering most professions, Islamic countries welcomed Jews, many of whom became doctors and civil servants, as well as serving as middle-men in East-West trade.

7.   Runciman, S. 1954. *A History of the Crusades, Vol.2.* Cambridge University Press.

8.   Ibid.

9.   Malouf. A. 1973. *The Crusades Through Arab Eyes.* London.

10.   Robinson, J. 1987. *Born in Blood.* New York: Evans & Co..

11.   Schonfeld, H. 1984. *The Essene Odyssey.* Longmead: Element Books.

12.   Sinclair, A. 1992. *The Sword and the Grail.* New York: Crown Publishers, Inc..

According to legend, 36 ox carts transported part of the Templar treasure to the French town of Carcassonne, located in Cathar territory, where it was hidden in nearby caves. Another part of the Templar enigma is to be found in a 19th. Century document *(Document Rubant)* that was based upon source material dated April 19th.,1308. According to the document, Count de Beaujeu was entrusted by his uncle, the Templar Grand Master, to hide arcane documents and precious relics in a remote castle at Arginy, in the Rhone Valley. During the past century, the castle has become the focal point for Freemasonic, Rosecrucian and Neo-Templar organizations. Constantin Melnik, the former head of the French Secret Service, allegedly participated in very dark occult rituals there.

At the present time, claims are being made on the Internet and on the lecture circuit that neo-Templar members of the Abwehr (the Nazi military counterintelligence force headed by Admiral Canaris) became founding members of the CIA. Some also became members of the United States Office of Naval Intelligence. This claim is correct. The same sources also claim that a great deal of Nazi gold was transferred to the Phillipines. This is also correct, according to the author's informants, who were very close confidantes of President Ferdinand Marcos, who became custodian of the treasure. Marcos was deposed when he attempted to use the gold for the purpose of upgrading the nation's infrastructure; what is not generally known is that Marcos faked his own death, and lived longer than the media would have us believe.

In conversations with the author, former Illuminati Mother Goddess Arizona Wilder has made mention of a Jesuit psychiatrist of Ibero American ethnicity. According to Ms. Wilder, this person has associated with Josef Mengele in the programming of mind control victims; she also claimed that he plays a major role in high-level Illuminati rituals, where he is clad in a black robe with red trim, and slits the throats of human sacrificial victims. Improbable as her claims may appear, sources associated with the Illuminati have confirmed her comments. The author has learned that this particular psychiatrist, who keeps chickens in his backyard (presumably for Santeria rituals, is in charge of a project initiated by the Illuminati High Council of the United States, whereby psychiatric staff members who also are Satanic cult members, are establishing a fifth column among the staff of a psychiatric facility located in Orange County, California. Upon completion of the project, mind control victims whose programming has begun to unravel, will be brought to this particular facility for reprogramming. Two years ago, one of the persons previously alluded to in this note, who is a proponent of the Canaris cabal, was taken to a party by this particular psychiatrist and introduced to prominent Illuminati members, according to one of the author's sources, who also attended the same party.

These various Internet sources, who appear to be apologists for the Templars and the Canaris faction, claim that this Canaris-created intelligence cabal is in collusion with the Saudi Royal Family and arms dealer Adnan Kashoggi (uncle of Dodi Fayed) and is attempting to overthrow the New World Order group. The author has monitored the dispersion of Nazi gold for several years. A considerable amount of it has been smuggled into the United States by some of the very worst elements of the Nazi Internationale (fifty-two tons of it are currently being used as collateral in a Mexican real estate development). Incredibly, these Internet sources claim that the Templars were bastions against feudalism and represented the interests of the public. As we have seen in this chapter, the Templars have had a long history of perpetrating genocide and exhorbitant usurious practices. As for collaborating with the Saudi Royal Family, the United States Justice Department is well aware (and ignores) the fact that numerous prepubescent American girls are abducted and sold for approximately $50,000 apiece as sex slaves, at slave auctions held in various locations, including Reno, Las Vegas and the California wine country. As the corruption mired Saudi Royal Family is well aware, many of these hapless children end up in Saudi brothels.

It would appear to the author that this particular intelligence faction is controlled by members of the Hapsburg bloodline, who are attempting to acquire a slice of the New World Order pie for themselves, when it is divided among the various other Illuminati factions, such as the Windsors, Braganzas and Rothschilds.

CHAPTER 13

1.   The Peace Corps, like the International Red Cross, primarily was created for infiltration of intelligence operatives into foreign nations.

2.   Sept. 11th., 1993. *The Manchester Guardian.*

3.   1994. *Paranoia Magazine, Issue 6.*

4.   Ibid.

5.   Sept., 1994. *Time Magazine.*

6.   H.G. Wells was a member of the *Coefficients Club,* a geopolitical think tank which planned World War I.

7.   Moreau de Tours, J. 1973. *Hashish and Mental Illness.* New York: Raven Press.

8.   German forensic toxicologist Svetla Balabanova has discovered the prescence of nicotine and cocaine in Egyptian mummies. These substances were probably brought to Egypt from Central America on Phoenician ships. Phoenician artifacts have been discovered in Brazil.

9.   The controlling stockholders of the world's second largest multi media company (Hachette Industries, Paris) are family members of Saddam Hussein. Hussein is also the publisher of *George Magazine.*

John Lennon publicly claimed that the Beatles single handedly introduced narcotics to the world's teen population. This suggests that the Beatles unwittingly may have been under covert Tavistock control, something Lennon alluded to in a magazine interview not long before his assassination; the lyrics to Lennon's song *"Imagine"* (purportedly written by a person who became President Clinton's speechwriter) are typical New World Order propaganda. Prior to his untimely death, Lennon clearly was his own person and therefore considered a political loose cannon by the Illuminati. This could be the motive for his assassination by CIA asset Mark Chapman, who displayed obvious signs of mind control at the time of his arrest.

10.   Chaitkin, A. October 7th., 1994. *Executive Intelligence Review.*

11.   The JFK assassination was perpetrated by the Defense Industrial Security Command, and masterminded by the Permindex Corporation, under the direction of Knight of Malta Louis Bloomfield. Bloomfield was the creator of the FBI Division 5 counterespionage group, which suppressed vital evidence in the case and misdirected public attention away from the true perpetrators of the crime.

12.   The author's duties as a Research and Development V.P. with several companies, has necessitated undergoing numerous frustrating phone calls to environmental agencies, for clarification of nebulous and

conflicting environmental rules. The calls were often handled, not by experienced and articulate personnel, but by environmental neophytes fresh out of college, answering in broken English.

13. Like his Illuminati overlords, the arrogant Brzezinski fails to comprehend that equally advanced technology exists in the private sector. A dozen partisans equipped with Gavreau infra-sonic cannons, Mossbauer beam weaponry, psychotronic systems and isochronous oscillators, could readily topple the Illuminati by destroying key subterranean facilities, EFT switching centers, satellites and the annual Bohemian Grove shindig, not to mention the de-activation of in-coming missiles, or catalysis of computer chips by means of MRX photonic coupling.

Two years ago, the author was sitting in his car in the parking lot of the Richard Nixon Library. A few yards away, Dr. Henry Kissinger was holding a book signing ceremony. If anyone intent on mayhem had the inclination, a readily obtainable magnetron, capacitor and transformer would have sufficed to have constructed a maser which would have cooked the brains of the good doctor, and his secret service personnel almost instantaneously. You were as vulnerable as when the Director of the Janus psyops group spies on you, Dr. Kissinger.

14. Many Native American children have been removed from their parents and subjected to intensive mind control programs in "Christian Schools" off the reservations. Some of these victims were sent to Britain and trained as multi-lingual special-operations assassins; posing as Viet Cong soldiers, they massacred many Cambodian women and children, collecting their ears as trophies. These soldiers were designated by the military as *"double veterans."*

15. The leader of the civilized group of global flood survivors who introduced agriculture to the hunter gatherer Sumerian natives, became known as *Tas Mikigal,* (Lord of Agriculture). With the passage of time, he became deified as *"Lord of the air,"* with the implication to the superstitious Sumerians that he had wings. We know him as Archhangel Michael.

16. Terry, M. 1987. *The Ultimate Evil.* New York: Doubleday & Co..

17. Leadership of the Theosophical Society was transferred to Annie Besant in 1894. Besant's brother Walter, was Grand Master of the Quator Coronati Masonic Research Lodge. The great grandfather of former Illuminati Mother Goddess Arizona Wilder, was statistician and authority on rituals for the Quator Lodge at this particular time period. The Quator Coronati, founded by one of the participants in the Jack the Ripper slayings, currently controls the activities of both the leading Christian Fundamentalist and Jewish Fundamentalist organizations, as a precursor to the destruction of the Dome of the Rock and the al Aqsa mosques on Jerusalem's Temple Mount.

18. The Nazis were adept at introducing psycho-manipulative techniques into German Youth Programs during the 1930's, in order to persuade children to inform on their parents, if the latter opposed Nazi ideologies. Kurt Hahn, the creator of the Hitler Youth movement, later became headmaster of Scotland's Gordonstoun School. The Duke of Edinburgh and Prince Charles were students there; the school buildings originally were built as the residence of satanist Robert Gordon. A similar insidious psycho-manipulative program is currently taking place in American schools, known as Drug Abuse Resistance Education (DARE). Claiming to be an anti drug program, in reality it is a psycho-profiling operation conducted by robocop police officers who are trained in techniques developed by behavioral psychologist Carl Rogers. Hearsay information about parents obtained through group dynamics is documented—a violation of privacy laws.

Various studies undertaken by behavioral psychologists have demonstrated that the DARE program has a negative effect on drug abuse prevention, as evidenced by a paper prepared by University of Southern California psychiatrists in 1989, and published in the *Journal of Preventive Medicine.* It stated: "….by the final post-test, classrooms that had received the affective program had significantly more drug use than controls." The DARE program was initiated by former Los Angeles

Police Chief Daryl Gates. According to former LAPD detective Mike Ruppert (w.w.w. copvcia.com): "Daryl Francis Gates was a CIA agent from the time he became a policeman." This is not surprising since in order to qualify for federal Law Enforcement Assistance Agency funding, American police departments have to permit some of their personnel to receive training by the CIA. This devious ploy has enabled the CIA to acquire control of major city police departments—a violation of the CIA charter.

Since the CIA has been heavily involved in narcotics trafficking for many years, it follows that it would not condone a meaningful drug-prevention program to be conducted in American schools. If DARE operatives were serious about curbing drug trafficking, they would vociferously be campaigning for anti drug legislation and the prosecution of bank executives who launder drug money. There is evidence that the last Los Angeles riot was a carefully orchestrated event, involving sophisticated incendiary devices. Many Korean owned stores were destroyed during the riot; a black activist who had fomented hostility toward Korean liquor store owners, in the days prior to the riot, had received funding from an extreme conservative Foundation, whose founder has publicly called for the establishment of a Fascist American government.

LAPD Chief Daryl Gates was out of town attending a fund raising event at the time that the riot began, even though a potential riot was anticipated on that particular day. Some of the victims who were killed during the riot were the subject of politically-ordered assassinations. A former U.S. Military assassin has privately admitted to the author of participating in the assassinations.

19. Hellenbroich, E. Jan.19th, 1989. *Address to the Martin Luther King Tribunal,* Rome, Italy.

20. Douglas, R. June 9th, 1989. *New Federalist.*

CHAPTER 14

1.   The Paleologues were a Greek branch of the Viterbo family of Italy. Their statesman George Gemithos established an alliance with Cosimo de Medici of Florence, which led to the Ecumenical Council of Florence, held in 14 39 A.D..

2.   In establishing their clients the Hapsburgs, as rulers of the fledgeling Austro-Hungarian Empire, the Venetian bankers were able to play the Hapsburgs and the Ottoman Empire against each other, to the advantage of the Venetians. The sacking of Rome by the Hapsburgs in 1527, enabled the Venetians to gain political control of all of Europe except for France and Tudor England. The Venetians and their Genoese banking allies funded the Stuart coup involving the Cecil family, which established King James 1st, on the English throne. In return, James appointed the Venetian/Genoese owned Levant Corporation as the official collector of British taxes. This appointment enabled the corporation to attain a prominent position in the commercial affairs of Britain.

3.   During the year prior to becoming Russia's Head of State, Vladimir Putin covertly flew to Gibralter, then boarded a fast launch, which secretly transported him to Boris Borezovski's Spanish beach-front estate on five separate occasions. The fact that his plane clandestinely landed at Gibralter on each of the five visits, suggests that Britain was privy to the meetings.

4.   The death of Czar Nicholas II and his family remains a mystery. The official version, which holds that the entire family was shot, then buried in a wooded area is false. Some investigators claim that others were shot to conceal the fact that the Romanov's lives were spared after signing away the Czar's right to the Romanov fortune, much of which was residing in Rothschild and Rockefeller banks. What the author knows from personal experience, is that Princess Marie Nikolayevna Romanova was named Empress of Russia by her father, then ransomed

for a large sum of money. Assuming the alias Countess Czapska, she later married and quietly settled in the south of France.

5.   Stalin's principal ally in accomplishing his coup was a powerful Raskolnik faction in the Ukraine.

6.   President Clinton paid tribute to his Jesuit mentor and New World Order asset Quigley, in his first presidential address.

7.   Cohn was a director of Permindex, a trading company linked to the assassination of President Kennedy. The Permindex C.E.O. was British Intelligence operative Major Louis Bloomfield.

8.   A former OSS operative has informed the author that his wife was the private secretary to British anthropologist Margaret Meade. Upon the first day of her employment, which was at the peak of the supposed cold war, she answered the phone and found that it was a social call from Nikita Kruschev to Meade!

9.   According to Sherman Skolnick, the founder of the Citizens Committee to Clean Up the Courts, an organization with an excellent track record in accurate investigative reporting, the Chinese Secret Police are firmly entrenched in America. Wang Jun, the alleged head of the Chinese Secret police in America, has visited President Clinton on several occasions. Moreover, he is the alleged law client of Whitewater investigator Kenneth Starr. Is this the reason why Starr appeared to be so lax in pursuing the dissemination of American secret military technology to the Chinese by Clinton?

CHAPTER 15

1.   According to investigative reporter Sherman Skolnick, the importation of "China White" heroin is being supplemented by the illicit importation of human organs from China. He alleges that healthy young Chinese prisoners are being beheaded by Chinese government officials, in order to provide top quality organs requested by the Rockefeller owned University of Chicago Hospital.

2.   Lewis Cass Payseur was a descendant of King Louis VI of France. With the wealth accrued from his North Carolina goldmines, Payseur constructed most of the railroads that were built in America during the 19th century, then leased them to operating companies. Payseur employed trustees such as J.P.Morgan, J.D. Rockefeller, Andrew Carnegie and Cornelius Vanderbilt, to serve as front men for his numerous companies. A.A. Springstein, a Rothschild cousin and father of principal Payseur trustee Leroy Springs, had an affair with Mary Hanks, in Lincolnton, North Carolina. The illegitimate offspring of this relationship was Abraham Lincoln, who was bequeathed land by Springstein. Lincoln in turn, had an illicit affair in 1856, which resulted in twin girls. Descendants included the astrologer Linda Goodman and Howard Hughes.

3.   At the end of the 19th century, Russia's petroleum industry was technologically years ahead of the rest of the world, and its naval vessels had been converted from coal to oil burning, years before those of any other nation. These technological advancements had been implemented due to the efforts of political reformer and visionary, Russia's Foreign Minister Count Witte. To counter Witte's on-going industrialization of Russia, Britain arranged to have the Baku oilfields destroyed by British directed Islamic terrorists. The act forced the ousting from office of Witte.

4.   The Nazi aircraft that flew to Scotland, possessed a different registration number from the one that the real Hess disappeared in, that same day. The real Hess bore the scar of a bullet wound received in W.W.I; the Hess look-alike at Spandau Prison did not possess a similar scar and lacked the aristocratic mannerisms of the real Hess.

5.   The British apparently traded flying saucer and rocket technology acquired from the Nazis, to America, in return for classified nuclear technology. Laurence Rockefeller allegedly had been involved in the deal. The Soviets also acquired German technology, including a bismuth/magnesium laminate, which degravitated when subjected to a

seven megahertz radio-frequency, while immersed in a high-voltage field. This was the invention of a German graduate exchange student circa 1935, who was detained by the Soviets. This invention is reminiscent of the laminated bismuth Hall-effect transistor that was invented by Dr. Palmer Craig, in 1925.

6.   U.S.Patent 2,939,648.

7.   It is rumored that shortly after this event, a convoy of U-Boats departed Norway, heading for Antarctica. Some of the fleet allegedly were powered by closed-loop Walter hydrogen peroxide engines, or Coler electromagnetic drive systems. The flotilla, armed with wire guided torpedoes and *Kraftstalhkannone* directed energy weapons, purportedly sank several British naval vessels en route. It is known that Nazi flying saucer facilities were established in the foothills of the Andes mountains at the conclusion of W.W.II. A large cigar-shaped craft resembling the Nazi designed Andromeda mother ship, was sighted over Central America several years ago by the crew and passengers of an American Boeing 727 airliner. The Andromeda was designed to carry on board several Vril scoutcraft and Haunabu flying saucers, and possessed a length of 139 meters.

8.   "Project Panic" was developed in order to create aerial holograms similar to those of Project Blue Beam, by means of opto-explosive systems which generated many terrawatts of energy.

9.   Eckankar was founded by Scientologist and Ron Hubbard aide Paul Twitchell, in 1955. Twitchell met Indian mystic Kirpal Singh during the latter's American tour, and was subsequently initiated by him. Twitchell corresponded with Singh for several years, allegedly admitting to Singh that he was unable to astrally project. Twitchell became a Scientologist after Singh refused to publish Twitchell's book *"The Tiger's Fang."* Twitchell later edited Kirpal Singh's name out of his earlier published books, replacing it with the name "Sudar Singh."

10.   During the genocidal Iraq/Iran war, Iraq made widespread use of chemical warfare agents, manufactured from chemicals supplied by

the French company American Lafarge. A principal stockholder in this company was President George Bush Sr, while one of its board-members was Hillary Clinton.

11.   In the 19th century, American inventor Nathan Stubblefield developed some of this wonderful science, converting the earth's ætheric energy into heat, light and sound. The Illuminati controlled Vatican established the solar oriented Gregorian calendar, in order to disengage human conciousness from true planetary attunement, with its attendant lunar overtones. This is why it is imperative that humankind returns to a thirteen-month lunar year.

CHAPTER 16

1.   Lyne, W. 1993. *Space Aliens from the Pentagon.* Texas: Creatopia Productions.

2.   The process was developed in Germany during the 1930's.

3.   Known as the air bomb, this was a German invention.

4.   National Geographic magazine. August, 1940. *Wanderers Awheel in Malta.*

5.   Anjard, R. Summer, 1978. *Pursuit Magazine.*

Crabb, R. *The Reality of the Cavern World.* Borderland Sciences Foundation.

6.   Allen, W. 1966. *Enigma Fantastique.* California: Health Research.

The late W. Gordon Allen, Ph.D, was an associate of the author in the research of transmutation and free energy devices.

7.   Arizona Gazette. April 5th, 1909. *Explorations in the Grand Canyon.*

8.   1969. *Scientific Study of UFO's.* Bantam Books.

9.   During the evening of July 2nd, 1947, a glowing UFO was sighted travelling in a northwesterly direction over Roswell, New Mexico; before reaching Corona, debris was ejected from the wedge

shaped craft, which abruptly altered course before crashing on the San Augustin plains. According to eyewitnesses, one alien occupant purportedly survived the crash. The autopsy report (viewed by the author) stated that another victim was in a comatose state. It would appear that these survivors did not require life support equipment in order to breathe our atmosphere, suggesting that these beings may be of terrestrial origin. It is highly probable that the crash may have resulted from destabilization, due to a high intensity experimental radar, or a captured German infra-sonic cannon operating at a 12 Hertz frequency, both of which allegedly were being tested in the area at the time.

10. It is claimed in some circles that the report was a hoax perpetrated by writers Leonard C. Lewin, E.L. Doctorow and publisher Victor Navasky. Even if so, their recommendations already have been implemented, e.g. the creation of an enormously expensive and wasteful space program when we already had operational flying saucers, E.T. invasion fear mongering, and the establishment of a prison industrial complex utilizing what amounts to an African American slave labor force (the infamous Wackenhut Corporation is a major builder and operator of privately-run prisons).

11. The world's largest military truck assembly plant was constructed in Russia during the cold war by Fiat, with U.S. Eximbank funding.

12. Dement, J. Feb, 1973. *Nuclear Explosive Light Generator.* Patent No. 3,715,596.

13. A typical case was described by Budd Hopkins in his book *Intruders,* in which he would have us believe that the principal percipient ("Kathy Davies" a.k.a. Mrs. Debbie Jordan-Kauble) was abducted by E.T.'s. No mention is made in the book that the various types of phenomena encountered are characteristic of geopathic stress-induced events—the shaking of a neighbor's house, accompanied by a loud roaring noise (geosound); a ball of luminous plasma; plant growth stimulation due to residual microwave energy in the soil; irradiated

patch on the lawn; malfunction of transistorized circuitry, nausea and dizzyness, etc.. The location where the phenomena occurred appears to be a geo-electrical "hotspot." Mrs. Jordan-Kauble exhibits the classic symptoms of electromagnetic hypersensitivity: allergic reactions, vasopressive condition etc., and in keeping with the other witnesses, apparently experienced temporal lobe lability, induced by the electromagnetic field effect. Such geo-electrical zones facilitate the temporary materialization of Carl Jung's humanoid "psychoidal energies," who possess the ability to pass through walls and closed doors.

14. Persinger, M., Ruttan, L., Koren, S. *Exposures to Milligause Intensity ELF Magnetic Fields.* Journal of Biochemistry, Vol. 9, No. 1.

15. Gallimore, J. 1976. *Handbook of Unusual Energies.* California: Health Research.

16. The above-cited Mrs. Jordan-Kauble experienced increase spiritual awareness and allergic reactions, following her paranormal encounter.

17. Brown, T. *On the Possibilities of Optical-Frequency Gravitational Radiation.* Unpublished paper.

18. Press and Thorne. 1972. *Gravitational Wave Astronomy.* Annual Review of Astronomy and Astrophysics, Vol. 10.

Jansky, K. 1932. *Directional Studies of Atmospherics at High Frequencies.*

Vasilatos, G. 1992. *Vril Compendium, Vol. IV.* Borderland Sciences, California.

The late Dr. Townsend Brown was the discoverer of the Biefeld-Brown electrogravitic effect, and was the progenitor of the electromagnetic field effect experimentation conducted at the Philadelphia Naval Shipyard in 1943, involving the USS Eldridge. According to Brown, the vessel only advanced in time five seconds, not forty years as claimed by some New Age lecturers. Dr. Brown later conducted precious metal enrichment studies in conjunction with the author's former research associate, the late Dr. Gordon Allen.

In order to comply with the requirements of energy conversation, re-radiated energy which is not converted into electricity by rocks, may be gravitic in nature, the frequency of which being determined by the natural resonance of the rock. If secondary gravitic radiation decay occurs deep within the earth, it may result in photonic emission, thus suggesting an explanation for the natural illumination purportedly observed by some explorers of very deep subterranean regions. Secondary gravitic emissions may also explain localized anomalies in biological growth and emotional stress.

Gravity waves may be a resultant effect arising from the creation of sub-atomic particles. If a localized region of the ætheric continuum is tightly wound into a catenoidal geometric form, additional torqueing presumably would cause a toroidal knot at the midpoint of the structure, resulting in the creation of a sub-atomic particle, and a surrounding void. The inflow of æther to fill the void would be what we perceive as gravity. Unravelling of the toroid would result in an emission of electromagnetic force.

In 1934, physicist P. Dirac postulated the existence of magnetic monopoles. Their presence was eventually detected in flowing water by the late Dr. Freeman Cope. Dr. Philip Callahan later verified the existence of tachyon monopoles (superluminal particles). Monopoles are created when magnetoelectric dipoles, ejected from the sun, are torn apart by cosmic forces. Certain people absorb such high levels of south monopoles that they are able to levitate, e.g. Saint Teresa of Avila.

Callahan, P. 1984. *Ancient Mysteries, Modern Visions.* Kansas City: Acres USA.

18.   American inventor Sonne Ward has reproduced the effect under controlled conditions.

19.   Sheldrake, R. 1981. *A New Science of Life.* Los Angeles: J.P. Tarcher, Inc..

20.   Persinger, M. 1981. *Perceptual and Motor Skills.*

21. The problem is frequently compounded by entities allegedly materializing accompanied by ghosts of the percipient's dead relatives, as reported by author Whitley Streiber in his book *Breakthrough.*

22. Geopathic stress is a geographically localized zone of geomagnetic disturbance, which disrupts the homeostasis of electromagnetically hypersensitive persons. The stress becomes intensified if the zone is concurrently irradiated by microwave transmissions or gamma-ray communication satellite signals and surveillance beams. Structures built over such zones frequently exhibit "cold areas." Other anomalies include variations in electrical resistance and radio reception. Geopathic stress encompasses two distinct categories:

a) A discharging field effect (yin) which occurs mainly at the intersection of subterranean streams, or over cavities in rock.

b) A charging field (yang) is often found over mineral deposits, which tend to emit infra-red radiation (this is why a light covering of snow melts quickest over veins of precious metals). Lightning often strikes these zones.

The flux intensity of such zones is intensified if they are located at the intersection of earth energy grids; the best known of these are the Hartmann Net and the Curry Grid. The Hartmann Net consists of a rectangular energy lattice oriented north-south and east-west. Grid lines running north-south are spaced 2.5 meters apart, and east-west lines are spaced 2.0 meters apart. Adjacent lines on the grid are of opposite polarities. Geopathic flux is greatest wherever grid lines of similar polarity intersect. Grid lines are usually 20 cms. in width, which increases to 80 cms. during full moon periods. The flux is stronger at night.. The Curry Grid, which runs diagonally to the Hartmann Net, has a grid spacing of 22 meters. Other important earth energies are Bloch Wall vortices and the World Grid system.

An "abduction event" is a signal that the phenomena site possibly is a geopathic stress zone, and may be affecting the general health of the percipient. Geopathic stress modulates the spin oscillation and proton resonance of protein molecules in the human body, and affects the polarity of cell membranes, as well as altering the hormonal balance of the body. The *Institute of Bioenergetic Medicine,* located in Bournemouth, England, has conducted excellent research on the physiological effects of geopathic stress. Sadly, the typical UFO field investigator is abysmally ignorant of earth energies, even though these exert a profound effect in many abduction scenarios

The awesome ability of the human mind to create physical constructs, such as humanoid beings, when subjected to intense electromagnetic fields, is probably due to the presence in the brain of neuromelanin. Extremely difficult to analyze, neuromelanin is a semiconductor which is responsive to stimulation by electromagnetic energy, light and sound. It is able to synthesize itself from various neurotransmitters, and appears to direct the activities of DNA and RNA. According to neuroscientist Frank Barr, M.D., neuromelanin modifies states of conciousness. Aging probably is linked to a depletion of neuromelanin.

The human brain is quite possibly both a generator and a detector of scalar waves. These waves are generated whenever a mechanical or electromagnetic stress is applied to the constrained energy potential of the virtual state. When two scalar waves converge at a location distant from their source (this is known as scalar wave interferometry) kindling occurs. This in turn results in the creation of energy in a variety of forms which are observable in the physical state. Crystalline rocks such as granite, and even the very planet itself, appear to be scalar wave generators.

It would appear that it is the kindling effect arising from the interaction of scalar waves of various frequencies, generated by the human mind and also by geopathic stress, which results in the quasi-physical manifestation of humanoid figures. Even conciousness itself is quite possibly a scalar wave phenomenon involving the use of tachyons. As experimentally verified by Dr. Freeman Cope and Professor Phillip Callahan, tachyons are elementary particles which travel at velocities exceeding that of light, and create a field in which space and time converge. This explains why remote viewers are able to attune to past, present or future events.

23.   Terziski, V. 1994. *Close Encounters of the Foo Fighter Kind.* Los Angeles: TR2 Consultants.

24.   Cockburn, A. March 27th., 1992. *Meteors and Mortars.* New Statesman.

25.   The Haunabu 3 craft is a typical example.

26.   Private communication with the writer.

Stefula, J. 1993. *Possible CIA Links to a Famous UFO Case—the Budd Hopkins Case of the Abduction of Linda Napolitano.* Privately-published paper.

Steiner, R. Undated. *Sting / Countersting: Unmasking the Disinformers.* Berkely: Global View Publications.

There is an interrelationship between Aviary disinformers, and U.S. Army Intelligence, NSA, ONI, DIA. Such personnel are represented on the board of directors of at least one "private" remote viewing company. One must question the claim of certain supposed remote viewers and channelers that they have communicated with Jesus Christ, since the data presented in this book clearly demonstrates that such an individual never existed. This explains why major writers and historians who lived in the religiously tumultuous 1st century A.D. (e.g. Philo Judaeus) never referred to him.

27.   Jung, C. 1959. *Flying Saucers.* New York: Harcourt Brace.

Jung, C. 1960. *On the Nature of the Psyche.* New Jersey: Princeton University Press.

Budden, A. 1995. *UFO's.* London: Blandford Press.

Mr. Budden is to be honored for his excellent grasp of the true nature of UFO phenomena.

28.   Dane. C. 1973. *The American Indian and the Occult..* New York: Popular Library.

29.   Little, G. 1994. *Grand Illusions.* Memphis: White Buffalo Books.

30. A key conspirator in attempting to drive Mr. Bennewitz to the brink of insanity, by means of psychological warfare, was a U.S. Air Force special agent, whose codename was "Falcon."

31. Streiber, W. 1995. *Breakthrough*. New York: Harper.

Mr. Streiber's cabin was located on iron-rich ground, suggestive that the phenomena encountered at the site was geopathic

32. Barclay, D. 1995. *Aliens—the Final Answer*. London: Blandford Press.

33. Silica possesses the ability to transform electromagnetic energy into scalar waves.

34. Temple, R. 1976. *The Sirius Mystery*. London: Sidwick and Jackson.

35. Adams, H. 1990. *African-American Baseline Essays*. Portland, Oregon.

36. Van Beek, W. 1991. *Dogon Restudies*. Current Anthropology Journal.

37. Boujou, J. Ibid.

38. In posing for the famous photograph in which he is seated adjacent to his Magnifying Transmitter, Tesla, in keeping with Leonardo da Vinci when he painted the Mona Lisa, is shielding from the eyes of the profane, a secret only to be revealed to the esoteric initiate: he would not be so foolhardy as to sit so close to lethal bolts of conventional 60 Hertz electricity. Tesla incorporated into his high frequency D.C. primary circuit, a spark gap which was subjected to a powerful magnetic field. The magnetic field caused the electrical current to pulse *unidirectionally* in the nanosecond range, apparently splitting off the unwanted positrons from the magneto-electric dipoles with which the earth is continuously bombarded. The space stressing effect created by the extreme rapidity of the pulses, induced a massive energy inflow into the circuit, thus enabling the device to produce far more electrical output than the energy input required to initiate the cycle, hence the term "free energy." The rapidity of the pulses resulted in a form of electricity

which did not shock the human body, since it flowed over, instead of through, the body, with oscillations so rapid that they could not be detected by nerve endings. In addition, light bulbs remained cool to the touch when this form of electricity passed through them.

The Mona Lisa's enigmatic smile masks the secret that the painting is a self portrait of a young Leonardo in drag!

For those wishing to acquaint themselves with free energy systems, the author strongly suggests that they commence with the following excellent book by scientist Peter Lindemann, DSc., which presents an in-depth analysis of the very successful Edwin Gray free-energy motor. Gray was given an award of merit by then Governor Ronald Reagan, after his motor had been tested to the satisfaction of company stockholders. The motor and relevant equipment was then seized by the Los Angeles District Attorney, forcing the company to declare bankruptcy. Gray's body was discovered by his sister, who notified the Riverside, California, police department. His death was ruled due to cardiac arrest, even though bloodstains were present. He purportedly was not given an autopsy. Why?

Lindemann, P. 2000. *The Free Energy Secrets of Cold Electricity.* Metaline Falls, Wa.: Clear Tec, Inc..

39. Raw sewage pumped into the depths of a depleted oilfield, is converted into high grade crude oil after a decade by anerobic bacteria; the patented (and suppressed) procedure is well known to the energy cartel.

The claim made by academia that petroleum is formed from the flesh of animal and marine life, simply because the oil bearing rock sometimes contains such fossils, lacks credibility. Petroleum is also found in terrains much older than the Carboniferous period. In reality, petroleum is almost certainly derived from magnesium, which has been transmuted into carbon by microorganisms. The carbon would then readily combine with hydrogen to form petroleum.

40. To their eternal shame, United States State Department personnel have elected not to take any action over the documented practice of
Saudi white slavery.

41. Whistlers are generated by lightning discharges.

42. Nikola Tesla invented a device for communication with entities;
it incorporated an electrostatically-charged wire screen which was over-
layed with an oil film, reminiscent of an Eidophor projection television
system.

43. Americans surrender their national sovereignty when a Social
Security number is issued in their name; they then become a franchisee
of the United States of America—a private corporation and body
politic formerly known as the Virginia Company. This company was
established in England in 1604, in order to fund the first Virginia settlement. Because King John of England deeded England and her dominions to the Vatican Corporation Sole in 1203 A.D. *in perpetuity,* the
United States of America is, in actuality, a possession of the Vatican,
which helps to explain why so many people who occupy the corridors
(or labyrinths) of power in North America have been Jesuit educated,
and why a parcel of land named Rome was selected for the site of the
District of Columbia.

In 1971, the United States Congress passed the super-secret Potomac
Water Resources Act. The bill, which passed with only one dissenting
vote, mandated the division of North America into ten water resource
regions. It states that the President of the United States, all law enforcement and military personnel, together with the general public, are subservient to the Commissioners of the Potomac Water Resource
Compact (who do not even have to be United States citizens). This treasonous bill, which has never been revealed to the public, defines a water
resource as a person or property located within a water resource region,
and is similar to the water resource bill used by Stalin in order to consolidate his political clout. In actuality, the bill is a title of conveyance of
North America and her peoples to the Potomac Commission. Congress

is not empowered to overturn a title of conveyance. The only peaceful remedy to this act of treason, is for American flag officers not born with a yellow streak, to effect the military arrest of those elements within and without the United States Government who have supported this shameful act, and restore the Constitution of these united Sovereign States of America—a document which was rendered null and void by passage of the Potomac Compact. Similarly, the Jesuit engineered 14th Amendment to the U.S. Constitution, granted the United States Government judicial governmental supremacy over the sovereign states of America.

44. A move in this direction would be not only the repeal of the National Security Act (which protects Project Monarch and similar mind control programs) but also replacement of usuary banking practices with the usuary-free tally system of banking, which provided western Europe with financial stability during the era which saw the construction of the magnificent Gothic cathedrals.

45. Heraclitus (circa 500 B.C.) hated the masses; fragments of his warped teachings are contained in the Hippocratic corpus. He stated that the aristoi (the elite) seek immortal glory among mortals, while the hoi polloi (the masses) merely glut themselves like beasts. As to be expected, the Illuminati hierarchy privately refer to themselves as "the Olympians," even though many of them are not very bright, but merely ruthlessly cold blooded.

46. Born in 1766, Malthus was the precursor to the eugenics movement, so avidly pursued in the 1930's by the Nazis and fellow travellers—the Harrimans, Rockefellers and Kennedys. He proposed that impoverished families be forced to live in overcrowded locations, in order to promote the spread of plague.

If the present global population were to be divided into groups of four persons, and each group allotted one eigth of an acre of land, the entire global population could be accommodated in the State of Texas. The U.S. Department of Agriculture has estimated that the current global agricultural capacity is sufficient to support a population of twelve billion people. This latter figure could be greatly increased by substituting cost-effective powdered rock mixed with vesicular micorrhizae soil fungi, for the presently used artificial fertilizers and pesticides. Such an approach would enable the arid regions of Afghanistan, Africa and Western China to produce ultra high yield, pest free crops with minimal irrigation requirements.

CHAPTER 17

1.   In 1836, Zevi Husch Kalischer proposed that the House of Rothschild purchase all of Eretz Israel, for the resettlement of Jewish refugees. Baron Edmund de Rothschild (1845—1934) financed Russian Jews emigrating to Palestine, in order to escape Czarist pogroms.

2.   Fearful that he might be the target of remote viewers, Hitler placed a price on the head of Austrian psychic and Luciferian, Rudolph Steiner, the founder of the Anthroposophy movement, and a member of the Ordo Templi Orientis.

3.   Infield, G. 1981. *Secrets of the S.S.* Miltary Heritage Press.

4.   That Baron Otto von Bolschwing was closely associated with President Ronald Reagan should not come as a surprise, considering that at the outbreak of W.W.II, Reagan accompanied Nazi sympathizers the Duke of Windsor and actor Erroll Flynn to the Bahamas, for a clandestine meeting with Gestapo executive Dr. Erdmann (Reagan is believed by some investigators to have been a member of Erroll Flynn's Nazi spy ring).

Only an outpouring of public opinion prevented Reagan from establishing a covert behavior modification facility in the Santa Monica Mountains of Southern California. The mind control facility was intended to be under the direction of the notorius mind control programmer Dr.Jolyon West, who "interviewed" Sirhan Sirhan—the patsy framed for the assassination of Senator Robert Kennedy. During his presidency, Reagan initiated *Rex 84,* which authorized the construction of concentration camps in America. This project evolved from an earlier plan which proposed the internment of African Americans in the event of civil unrest.

Ms. Arizona Wilder, the former Illuminati Mother Goddess, has claimed to have observed Ronald Reagan at Illuminati Satanic blood rituals. As far fetched as this claim appears to be, it should be noted that wealthy satanists attempt to acquire a residence bearing a number 666 postal address. In checking Ms. Wilder's claim, the author found that President Reagan's current Bel Air, California, postal address is listed as: 666 and 668 Saint Cloud Road.

During W.W.II, the S.S. created a continuity of government organization known as *Vertribene,* which was continued after the war by the Jesuit-controlled Reinhard Gehlen intelligence organization. This organization established fifth-column groups within transnational corporations which had been sympathetic to the Nazis. Until his death, Martin Bormann was involved in the project, which owns numerous corporations in Europe and America, especially in the media field. Its media influence enabled it to exaggerate the Soviet threat to the West, thus subliminally influencing the American public to support the overly excessive budgets of the military/industrial complex.

World Federalist supporter Ronald Reagan implemented the disastrous National Security Policy Directive No. 68, which called for a massive arms escalation in an attempt to bankrupt the Soviet Union, as a ploy for acheiving the Gehlen objective of recovering Germany's lost territories. The outcome was the largest budget deficit in American history, and a crippled economy. For all practical purposes, the Reagan cabinet, mired by the scandal ridden murder of model Vicky Morgan, presented the appearance of being an arm of the Third Reich.

5.   Noriega was ousted for refusing George Bush, Sr.'s request for Noriega to provide assistance to the narco trafficking Nicaraguan Contras, and also for refusing to quell Panamanian demonstrators who

were protesting proposed International Monetary Fund austerity measures. George Bush's Panamanian invasion force, under the command of General Max Thurman, razed the working class suburb of San Miguelito. American troops surreptitiously buried many of the five thousand dead civilians, including women and children, at night, in unmarked mass graves. And we thought only the Nazis were evildoers.

After the massacre, Bush appointed Guillermo Endara as the new Panamanian President. Endara previously had been a director of a bank used by the Colombian drug cartel. Endara's Attorney General was Rogelio Cruz, a director of First Interamericas Bank, owned by the Calli drug cartel. It is precisely because of such unlawful and brutal extraterritorial excursions, that the United States and Britain have become the most hated and reviled nations on earth.

6.   The two other branches of the Hospitallers are the Lutheran Church-affiliated *Johanniterorden,* which is primarily under the direction of the Swedish royal family, together with co-founder of the Bilderberg Society, Prince Bernhard of the Netherlands. The last of the four branches is the *Sovereign Order of Saint John of Jerusalem,* popularly referred to in Illuminati circles as the *Russian Order,* which has ties to the Russian Orthodox Church and the *Foreign Intelligence Service* (the former KGB). The Russian Order is involved in the operation of a hospice in Lakewood, Colorado—the town where John Hinckley, Jr., received some of his mind control programming prior to his failed attempt to assassinate President Reagan.

7.   Lest the Illuminati hierarchy are under the impression that we, the people, are unaware of the Illuminati's most closely held secrets (Illuminati walls have many ears) perhaps it is opportune to inform them that the author is quite conversant with the bizarre banquets hosted by Lord Louis Mountbatten, at which some of the place settings remained seemingly unoccupied, yet food placed on the plates dematerialized during the course of the banquet.

For those readers who aspire to become members of the Illuminati and serve the dragon, it is well to know that Illuminati satanic rituals incorporate the former Roman military custom of decimation, in order to instill terror among its members. Whenever a Roman Legion lost a battle, its troops were ordered to form into groups of ten, and draw straws. The soldier who drew the shortest straw was then clubbed to death by the remaining nine. In similar fashion, Illuminati non-reptilian members attending rituals suddenly find that they have been selected as sacrificial victims. At a recent satanic ritual of the Illuminati Council of the United States, held in the California town of San Juan Capistrano, three of its most loyal aides were sacrificed. You have been warned, dear reader.

8.   "M" Group was a very clandestine British Intelligence organization created in 1934 by Sir Desmond Morton, without the knowledge of the British Prime Minister, and with funding provided by King George V. Morton later formed the Special Operations Executive, after Winston Churchill became Prime Minister.

9.   Wiesenthal, S. 1967. *The Murderers Among Us: the Simon Wiesenthal Memoirs.* New York: McGraw-Hill.

10.   Le Chene, E. 1971. *Mauthausen: The History of a Death Camp.* London.

One of the propulsion systems for the very successful German flying saucer program, was designed by the brilliant Victor Schauberger, who directed a design team of inmates at the Mauthausen camp.

11.   Quote by Arnold Forster, General Counsel to the Anti-Defamation League.

INDEX

0-595-21957-8

Printed in the United States
61109LVS00003BC/34-39